Southern Literary Studies
Louis D. Rubin, Jr., Editor

Winner of the Jules F. Landry Award for 1983

Tell About the South

TELL ABOUT THE SOUTH

The Southern Rage to Explain

Fred Hobson

LOUISIANA STATE UNIVERSITY PRESS

BATON ROUGE

Designer: Albert Crochet
Typeface: Linotron Palatino

Louisiana Paperback Edition, 1998
07 06 05 04 03 02 01 00 99 98   5 4 3 2 1

LIBRARY OF CONGRESS CATALOGING IN PUBLICATION DATA

Hobson, Fred C., 1943–
    Tell about the South.

    (Southern literary studies)
    Bibliography: p.
    Includes index.
    1. American literature—Southern States—History and
criticism.   2. Southern States in literature.   3. Southern
States—History.   4. Southern States—Civilization.
5. Confession in literature.   I. Title.   II. Series.
PS261.H54   1983   810'.9'975   83-5477
ISBN 0-8071-1112-0
ISBN 0-8071-1131-7 (pbk.)

For Jane

For Louis D. Rubin, Jr.

Contents

Acknowledgments

This book had its beginnings in 1976 and 1977 during a year of reading and writing about Southern history and literature made possible by a Fellowship for Independent Study and Research from the National Endowment for the Humanities. I am grateful to the NEH for its generous support. I also thank the Research Grants Committee of the University of Alabama for its generosity.

Parts of the book were published as essays in the *Southern Literary Journal* and the *Virginia Quarterly Review*, whose editors I thank for their permission to include those essays. Other parts were included in a paper given before members of the Program in American Civilization at Harvard University.

My personal debts are great and numerous: to Louis D. Rubin, Jr., David Donald, and Daniel Aaron, all of whom made valuable suggestions in the early stages of the study, and to several colleagues who have read chapters, discussed the work with me, or helped in various ways—William Barnard, Phil Beidler, Ralph Bogardus, John Burke, Rose Gladney, Robert Halli, Claudia Johnson, and George Wolfe.

Many others—scholars, librarians, and friends—have helped in ways too various to enumerate: among these are Lewis Baker, Staige D. Blackford, John Milton Cooper, Alice and Ambrose Dudley, Leslie W. Dunbar, Jane Hobson, Linda Whitney Hobson, Hunter James, Thomas L. Johnson, Catherine Jones, Joyce Lamont, Fran Schell, Derek Williams, Clyde Wilson, Thomas Daniel Young, and Dave Zielenski, as well as the manuscript librarians of the New York Public Library, the Enoch Pratt Free Library of Baltimore, and the Southern Historical Collection of the University of North Carolina and librarians of the University of Alabama, Duke University, Emory University, Princeton University, Vanderbilt University, and the University of Virginia.

I am grateful to Polly Weaver Beaton, Mary Davidson Bell, Mary Cash Maury, Nancy Nilsson, Mary Frances Odum Schinhan, LeRoy P. Percy, the New York Public Library (Astor, Lenox, and Tilden Foundations), the Princeton University Library, and the Enoch Pratt Free Library for permission to quote from unpublished correspondence; to Karen Nelson, who not only typed the manuscript, finding her way through a maze of insertions and modifications, but also found and corrected errors of all sorts; and to Roger Sayers, Academic Vice-President, and Douglas Jones, Dean of the College of Arts and Sciences, of the University of Alabama. I wish to thank the Louisiana State University Press, particularly Beverly Jarrett, Catherine F. Barton, and Barbara Phillips, for encouragement, guidance, and deadlines; and, finally, I thank Cynthia Graff Hobson, who has served expertly as editor, word-suggester, encourager, and critic, and who, despite her Iowa roots, has come to know and appreciate an earlier South.

Tell About the South

Tell about the South. What's it like there. What do they do
there. Why do they live there. Why do they live at all.

Shreve McCannon in conversation with Quentin Compson
Faulkner, *Absalom, Absalom!*

Prologue

We need to talk, to tell, since oratory is our heritage. We seem
to try in the single furious breathing (or writing) span of the
individual to draw a savage indictment of the contemporary
scene or to escape from it into a make-believe region of swords
and magnolias and mockingbirds which perhaps never existed
anywhere. Both of the courses are rooted in sentiment; perhaps the one who writes savagely and bitterly of the incest
in clayfloored cabins are [*sic*] the most sentimental. Anyway,
each course is a matter of violent partizanship, in which the
writer unconsciously writes into every line and phrase his violent despairs and rages and frustrations or his violent prophesies [*sic*] of still more violent hopes. That cold intellect which
can write with calm and complete detachment and gusto of its
contemporary scene is not among us; I do not believe there
lives the Southern writer who can say without lying that writing is any fun to him. Perhaps we do not want it to be.
Faulkner
Unpublished manuscript, 1933

The radical need of the Southerner to explain and interpret the South
is an old and prevalent condition, characteristic of Southern writers
since the 1840s and 1850s when the region first became acutely self-
conscious. The rage to explain is understandable, even inevitable,
given the South's traditional place in the nation—the poor, defeated,
guilt-ridden member, as C. Vann Woodward has written, of a prosperous, victorious, and successful family.[1] The Southerner, more than
other Americans, has felt he *had* something to explain, to justify, to
defend, or to affirm. If apologist for the Southern way, he has felt
driven to answer the accusations and misstatements of outsiders and

1. See C. Vann Woodward, "The Search for Southern Identity," *The Burden of South-
ern History* (Rev. ed.; Baton Rouge, 1968), and "The Irony of Southern History," in
Louis D. Rubin, Jr., and Robert D. Jacobs (eds.), *Southern Renascence: The Literature of the
Modern South* (Baltimore, 1953).

3

to combat the image of a benighted and savage South. If native critic, he has often been preoccupied with Southern racial sin and guilt, with the burden of the Southern past—and frustrated by the closed nature of Southern society itself, by that quality which suppressed dissent and adverse comment.

I do not mean, in particular, the Southern novelist; his story, at least in the most notable cases, has already been told. Nor do I necessarily mean the historians and scholars. They too have pondered and told about the South, but they have told about it—at least if they have done their jobs in a reasonably orthodox manner—not in passion but, insofar as possible, with something approaching calm and deliberate reflection. I mean, rather, certain individual Southerners—some journalists, some teachers, some belletrists, some writers of no precise description—who have approached the South with a purpose that went beyond professional interest or intellectual curiosity, who have responded to it emotionally, even viscerally, and have written books, usually of a highly personal nature, in which they have set forth their feelings. I mean Southerners such as Edmund Ruffin of Virginia, who came to identify his own destiny with the Southern cause, who loved the South so intensely that the spring the Civil War ended he scribbled in his diary his "unmitigated hatred" to all Yankees and moments later put a bullet through his brain; or Hinton Rowan Helper of North Carolina, who wrote at the same time as Ruffin, and with the same zeal and fervor, but from an entirely different point of view: he wanted to reshape the South, not to preserve it. I mean other Southerners who saw a divine mission for the South, an obligation to provide a model for the rest of the world—a mission articulated with all the conviction and moral rectitude of seventeenth-century New England Puritans: Robert Lewis Dabney of Virginia, who was convinced in the 1860s and 1870s that the South could show the way to a confused and fragmented world, as were, in later times, Thomas Nelson Page of Virginia, Donald Davidson of Tennessee, and Richard M. Weaver of North Carolina. Other Southerners wrote less from pride than from disapproval, frustration, or consuming fascination: W. J. Cash of North Carolina, who spent most of his adult life pondering the Southern past and the Southern mind, then committed suicide in 1941 only five months after publication of the book that attempted to explain that mind, the book he had agonized over for twelve years and had been reluctant to relinquish; George Washington Cable, who, a half-century before Cash, dared to speak truthfully and forcefully about Southern race relations, invoking the wrath of his fellow Southerners and proving the truth of what Cash later called the "savage ideal"; or James McBride Dabbs of South Carolina, sitting in his antebellum home, preoccupied with both Southern sin *and* Southern mission, talking about a divine plan of Southern history and God's Providence in the working of Southern affairs.

It would be an oversimplification to say that the apologists, at least those after 1865, belong to a Southern school of remembrance, and the critics—Cable, Cash, Dabbs, Lillian Smith, and others—to a school of shame and guilt, although something of the sort comes close to the truth. It is salvation in Southern values—and a glory of the past not always properly captured in written history—that the apologists have seen; it is the burden of that past the critics have stressed. But whatever their differences, the quality almost all of these writers, apologists and critics, shared was a need, in some instances nearly a compulsion, to—in Faulkner's words—"tell about the South." As Southerners who brooded over the South, its promise and its failure, they wrote with deep commitment and often outrage but rarely with humor and sometimes not even with perspective. Indeed, in some few cases, they seemed tortured by their Southernness.

If this Southerner with a rage to explain himself and his region has a prototype in the fiction of the American South, it surely is Quentin Compson of Mississippi—the Quentin of *Absalom, Absalom!* who on a January night in 1910 sat in the tomblike chill of his room in Cambridge, Massachusetts, and tried to explain the South to his Canadian roommate, Shreve McCannon. He told the story of Thomas Sutpen, a Virginian who had come to Mississippi in the early nineteenth century, but in fact it was Quentin Compson's own story that he told as much as it was Thomas Sutpen's, and it was told for Quentin himself as much as for Shreve. Haunted by the Southern past as much as he was drawn to it, Quentin told his story not with intellectual detachment but with a visceral commitment to the importance of what he was telling. Both blessed and cursed with an excess of consciousness, possessed of a rage to order as well as to explain, he agonized over the larger meaning of Thomas Sutpen's story, over the significance of what had happened in the South during the century just past. He told *his* story in love and in anger, in pride and in shame; he told it not so much by choice as by compulsion, the very telling rendering him oblivious to the presence of the bespectacled, analytical Shreve. Quentin hoped, one suspects, to escape his past by pouring it out, by confessing it to this rational and objective friend separated from him by geography and history—but in the telling he was only drawn in more deeply. He had come to New England only to return to Mississippi in his mind, and the burden of the Southern past, of Southern values, of Southern myths, of himself and his family as Southerners was too great to bear. Five months after he told his story in Cambridge—five months after he had answered Shreve McCannon's question, "Why do you hate the South?," by protesting, "I dont hate it . . . I dont. I dont!"[2]—he was dead by suicide, a Southerner consumed in large measure by his Southernness.

Quentin Compson of Mississippi, of course, was not a historical personage—he sprang from the mind of William Faulkner of Mississippi—and not all the writers to be discussed herein were tortured and consumed by their inheritance as he was. All did not even rage as Edmund Ruffin (who *was* consumed) and Helper and Dabney. A few were not absolutists, all-or-nothing men. Indeed, Thomas Nelson Page, a Virginian who prized moderation whether he always practiced it or not, would have considered it a bit ungentlemanly to rage, to reveal too much of himself, although one should not on this account doubt his sense of mission or dedication to the Southern cause. Indeed, to Page, his telling about the South was a calling, a sacred duty, an obligation to redeem the Old Dominion and the South, and if he spoke more calmly than Ruffin or Helper it was partly because he felt that a restraint, an appearance of calm deliberation, best suited his purpose. Nor should one doubt the fervor and mission of Howard W. Odum of North Carolina just because Odum was never fully able to break through sociological jargon to display the anger of a Helper or the eloquence of a Donald Davidson. Nor that of James McBride Dabbs (less Quentin Compson than Isaac McCaslin in any case), who dispensed sweetness and light as well as wrath and warning. Conviction and intensity drove all these men, as did an identification of themselves with the meaning and destiny of the South.

Few of the writers I shall discuss could be called truly representative Southerners. And though all of them were certain of their calling

2. William Faulkner, *Absalom, Absalom!* (1936; rpr. New York, 1972), 174. Wherever possible, page references to specific works are cited parenthetically in the text.

as truth-sayers, none of them told the entire truth about the South. Henry Adams once wrote that the South had no mind, but in fact it has had many minds, and nowhere is its diversity illustrated better than by the subjects of this book. Each of them suggests some aspect of that mind, and each was too deeply committed to a particular point of view, a particular vision of the South, to attain the great calm, the later Faulknerian perspective, the ability to muse upon the Southern past, affecting cosmic disinterestedness. Liberal or conservative, critic or apologist, each felt compelled to explain the South, and if any generalization might be made at the outset it is that the apologists, the defenders, tended to be of a poetic nature and, since poetry is ahistorical, to protest the injustice that the South should be judged only through its recorded history and not through the integrity of its vision as well; while the critics (to call them liberals is generally accurate) tended to rest their case on history, on observed fact, and draw their position, their attitude, from the documented Southern past. Whatever their differences, however, all these writers shared a belief in the uniqueness of Southern history, a conviction that the South is substantially different from the rest of the United States, "not quite a nation within a nation," as W. J. Cash observed, "but the next thing to it."[3] And they believed not only in the uniqueness but in the *importance* of that uniqueness—which is to say that these particular Southerners seem rarely or never to have entertained the secret doubt that Southern scholars, no matter how committed to the task, sometimes have: that the South's uniqueness may not really be as important as its similarities to the rest of the Union.

It is obvious that many of the Southerners in this book were persons of complex personality, and in some cases their reasons for telling about the South cannot easily be separated from their biographies. Many, like Quentin himself, were afflicted with an excess of consciousness, and in those cases my discussion will be in part a study in the perils of such excess. Many—Ruffin, Helper, Dabney, Davidson, Cash, and Richard Weaver—were no strangers to alienation, to loneliness, and certainly their rage to explain the South was a product in part of spiritual or intellectual isolation and the contemplation and introspection it engenders. One considers further that the act of telling about the South (particularly when shame and guilt mo-

3. W. J. Cash, *The Mind of the South* (1941; rpr. New York, 1960), viii.

tivate the telling) can be among other things an act of confession, even catharsis—of purging oneself of haunting memories and fears in the hope that they will haunt no more, but always with the dangerous possibility that to explore and reveal is to dredge up painful memories which without confession would not be brought to the surface. Truth-telling, which could be cathartic, could also—as with Ruffin and Cash—become one's *raison d'être*, and when one's task was completed, one's truth told, one ran the risk of finding a great vacuum in his life.

V. O. Key has remarked upon the "depressingly high rate of self-destruction" that "prevails among those who ponder about the South and put down their reflections in books," the "fatal frustration [that] seems to come from the struggle to find a way through the unfathomable maze formed by tradition, caste, race, poverty."[4] Indeed, in this study alone, one is struck by the remarkable fact that four of the dozen and a half subjects (as well as their prototype, Quentin) committed suicide; and although organic or personality disorders may have contributed to the self-destruction of Ruffin, Helper, Clarence Cason, and Cash, it is indeed striking that three of the four suicides came at that moment—or just after it—when the writer had most deeply pondered the meaning of the South and his own identity as Southerner, and had gone on record with his feelings and conclusions. One wonders at the suicides of Cason and Cash (like Quentin himself) within months of pouring out their thoughts about the South and that of Ruffin at his most heightened moment of Southern self-awareness. One recalls Hawthorne's Ethan Brand and remembers well the price of looking into the fire too long, of searching too deeply for the truth. This is not to say that suicide is necessarily an occupational hazard of serious and committed South-watching: Cable, Dabney, Dabbs, and Thomas Nelson Page died, though not in all cases peacefully, in old age, and nearly all the scholars seem to endure. It is to suggest, however, that an unbalanced personality and a deep personal identification with a troubled land, added to the fear of public reaction to what one might say about that land, have been in some instances an explosive mixture.

But the Southern rage to explain, the compulsion to tell about the South, must be adjudged something other than a manifestation of

4. V. O. Key, *Southern Politics in State and Nation* (New York, 1949), 664.

personality disorder. Various Southerners of the nineteenth and twentieth centuries have been seized by the same compulsion, to the extent that explaining the South is almost a regional characteristic in itself. In one sense, of course, this Southern impulse for self-exploration and self-explanation is but a variation of the greater American rage to explore and explain, a desire dating back to the Puritans to justify themselves before the critical eye of the world. But it is something apart from and beyond that. No other American region has been nearly so self-conscious as the South; only New England has come close, only it has shared the South's position, as Lewis P. Simpson has written, as "spiritual nation,"[5] and even New England in the twentieth century is no longer the homogeneous land with a mission it once was.

Thus the South has stood alone as an alien member of the national family, and as the most frequently analyzed member of that family. A national enigma, a "kind of Sphinx on the American land," David M. Potter has called it, an enigma that not only the South but all America has attempted to penetrate. A distorted mirror for the rest of America, another writer has suggested, a mirror that reflects and magnifies the nation's vices and a few of its virtues. "America's exposed nerve," still another has written, where national issues are "most intense, or at least most apparent."[6] Americans have long been fascinated with the South as spectacle, as land of extremes—the most innocent part of America in one respect and the guiltiest in another—a "great Sodom" to William Lloyd Garrison, a semibarbarous region to scores of other Northerners, but the veritable primal Garden to many other observers, North as well as South.

The South's "uniqueness" and thus the roots of its rage to explain lie primarily, of course, in its history, in what it has done and what has been done to it. The American South was forced on the defensive in the 1820s and 1830s because of its peculiar institution, Negro slavery, and it has been on the defensive ever since, at least until very recently. It is the only American region to have been a separate nation, the only region to have suffered military defeat on its own soil and to have withstood occupation and reconstruction by the enemy. The South

5. Lewis P. Simpson, *The Man of Letters in New England and the South: Essays on the History of the Literary Vocation in America* (Baton Rouge, 1973), 209.
6. David M. Potter, "The Enigma of the South," *Yale Review*, LI (October, 1961), 142; Howard Zinn, *The Southern Mystique* (New York, 1964), 13; Leslie Dunbar, "The Changing Mind of the South: The Exposed Nerve," *Journal of Politics*, XXVI (February, 1964), 3.

has been and remains the most homogeneous of regions, the most provincial, the most insular—and, until recently, the most insecure. As Sheldon Hackney has observed, "The southern identity has been linked from the first to a siege mentality. . . . Being southern . . . inevitably involves a feeling of persecution at times and a sense of being a passive, insignificant object of alien or impersonal forces." Not only is the Southerner no stranger to failure and frustration, he has also been confused and bewildered by the outside world and what it expects of him. "The average Southerner," Richard M. Weaver has remarked, "pushed beyond the rather naive assumptions with which he sanctions his world, becomes helpless and explodes in anger."[7] The Southerners discussed in this study are hardly average, but many of them—particularly the apologists, Ruffin, Dabney, and Davidson—have exploded as well, if not in helpless anger, in a sort of eloquent rage.

A constant assault from without, an indictment of every aspect of their civilization, was the burden under which Southerners lived for more than a century (as if defeat and poverty and failure were not enough), and it is little wonder that such a legacy created men and women who sought to justify their past and their tradition. But the siege from without was not all, was not even the principal factor in turning the Southern mind upon itself. Even greater was the pressure from within—the doubt honest Southerners had about themselves and their own past—for the burden of Southern history was a burden primarily self-imposed. If guilt and shame were not dominant in the antebellum mind—and the works of George Fitzhugh, Daniel R. Hundley, Ruffin, Helper, and most other Southern writers of the 1840s and 1850s show a remarkable absence of guilt—shame and guilt have been central in Southern self-exploration since that time. Cable, Cash, Dabbs, Lillian Smith, all wrote of guilt, not so much a personal guilt as a guilt acknowledged and confessed for their homeland. They and others have pondered the injustice of Negro bondage, have (with the possible exception of Cash) been obsessed with slavery and its aftermath. "The negro," they—like Melville's Don Benito—would exclaim if asked what cast a shadow over their land.[8]

7. Sheldon Hackney, "Southern Violence," *American Historical Review*, LXXIV (February, 1969), 924–25; Richard M. Weaver, *The Southern Tradition at Bay: A History of Postbellum Thought*, ed. George Core and M. E. Bradford (New Rochelle, N.Y., 1968), 389.

8. Herman Melville, "Benito Cereno," in *Selected Tales and Poems*, ed. Richard Chase (San Francisco, 1950), 90.

To some psychologists amateur and professional the South has been a neurotic society, one that repressed its true feelings about the Negro and constructed defense mechanisms to conceal its guilt over slavery[9]—a society, by this reasoning, that lived a lie for years, convincing itself that slavery was a positive good ordained by God and nature, and then was forced to live after 1865 with the knowledge of and guilt for that lie. But the Southerner, after 1865 as before, did not always face that knowledge and guilt. It was principally the critics— the school of shame, we may as well call them—who acknowledged the darkness in the Southern past. The apologists, or the school of remembrance, never fully acknowledged or, in some cases, even felt that shame and guilt. At least in the years after Appomattox, they preferred rather to celebrate the antebellum past, the noblest civilization, wrote Thomas Nelson Page, the world had ever seen. Indeed, for the Southern apologist, the rage to explain in these immediate postbellum years (as ever since) arose from a source different from that which impelled the Southern critic. The apologist continued to respond to the old attack from without, even in the 1880s and 1890s after the attack had largely ceased to pour down from the North; he felt he had to state his case persuasively and absolutely for the civilization of the Old South before that civilization slipped from memory. The critic, by contrast, was disturbed not by censure or pressure from without but rather by the closed nature of Southern society itself, a quality that threatened to stifle his own free expression. But critics were few in the years after the war: the literature of remembrance carried the day before 1900. Not until the mid-twentieth century would the literature of shame and guilt gain preeminence.

Still another intriguing quality in the self-conscious Southerner arose in the years after Appomattox and is seen to this day, still another paradox to add to the scores already detected in the Southern character: the Southerner, apologist or critic, began to perceive a certain value in his defeat, his poverty, even (if he acknowledged it) his guilt and his shame. If one at first believes that the Southern rage to explain stems from a regional inferiority complex, a recognition of failure, he soon realizes that there exists as well a perverse and de-

9. See D. A. Hartman, "The Psychological Point of View in History: Some Phases of the Slavery Struggle," *Journal of Abnormal and Social Psychology*, XVII (October-December, 1922), 261–73; and, for a Freudian reading, Earl E. Thorpe, *Eros and Freedom in the Old South* (Durham, N.C., 1967) and *The Old South: A Psychohistory* (Durham, N.C., 1972).

fiant pride in the Southerner, a sense of distinction, of superiority, stemming *from* this inferior status. The Southerner, that is to say, wears his heritage of failure and defeat as his badge of honor. He would not have it any other way. He also carries his legacy of failure with an attitude akin to arrogance, an intolerance of less sensitive beings who do not understand and feel the complexities of life. "You would have to be born there" (p. 361), Quentin protests impatiently and with a certain superiority to his Canadian friend at Harvard (a superiority if not on Quentin's part at least on the part of his creator), and other Southern interpreters echo this claim. In fact you do not have to be born there, as evidenced by several non-Southerners who have told about the South with as much comprehension, if not commitment, as have most native interpreters. But still resounds the Southern boast: we at least have our history, our defeat, therefore we are deeper, we possess the tragic sense. And the Southerner who so claims has also a deep conviction that the rest of the nation really wants and needs to know about his history and his defeat. That in part is why he writes, to convince the outsider of the importance and transcendent meaning of the South and himself as Southerner, although most of all, like Quentin, he tells his story for himself, to work out certain questions and doubts that weigh heavily on his mind.

Any study of Southern self-explanation must have boundaries, for in essence all writing about the South, fiction or nonfiction, seeks in one way or another to explore and explain the region. Thus this study is limited not only to those writers who had a particular vision of the South and identified very personally with its destiny but also, as I have said, it focuses on nonnovelists and nonscholars. It is concerned only with those Southerners who wrote after 1850. Although Southern sectionalism and self-consciousness existed before that time, there did not exist until then the idea of the South as "spiritual nation" with a separate destiny and mission. Finally, I limit the study to white Southerners, although agreeing fully with C. Vann Woodward that "there is no one more quintessentially Southern than the Southern Negro."[10] I go further and maintain that if any Southern writer possessed, and was entitled to possess, a rage to explain the South, it was the Southern Negro, and I omit black writers—Richard Wright

10. C. Vann Woodward, *American Counterpoint: Slavery and Racism in the North-South Dialogue* (Boston, 1971), 6.

and Ralph Ellison most prominently—only because it would be impossible to do them justice in a work of this scope. The story of their rage to explain is a book in itself.

I should also set forth some other assumptions and intentions with which this study is undertaken. I have no particular position to advocate—except that position held by all the subjects of this study, that the South is different and significantly so from the rest of the United States. I am skeptical, however, of excessive claims for Southern virtue, and at least mildly skeptical of certain assumptions about the Southern temper and character. The definition of the "representative" Southerner has generally run something like this: he is conservative, religious, and suspicious of science and progress, he loves the land, has a sense of tradition and a sense of place, and he prefers the concrete to the abstract. Granted, these qualities describe the Southerner, and they continue to describe him, as John Shelton Reed has shown, even after he moves to the city.[11] I cannot help but think, however, they also describe any number of inhabitants or former inhabitants of farms and small towns in upper New England and even sections of the Middle West. That is to say, many of these qualities are not so much Southern as traditional American rural (and I omit those qualities such as poverty and a legacy of defeat which stem largely from the Civil War and *are* largely Southern). Further, I question to some extent the assumption stated by Robert Penn Warren and numerous others that the Southerner possesses a far greater rage against abstraction than do other Americans. Certainly antebellum Southerners as diverse as Thomas Jefferson and John C. Calhoun, and postbellum Southerners as diverse as Thomas Nelson Page and Howard W. Odum, shared a predisposition to abstraction. The Civil War was begun at least in part because of a quarrel over abstractions—states' rights and the extension of slavery into territories to which it was unsuited anyway—and never has a nation stressed those abstractions, honor and duty, more than the Confederacy did. Indeed, the very act of constructing a model of the "representative" Southerner—conservative, religious, with a rage against abstraction—itself violates the taboo against abstraction.

All of this is to say that in the following study I am more inclusive in my allowance of who and what is Southern than some others who

11. See John Shelton Reed, *The Enduring South: Subcultural Persistence in Mass Society* (Lexington, Mass., 1972).

have preceded me. I prefer to think of all the writers treated herein as equally Southern: Southerners, that is, can be sociologists as well as poets. One might envision these interpreters of the South as E. M. Forster once pictured the English novelists of various periods—writers of differing points of view seated simultaneously in a room, a sort of British Museum reading room, Forster said, but for our purposes perhaps the library at Monticello. Our task might be more difficult than Forster's: the angry men, Helper and Ruffin and Robert Lewis Dabney, might refuse to take their seats. As for the others, they would soon begin to speak, sharing certain elements of a common experience, in different Southern accents.

This study begins with one other assumption: that it is now intellectually respectable, even outside Agrarian circles, to be Southern in sentiment, that it had already begun to be so before the election of a Southern president, and that such is the case for the first time in the twentieth century, and perhaps since 1830. If the prevailing national image of the South in the 1850s was that of a semibarbarous land, and if the image in the 1920s and 1930s was, as George B. Tindall has written, a benighted South, the image today is of what one might call a superior South—a region cleaner, less crowded, more open and honest, more genuinely religious and friendly, and suddenly more racially tolerant than any other American region (although, a sociological survey assures us, still much more likely than other American regions to believe in the devil).[12] The South is now more acceptable not only to its traditional defenders but also to its traditional native critics. Even the liberals seem to assume that the good is within the South and the threat is from without. The "Americanization of Dixie," encouraged by Walter Hines Page in the 1890s and Howard W. Odum in the 1920s, is now perceived by many of their liberal descendants as the worst fate that could befall the Southern states.[13]

The South thus assumes a curious new role in American life—the nation's second chance, a relatively unspoiled land whose cities are new and sparkling and whose people retain the mythical innocence and simplicity of an earlier America. It matters little that the South's current virtues derive in part from circumstances and in part from its past shortcomings—its relatively new and clean cities from its inability to industrialize and to grow as early as the Northeast and the

12. *Ibid.*, 60.
13. See John Egerton, *The Americanization of Dixie* (New York, 1974).

Middle West; its antimaterialism from its poverty; its protest against progress from its realization that progress would bring painful racial change; its sense of tragedy from its failure to win the Civil War; its sense of history and even to some extent its twentieth-century literary renascence from that same legacy of defeat and looking backward; and even its deep religious belief, in part, from its rural isolation and lack of exposure through education and commerce to other ways of viewing life. One can easily be suspicious, that is, of the South's current claims to moral superiority. The reasons for its virtues become obscured to its champions, just as the reasons for the sins of a benighted South were often ignored by its critics. But in the eyes of its champions the South now presumably has the chance George Fitzhugh of Virginia saw for it more than a century ago—the opportunity to be a model for the rest of the United States.

How the new image of a superior South will affect the traditional Southern rage to explain will be curious to behold. For the compulsion to tell about the South as it has existed since the 1830s has rested on the assumption that the Southerner spoke from a defensive position, a position of inferior status within the nation. A further assumption—and this has been especially important in the case of the anguished native critic—is that the Southerner spoke to and within a society that would not tolerate critical examination. Now, neither of these conditions necessarily exists any longer, and as a result the despairing Southern confession of guilt and shame, as well the impassioned defense, as they have existed over the last century and a half may be no more. The Southerner had a true rage to explain only when he had an enemy across the line issuing an indictment that had to be answered, or when he had an enemy within Southern society forcing him to repress his feelings until the internal pressure became so great he had to spew them out. Now there is need neither to defend nor to attack the South with passion and intensity, and as a result the region is no longer likely to produce rigid absolutists such as Edmund Ruffin, Hinton Rowan Helper, Robert Lewis Dabney, and Donald Davidson. The newest of New Souths is not a likely partner in a love-hate relationship.

The Southern confessional literature will no doubt continue, partly because the South, whatever its changes, is still distinctive and picturesque. But one questions, again, whether the new confessional literature will be written from the same mixture of love and anger, shame and pride, whether an all-consuming passion to explain will constitute the basis for future Southern writing as it did for that of Ruffin and Dabney, Davidson and Cash. The confessional literature has already become in part, one suspects, a habit in the South, a function, an aesthetic ritual. The young creative Southerner who leaves his home now writes the obligatory confessional because his predecessors have. What we have in the South in the last few decades is nothing short of a new literary mode, a subgenre as it were: a Southern confessional literature has grown up and is firmly established in the twentieth century, a particular kind of literature not seen in any other American region since perhaps New England in its colonial days.

And the literature that explores and explains the American South will continue for another reason, one that did not exist until the last decade—that is, the Southern experience is now more than ever not only the South's but the nation's. Not only has the South long provided a mirror image for America's flaws and blemishes, but in post-Vietnam America those qualities we have identified as Southern—frustration, failure, defeat, guilt—can be shared by the rest of the nation. Dixie has to some extent become Americanized, but America has absorbed much of Dixie too. Country music, fried chicken, stock car racing, evangelical religion, and opposition to busing school-children—all these have replaced cotton as Dixie's leading export, not to mention a general distrust of analysis, bureaucracy, big government, and impersonality in human affairs.

To tell about the South, then, becomes increasingly to tell about America. Indeed, the temptation in writing a book such as this, especially if the author is a Southerner, is that he will try to do what his subjects have done—to make his own case for or against the South. I hope I have resisted this temptation, for this study is offered not as another in that series of books that attempt an explanation for the South's uniqueness, but rather as a study *of* those books and their authors. My role, finally, presumes to be that of fascinated observer, not advocate a priori—of Shreve McCannon, not Quentin Compson.

PART I

Ante Bellum

We alone are a new people. . . . New, original, and valuable combinations of thought will be suggested by our peculiar social organism, so soon as we dare to think independently, and to justify ourselves before the world.

George Fitzhugh,
De Bow's Review (September, 1860)

And now with my latest writing and utterance, and with what will be near my latest breath, I here repeat and would willingly proclaim my unmitigated hatred to Yankee rule—to all political, social and business connections with Yankees, and the perfidious, malignant and vile Yankee race.

Edmund Ruffin,
Diary, 1865

The need to defend and to explain the American South began almost as soon as the inhabitants of that region below the Potomac realized they *were* Southern, even before they fully realized they were American. By the time of the American Revolution, John Alden has written, the South had already become, to some degree, a self-conscious section, one which feared becoming "a minority in an American union dominated by a Northern majority."[1] Indeed, one might contend, sectional consciousness—and self-justification—precedes the Revolution by a great many years. As early as the seventeenth century inhabitants of the Southern colonies—although they would have identified themselves as Virginians and Carolinians, not "Southerner"—wrote books, pamphlets, and letters which attempted to defend if not the South at least particular parts of it. John Hammond's *Leah and Rachel, or, The Two Fruitfull Sisters of Virginia and Mary-land* (1656), Robert Beverley's *History and Present State of Virginia* (1705), and Hugh Jones's *The Present State of Virginia* (1724) were all written in large measure to set the record straight, to correct misconceptions— albeit British, not Yankee ones at this point. Although no book this early could with any real conviction be called "Southern," these works did anticipate the defensive posture of much Southern writing

1. John Alden, *The First South* (Baton Rouge, 1961), 4.

19

of the next two and a half centuries. Similarly, Thomas Jefferson in his *Notes on the State of Virginia* (1785) defended not precisely the "South" but his part of the New World against accusations that American soil, air, climate, and animals were inferior to their European counterparts. In the same work he expressed his anguish over slavery, and thus in one book became a forerunner of the Southern traditions of defensiveness *and* guilt. The same year Jefferson's *Notes* appeared he demonstrated as well a keen awareness of American regional differences when he reported in a letter to the Marquis de Chastellux that Northerners were "cool, sober, laborious, independent . . . and hypocritical in their religion," Southerners "fiery, voluptuary, indolent, unsteady . . . generous, candid, without attachment or pretentions to any religion but that of the heart."[2] His was a list of attributes not unlike those assigned Southerners by W. J. Cash a century and a half later.

But if the American South had some sense of separate identity as early as the eighteenth century, certainly it linked its destiny with that of the new American nation; how could it do otherwise when Virginians served as the new nation's president for thirty-two of its first thirty-six years? The South as a whole did not achieve even a moderate sectional identity until the 1820s, and then as a result of the congressional debate over the Missouri Compromise. The individual states below the Potomac and Ohio, that is, came to think of themselves as a section, a community of spirit rather than individual political units with state allegiances, only when they were forced on the defensive with the debate over slavery and the tariff. The Southern need to explain and to justify thus had its origin, in part, in a defensive response to a national dilemma, and it was on the defensive that most Southerners were to remain for the next century and a half. Southern novelists of the mid-nineteenth century—William Alexander Caruthers, Nathaniel Beverley Tucker, John Pendleton Kennedy, William Gilmore Simms—stated their case for the South, but the most fervent support of Southern institutions come in the writings of proslavery polemicists such as Thomas Dew, George Frederick Holmes, George Fitzhugh, W. A. Smith, and Alfred Taylor Bledsoe of Virginia, Thomas Cooper, Edward B. Bryan, James H. Hammond, James H. Thornwell, William Grayson, and William Harper of

2. Thomas Jefferson, *Notes on the State of Virginia* (1785; rpr. Chapel Hill, 1955); Jefferson to the Marquis de Chastellux, quoted in Alden, *The First South,* 17.

South Carolina, Henry Hughes and E. N. Elliott of Mississippi, and George S. Sawyer of Louisiana.[3]

Both William S. Jenkins and William E. Dodd have emphasized the centrality of Dew in proslavery thought.[4] A professor in the College of William and Mary, he led in the process that turned educated Virginians from Jeffersonian liberalism to a social philosophy that assumed slavery to be a "normal" condition of mankind. As Edmund Ruffin of Virginia wrote in his diary, Dew's essay on slavery, *Review of the Debate in the Virginia Legislature of 1831 and 1832*, had "more effect than any argument I ever knew in changing and giving a new direction to public opinion."[5] By the late 1830s, after absorbing Dew's ideas and John C. Calhoun's "positive good" theory of slavery, many Southern-

3. See Thomas Dew, *Review of the Debate in the Virginia Legislature of 1831 and 1832* (Richmond, 1832); Alfred Taylor Bledsoe, *An Essay on Liberty and Slavery* (Philadelphia, 1856); Edward B. Bryan, *The Rightful Remedy, Addressed to the Slaveholders of the South* (Charleston, 1850); William J. Grayson, *The Hireling and the Slave* (Charleston, 1856); Henry Hughes, *Treatise on Sociology* (1854; rpr. New York, 1965); George S. Sawyer, *Southern Institutes; or, An Inquiry into the Origin and Early Prevalence of Slavery and the Slave Trade* (Philadelphia, 1858); William Harper and others, *The Pro-Slavery Argument* (Charleston, 1852); E. N. Elliott and others, *Cotton Is King, and Pro-Slavery Arguments* (Augusta, 1860); George Fitzhugh, *Sociology for the South* (Richmond, 1854) and *Cannibals All!* (Richmond, 1857).

4. William S. Jenkins, *Pro-Slavery Thought in the Old South* (Chapel Hill, 1935); William E. Dodd, "The Social Philosophy of the Old South," *American Journal of Sociology*, XXIII (March, 1918), 735–46. See also, for more recent discussions of many of the proslavery writers, David Donald, "The Pro-Slavery Argument Reconsidered," *Journal of Southern History*, XXXVII (February, 1971), 3–18; Drew Gilpin Faust, *The Sacred Circle: The Dilemma of the Intellectual in the Old South, 1840–1860* (Baltimore, 1977); William R. Taylor, *Cavalier and Yankee: The Old South and American National Character* (New York, 1961); Eugene Genovese, *The Political Economy of Slavery* (New York, 1965) and *The World the Slaveholders Made* (New York, 1969); George M. Fredrickson, *The Black Image in the White Mind* (New York, 1971); Lewis P. Simpson, "The Antebellum South as a Symbol of Mind," *Southern Literary Journal*, XII (Spring, 1980), 125–36; Robert J. Brugger, "The Mind of the Old South: New Views," *Virginia Quarterly Review*, LVI (Spring, 1980), 277–95. Faust's book and Simpson's essay concentrate on Beverley Tucker, Edmund Ruffin, William Gilmore Simms, James H. Hammond, and George Frederick Holmes as antebellum intellectuals who were critical of the South in many respects, whose sense of "moral stewardship" led them to undertake its proslavery argument, and who finally considered themselves failures because they could not capture the attention of their fellow Southerners. Donald, in his excellent essay, contends that many of the Southern apologists wrote because they were personally unhappy and because they were romantics longing for a "by-gone era," rather than because they were driven by guilt over slavery or hoped to persuade Northerners or doubtful Southerners that slavery was right. See also, for a discussion of Southern life during the 1850s (although not of the proslavery writers in particular), Avery O. Craven, *The Growth of Southern Nationalism, 1848–1861* (Baton Rouge, 1953); and David M. Potter, *The Impending Crisis, 1848–1861*, edited and completed by Don E. Fehrenbacher (New York, 1976).

5. [Edmund Ruffin], *The Diary of Edmund Ruffin*, ed. William Kauffman Scarborough (2 vols.; Baton Rouge, 1972), I, 136.

ers had indeed rid themselves of whatever guilt they might have felt over owning slaves, and had begun to accept as truth what the pro-slavery writers affirmed: that slavery was justified by Aristotle, Greek democracy, Roman law, the Bible, and the Christian church. A slave society was not only defensible, it was preferable to a free society. Some Southern apologists saw the South as the European feudal society transplanted to the New World. Others, like Calhoun, saw it as a latter-day Greek democracy, resting on a foundation of slavery. Rollin Osterweis has written of the antebellum Southerner's desire for "the establishment of a free state based on a slave proletariat after the manner of Pericles' Athens. . . . Here was an ingenious attempt to bring into harmony two obviously irreconcilable facts: the system of Negro slavery and the rising spirit of democracy." As Allen Tate has written, however, the Southern plantation ideal was "actually nearer to Republican Rome, a society which, like the South, was short in metaphysicians and great poets, and long in moralists and rhetoricians." The South "was an aggregate of farms and plantations, presided over by our composite agrarian hero, Cicero Cincinnatus." But nearly all the early apologists were seeking historical roots and identity for the South, and the fact that the Southern system was in many ways unlike the Greek, Roman, and European feudal societies did not dissuade them. Some few Southerners, in fact, recognized the dissimilarities and struck out even more boldly to portray the South not as successor to Greece and Rome and medieval Europe but as an essentially new society with a new mind, a "budding mind" as Lewis P. Simpson has written.[6]

But despite the many defenses of slavery and claims for Southern civilization, very few Southerners before 1848 actually thought of the South as a potentially new nation, and very few, before the Nashville Convention of 1850, spoke openly and seriously of secession. One who did was James H. Hammond of South Carolina, the "Hamlet of the Old South" according to Clement Eaton, but a man in the 1830s

6. Rollin Osterweis, *Romanticism and Nationalism in the Old South* (New Haven, 1949), 94; Allen Tate, "A Southern Mode of the Imagination," *Essays of Four Decades* (Chicago, 1968), 587, 588–89; Lewis P. Simpson, "The South's Reaction to Modernism: A Problem in the Study of Southern Letters," in Louis D. Rubin, Jr., and C. Hugh Holman (eds.), *Southern Literary Study* (Chapel Hill, 1975), 55. Simpson writes elsewhere that far from representing a culturally conservative force, the slaveholding South was "the most novel part of the novel nation in history," because the institution of chattel slavery in the South was without precedent in medieval Europe or antiquity (*The Dispossessed Garden: Pastoral and History in Southern Literature* [Athens, Ga., 1975], 36).

speaking with a voice more decisive than that of his fellow Southerners. Hammond, indeed, was that rare apologist who was more vocally pro-Southern in the mid-1830s than in the late 1850s. If legislation which could lead to abolition were even considered, he proclaimed on the floor of Congress in 1836, he would "go home to preach, and if I can, to practise disunion, and civil war, if needs be. A revolution must ensue, and this Republic sink in blood." "The sans-culottes are moving," he wrote the same year:

On the banks of the Hudson, the Ohio and the Susquehannah [sic]—on the hills, and in the vales, and along the "iron-bound coast" of *immaculate* New England, they are mustering their hosts and preparing for their ravages. Let them come! we will be ready. . . . Painful as it is, the truth should now be told, for shortly it will speak itself, and in a voice of thunder. . . . Nor can we justify ourselves before the world for the course which we may be compelled to take in order to maintain our rights, without boldly declaring what those rights are, defining them and showing that they are inestimable.[7]

To "justify ourselves before the world": such was Hammond's calling, and an expression which anticipated the Southern mission of the 1850s.

But Hammond, to repeat, was an exception: most Southern polemicists were nowhere near so fervent in the 1830s and early 1840s. Indeed, the South as a whole, Avery O. Craven has written, lacked a strong sectional identity as late as the 1840s.[8] The remarkable fact is that, so shortly after that, the South came to think of itself not only as a unified section but potentially, and soon actually, as a nation. It was only at that point—more precisely, in 1848, 1849, and 1850 with the great debate in Congress over slavery—that the South began seriously to consider the secession that Hammond had threatened in 1836, and with that consideration came, even more emphatically than before, support for the idea of the South as a unique civilization, superior in every way to the American North. The publication in 1851 of

7. James H. Hammond, "On the Justice of Receiving Petitions for the Abolition of Slavery in the District of Columbia," in Clyde N. Wilson (ed.), *Selections from the Letters and Speeches of the Hon. James H. Hammond* (Columbia, S.C., 1978), 35, 45, 46. Compare Hammond's 1836 speech with a more moderate appeal delivered in 1858 in Barnwell, South Carolina (pp. 323–57), in which he spoke against disunion, acknowledged that expansion of slavery into the Western territories was unrealistic (because they were unsuited for slavery), and expressed the belief that the South could achieve its objectives within the Union.

8. Craven, *The Growth of Southern Nationalism*, 6.

Uncle Tom's Cabin, followed by Frederick Law Olmsted's three books describing the economic, social, and cultural poverty of the South, turned Southerners more resolutely than before to a defense of their civilization and to a counterattack against the North.[9] More than a dozen novels and many more pamphlets were written in response to *Uncle Tom's Cabin*, and literally hundreds of tracts appeared defending slavery and the Southern way. As the great debate of the 1850s began the South saw itself more consciously than before as a land with a destiny separate from that of the North and West, with a special cause and mission. It was at this point that the South became a nation of the spirit envisioning itself a nation in fact.

The most notable proponent of the South as unique civilization and Southerners as a people of destiny was George Fitzhugh of Virginia, a planter and failed lawyer whose two books, *Sociology for the South* (1854) and *Cannibals All!* (1857), won him a reputation as the "Garrison of the South"—or, to William Lloyd Garrison himself, as the "Don Quixote of Slavedom." Fitzhugh's reputation, if not his influence, endures in the twentieth century. Edmund Wilson, C. Vann Woodward, David Donald, Louis Hartz, Harvey Wish, and Eugene Genovese are among those who have written at length about him.[10] But Fitzhugh was a most curious Southern advocate. Not particularly well regarded by his fellow Southern polemicists, more a popularizer than a generator of ideas, he had read the classics sporadically, had read British periodicals and Southern proslavery tracts more carefully, had absorbed the works of Thomas Carlyle, and, as a slaveholder in an area of Virginia in which Negroes outnumbered whites, had become convinced that slavery was a positive good not only for Negroes but—ideally— for some whites as well. Thus he issued in the 1850s the two books setting forth his views: slavery was "natural," and Southern society, as a slave society, was more nearly in harmony with nature than were

9. Harriet Beecher Stowe, *Uncle Tom's Cabin* (Boston, 1851); Frederick Law Olmsted, *A Journey in the Seaboard Slave States* (1856), *A Journey Through Texas* (1857), and *A Journey in the Back Country* (1860), all in Arthur M. Schlesinger (ed.), *The Cotton Kingdom: A Traveller's Observations on Cotton and Slavery in the American Slave States* (New York, 1953). For a discussion of budding Southern nationalism during the 1850s, see Craven, *The Growth of Southern Nationalism*, especially Chapter 3.

10. Edmund Wilson, *Patriotic Gore: Studies in the Literature of the American Civil War* (New York, 1962), 341–64; C. Vann Woodward, "George Fitzhugh, *Sui Generis*," introduction to Fitzhugh, *Cannibals All!*; Donald, "The Pro-Slavery Argument Reconsidered"; Louis Hartz, *The Liberal Tradition in America* (New York, 1955); Harvey Wish, *George Fitzhugh: Propagandist of the Old South* (Baton Rouge, 1943); Genovese, *The World the Slaveholders Made*.

competitive industrial societies in western Europe and the American North. Slavery was natural because men were unequal, and not only unequal but endowed with a social instinct which ensured that the strong would provide for the weak. Slavery was an extension of the family: just as the head of the home cared for his wife and children, so he cared for his slaves. Southern society was thus in the tradition of classical civilizations; Northern society was a radical experiment in liberalism, a modern departure from tested and established ways of living. Industrialism was fiercely competitive, stressing freedom and liberty, but according to Fitzhugh freedom and liberty were far less desirable than security to the mass of men. Southern slaves fared better than "free" Northern and British factory workers.

Fitzhugh's thesis, in many respects, was that which other proslavery writers, particularly Grayson and Bryan of South Carolina and Bledsoe of Virginia, had been arguing—somberly, earnestly—for two decades. Parts of his argument were as old as Aristotle. But this failed attorney from the Northern Neck brought to his new calling a flair for drama and a penchant for verbal fireworks, a lively wit and a sense of irony and paradox which other Southern defenders lacked. "Weakness is strength," he declared, and "the master is the slave." He attacked capitalism, proclaimed himself a "socialist" and railed against John Locke, Adam Smith, and Thomas Jefferson. He expressed even more forcefully than his contemporaries a conviction that the South was a spiritually elevated civilization, superior in values and in goals to the American North. The South, he wrote in *De Bow's Review* in 1857, "is about to lead the thought and direct the practices of christendom," and Christendom, if it were to survive, had to "adopt and follow Southern thought." Such a direction would "put the South at the lead of modern civilization."[11]

If Fitzhugh's message of the mid-1850s did not depart radically from that of other Southern advocates who had held that Southerners were a people of destiny, his essays of 1859 and 1860 began to stress a different theme. After insisting for a decade that the South was following in the tradition of tried-and-true classical civilizations, in 1860 he ventured that Southerners were a "new people" and the American South a "peculiar social organism." "Our social relations and institutions differ widely from those of other civilized countries of modern

11. George Fitzhugh, "Southern Thought," *De Bow's Review*, XXIII (October, 1857), 337.

times," he wrote, "and in some respects from those of antiquity." In words reminiscent of Emerson's declaration of intellectual independence from Europe in "The American Scholar," he pronounced a Southern independence from the American Northeast *and* the Old World: "When we cease to study Northern and European books, to depend on their commerce and manufactures, to ape their fashions, manners, and customs, and to be guided by their thought and opinion, we shall begin to think, to act, and to write for ourselves, and may build up a Southern literature, more truthful, more Christian, more natural, and therefore superior to any that has preceded it." Fitzhugh envisioned a Southern version of John Winthrop's "City Upon a Hill." And like the earlier Puritans, whom he despised but whose vigor he admired—and like James Hammond twenty-five years before—Fitzhugh announced in 1860 that Southerners must dare to "justify ourselves before the world." [12]

In proclaiming Southerners a "new people" with a "new philosophy," George Fitzhugh proved himself the most imaginative of those writers who sought to make a case for the South in the decade preceding the Civil War. But his was only the most distinctive voice in the rising Southern chorus. In no other decade, indeed, has the Southerner's desire to explain and justify his homeland possessed quite the conviction and intensity it possessed in the 1850s. For Fitzhugh and the other apologists of that charged decade were like no other Southerners before or since in one important respect: the object of their vision was not past, not imagined or conditional, nor was it in the distant future. It was imminent and real. The idea of Southern nationhood before 1848—the year in which the debate over slavery had grown particularly heated—was conceivable but remote; the Southern nation after 1865, no matter how powerful in the Southern imagination, would be but a nation of the spirit and the soul. But what Fitzhugh and many of the other apologists of the 1850s were envisioning—were preparing for, were justifying and thus were helping to create—was a political and cultural entity separate and independent from the rest of the United States. These particular Southerners, especially toward the end of the decade, wrote with a sense of destiny, an actual expectation of nationhood, a conviction that neither the Southerner before 1848 nor the Southerner after 1865 could muster.

12. George Fitzhugh, "German Literature," *De Bow's Review*, XXIX (September, 1860), 290.

Their purpose was not to memorialize and to lament—the primary roles of Southern apologists of later times—but to persuade, to move to action. The heirs and beneficiaries of the earlier American Revolution they proclaimed themselves, the oppressed colonials fighting centralized authority. As the American colonists of the 1770s had done, they would form a new nation. And one other trait distinguished George Fitzhugh and the Southern apologists of the 1850s from their successors and even some of their predecessors: they wrote with a remarkable absence of guilt and shame, and what is more, with very little *awareness* of guilt—neither the guilt over slavery expressed by Jefferson and by other Southerners as late as the 1830s, nor the even greater guilt and shame expressed by numerous Southerners after 1870 and recognized as part of the Southern legacy even by those writers who did not experience it personally. There were few troubled consciences among the Southern advocates of the 1850s. They looked ahead with a confidence that would be impossible for the Southern apologist after 1865—who could only look back—and they wrote with a sense of the tangible, the immediate that was impossible before 1848. Their cause was not lost; it was at hand.

Edmund Ruffin

If George Fitzhugh of Port Royal was the "Garrison of the South"—its theoretician and propagandist who could reflect upon its transcendent meaning, defend its institutions, and justify its existence as a nation—his fellow Virginian Edmund Ruffin was surely its John Brown. While Fitzhugh in 1860 remained in Virginia envisioning Southern nationhood, Ruffin rushed frantically from Virginia to North Carolina, South Carolina, Georgia, Florida, and Kentucky, urging a Southern secession which would bring about the new nation in fact. While Fitzhugh shortly after the beginning of the war accepted a position as an auditor for the Confederate government in Richmond—and contemplated a book on "moral science"—Edmund Ruffin at sixty-seven, twelve years Fitzhugh's senior, enlisted in the Confederate army and soon became a symbolic military hero. And while Fitzhugh at war's end accepted the Union victory, became friends of Union officers stationed in Virginia, and went to work for the Freedman's Bureau, Ruffin took his own life rather than endure Yankee rule.

George Fitzhugh, thus, was not one of those Southerners who linked his own destiny body and soul with the fate of the American

South. He served his homeland but he served it intellectually, not viscerally, and his writing—in *Sociology for the South* and *Cannibals All!* if not always in his *De Bow's Review* essays—suggests more the eighteenth-century English gentleman than the Southern firebrand. Like that expansive and tolerant gentleman, Fitzhugh maintained a broad perspective, wrote with a sense of humor, and revealed little of himself directly, often preferring to hide behind his gentle narrator, a kind of literary persona. Possessing a temper as much classical as romantic, guided by a vision more comic than tragic, he did not commit himself so personally and indulge in suffering so dramatically as certain of his contemporaries. He was not, at least in the manner of others we shall discuss, one of the truly committed, the consistently high-minded.

If one seeks those men of awesome earnestness and little humor, then, in the South on the eve of war, one turns not to George Fitzhugh of Port Royal but rather to Edmund Ruffin and to two other, terribly intense younger writers who, like Ruffin, produced books about the South in the year 1860: Hinton Rowan Helper of North Carolina, a noncompromiser like Ruffin who could see the right in no path save his own; and, in a quite different way, Daniel R. Hundley of Alabama. Driven by a desire to be known and respected, feeling more keenly than others the pains and burdens of life, Helper, like Ruffin, ended his life in suicide. Hundley, at least by contrast, was a balanced, moderate man who stated his case with a surface assurance; but he too possessed a high seriousness, a terrible earnestness, a great sense of self-importance, and a burning desire to be known; he too was tough-minded and uncompromising. The books these three Southerners produced in 1860 were written from vastly different points of view. Ruffin's novel, *Anticipations of the Future*, was a fervent plea for Southern nationhood and victory over the "perfidious" Yankees, Helper's *The Impending Crisis of the South* (an earlier but less publicized version of which had appeared in 1857) a violent antislavery tract which would earn its author the title the "Hated Helper." No other book, not even *Uncle Tom's Cabin*, would so stir the ire of loyal Southerners as his did. Hundley's *Social Relations in Our Southern States* was neither an attack upon nor a defense of Southern institutions, or rather it was both—ostensibly a defense of the South, it was in a deeper sense a severe indictment of the Cotton Kingdom. Hundley, the critic *malgré lui*, disproves the assumption that virtually no

Southerner except Helper—and no man at all from the Deep South—dared criticize Dixie in the year 1860. These three writers of vastly differing backgrounds and persuasions were similar in two important respects: each was in some measure outside the mainstream of Southern thought—either too fervent, too unorthodox (or, in Hundley's case, too little known) to be fully accepted by his contemporaries—and each perceived himself a Southerner with a mission, a compelling need to tell his truth about the South to outsiders, to fellow Southerners, and most of all to himself.

Edmund Ruffin of Prince George County, the first of the three to achieve recognition, was in many respects an unlikely candidate to lead a crusade for Southern nationhood. Indeed, as a stimulating thinker and theoretician, he was far less impressive than his fellow Virginian Fitzhugh. His vision was neither so broad nor so majestic, and compared to Fitzhugh's his was a mean and petty mind, lacking the range and the imagination to see the South in a larger perspective. If George Fitzhugh seized the Southern offensive in the 1850s, Ruffin stood on the defensive, and because his stance was defensive it was limited. While Fitzhugh and other apologists expounded on what the South could offer to the world, Ruffin concentrated on what the South was suffering, how it—and he—could obtain revenge. His tragedy was that his world was too restricted in place and time, that he could not transcend his region and his age. So close became his identification with the fate of the South that he himself burned brightest in those moments when the chances of a permanent Southern nation seemed strongest; and when the dream of the Confederacy ended in 1865, he could no longer bear to live.

Edmund Ruffin, the master of Beechwood and Marlbourne plantations, had gained a reputation in the 1830s and 1840s as the editor of the *Farmer's Register* and as the foremost scientific agriculturist in the South. Today he is remembered principally for two dramatic acts, one coming at the beginning of the Civil War, the other at the end: he fired probably the first shot at Fort Sumter in 1861, and he was so broken by the Confederate defeat in 1865 that he wrote a note proclaiming his "unmitigated hatred to . . . the malignant and vile Yankee race" and thereupon took up a gun and killed himself. If the legitimacy of the claim that he fired first at Sumter has been challenged,[13]

13. Martin Abbott, "The First Shot at Fort Sumter," *Civil War History*, III (March, 1957), 41–45.

his suicide is an established fact, and the reasons for it as given in Ruffin's final note stand undisputed. Never did a Southerner hate Yankees more, and never did a Southerner take defeat harder.

In many ways Edmund Ruffin seems to have been one of those men who, feeling a lack of meaning or purpose, an overwhelming emptiness or pain in his own life, attaches himself to a public cause and allows that cause to become the totality of his life, allows himself to live and die, literally, for it. The son of a wealthy planter and the descendant of a family important in Virginia affairs since the seventeenth century, Ruffin felt destined from an early age to play an important role in public life.[14] But, like George Fitzhugh, he failed in his earliest attempts. Elected to the Virginia Senate at twenty-nine, he did not succeed because he was a poor speaker and because he did not like to stoop to political expediency or to be beholden to his constituents. He resigned his seat and returned to his plantation in Prince George County, feeling that he was a failure for not having lived up to that Virginia ideal—the man of affairs as orator—but still determined to make himself known. His voice stilled, he turned to the pen, and one can only guess the extent to which his desire to be heard had its origins in his failure to be heeded as a young senator. His first important task was to tell the farmers of Tidewater Virginia that their worn-out soil could be replenished by the use of marl as fertilizer. At first his neighbors were skeptical, later all Virginia heeded and then hailed him—but not sufficiently for the giant ego of Edmund Ruffin. Feeling unappreciated in Virginia, he adopted South Carolina as his spiritual home, and although he later forgave Virginia, South Carolina remained the state in which he found kindred spirits, James H. Hammond and William Gilmore Simms in particular. The leading South Carolinians shared his views on slavery and Southern nationalism; many of the leading Virginians did not.

In 1855, Ruffin gave up active management of his plantations, Marlbourne, just northeast of Richmond, and Beechwood, on the James River, and turned with even more urgency to stating his case for an independent South. He soon adopted the Southern cause as his own. He wrote to William Lowndes Yancey in 1860 urging the fiery Ala-

14. This and other biographical information I take from Avery O. Craven, *Edmund Ruffin, Southerner* (1932; rpr. Baton Rouge, 1966), and Betty L. Mitchell, *Edmund Ruffin: A Biography* (Bloomington, 1981).

bamian to become the Patrick Henry of the South,[15] but in fact that was a role Ruffin himself had already assumed, along with that of Thomas Paine. In his articles in Southern newspapers and journals, including *De Bow's Review*, in his own pamphlets, and in his travels around the South, Ruffin urged, much earlier than George Fitzhugh, the secession of the Southern states. In his activity Ruffin found a purpose, a gratifying sense of his own importance, that had been missing in his life. This slight man with the long white hair and the deep-set eyes became totally immersed in the excitement of the times. Finding himself obsessed with John Brown and his raid, he went to Harper's Ferry to witness Brown's execution. Dressed in a cadet's uniform from the Virginia Military Institute in order to be present at the hanging, he collected some of the pikes with which Brown's men had hoped to free the slaves and sent the pikes to Southern governors with these words attached: "SAMPLE OF THE FAVORS DESIGNED FOR US BY OUR NORTHERN BRETHREN" (*D*, I, 443). Not only did he crusade for secession in various Southern states, but when he saw war was imminent he went to Charleston, joined the Palmetto Guard, and at age sixty-seven fired the war's first shot—then sent Jefferson Davis a fragment of one of the bombshells that fell within Sumter (*D*, I, 604). And after Sumter, when he returned to Virginia, he fed hungrily on news of the war. The coming of the mail became the supreme event in his day. As he wrote in his diary, "We have now so many papers, that to get through them will occupy me for the half of every mail day" (*D*, I, 415). During the last year of the war he sent most of his income and much of his dwindling fortune to the Confederate government.

Ruffin, thus, in the last ten years of his life became almost exclusively the public man, a Southerner who, more than any other, saw his own destiny as one with that of the South. As war grew near he was hailed in South Carolina, Alabama, Mississippi, Florida, and, finally, in 1861, even in Virginia. On November 27, 1860, he confided in his diary: "The time which I have spent in South Carolina (especially) & elsewhere since I left home on the 6th inst. has been to me the most gratifying of my life, both on personal & general grounds. In addition to the exciting & important, & most gratifying political events, of the program of secession, I have myself been made the subject of kind

15. [Ruffin], *Diary*, I, 634.

feeling & favor, & of general appreciation, such as I had never before experienced, & never expected to receive" (*D*, I, 505). The enthusiasm was dampened by Ruffin's initial lack of widespread recognition and appreciation in Virginia, where there were "far more enemies to depreciate, & to censure me, & many to calumniate, than there are friends & approvers to applaud" (*D*, I, 505). But all things considered, Edmund Ruffin believed he was at last receiving his just due, the fame he had long craved and believed he more than any other man deserved. The fame was accompanied in the North by notoriety, but this, too, Ruffin welcomed. To be recognized, and especially to be known for his devotion to a great cause: such was Edmund Ruffin's obsession, just as fully as it was John Brown's in the late 1850s. Indeed Ruffin, who was fascinated with Brown, must have seen something of himself in "Old Osawatomie" as he watched the execution at Harper's Ferry on that clear, cold December day in 1859—Brown's single-mindedness, his refusal to compromise, his extremism. An "atrocious criminal," he called Brown, but he also wrote in his diary, "It is impossible for me not to respect his thorough devotion to his bad cause, & the undaunted courage with which he has sustained it, through all losses & hazards" (*D*, I, 350). The same might have been said for Edmund Ruffin.

Ruffin was an extremist in part, however, because during the last decade of his life he felt he had nothing to lose; and this fatalism, this plunge into the unknown and the devil fetch the hindmost, played a great part in the making of Edmund Ruffin, Southern crusader. For Ruffin's emergence as a fire-eater in the mid-1850s was not altogether a result of the times; it was also the result of his personal circumstances. The tension between North and South began to grow most heated just as Ruffin came to experience a void in his own life that he could fill from nothing within himself. He seems always to have been cursed with ill luck. He had lost his mother when he was young, had lost three of his own children in infancy, and in 1846 had seen his wife die in her early fifties. Then, in the terrible summer of 1855, *three* of his surviving daughters died unexpectedly. The next year his retirement from farming, in addition to his daughters' deaths, created a great vacuum in his life. He wished for death as an end to suffering. Ruffin had long had a fascination with self-destruction, seen best in a lengthy description he had written in 1840 of the suicide of his friend Thomas Cocke—a description which anticipates in many details Ruffin's own suicide a quarter-century later. Now in the late 1850s there seemed to be little to live for. "I do not deem the coming of death, without long delay, as to be dreaded or deplored," he wrote on January 5, 1859, "provided the death shall be sudden & unexpected, & without suffering" (*D*, I, 262). The next October he lamented, "If I had died five years ago, how much of unhappiness would have been escaped" (*D*, I, 346), and two weeks later, again: "I have lived long enough & a little more time of such unused and wearisome passage of time will make my life too long" (*D*, I, 348).

Ruffin, then, in the late 1850s was a man literally hoping for death, one with little to preserve, little to anticipate. But all the while he desired death, he desperately sought something to ease his terrible loneliness. At the same time that he must have raged at fate for his personal misfortune of 1855, in addition to what he felt had been a cosmic injustice his entire life, he also looked outward for a cause to fill the void in his life. It is no coincidence that Ruffin began in 1856 to keep the diary on which he would spend a good portion of some days and which would reach twenty-five manuscript volumes before he made his last entry moments before his death in 1865. Ruffin later said he began his diary, as well as undertook his other written work, in order to "avoid the misery of idleness," and indeed it was idleness, which created opportunities for dwelling on past misfortune, that he most feared. Thus into the diary he poured not so much his sorrow as his reflections on public affairs. Curiously he passed off the deaths of his three daughters with a single reference to "the successive illness and deaths of my children in 1855" (*D*, I, 8). But he devoted page after page to his travel, his reading, and his growing fervor for the Southern cause.

This is not to say that Edmund Ruffin would never have become a Southern extremist if he had not suffered intense personal tragedy in the mid-1850s. He was already a committed Southern nationalist keenly aware of Northern injustices toward the South even before that time, and his temperament easily adapted itself to extremism. But it is undeniable that his need to write voluminously, to pour out his thoughts in diary, pamphlets, and newspaper and journal articles, was greatly motivated by the emptiness and misery which he found in his own life. In one sense, his rage to explain was gratified most by his diary, a work presumably not intended for public consumption at all—although a large part of it has now been published. It was in the diary that Ruffin's undisciplined intensity found its form: "I have the defect of never being able to arrange my words in advance of my writing," he confessed in January, 1857 (*D*, I, 21), but in the diary the defect became a virtue: it ensured spontaneity and it also ensured earnestness, never a deficiency for Ruffin in any case.

We see in the diary the master of Marlbourne railing against "these degenerate times," against New England and the Puritans, against Southerners who courted Northern favor, against various other Southerners who offended him. The remarkable fact, again, in the private diary is the public nature of the entries. Ruffin seized upon events, and his reactions to them came to constitute the greater meaning of his life. As secession approached he could think of little else. On December 8, 1860, he recorded in his diary that still another daughter had died after giving birth (*D*, I, 508), but he did not mention it again. Ten days later he left for Charleston and the South Carolina secession convention. On December 26 he began: "A letter from Julian [his son], with the information, not unexpected, that the infant of Mr. Sayre had died" (*D*, I, 516). Thus disposing with the death of a grandchild, he turned straightaway to the business at hand: "As usual, went to the opening of the session of the Convention" (*D*, I, 516), and we hear no more about the deaths of daughter and grandson. This is not to say that Ruffin was insensitive; perhaps he had previously been too sensitive and now had been numbed by family tragedy, by a fate that he could not control or even fathom. It was useless to comment. The act of secession he *could* influence, and secession provided release from family tragedy. Only on rare occasions did family misfortune creep into the diary, and on those occasions one sees why Ruffin preferred to dwell on politics. An entry of September, 1860, mentioned a friend who played for Ruffin on the melodeon the tunes that he and his three unmarried daughters had formerly played and sung together. "How lonely & desolate now, in comparison!" wrote the old man (*D*, I, 468).

Life was to grow no better for Ruffin following secession, although for a time it did become more dramatic, which to Ruffin was the next best thing. After Sumter he returned to Virginia and participated in the first battle of Bull Run. "The venerable Edmund Ruffin," he entered in his diary on July 23, 1861, "who fired the first gun at Fort Sumter, who, as a volunteer in the Palmetto Guard, shared the fatigue & dangers of the retreat from Fairfax C.H., & gallantly fought through the day at Manassas, fired the first gun at this retreating column of the enemy, which resulted in this extraordinary capture" (*D*, II, 91). After the battle Ruffin walked among the Union dead, spoke kindly to the wounded, and offered them water. "No one more bitterly hates the northerners as a class than I do," he wrote, "or would be more rejoiced to have every invading soldier killed—but all my hatred was silenced for the wounded, seen in this long continued & wretched state of suffering" (*D*, II, 93).

Shortly afterward Ruffin, largely deaf as a result of the loud cannon fire at Sumter and Bull Run, gave up the battle and settled into a life of war-watching and painful introspection at Beechwood. He retreated into weariness and depression. He could not fight, and even his writings, he wrote in August, 1861, "neither attracted attention of or produced benefit to the public, nor added anything to my own reputation or appreciation" (*D*, II, 108). He read and reread the novels of Sir Walter Scott—*The Antiquary* for "the fifth or sixth time"; he awaited the invasion of the Yankees; he learned that a grandson, Julian Beckwith, had died in battle; and for himself he wished only "an [early] and sudden death" (*D*, II, 120). Only "the progress of the war, & all connected matters . . . now are greatly interesting to me," he wrote on September 30, 1861. "And to know the issue is the only thing now left for me to desire my life to be continued longer. . . . Would that I may be soon relieved of the continuance, by a sudden, unexpected, & painless death. If a cannonball, at Bull Run, or Manassas, had then been the means, it would have been the most desirable termination of my life" (*D*, II, 139).

It is in the diary, then, that the tortured and quixotic mind of Edmund Ruffin finds its fullest expression, but the diary would have virtually no readers for more than a century. It is a poignant comment on Edmund Ruffin's life that his most honest written communication was not with those Southerners of his own generation he wanted to persuade and to lead but with those three generations later. His most truthful message—in the words of another unappreciated soul, Emily Dickinson, at almost precisely the same time—was "committed to hands" he could not see. But if in the diary he was more true to himself, and suggested the reasons for his fascination with the war and his desire for Southern victory, he also wrote pamphlets and essays in which he made a more conventional case for the South. The articles in the Richmond *Enquirer*, the Charleston *Mercury*, *De Bow's Review*, and other journals spoke specifically and forcefully of the issues of the day. Ruffin often appeared beside George Fitzhugh in the pages of *De Bow's Review*, but his work was far more topical, less philosophical (or aspiring to philosophy) than Fitzhugh's. In essays just before the outbreak of war Ruffin wrote about colonization, the high price of slaves, the consequences of abolitionist agitation, and the abuses suffered by the South, but he was unable to envision the South's greater destiny, to state its larger meaning, as Fitzhugh was.[16] He was unable to see a mission for the South other than its—and his—own self-preservation.

Ruffin's principal contributions to the proslavery argument came in several pamphlets, the most significant of which, *The Political Economy of Slavery* (a title later appropriated by Eugene Genovese), appeared in 1858. He had read Fitzhugh by this time, and he evidently drew on *Sociology for the South* and *Cannibals All!*, as well as the works of Thomas Dew and other proslavery writers. Like Fitzhugh, he saw slave society as a more "normal," more humane society, and he believed the condition of the slave preferable to that of the industrial worker in England and the American Northeast. He also echoed Fitzhugh's belief that, in Ruffin's words, "the dreams and sanguine hopes of the socialistic school of philanthropists" were most completely realized "in the institution of domestic slavery."[17] But Ruffin, like his friends George Frederick Holmes, James Hammond, and Beverley Tucker, generally disapproved of Fitzhugh and disagreed with him in several particulars. Ruffin admired Fitzhugh's bête noire Adam Smith, whose *Wealth of Nations* he believed "one of the greatest & most useful works ever written" (*D*, I, 298–99). Although Ruffin wrote in 1859 that he had come to "distrust or to deny some of [Smith's] minor positions or premises" (*D*, I, 287), he remained sympathetic to capitalism, and as such was far more representative of the Southern planter class than was Fitzhugh. But his objections to the author of *Sociology* and *Cannibals All!* went beyond matters of substance. It was Fitzhugh's informal tone, which Ruffin mistook for his "careless" manner, that disturbed him. A man so earnest and intense as Edmund Ruffin could not appreciate the wit and irony, at times the

16. For a discussion of four of these essays, "The Influence of Slavery, or of Its Absence, on Manners, Morals, and Intellect," "The Political Economy of Slavery," "African Colonization Unveiled," and "Slavery and Free Labor Described and Compared," see Craven, *Edmund Ruffin*, 129–42.

17. Ruffin, quoted in Craven, *Edmund Ruffin*, 133.

sheer funning, of a man like Fitzhugh. Ruffin as essayist, or polemicist in essay form, was inferior to Fitzhugh. His forte was not wit but
conviction and deep personal commitment to the South, and Ruffin is
significant as Southern commentator only when he could bring his
conviction and commitment, his personal outrage, directly to bear on
Southern affairs—only, that is, when he felt unrestrained by an editor
and unrestricted by the essay form.

Aside from his outbursts in his diary, Ruffin achieved this freedom
only once, in a novel which was published in 1860 but has been virtually ignored, even by Ruffin scholars, ever since. *Anticipations of the
Future*, his one attempt at fiction, might more accurately have been
entitled "The Wish Fulfillment of Edmund Ruffin." [18] It tells us more
about his dreams, his hopes, and his total identification with the
Southern cause than anything else he ever published. It also demonstrates just how limited and petty his vision really was.

Written in the winter and spring of 1860, *Anticipations of the Future*
prophesies and describes a war between North and South, and in his
narrative Ruffin lets his hatred of Yankees and his fury toward abolitionists in particular run unrestrained. In fiction he was able to create
events he wished to see in fact—the secession of the Southern states,
the massacre of Northern troops, the financial failure of the Northeast, the rejection of Northern abolitionists by the Northern masses,
the hanging of John Brown's son, the burning of New York City (destroying every house in Manhattan and Brooklyn and leaving as well
"many thousands of charred and partly consumed skeletons" [p.
296]), and, ultimately, the triumph of an independent and prosperous
South and the total defeat and humiliation of New England, its political and economic position left "scarcely superior to those conditions
of the present republic of Hayti" (p. 342). Ruffin's desire to express his
love for the South and his hatred for the North was never more evident than in this work, and the author himself realized just how
much rein he had allowed his imagination. "I fear this writing of mine
(if not also some previous) would offer to a capable judge, indications
of a failing mind," he wrote in his diary the week he completed the
work (*D*, I, 416).

Ruffin was not the first Southerner to write a novel prophesying

18. Craven, in his otherwise sound biography, gives *Anticipations of the Future* only
one page. Mitchell devotes fewer than three pages to the novel. Edmund Ruffin, *Anticipations of the Future: To Serve as Lessons for the Present Time* (Richmond, 1860).

war between North and South. In 1836, Nathaniel Beverley Tucker had published pseudonymously *The Partisan Leader*, a work depicting a war beginning in 1849 with the secession of the Deep South states.[19] The war Tucker described, however, was on a much smaller scale than the one Ruffin foresaw—or, in fact, the actual war that was to come. Tucker's novel also lacks the intensity, the repeated scenes of death and destruction, and the unrestrained glee at Yankee misfortune which characterize *Anticipations of the Future*. Sir Walter Scott, rather than some private demon, was the force behind *The Partisan Leader*. Indeed, Tucker's novel ends unresolved; the struggle for Southern independence has just begun, although Tucker assures us that independence will eventually come.

But Ruffin in *Anticipations* gives us both gory spectacle and decisive Southern victory, and he delights in doing so. Writing the novel brought him both pleasure and satisfaction, he wrote in his diary, and it also brought a release from further personal sorrow. In the fall of 1859, Ruffin's remaining unmarried daughter had taken a husband and moved to Kentucky, thus leaving her father weary and alone. He again recorded in his diary his wish for death. But it was precisely at that point—the very day, in fact, after he had expressed his wish to die—that he learned of John Brown's raid at Harper's Ferry; and his interest in the raid, the fate of John Brown, and the larger implications of the raid for North and South are what saved Edmund Ruffin from himself in the fall of 1859. Shortly after he returned from Harper's Ferry he read a book entitled *Wild Scenes of the South*—"a very foolish book," Ruffin wrote, but "a *prospective* narrative of the supposed incidents & results of a separation of the Union" (*D*, I, 407)—and he had his idea. He concluded that he himself could better tell the story of disunion and war, and thus he began to work feverishly on the book which became *Anticipations of the Future*. In fact, Ruffin himself had four years earlier considered the consequences of Southern secession and had published his thoughts in the Richmond *Enquirer*. Southern rights, he had insisted, could be protected only by secession; further, the North would not make war to preserve the Union, and even if it should, the South would win. Now, in 1860, he put his ideas into an epistolary novel—but one only in the most general sense. In fact, Ruffin's projected work of propaganda would have little concern for

19. [Nathaniel Beverley Tucker], *The Partisan Leader* (1836; rpr. New York, 1933).

the requirements of good fiction. "My plan," he wrote in his diary on February 29, 1860, "is to assume the position of an English correspondent of the London Times, residing in America, & whose letters of news and comments thereon will commence with Seward's second election to the presidency [in 1864]—& will show how extreme opposition may be inflicted on the southern states, & their virtual bondage to the north, without any infraction of the federal constitution" (*D*, I, 408).

By late April, 1860, Ruffin had completed more than four hundred pages, and the project had come completely to occupy his mind: "I have passed many separate portions of what otherwise would have been wearisome time of solitude or wakefulness, in imagining what would be the probable results of even improbable incidents & political causes, & planning suitable succeeding incidents & consequences" (*D*, I, 413). If Ruffin could not shape life, he could at least shape and structure the world of his imagination. The early chapters appeared in the Charleston *Mercury*, and Ruffin hoped he was convincing the South that secession was the right course of action, since, according to *Anticipations of the Future*, to remain within the Union was eventually to lose all Southern rights. In order to reach an even larger audience, he persuaded a Richmond publisher to bring out the work as a book. To ensure that the reader did not miss his message, Ruffin gave his book the subtitle *To Serve as Lessons for the Present Time*.

Ruffin begins his book with a note to the reader disclaiming any gifts of prophecy, but he makes clear his intent to instruct as well as to entertain. His strategy is evident from the first: he will write of war between North and South because, he says, some believe war inevitable—and also, one suspects, because Ruffin himself revels in the possibility of such a spectacle. At the same time he assumes a sober pose in his introduction and writes that he himself does *not* believe war will follow secession; rather the Northern states will not "deem it expedient, or safe" to attack the seceded states or blockade their ports or promote service insurrection. Ruffin wants, that is, to assure his Southern readers that secession is not, after all, a radical course, that indeed it is respectable. But he also wants to warn any Northern readers that the South is serious about secession—that it will retaliate if the Northern "sectional party" seizes control of the federal government and degrades and ruins the South, even if the degradation comes through constitutional and nonviolent means.

Ruffin's story begins on November 11, 1864, when his narrator, the English correspondent, reports that William Seward has just been elected president by a larger majority than Lincoln's in 1860. (Ruffin had changed his original plan and had delayed Seward's first term until 1864.) The correspondent then traces the events of the late 1850s and early 1860s which had brought affairs to this point. Lincoln, he reports, had been an acceptable president; he had not attempted to abolish slavery. But an abolitionist Congress had slowly eroded Southern rights through enacting higher tariffs, improving Northern rivers, harbors, ports, and military posts while neglecting Southern ones, and reorganizing the Supreme Court to the North's advantage. Seward's appointees include abolitionists such as Horace Greeley, Wendell Phillips, and "the notorious [Hinton] Helper" who "was made one of the new Receivers of the Land Office" (p. 38). The South, Ruffin's Englishman reports, takes its punishment without resistance. He finds a "silent and subdued and sullen discontent of all the southern section and people" (p. 33). Later there is bluster but no action. The South is "noisy but impotent" (p. 48).

Soon the Seward administration attacks slavery directly, first by abolishing it in the District of Columbia, then by encouraging and helping slaves to escape, and finally by dividing the Northern states and creating more free states, thus providing a three-fourths majority which will enable the North to abolish slavery by constitutional amendment. Finally, in 1868, six states from the Deep South secede, South Carolina forces seize Fort Sumter, and Ruffin's correspondent leaves for Charleston "for nearer observation of the events most likely to be interesting" (p. 103). Virginia and the other states of the upper South decide against secession at this point. Despite Edmund Ruffin's disclaimers of prophetic gifts, writing in March, 1860, he came close to describing the early days of the American Civil War.

Soon after the first shot is fired in Charleston—a shot Ruffin himself would fire one year after he wrote—Union troops march into western Virginia, and Virginia responds by leading the remaining Southern states, except Texas, into the Confederacy, after which the Southern army occupies Harper's Ferry and the District of Columbia. The Union has already been forced to move its capital to Albany. It is at this point in the novel that Ruffin's fantasies assume even greater proportions, and his writing becomes particularly fevered. A group of eight hundred Ohio abolitionists and twenty-seven hundred Negroes—most of them fugitive slaves—swoop across the Ohio into Kentucky with the intention of freeing every Negro and massacring every white they can find. John Brown's body lay "a-mould'ring in the grave," but Ruffin's obsession with Brown remained, for leading the invaders is John Brown's son, General Owen Brown, his commission signed by President Seward. The abolitionists and Negroes butcher all the men, women, and children they can find "after the infliction of still greater horrors" (p. 254), but their plan to rescue slaves from Kentucky plantations is thwarted because, Ruffin tells us, very few slaves want to be rescued. Indeed, we discover, many of Brown's Negro recruits had joined his band in the first place with the sole purpose of getting back to the South so they could rejoin their old masters; or, if they could not find their old ones, any master would serve. Finally the Kentucky sharpshooters rout the invaders. Most of the Negroes run, being "naturally" timid, Ruffin writes, and having "the acquired sense of inferiority to the white race" (p. 262).[20] Owen Brown is captured, and "from the different spreading branches of one gigantic oak were hung Gen. Brown, with twenty-seven of his subordinate white officers." Their bodies "were left there, to be devoured by carrion vultures." Of the eight hundred whites in the invading force, "every one was either killed, or, if captured, was afterwards hung" (pp. 264–65). Ruffin's revenge on John Brown was complete.

In the following chapters Ruffin continues to revel in Yankee suffering. In a naval battle off Charleston in which Northern sailors attempt to board a Southern steamer, "streams of boiling water were directed upon the boarders" (p. 274). And when their Northern vessel, badly damaged, sailed north for repairs, it foundered off Cape Hatteras and "the whole ship and armament with nearly all the crew were lost" (p. 275). Meanwhile, the North suffers economically from the loss of Southern trade, and riots break out in Northern cities. Mobs take over New York in a scene that anticipates actual events in the summer of 1863. "There was no order—no command," writes Ruffin in lines which Herman Melville would echo three years later in "The House-Top," his poem on the New York riots. In Melville's poem, "Wise Draco comes, deep in the midnight roll / Of black artillery," and the rioters are brought under control. But in Ruffin's fantasy the militia

---

20. Ruffin's use of the word *acquired* is curious. He seems to suggest that he believed Negroes not innately inferior, a view that would not have been shared by most other white Americans, Northern or Southern, of his day.

has little effect. Churches and banks are rifled and robbed, the entire city is burned: "In two hours, this great and rich city . . . was so covered by flames, that no possible human means could have prevented the full consummation of the calamity." The city is "one raging sea of flame, rising in billows and breakers above the tops of the houses" (p. 295), and many thousands die. Philadelphia and Boston explode in a similar fashion, and in Boston the rioters turn against the abolitionists whom they hold responsible for the war.

Ruffin then brings his war, and his book, to a rapid conclusion. In September, 1868, less than six months after the conflict had begun, the North agrees to a truce, and although the Union refuses at this point to grant the South independence, it is obvious that independence will follow. The Northeast has collapsed, and Southern commerce prospers through direct trade with Europe and the American Northwest. Ruffin's correspondent predicts that the Northwestern states—those on the upper Mississippi—and eventually the Middle Atlantic states will join the new Southern nation and will accept slavery. They will do so because they have tired of the fanaticism of New England. Ruffin's final comfort is that after Southern victory New England will be isolated and the Southern Confederacy (including the Middle Atlantic and Northwestern states) will refuse to take it back into the Union. The original secession of the South will have led, through war, to the ultimate alienation of New England, and again Edmund Ruffin would be vindicated.

Such was Edmund Ruffin's wish fulfillment and also his revenge— a premature revenge, to be sure, since as he wrote in 1860 the acute Southern suffering at Northern hands had not yet begun. Southern pride, and Ruffin's own, had been wounded, but the South had not yet experienced defeat. Ruffin launched his book in the fall of 1860, well aware of its literary inadequacies but eager to see its reception. It had little to recommend it artistically except a sometimes lively prose style, an occasional power of description, and a sense of the grotesque. It offered little plot and even less development of character. The narrator, the English correspondent, spoke with Ruffin's own voice and took a delight in Northern misfortune which no detached reporter would have evinced. Ruffin, then, justifiably feared "deserved censure for literary demerit," but at the same time he could not "help sanguinely hoping that the book, as an argument & incentive to defense & resistance by the South, & for disunion, will have noted &

good effect" (*D, I,* 463). He hoped for too much. Although one reviewer said his book "bids fair to create a furor in the South, similar to
that caused at the North by the notorious Helper book" (*D, I,* 554, n.
15), and the *Southern Literary Messenger* remarked that *Anticipations of
the Future,* if it were read, would "be productive of much good," in
fact it was not read.[21] Most journals ignored the book, and Ruffin later
wrote in his diary that "little more than 400 copies have been issued in
sales & *gifts*" (*D, II,* 232). Ruffin's one venture into fiction may have
been early Southern Gothic, but it went largely unrecognized in his
own day as it has gone unrecognized since. His diary, written in confidence, would eventually attract more readers than the novel for
which he had such great hopes.

But given the centrality of Edmund Ruffin in Southern secessionist
thought and action in the years before the war and in the developing
tradition of Southern self-justification, the novel does have value: it
tells us what an important Southern extremist—unique, but still representative in many ways of other extremists, as Avery Craven em-
phasizes—*wished* would happen in the year 1860, and also the manner in which he wished it would take place. Edmund Ruffin wrote
little else for publication after 1860; but one wonders what he would
have written if he had waited until 1865 to write his fantasy of revenge. It was to be Atlanta and Columbia, after all, not New York and
Boston, that would be destroyed by fire, and the South, not New England, would be left paralyzed and friendless after the war. And Ruffin
himself would suffer even greater personal tragedy before 1865—
the deaths of two more daughters, the death in combat of his son Julian as well as a grandson, the ransacking and partial destruction by
Union forces of Beechwood in 1862 and Marlbourne in 1864. Ruffin,
who saw the Civil War as a personal vendetta, had challenged the
Yankees and the Yankees had responded in kind. A wood engraving
identified as the burning of Beechwood (in fact, only the outbuildings
were burned) appeared in *Harper's Weekly,* and a Union nurse, present at the burning, described a "splendid sight": "such bursts of flame
& volumes of black, dun-colored & white smoke I have never seen."[22]

If he had waited until 1865, then, Edmund Ruffin's revenge would

21. Review of *Anticipations of the Future,* in *Southern Literary Messenger,* XXXI (October, 1860), 320.
22. See "A Volunteer Nurse in the Civil War: The Diary of Harriet Douglas Whetton," ed. Paul H. Hass, *Wisconsin Magazine of History,* XLVIII (Spring, 1965), 213.

have been the bloodier. Or, perhaps, it would not have come at all. For Ruffin, when he wrote in 1860, was buoyant in spirit; he wrote with expectation and pleasure, with demonic energy. But as he stood at war's end he was a weary and defeated man, numbed by sorrow, too weak for revenge, bereft of imaginative strategy, certainly unable to envision the destruction of the entire Northeast. When his three daughters had died in the summer of 1855, Ruffin had at least the Southern cause to turn to, but when the Confederacy died ten years later he had nothing at all. Reality had intruded too deeply into his life by that time, and in 1865 he could only contemplate Southern defeat and the end of the Confederacy, scribble his "unmitigated hatred" to Yankees, and, four years after he had fired the shot that began the war, fire another that would end his own life. "The Yankees have just as certainly killed your Grandfather," Ruffin's son wrote to his own sons, "as they did your beloved uncle who fell gloriously on the field of battle." [23] It was good, then, that Edmund Ruffin had had his public revenge in 1860 in *Anticipations of the Future* before it was fully due. In 1865 he would be incapable of it.

Hinton Rowan Helper

If the Old South was ancient Greece reborn, as Southern polemicists sometimes claimed, Edmund Ruffin was its self-proclaimed truth-sayer, its Empedocles poised upon Etna, fearing the Golden Age gone, seeing ahead only commercialism, competition, weakness and deficiency of character. Empedocles had lived too long, had lived—in the words of Matthew Arnold—"on into a time when the habits of Greek thought and feeling had begun fast to change, character to dwindle." [24] Just as Empedocles leaped into Etna, Edmund Ruffin, who had also lived too long and pondered too deeply the condition of his homeland, chose to end his life rather than to face whatever the future might bring.

Suicide, as we have noted, has been an occupational hazard for those Southerners who pondered their region and themselves too deeply, without the leaven of wit or humor or the relative detach-

23. "The Death of Edmund Ruffin," *Tyler's Quarterly Magazine*, V (January, 1924), 193–95. A letter from Edmund Ruffin, Jr., to his sons, dated June 20, 1865, gives details of Ruffin's suicide.

24. Matthew Arnold, "Preface to *Poems*, 1853," in Lionel Trilling (ed.), *The Portable Matthew Arnold* (New York, 1949), 185.

ment of scholarly pursuit, for those who identified their own fate too closely with the fate of their region. Edmund Ruffin was one such Southerner, and so in a quite different way was Hinton Rowan Helper of North Carolina. Although Helper's self-destruction came long after he wrote most fervently about the South, the roots of that destruction were present in his personality and his work from the beginning. Like Ruffin an absolutist, an all-or-nothing man, he was earnest, intense, and unable to see himself or any subject with detachment. He was no Empedocles: when he contemplated the South he had not lived too long. Neither did he fear change. To the contrary, he advocated it as long as it proceeded as he wished.

In many respects Edmund Ruffin and Hinton Rowan Helper can be seen as linked Southern antagonists, both impulsive men of great ego and exaggerated self-importance, driven by ambition and by a belief, from their early years, that they were meant for a nobler destiny than that of other men; both seeing themselves in the late 1850s as Southern prophets, messengers with the truth, and both in the end giving in to a long-standing self-destructive urge. But if Ruffin and Helper were similar in temperament, they were at opposite poles in nearly every aspect of belief and of background. They form one of the many pairs of curiously similar adversaries from those states separated by William Byrd's Dividing Line: Ruffin the planter from Virginia who prized hierarchy, Helper the Piedmont Carolinian of lower birth who hated the slave-owning oligarchy and longed for a white-only democracy.

Hinton Rowan Helper has lived long in infamy, championed by neither Southerner nor non-Southerner. For not only was he an abolitionist but one who professed a hatred of Negroes, thus a man who eventually managed to antagonize both camps, North and South. "The Notorious Helper" he was called after the first version of *The Impending Crisis of the South* appeared in 1857, and his later books earned him a reputation as racial monomaniac. Ruffin was also a monomaniac but one, like Melville's Ahab, who had "his humanities": he had lost six children and two homes and was an object of pity rather than scorn by the time he ended his suffering in 1865. But Helper seems to have had no such excuse for his excesses. He was young, in his twenties—tall, broad-shouldered, bearded, handsome—when he wrote *The Impending Crisis,* and still relatively young and unscarred when he wrote his virulent anti-Negro works, *Nojoque* (1867), *The Negroes in*

Negroland (1868), and *Noonday Exigencies in America* (1871).[25] "A new Moses," Helper was acclaimed in the North after *The Impending Crisis* appeared, although a Jeremiah would have been nearer the truth. But in his own country Helper was not prophet so much as he was, according to a newspaper in his home state, a "poor traitor to his native sod and native skies." Possession of his abolitionist tract was a crime in most Southern states, one often prosecuted to the fullest: three men were reported hanged in Arkansas for owning copies, men were jailed in other states, and university professors were fired in North Carolina, Virginia, and Georgia.[26] Never did a Southern book cause such a furor, and never was a Southerner hated more by his countrymen than this obscure backwoodsman from North Carolina.

Little has been written since to redeem the reputation of Hinton Rowan Helper. The Northern abolitionists who embraced him in 1857 denounced him when they read his later works of Negrophobia. Southerners who reviled him for his abolitionist views in 1857 continued to revile him even after he became a strident spokesman for the most extreme racists among them. Biographers have pictured Helper as an opportunist, a thief, and a madman,[27] and indeed he serves as an example of that writer whose work as a whole is denounced because a large part of that work was eccentric and because he himself was deemed unbalanced and unfit. That is, because of the instability and bitterness of his later years, and the fanatical books of his middle years—in which he proposed, among other things, writing the Negro "out of existence," flooding the Sahara, and annexing all of British America—it might be assumed that he was equally mad in his twenties when he wrote his most important book, *The Impending Crisis*. Edmund Wilson, for example, writes in *Patriotic Gore* that

25. Hinton Rowan Helper, *The Impending Crisis of the South* (New York, 1857); *Nojoque: A Question for a Continent* (New York, 1867); *The Negroes in Negroland; The Negroes in America; and Negroes Generally* (New York, 1868); *Noonday Exigencies in America* (New York, 1871).

26. William T. Polk, "The Hated Helper," *South Atlantic Quarterly*, XXX (April, 1931), 182; Hugh T. Lefler, *Hinton Rowan Helper: Advocate of a "White America"* (Charlottesville, 1935), 6. See also Joaquin Jose Cardoso, "Hinton Rowan Helper: A Nineteenth Century Pilgrimage" (Ph.D. dissertation, University of Wisconsin, 1967), 130–68. Most subsequent biographical information is taken from Cardoso's excellent dissertation, the most thorough and the most accurate biographical study of Helper. I also draw from Hugh C. Bailey, *Hinton Rowan Helper: Abolitionist-Racist* (Tuscaloosa, Ala., 1965).

27. As a youth Helper took $300 from a Salisbury shopkeeper, but later he confessed the embezzlement and repaid the debt. Helper's earlier biographers, Bailey and Lefler, treat Helper less sympathetically in their accounts of this episode than does Cardoso, who dismisses it as a youthful indiscretion.

Helper "already in the *Crisis* . . . is exhibiting the symptoms of a rabid crank with delusions of persecution." Wilson may be partially correct, but to focus on Helper's delusions of persecution—or, as other critics have done, on his misuse of statistics in the book or on a racism which in fact is hardly evident in *The Impending Crisis* and becomes virulent only later on—is to miss the point about Helper's book; and that is, the *general* truth of his indictment in *The Impending Crisis*. What he said—that slavery was economically unfeasible—was nothing more than what the most prominent Southerners were saying ten and fifteen years after he wrote. Slavery had been the worst curse ever brought upon the Southern people, proclaimed Henry A. Wise, the former proslavery governor of Virginia to whom Fitzhugh had dedicated *Cannibals All!*, in a speech in 1873.[28]

Similarly, the most basic details of Helper's life have often been misstated. Helper, Wilson wrote in *Patriotic Gore*, was a man of "lower-class German blood" (p. 377) from "all but the lowest stratum" of society (p. 371), the son of "an illiterate farmer" whose "parents had died early and left him nothing" (p. 365). Such information is misleading at best, inaccurate at worst, and suggests more about the prejudices of Edmund Wilson than about the background of Hinton Helper. In fact, Helper came from the upper stratum of the rural middle class of Piedmont North Carolina. His mother's family was well educated, highly respectable, and far from poor. His maternal grandfather had been one of the most influential citizens of Rowan County. Helper's own father owned more than two hundred acres of land, and left both land and money at his death. It is uncertain whether Helper's immediate family owned slaves: no records exist showing ownership, yet Helper claimed in *Nojoque* (p. 13) that his father owned four slaves, and he wrote years later in a letter to Thomas Nelson Page that he "had the misfortune of being born a slaveholder"—a claim which leads one to wonder if Helper, the great critic of the slavocracy, was a pretender to it himself.[29] In any case, that the Helpers owned few slaves, if any, may have led Wilson to conclude they were "lower-class"; but in fact the section of North Carolina in which they lived, settled in large part by Germans, Moravians, and Quakers, was not a

28. Wilson, *Patriotic Gore*, 375; Clement Eaton (paraphrasing Wise), quoted in George B. Tindall, "Onward and Upward with the Rising South," *The Ethnic Southerners* (Baton Rouge, 1976), 233.

29. Hinton Helper to Thomas Nelson Page, May 6, 1903, in Thomas Nelson Page Papers, Duke University Library, Durham.

large slaveholding area and indeed had much antislavery sentiment. Moreover, Helper's own basic position as he set it forth in print—disliking both slavery and Negroes—was not nearly so rare as it might now seem. It was not uncommon in the North Carolina Piedmont, as well as in the free states, in the 1840s and 1850s to hate both slavery and the slave, to want no part of either. "Hatred to slavery is very generally little more than hatred of negroes," George Fitzhugh had written in *Cannibals All!* (p. 297), the same year the earliest version of *The Impending Crisis* appeared, and although he was not correct in the case of most New England abolitionists, he was correct in Helper's case. Neither was it uncommon, W. J. Cash notwithstanding, for the nonslaveholder to resent the power and sway of the slaveholder. Hinton Helper—as C. Vann Woodward has written of Fitzhugh—was *sui generis*; yet he was also a product of his society, a spokesman, albeit an extreme one, for his people.[30]

Helper was hardly the first such spokesman. Although it is sometimes assumed that the critical spirit in the South disappeared in the 1830s with the waning of Jeffersonian liberalism, in fact, as Carl Degler has shown, there were protesters, particularly in the upper South, up until 1859 and John Brown's raid. Moncure Daniel Conway, Henry Ruffner, and Samuel Janney of Virginia; Cassius Marcellus Clay and James B. Birney of Kentucky; Benjamin Sherwood, Benjamin Hedrick, and Daniel Goodloe, like Helper, from the North Carolina Piedmont: all opposed slavery, and most for the same social and economic reasons which motivated Helper.[31]

Goodloe, who along with Hedrick became a friend of Helper's, most nearly anticipated the author of *The Impending Crisis* although he was far more moderate. Some fifteen years Helper's senior, Goodloe went to Washington in the 1840s and became an editor of the antislavery *National Era*, thus launching most of his attacks on slavery from the relative safety of a border city. Like Helper, he stressed the South's inferiority to the North in nearly every measurable particular, introduced statistics to support his position, and concluded that slavery was the cause of this inferiority. He stated his case primarily in widely circulating pamphlets, of which his *Inquiry Into the Causes Which Have*

30. See Clement Eaton, *The Mind of the Old South* (Baton Rouge, 1964), 152–69.
31. See Carl N. Degler, *The Other South: Southern Dissenters in the Nineteenth Century* (New York, 1974), especially 13–96; and Eaton, *The Mind of the Old South*, especially Chapters 1, 4, 5, and 7.

Retarded Accumulation of Wealth and Increase of Population in the Southern States (1846) was perhaps most representative. Here he focused on Southern economic inferiority and, like Helper, stressed that the South was behind the North even in that area for which it claimed so much, agriculture. Also anticipating Helper, he compared slave and free states, beginning with Virginia and New York, the two states with which Helper also was to begin. "Slavery," he concluded, "sits like the Old Man of the Sea upon the necks of the people, paralyzing every effort at improvement." Goodloe in this pamphlet and others differed from Helper, however, in several important ways: he wrote with little rancor; he did not propose an actual platform for abolition; he was not a Negrophobe; and he wrote anonymously, signing at least two works merely "By a Carolinian," rather than identifying himself as Helper was to do.[32] The anonymity Goodloe sought is significant: never would his friend Helper seek to remain anonymous in any writing venture. To escape anonymity was perhaps his life's goal. For him, being known was at least as important as being heard.

Helper first sought to be heard in *The Land of Gold*, his highly impressionistic study of life in California.[33] He had traveled to the Far West at twenty-one seeking adventure and wealth. The first he had found but not the latter, although he did not fare so poorly as his earliest biographers supposed. When he returned to North Carolina in 1854 he saw an opportunity both to gain recognition and to puncture myths about California. In *The Land of Gold* he sought to expose the "rottenness, corruption, squalor, and misery" of California, and he did his job well enough. This, as Joaquin Jose Cardoso notes, was the most temperate book Helper ever wrote. It was also the only one which was not preoccupied with race. Helper included only the mildest criticism of Negro slavery, and indeed at one point he felt compelled to attack "meddling abolitionists" (p. 276). At another, the author, who had stopped in Central America on his voyage home, insisted that Nicaragua could "never fulfil its destiny until it introduced negro slavery. Nothing but slave labor can ever subdue its forests or

32. [Daniel Goodloe], *Inquiry Into the Causes Which Have Retarded Accumulation of Wealth and Increase of Population in the Southern States* (Washington, D.C., 1846), 13, and *The South and the North* (Washington, D.C., 1849). Goodloe's later work, *The Southern Platform: or, Manual of Southern Sentiment on the Subject of Slavery* (Boston, 1858), he did sign, but this was a compilation of statements against slavery by earlier Southerners, rather than Goodloe's own expression.

33. Hinton Rowan Helper, *The Land of Gold* (Baltimore, 1855).

cultivate its untimbered lands" (p. 221). Although there is some doubt whether these were Helper's original words—his publisher in Baltimore forced him to alter the original text to conform more nearly to a proslavery position—the young North Carolinian apparently was willing to go on record as a mild supporter of slavery under certain conditions.

Helper's trip enabled him to become an author, and *The Land of Gold* revealed for the first time his need to tell the truth as he saw it—as well as, Cardoso suggests, the corresponding fear that he might not be believed. The trip had also afforded him a perspective on the South, a vantage point Edmund Ruffin, despite his greater age and experience, never had. Helper's perspective, given his early years in the Carolina Piedmont, had been somewhat different even before, but in many regards he was still a rather typical Southerner when he went to California. Only in the West did he view slavery and the South with new eyes. If he was disturbed by the lack of order and decorum on the California frontier, he was also impressed by the social democracy and, his later observations in Nicaragua notwithstanding, he came to see advantages in free labor.

The Land of Gold had convinced Helper he could write, but just what in 1855 led him to begin such an iconoclastic work as *The Impending Crisis* is uncertain. Helper himself later told a correspondent that he had been inspired by "the sagacious and salutary and statesmanlike writings of Thomas Jefferson"; and William T. Polk, one of his few sympathetic critics, has written that he was "inspired by the purest love of the South."[34] Polk may be partially correct; yet what ignited Helper at the time was his anger at Charles Mortimer, the Baltimore publisher who had removed certain antislavery passages from *The Land of Gold*. When he returned to North Carolina he began to correspond with Northern abolitionists and to gather information which would "prove" free labor superior to slave labor. He drew on statistics provided by the Seventh United States Census, which had been directed, curiously enough, by James D. B. De Bow. One pictures Helper, the intense man in his mid-twenties, still accepted at this point by the unsuspecting townsfolk of Salisbury, writing a book that would later be denounced by even his closest friends. Helper surely

34. Hinton Rowan Helper to John Sherman, October 19, 1896 (typed copy), in Southern Historical Collection, University of North Carolina Library, Chapel Hill; Polk, "The Hated Helper," 177.

realized what he was doing, and also determined that he needed further information to complete his study. Thus in the spring of 1856 he sold his interest in the family farm (an interest Edmund Wilson would deny him) and traveled to Baltimore, then to New York, where he completed the writing early in 1857. When he left North Carolina with the uncompleted *Impending Crisis* in hand, he must have known he was leaving the South for good.

Since Helper was unable to find a publisher in Baltimore, he peddled his manuscript in New York and finally offered to give it away. Since commercial publishers feared they would lose Southern trade if they published such a book, he gave a bond protecting his publisher against loss. Finally, in June, 1857, the first version of *The Impending Crisis of the South* appeared. It was a book which eventually would reach more Americans than any work of nonfiction to that time, but its popularity did not come at once. *The Impending Crisis* sold thirteen thousand copies in 1857—respectable enough when compared to the fewer than four hundred copies of Ruffin's *Anticipations of the Future*—but its fame did not come until late 1859 when the new Republican party adopted the book for circulation in the 1860 campaign. The 1859 *Compendium* was basically the same as the 1857 book, although Helper toned down the language, eliminated some of the most savage references to slaveholders, and added a chapter in which he quoted other antislavery writers.

The 1857 edition of the book is the one in which the essential Helper emerges, the man filled with class resentment who later said he was "pushed and twirled by an involuntary impulse" to write[35]—but in fact was driven by the purely voluntary impulse to become the champion of the plain Southern white and make himself known in the process. Helper began his book humbly enough, insisting that "it has been no part of my purpose to cast unmerited opprobrium upon slaveholders, or to display any special friendliness or sympathy for the blacks" (p. v) and maintaining that he was more interested in the economic aspects of slavery than in the moral or humanitarian. He identified himself as a Southerner, assured the reader that the discussion to follow was "but a fair reflex of the honest and long-settled convictions of my heart" (p. v), and explained further that he had undertaken his book because of "an irrepressibly active desire to do

---

35. Hinton Rowan Helper, quoted in Cardoso, "Hinton Rowan Helper," 267.

something to elevate the South to an honorable and powerful position among the enlightened quarters of the globe" (p. vi). Helper's
stated mission, thus, was more modest than George Fitzhugh's in
Cannibals All!, which appeared the same year. Fitzhugh wanted the
South to point the way for the world; Helper presumed only to elevate the South itself.

Helper continued in a tone almost contrite for the first few pages of
his book. As a "true-hearted southerner" (p. 12) he was "heartily
ashamed of the inexcusable weakness, inertia and dilapidation" of
the South (p. 20). He deplored the colonial status of the South, anticipating Henry Grady's later complaint of Southern dependence on the
North, nearly in Grady's words. As Helper wrote: "In infancy we are
swaddled in Northern muslin; in childhood we are humored with
Northern geegaws; in youth we are instructed out of Northern books
. . . in the decline of life we remedy our eye-sight with Northern
spectacles and support our infirmities with Northern canes . . . and
finally, when we die, our inanimate bodies, shrouded in Northern
cambric, are stretched upon the bier, borne to the grave in a Northern
carriage, entombed with a Northern spade, and memorized [*sic*] with
a Northern slab!" (pp. 22–23).[36]

To this point Helper had said little that many a respected Southerner had not said before; his indictment of the South's colonial status could have come from Fitzhugh or De Bow. But it was here that
his tone abruptly changed and the seething resentment which he
had suppressed during his first dozen pages spewed forth. Why, he
asked, is the South inferior to the North "in a commercial, mechanical, manufactural, financial, and literary point of view?" (p. 23). "*Slavery!*" he answered (p. 25), but before he answered he insisted on his
right to give such a response. As a Southerner, "we have the right to
express our opinion . . . on any and every question that affects the
public good; and, so help us God, 'sink or swim, live or die, survive
or perish,' we are determined to exercise that right with manly firmness, and without fear, favor or affection" (pp. 24–25).

The challenge Helper had accepted and welcomed, and he wanted

36. Compare Grady's description of a Southern funeral in his speech to the Bay
State Club of Boston in 1889: the deceased had "a tombstone . . . from Vermont," a
"pine coffin from Cincinnati," and a shovel to dig his grave made of iron "imported
from Pittsburgh." "The South didn't furnish a thing on earth for that funeral," Grady
said, "but the corpse and the hole in the ground" (*The New South and Other Addresses*
[New York, 1904], 133).

to make one other thing clear. In the same passage in which he condemned slaveholding, he identified himself as the son of "a considerate and merciful slaveholder" (p. 24), a claim which may or may not
have been true but which, in any case, Helper wanted to put on record. Such a statement could be justified as being of strategic importance: it would assure his readers that Helper was no stranger to slavery and spoke with a certain knowledge and experience. But it also
served to ally him not with the nonslaveholding plain whites for
whom he presumably wrote but rather with those few "enlightened"
slaveholders—with Jefferson, Madison, and other slave-owning opponents of slavery whom he quoted later in *The Impending Crisis* and
with whom he wanted to be identified. This man of "lower-class
blood"—to quote Wilson—who is said in *The Impending Crisis* to have
stated the case for the common man, who himself wrote on the final
page of his book that his was the voice of the nonslaveholding whites
of the South (p. 413), initially wanted to give the impression of speaking not from the point of view of the exploited white Southerner, as is
often asserted, but rather from the position of the slavocracy itself.
Only once in the first four hundred pages of the 1857 *Impending Crisis*
did he suggest that he himself might be a plain white.

Once having defined himself as a critic of slavery, Helper realized
there was no turning back: "Then we are an abolitionist? Yes! not
merely a freesoiler, but an abolitionist, in the fullest sense of the
term" (p. 25), and one in favor of "immediate and unconditional abolition" (p. 26). Helper expected criticism and violence, he added, but
he had written with a "conviction that we are right" (p. 26) and asked
Southerners to join him in overthrowing the "slave-driving oligarchy." To show his readers the virtue of his course, he proceeded to
introduce pages of tables, statistics, and quotations from authorities
which showed the slave states behind the free not only in wealth and
commerce but also in that very agriculture of which the South so
boasted. When armed with facts and statistics, Helper seized the
offensive and began to speak even more boldly to the reader and
more defiantly to the slaveholder. Contending that slaveholders were
"more criminal than common murderers" (p. 140) and that slavery,
"the monstrous enemy that stalks abroad in your land" (p. 53), was
responsible for all Southern ills, he urged nonslaveholders to follow
his plan of action: organize; vote to make slaveholders ineligible for
office; boycott slaveholding merchants; tax slaveholders. Helper went

on to present an eleven-point plan of action. Then, his language becoming even more explosive, he turned directly to the slaveholders:

> But, Sirs, knights of bludgeons, chevaliers of bowie-knives and pistols, and lords of the lash . . . Terror-engenderers of the South . . . we have no modifications to propose, no compromise to offer, nothing to retract. Frown, Sirs, fret, foam, prepare your weapons, threat, strike, shoot, stab, bring on civil war, dissolve the Union, nay annihilate the solar system if you will— do all this, more, less, better, worse, anything—do what you will, Sirs, you can neither foil nor intimidate us; our purpose is as firmly fixed as the eternal pillars of Heaven; we have determined to abolish slavery, and, so help us God, abolish it we will! (pp. 185–87)

Thus spoke twenty-seven-year-old Hinton Helper, but it could as well have been Melville's Ahab crying defiance of the gods: "nay annihilate the solar system if you will . . . our purpose is as firmly fixed as the eternal pillars of Heaven." The single-minded vision, the monomaniacal rhetoric, the defiant tones: Helper, fully as much as any transcendentalist-turned-nihilist, was unwilling to compromise.

Having spent most of his fury, the author settled into relative calm for the remainder of his book, citing antislavery authorities from North, South (primarily the early Virginians), church, and Bible. He introduced more statistics to prove Southern inadequacy in industry, education, and transportation, and again deplored the colonial status of the South: "See [even the slaveholder] rise in the morning from a Northern bed, and clothe himself in Northern apparel; see him walk across the floor on a Northern carpet" (p. 355). And not only had slavery affected Southern prosperity, it had closed the Southern mind. The South was barren in all fields of intellectual endeavor, Helper insisted, and in an indictment that anticipated H. L. Mencken's "Sahara of the Bozart" sixty years later, he enumerated the inadequacies of Southern intellectual life:

> Whence come our geographers, our astronomers, our chemists, our meteorologists, our ethnologists, and others, who have made their names illustrious in the domain of the Natural Sciences? Not from the Slave States, certainly. In the Literature of Law, the South can furnish no name that can claim peership with those of Story and of Kent; in History, none that tower up to the altitude of Bancroft, Prescott, Hildreth, Motley and Washington Irving; in Theology, none that can challenge favorable comparison with those of Edwards, Dwight, Channing, Taylor, Bushnell, Tyler and Wayland; in Fiction, none that take rank with Cooper, and Mrs. Stowe; and but

few that may do so with even the second class novelists of the North; in
Poetry, none that can command position with Bryant, Halleck, and Per-
cival, with Whittier, Longfellow, and Lowell, with Willis, Stoddard and
Taylor, with Holmes, Saxe, and Burleigh; and—we might add twenty other
Northern names before we found their Southern peer, with the exception
of poor Poe. (pp. 403–404)

"WHAT HAS PRODUCED THIS LITERARY PAUPERISM OF THE SOUTH?"
Helper asked. "One single word, most pregnant in its terrible mean-
ings, answers the question. That word is—SLAVERY!" (p. 404). Further, "a free press is an institution almost unknown at the South. Free
speech is considered as treason against slavery: and when people
dare neither speak nor print their thoughts, free thought itself is well
nigh extinguished" (p. 409). Thus the closed society—the savage
ideal, as another Piedmont Carolinian, W. J. Cash, would later call
it—had triumphed in the South.

That it had not fully triumphed, of course, was shown by those few
Southerners such as Helper himself who continued to attack slavery,
but that its victory was nearly complete was suggested by the Northern residence of Helper, Goodloe, and others when they issued their
indictments. It was fortunate for Helper that he had gone north; otherwise, as one North Carolina editor wrote, the wish he expressed in
The Impending Crisis to die in his native state might well have been
granted sooner than he expected. He was so well liked that if he returned, "he will never be permitted to go away again. We will give
him *a home in the bosom of his native soil*." The *Carolina Watchman* in
Helper's hometown, Salisbury, was particularly indignant because
Helper had written most of his book while living there. Most of the
Southern reaction to the book came from the upper South; Deep
South newspapers and journals hardly responded at all, the New Orleans *Picayune* and *De Bow's Review* being notable exceptions. De Bow
in a pamphlet issued in 1860 did not mention Helper by name, but
refuted many of the contentions of *The Impending Crisis* and insisted
that the nonslaveholder benefited from slavery.[37] And up in Richmond old Edmund Ruffin, having committed himself heart and soul
to the cause of the slave society, read a copy of the book which other

37. Editor of Raleigh *Weekly Register*, December 7, 1859, quoted in Lefler, *Hinton
Rowan Helper*, 26; Cardoso, "Hinton Rowan Helper," 130–68; James D. B. De Bow, *The
Interest in Slavery of the Southern Non-Slaveholder* (Charleston, 1860).

Southerners were jailed for possessing—read in fact the milder version, the 1859 *Compendium*—and entered in his diary his immediate reactions to this "infamous & lying" work. "He left home because guilty of, & detected in, stealing from his employer, & going to the North, sought & gained favor there by denouncing & calumniating his southern country & countrymen. It is an ultra violent assault on negro slavery. . . . Much the greater part is of false opinions or facts, & weak or foolish arguments" (*D*, I, 342–43, 445). Five months later, in the midst of composing *Anticipations of the Future*, Ruffin again looked over the book and blasted the renegade Helper and the many "lies & exaggerations" in his book, but at the same time, curiously, he welcomed it: "If Helper's statements & arguments are taken as good authority, the fanatical hatred of negro slavery, & of the southern people will be greatly increased, & also the wish to use, & the faith in the effects, of such action as led to, & induced [John] Brown's attempt. The greater the extent of their delusion, & madness in this respect, & the greater their perseverance, the better for us will be the result" (*D*, I, 408–409). The extremist Ruffin thus applauded the extremist Helper because the efforts of both would push North and South closer to war.

Some few Southerners agreed with Helper's book, notably Cassius Marcellus Clay of Kentucky and Helper's friend Benjamin Hedrick of North Carolina, but most of his support came naturally enough from the North. Abraham Lincoln, who earlier had read Fitzhugh's *Sociology*, read and marked *The Impending Crisis* in the spring of 1858 as he prepared his "House Divided" speech. But Helper found stronger allies in Horace Greeley, William Lloyd Garrison, and other abolitionists. The 1859 *Compendium* caused a furor North as well as South. The United States Congress debated its merits during the winter of 1859–1860 after John B. Sherman of Ohio, candidate for Speaker of the House, endorsed the book, which he had not even read. At least four books, three by non-Southerners, were written in response to *The Impending Crisis*. The one Southerner, Samuel M. Wolfe of Virginia, called Helper a "vile wretch" who must have had a "diseased brain" to have written such a work. In particular, Wolfe charged that Helper had manipulated statistics to prove Northern superiority.[38]

38. Bailey, *Hinton Rowan Helper*, 59–60; Samuel M. Wolfe, *Helper's Impending Crisis Dissected* (Philadelphia, 1860), 1–2.

Indeed, to some degree he had. Or, rather, he had chosen only those statistics which supported his argument, which after all was no more than proslavery Southerners had done. Critics particularly disputed his claims that New York was wealthier than seven Southern states combined and that the Northern hay crop alone was worth more than cotton and five other Southern agricultural products combined. They also challenged his method for determining population increase in the North and South by selecting for the South those seaboard states in which the population increase was minimal rather than the Cotton Kingdom, where it was greatest. And they noted correctly that he had neglected statistics favorable to the South, particularly the finding of the 1850 census that *white* per capita income was higher in the South than in the North. Fewer critics pointed to a fact obvious to the modern reader: the Southern weaknesses Helper catalogued were not due entirely to slavery. Land, for example, was worth less per acre in the South not so much because of slavery but because of the smaller population in the South compared to the settled Northeast.

Economic historians still debate the central contention of *The Impending Crisis* that slavery was unprofitable and economically destructive to the region. Although Robert William Fogel and Stanley L. Engerman conclude in *Time on the Cross* that the Southern economy was healthier in many ways than the Northern from 1840 to 1860 and that Southern agriculture was much more efficient than Northern, their evidence is not totally convincing, and more historians would disagree than would fully agree with them. To conclude whether slavery was profitable or not is a many-faceted question. Profitable to whom? To the individual slaveholder or to the region? Profitable only with cotton or tobacco or sugar, or profitable with other crops as well? And if so, profitable only in producing crops, or also in producing and selling slaves?[39] Whatever the findings of later scholars, it is significant that many of Helper's contemporaries agreed with him on the economic impact of slavery—not only outsiders such as Olmsted (who also supported Helper's contention that nonslaveholders would like to abolish slavery, if they could abolish slaves as well) but even so

39. See Robert William Fogel and Stanley L. Engerman, *Time on the Cross: The Economics of American Negro Slavery* (Boston, 1974); Hugh G. J. Aitken (ed.), *Did Slavery Pay? Readings in the Economics of Black Slavery in the United States* (Boston, 1971); Kenneth Stampp, *The Peculiar Institution: Slavery in the Antebellum South* (New York, 1956).

proslavery a Southerner as George Fitzhugh, who maintained that "free labor is cheaper than slave labor" (*CA*, 17).

If Helper's manipulation of statistics is one factor that has partially discredited *The Impending Crisis*, his racism is another. Hugh C. Bailey's work, the single published full-length biography of Helper, is subtitled *Abolitionist-Racist*, and many other writers have assumed that *The Impending Crisis* is laced with Helper's racism. In fact, it is not. Hinton Helper may well have been a racist when he wrote his *Crisis*, but he let very little racism creep into his book. In fact, he was not— that is, publicly—abolitionist and racist at the same time. He announced himself a virulent white supremacist only *after* the Civil War. One finds, indeed, far more humanitarian concern for Negroes in *The Impending Crisis* than has heretofore been acknowledged. Although Helper announced in his preface that he was only "in a very slight degree" concerned with the humanitarian dimension of slavery, that was a dimension to which he returned periodically in subsequent chapters. He acknowledged early "a reasonable degree of fellow feeling for the negro" (p. 26) and pointed to "the sin and the shame of slavery" (p. 31), the suffering of Negroes "who are bought and sold, and driven about like so many cattle" (p. 43). He was "deeply impressed," he wrote, "with the conviction that slavery is . . . *a sin and a crime*" (p. 118), that it was "a great moral, social, civil, and political evil" (p. 151), and that "it is not our business to think of man as a merchantable commodity" (p. 86). Indeed, at times, he seemed to envision Negroes as full participants in American democracy, particularly when he declared that the great American revolutionary movement "has not yet been terminated, nor will it be, until every slave in the United States is freed from the tyranny of his master. Every victim of the vile institution, whether white or black, must be reinvested with the sacred rights and privileges of which he has been deprived by an inhuman oligarchy" (p. 95). He acknowledged at one point that Negroes were "an undesirable population," but aside from that there was little to anticipate the violent racism of his later three works.

Certainly, when Helper wrote *The Impending Crisis* he might have been aware of the need to conceal his racism if he were to find a publisher in the North and, when he wrote the 1859 and 1860 versions, to gain support from Northern abolitionists. But he apparently first hoped to publish the book not in the North but rather in a city still largely Southern, Baltimore. Moreover, if he really hoped to persuade the Southern nonslaveholder as he maintained, it would have been to his strategic advantage to emphasize his white supremacy, not conceal it. Such concealment is only one of many puzzling aspects of *The Impending Crisis*, aspects which lead one finally to ask if Helper knew fully what he was doing when he wrote his *Crisis*, if he truly understood the South for which he presumably was writing. The major question about *The Impending Crisis*, in fact, is not whether Helper misused statistics or even whether he was a racist, but rather may be one of audience. For whom and to whom was Helper writing? For the plain and poor whites, he insisted, but he must have known that many of those plain and poor whites were illiterate or unaccustomed to reading anything other than the Bible and perhaps local newspapers. Beyond that, he must have known that the same oligarchy which, he charged, suppressed free thought would also suppress his book. He must have known too, or at least should have, that even if those plain whites by some chance should read his *Crisis*, they would not follow his suggestions, nor would they accept his opinion that slaveholders were "more criminal than common murderers" (p. 140). These plain whites, after all, had kind neighbors who were slaveholders, sons and brothers and cousins who were slaveholders, and they aspired in many cases to be slaveholders themselves. One wonders, therefore, for whom Hinton Helper told his story of the South, and one concludes that, like so many other Southerners in this discussion, he told the story primarily for himself. Communication, or rather persuasion, was less important to him than venting his own wrath, his rage against both the slave oligarchy and the publisher in Baltimore who had silenced him earlier. It is true that he began his book as one who wanted to state his case persuasively—his preface and his first twenty-four pages would not have appeared greatly unreasonable even to a Southern slaveholder—but at the point he announced himself an abolitionist he began to rage and to taunt. Driven by his "involuntary impulse," he sustained his anger to the end of the book. By that point the act of telling, of pouring out his truth, had become more important than persuading.

A curious fate awaited the author of *The Impending Crisis*. Helper gained fame from the book but not fortune, since he received no royalties from the 1859 *Compendium*. He was first ignored by the Republicans, to whose victory in 1860 his book had contributed, then in 1861 he was appointed consul to Buenos Aires by President Lincoln. The author of *The Impending Crisis*, who had been claimed by Northern abolitionists whether he wanted to be or not, showed them soon after his return to the United States in 1866 that if he had been in their camp before the war he could not be after it. And he demonstrated as well that his compulsion to tell his truth, whether well received or not, had grown even stronger since the war.

Upon his return from Argentina, he traveled to North Carolina, not to Salisbury but a hundred miles west to Asheville, and there wrote the first of his works of Negrophobia, *Nojoque: A Question for a Continent* (1867).[40] If Helper had expressed a "reasonable degree of fellow feeling" for the Negro in *The Impending Crisis*, he expressed only hatred in this next book. Had his experience in South America altered his view of darker people and thus his view of the Negro? Or was he in 1867 expressing for the first time what he had felt all along? His express purpose, he declared in *Nojoque*, was "to write the negro out of America" and "to write him . . . out of existence" (p. v). He desired "the whole habitable globe" to be peopled "exclusively by those naturally and superlatively superior races,—the pure White Races" (p. viii). He proceeded in his book to demonstrate to his own satisfaction the inherent inferiority of the Negro and other people of color, and to ground his prejudice in what he called man's natural antipathy to black ("a thing of ugliness, disease, and death") and the natural attraction to white ("a thing of life, health, and beauty").

Helper's two books after *Nojoque* (the title apparently meant only "No Joke") were in the same vein. *The Negroes in Negroland* (1868) was primarily a compilation of statements by other writers who shared Helper's belief in Negro inferiority, and *Noonday Exigencies in America* (1871) repeated the argument of *The Impending Crisis*: "the condition of the South is so generally and so obviously inferior to the condition of the North" because "of *negroes and slavery*" (pp. 154–55). But now the primary emphasis was on "negroes," not slavery, and thus Helper, in his *Noonday Exigencies*, proposed a new political party which would end Radical Reconstruction and work toward racial purity in the South by bringing in white Northerners and Europeans.

Noonday Exigencies was Helper's last book on the Negro question. In the 1870s he found another cause, the construction of an inter-

40. See Bailey, *Hinton Rowan Helper*, 133–56.

American railroad from Canada to Argentina. The railroad became his new obsession, the "truth" which Negro inferiority had previously been, and it remained so for the next quarter of a century. For it he lobbied in Washington, neglected his Argentine wife (who had long been secondary to his causes), and undertook various promotion schemes. Finally, he was unsuccessful, and in March, 1909—his wife and son having left him, his friends dead, his funds depleted, his railroad proposals rejected, and himself ridiculed in Washington—he committed suicide in his drab rented room on Pennsylvania Avenue. The man who earlier had craved recognition had taken the room under an assumed name. "There is no justice in this world," he is reputed to have said shortly before his death, and although the testimony of his acquaintances may be disputed, these last public words would have been appropriate.[41] They were in the tradition of Southern melodrama. They also expressed a sentiment with which old Edmund Ruffin, in his last moments nearly half a century earlier, would undoubtedly have agreed.

Only at his death did Hinton Helper again receive a portion of that attention he had been given long before as the author of *The Impending Crisis* but which had been denied him the fifty years after that. The South had largely forgotten him in 1909 because, like Fitzhugh and Ruffin after Appomattox, he had become irrelevant. Like them, he had little lasting influence. His descendants in racism, the worst of the Southern demagogues, needed no antecedents: their hatred and their flair for drama came naturally enough. The South had also forgotten him because what he had said in *The Impending Crisis* about the antebellum Southern economy was no longer disputed. Southerners had long accepted the truth of what men had been jailed for professing in 1860—that slavery had damaged the South. Not only did former governor Wise of Virginia in 1873 pronounce slavery a "curse," but two years earlier General Benjamin H. Hill of Georgia proclaimed that "Southern progress, Southern development, and Southern power have been in bondage to the negro; and Southern failure, Southern dependence, and Southern sorrow are the heavy penalties we suffer for that bondage." Not long afterward Atticus G. Haygood, a promi-

41. Helper, quoted by Gerald Gaither and John Muldowny (eds.), "Hinton Rowan Helper, Racist and Reformer," *North Carolina Historical Review*, XL (Autumn, 1972), 382.

nent Methodist minister in Georgia, would say, to the approval of
most of his congregation, "I am grateful that slavery no longer exists,
because it is better for the white people of the South. It is better for
our industries and our business, as proved by the crops that free labor
makes." [42] Such is precisely what Hinton Helper had said twenty years
before.

One is hesitant, however, to call Helper a Southern prophet. In
fact, he understood neither his own time nor the way of the future.
But one must to some extent grant his own claim for consistency in
his books: each of his works, from *The Impending Crisis* on, was written, as he claimed, in support of "poor whites." The emphasis shifted
in Helper's work only because the enemy, as he saw it, changed. In
the *Crisis* he opposed the slaveholder because he believed the slaveholder oppressed the poor and plain white. In the later works he opposed the Negro because then, he believed, it was the freedman who
most threatened the poor white. Helper himself insisted, at the very
time he was producing his most vicious anti-Negro books, that he did
not hate the black race so much as he simply loved the white. "It is
strange," he wrote Benjamin Hedrick in 1869, "how you, and others
who should know better, will persist in calling my preference for the
white man 'hatred' for the negro." [43]

Forever misunderstood, even by his friends: such was the way Hinton Helper perceived himself. Thus he always attempted to be heard,
to make himself clear, particularly to those who did not understand
that an abolitionist could also be a Negrophobe. So, if he had written
one book, *The Impending Crisis*, to advocate the abolition of slavery, he
wrote three others to advocate the abolition of Negroes—and even
then believed he had not made himself sufficiently clear. Helper
saw himself, above all, as a truth-teller, and he bitterly resented the
world's failure to heed him. His truth—the South of his confused
mind—was a purely white South, the ideal world he envisioned at
the end of his book *Nojoque*: "No new golden age, no general jubi-
lee, no Eden-like millennium, no prolonged period of uninterrupted
peace and joy, until in the total absence of all the swarthy and inferior
races of men, the happy time thus contemplated shall be ushered in

42. Benjamin H. Hill, quoted in Paul M. Gaston, *The New South Creed* (New York,
1970), 35; Atticus Haygood, *The New South* (1880; rpr. Atlanta, 1950), 9.
43. Hinton Rowan Helper to Benjamin Hedrick, May 4, 1869, in Benjamin Hedrick
Papers, Duke University Library, Durham.

amidst the rapturous melody of a grand and universal chorus of the Whites!" (p. 474).

Daniel R. Hundley

W. J. Cash, in the first chapter of *The Mind of the South*, refers briefly to Daniel R. Hundley, "a Charleston lawyer of good family" (p. 20). Hundley was not that at all—he was an Alabama lawyer who had no ties whatever to Charleston—but he would have liked the description. For Hundley was indeed of "good family," the son of a planter and slaveholder who was also a minister and a physician; and Daniel Hundley himself was a patrician who believed one's highest calling was to be a gentleman. He sometimes regretted that he had been born in Alabama: in his youth, in the 1830s and 1840s, it was still frontier, a shifty country with little regard for gentlemen. His family's roots were in Virginia—though Charleston would have served as well—and in spirit he was still a Virginian. He attended the University of Virginia (after having earned an A.B. at Bacon College in Kentucky), and at age twenty-three he took as his wife a wealthy first cousin from Virginia—"the daughter," he wrote, "of a Virginia gentleman." [44] Later he took a law degree at Harvard, moved to Chicago, and in 1860 returned to north Alabama, where, except for duty in the Confederate army, he remained until his death in 1899. He fit well enough into Alabama society, but he never forgot that he was descended from Virginians. Hundley is that specific case which supports the generalization: in the early and mid-nineteenth century Virginia was the ideal to which the Deep South aspired, the image from which the rest of Dixie sprang.

Cash's reference to Hundley in *The Mind of the South* does more than mistakenly identify him. It also suggests his place in Southern history, at least until recently. His reputation rests on a single full-length book, *Social Relations in Our Southern States* (1860), written when he was twenty-eight, and that reputation has been exceedingly modest. Few students of Southern history and literature know much about him, and those scholars who have accorded him brief mention—Ulrich B. Phillips, Clement Eaton, William R. Taylor, Kenneth Stampp, Carl Degler, and William J. Cooper, Jr.—have been principally concerned with his recognition, in *Social Relations*, of the importance of the yeoman farmer and of a multiclass structure in the Old South, or,

44. Daniel R. Hundley, *Prison Echoes of the Late Rebellion* (New York, 1874), 6.

in Stampp's case, with his remarks on slavery.[45] Of these writers only Cooper, in an excellent introduction to a reprint edition of *Social Relations* (1979), has given him much attention. Jay B. Hubbell, who included in *The South in American Literature* more than a hundred Southerners who wrote before 1900, not only neglected to mention Hundley but also wrote: "No Southern writer dared to follow Thackeray and satirize the 'cotton snobs,' who were too often in the Northern mind confounded with Southern gentlemen."[46] This is precisely what Hundley did—even calling his subjects Cotton Snobs and complaining that Northerners confused them with Southern gentlemen— and he did it in 1860, at least in part in the Deep South, at a time and in a place in which the critical spirit is often assumed to have been dead.

Daniel Hundley, thus, is something of an enigma: an Alabamian who sometimes wished he were a Virginian, and the author of a book undertaken largely to defend and justify the South but which became, despite its author's intent, a book more critical of the South than anything else written by an inhabitant of the Deep South in the years just preceding the Civil War—a book which, although no one realized it, was perhaps even more damning than Helper's, since Helper condemned only the slaveholders, Hundley the majority of slaveholders and most of the plain and poor whites as well. Such a book could perhaps have been expected of Daniel Hundley, a man full of ambiguities and conflicting loyalties who seemed sometimes to thrive on privation rather than on privilege. He was not a particularly happy man, if we are to judge by the entries in his unpublished diary, although he never actually sank to the depths reached by Ruffin and Helper.[47] He was, by temperament, introspective and melancholy,

45. For brief comment on Hundley, see Ulrich B. Phillips, "Economic and Political Essays," *The South in the Building of the Nation* (Richmond, 1909), VII, 188–89; Clement Eaton, *The Waning of the Old South Civilization, 1860s–1880s* (Athens, Ga., 1968), 4–6; Taylor, *Cavalier and Yankee*, 337; Stampp, *The Peculiar Institution*, 180, 256–57; Carl N. Degler, *Place Over Time: The Continuity of Southern Distinctiveness* (Baton Rouge, 1977), 56; Blanche Weaver, "D. R. Hundley: Subjective Sociologist," *Georgia Review*, X (Summer, 1956), 222–34; and, for the best discussion of Hundley's life, William J. Cooper, Jr., "Daniel R. Hundley," introduction to *Social Relations in Our Southern States* (Baton Rouge, 1979).

46. Jay B. Hubbell, *The South in American Literature, 1607–1900* (Durham, 1954), 343.

47. I am grateful to Mrs. J. Dexter Nilsson of Rockville, Maryland, a great-granddaughter of Daniel R. Hundley, for allowing me to read the unpublished diary for 1861 and 1864. (The 1862 and 1863 segments are missing.) The diary is in Mrs. Nilsson's possession, but she has deposited a copy of parts of the diary in the libraries of the

constantly searching for God's purpose in human affairs, but not averse to consulting phrenologists and clairvoyants. Like Ruffin, he experienced great family tragedy (the deaths of three young sons) and suffered greatly during the Civil War. But he never truly lost control as Ruffin did. Indeed, in many respects, he was a moderate man whose conduct and beliefs at various times were not atypical of at least a substantial minority of his fellow Southerners. A Unionist until 1860 and a supporter of Stephen Douglas for president, he became vocally pro-Southern only after Lincoln's election in 1860 and passionately so only in April, 1861, after a narrow escape from anti-Southern vigilantes in Chicago. He returned to north Alabama, organized a company which he served as captain and colonel during the war, endured injury, imprisonment, and financial ruin, and emerged from war and Reconstruction remarkably enough a Unionist again, a man not embittered by his experience.

But in the year 1860, and in a different way from 1861 to 1865, Hundley, fully as much as Ruffin and Helper, was an absolutist, a noncompromiser who stated his beliefs boldly and without qualification. Like them, he wrote partly—so he confided in his diary—to escape obscurity; but he also wrote because, from 1860 to 1865 if not particularly before or after, he was moved by a conviction that the truth about the South had not been told, or at least had not crossed the Potomac and the Ohio. He wrote—far more than did Ruffin and Helper—for the non-Southern reader, and the truth he felt compelled to tell, at least in 1860 in his *Social Relations*, was that Southern society was far more complex than the non-Southerner had imagined: many white Southerners were neither aristocrat nor poor white. He wrote his *Social Relations*, however, not only to set forth his own sociology for the South but also to answer Northern radicals. Or such was his intent at first. "I cannot remain silent," he wrote, "while the anarchists of the North are scattering broadcast the seeds of infidelity and neo-republicanism and all the time disguising their damnable heresies under the cover of hatred of the South. . . . God help me present the truth in a form acceptable to the public." [48]

To "present the truth," then, is what Daniel Hundley intended

---

University of Alabama and Louisiana State University. My biographical information about Hundley I take from the unpublished diary, as well as from the essays by Cooper and Weaver.

48. Hundley, quoted in Weaver, "D. R. Hundley," 222.

when as a young man in Chicago in the late 1850s he determined to write about the South. He had come to Chicago in 1856 to manage his father-in-law's real estate interests, but in fact he had spent more time reading, writing, and self-communing than tending to business. Although he continued to spend winters in Alabama, he "preferred living [in Chicago] to living in Alabama," he later wrote; and if he moved from Chicago, he vowed, it would be to New York, not Dixie. But at the same time Hundley remained very consciously a Southerner, and one who felt his Southernness intensified by his Northern residence. In an article for *Hunt's Merchant's Magazine* in 1857 he had taken issue with critics of Southern slavery.[49] But he soon determined that the urgency of the times required from him not only essays but a book explaining the South, and not a book, he wrote in the preface to *Social Relations in Our Southern States*, which would rely on "wit": "I have endeavored to speak my sentiments plainly, to narrate facts impartially, and to treat a grave theme in a manner becoming its gravity and great importance" (p. vi).

On several occasions in *Social Relations* Hundley departed from this high seriousness, at times affecting the jaunty tone and irreverent banter of George Fitzhugh. Like Fitzhugh, outside the mainstream of Southern social and political thought, he possessed a certain liberty that official spokesmen lacked. But for the most part he was the earnest, high-minded interpreter he claimed to be, and he began his book about the South by insisting on his own knowledge and objectivity. He knew both North and South, the vices and virtues of each. He had first gone north to Harvard University because he "had a strong desire to come in contact with the Northern people, and Northern prejudices, on their own soil; to correct [my] own sectional prejudices, should these require correction, as well as to demonstrate to those with whom [I] might have occasion to associate, that not all slaveholders are such 'outside barbarians' as the enemies of the South strive so laboriously to make the Northern public believe." He had traveled in most of the United States, he stressed, and had lived in the North for four years: "Indeed, [my] pecuniary interests in the North and South are about equal, so that there will not be a sufficient preponderance of selfish interests to bias [my] judgment one way or the other. We shall aim all the time at strict impartiality" (pp. 19–20).

49. Daniel R. Hundley, "Traffic in Coolies," *Hunt's Merchant's Magazine*, XXXVI (May, 1857), 570–73. Hundley also wrote, for the same magazine, "The Evils of Com-

This "young and unknown literary aspirant," as Hundley identified himself, intended in *Social Relations* to enlighten those outsiders who saw Southerners either as "so many Chevalier Bayards, *sans peur et sans reproche*" (p. 14) or as cruel barbarians. But in fact his long first section, "The Southern Gentleman," probably the least impressive part of his book, reinforces myths as much as it shatters them. "To begin with his pedigree," Hundley wrote, "we may say that the Southern Gentleman . . . comes usually of aristocratic parentage. . . . In Virginia the ancestors of the Southern Gentleman were chiefly English cavaliers" (p. 27). And besides being of "faultless pedigree," the Southern Gentleman was "usually possessed of an equally faultless physical development": his "average height is about six feet, yet he is rarely gawky in his movements, or in the least clumsily put together; and his entire *physique* conveys to the mind an impression of firmness united to flexibility" (p. 29). The Gentleman was a hunter, a fisherman, and a fine rider, and his love of the outdoors contributed to his physical perfection. So concluded Daniel Hundley, who himself loved the outdoors, loved hunting and fishing and riding, was descended from Virginians, was convinced of his fine bloodlines, was six feet, two inches tall and handsome.

Hundley's pro-Southern sentiments seemed clear in the first third of his book. Indeed, he wrote little in the first hundred thirty pages that would distinguish this book from any written by an uncritical Southerner in the years just before the war. He was lavish in his praise of the plantation system, Southern grace and hospitality and respect for family life. Southerners, he wrote, were happier than Northerners: a "smiling, rollicking spirit . . . seems to pervade the entire South" (pp. 126–27). The South rested on stronger financial ground than did the North; it stood "firm as a rock" (p. 126). And the South—particularly its son, Hundley—revered woman: "Ah! thou true-hearted daughter of the sunny South, simple and unaffected in thy manners, pure in speech as thou art in soul" (p. 72). The representative Southern woman

> lives indeed only to make home happy. She literally knows nothing of "woman's rights," or "free love," or "free thinking;" but faithfully labors on in the humble sphere allotted her of heaven—never wearying, never

---

mercial Supremacy" (XXXVI [March, 1857], 316–17), and in 1858 produced a pamphlet, *Work and Bread; or the Coming Winter and the Poor* (Chicago, 1858). See Cooper, "Daniel R. Hundley," xvii–xix.

doubting, but looking steadfastly to the Giver of all good for her rewards; and she is to-day the most genuine pattern and representative of the mothers of our Revolutionary history, to be found anywhere in the land. 'Tis true she wears no costly silks, and instead of fine linen every day, is simply arrayed in homely calico . . . yet, believe us, O ye spoiled children of Fashion . . . never once can you claim to be apparelled like unto her! For, as the Lady Countess of Godiva was "clothed on with chastity," so is she, as well as with unassuming modesty and Christian meekness, the peerless raiment of the daughters of heaven. (p. 99)

This was the best of the South—chivalrous, honorable, woman-worshipping. The North, by contrast, was money-mad, utilitarian, susceptible to "isms." Southerners were "far less nervous and spasmodic than their fellow-citizens of the Free States" (p. 40). Northerners were too cerebral: they shut themselves up in rooms and did not exercise. "Nor do we wonder that Spiritualism, and every other blind fanaticism of the hour, should possess the minds of men, whose bodies are unsound and whose secretions are altogether abnormal" (p. 41). Physically the Yankees virtually belonged to a different species, it appeared, and emotionally they were harder, less compassionate. Southern slavery was more humane than Northern wage-slavery, the slave happier than the North's "toiling poor." The Southern slaveholder loved his slaves and "his love is not theoretical but practical. He has tried theory and found it would not do" (p. 61).

Concluding his panegyric to the South a third of the way through his book, Hundley the patriot became the sociologist. In a lengthy discussion of the Southern "middle classes," he acknowledged that such Southerners constituted "the greater portion of [the South's] citizens, and are likewise the most useful members of her society" (p. 77). But Hundley the gentleman wrote with clear condescension toward these small planters and farmers, storekeepers, country schoolteachers, mechanics, "half-fledged country lawyers and doctors, [and] parsons" (p. 80). Again he based his case on heredity. Members of the Southern middle classes were descended not from the Cavaliers and Huguenots, as were Southern aristocrats, but rather from the Scottish, Irish, and "sturdy English." In physical appearance "the middle-class planter differs very materially from the Southern Gentleman"; he "does not possess that lithe, airy, and graceful carriage, that compactness and delicacy of muscle" (p. 84).

Hundley's praise for the energy and ambition of the Southern middle classes, then, was not so unqualified as it might at first appear; for out of the middle classes came those Southerners whom Hundley most disdained, and it was his discussion of the middle classes which led directly to his criticism of many aspects of Southern society. The four categories of Southerners he indicted—the Model Storekeeper, the Southern Yankee (a native Southerner, and a Yankee only in spirit and character), the Southern Bully, and the Cotton Snob—all sprang from the middle class. The Model Storekeeper was a dishonest fraud who aspired to be a gentleman but lacked the manners to become one. The Southern Yankee was a mean, tightfisted sort interested only in pursuing wealth, who was similar to but worse than the Model Storekeeper. The Southern Yankee was usually a trader or a speculator, but sometimes a planter or a farmer. When Hundley spoke of a particular variety of Southern Yankee located in Georgia, he described a creature almost mythical, belonging to a separate race, and in doing so again betrayed his tendency to classify people according to physical characteristics: "In [Georgia] they grow to enormous sizes, and seldom stand under six feet in their stockings, often, indeed, reaching six feet and a half. Muscular, heavy-jawed, beetle-browed, and possessed of indomitable energy, they are well calculated to command respect almost any where, did one only have it in his nature to forget that SELF is the only god they worship, and MONEY the only incense that ever ascends as a sweet-smelling savor to the nostrils of their idol" (p. 157).

But Hundley's indictment of the Model Storekeeper and the Southern Yankee, though harsh, could not after all be construed precisely as criticism of the *South*, since those characteristics Hundley assigned them, greed and callousness, he designated as Northern traits. It was with his criticism of "our Cotton Snobs and rich Southern Bullies," to whom he devoted more than fifty pages, that he launched an attack on those Southerners who by 1860 had gained control in much of the South, particularly the Deep South. By Cotton Snobs, Hundley explained, he meant not only cotton planters but also many of those who grew tobacco, rice, and sugar. But, clearly, it was the planters of the Cotton Kingdom, including his native state of Alabama, whom he particularly had in mind. The Cotton Snob might be at first mistaken for a gentleman, but closer examination revealed that he was not. He dressed well, but he drank, gambled, and boasted:

> The Cotton Snob is frequently to be seen in the Free States, and when seen is pretty sure to make himself a "shining mark," for he assumes to be the

very tip-top of the first families, and as such considers his individual cor-
porosity a thing too sacred to be touched even by the hands of Northern
canaille, "greasy mechanics," or what not. He also seeks every opportunity
to talk about "my niggers," (observe, a Southern Gentleman rarely if ever
says *nigger*) endeavors to look very haughty and overbearing; sneers at
whatever he considers *low*, and "their name is legion;" carries a cane not
infrequently; affects a military step and manner. . . . By such and other
similar displays of vulgarity and ill-breeding, the Cotton Snob pretty soon
renders himself both ridiculous and contemptible; and, what is more and
worse, brings a reproach upon the true Gentlemen of the South. (p. 170)

Hundley grew bolder as he catalogued the sins of Cotton Snob: he
flaunted his wealth, he had no taste, he adopted affectations, he consciously dropped his *r*'s and said "pawty" rather than "party," and
most of all he was a slave to fashion—which to Hundley, as to Fitzhugh, was one of the worst of offenses:

And the Cotton Snob verily, if persuaded it was *the thing* to have a juvenile
African served up whole on state occasions, stuffed like a young grunter or
prepared like a baron of beef, would never once hesitate to have young
Sambo served with parsley and egg-sauce, or whatever else might be the
taste of the hour; and what is more, he would pretend to enjoy the deli-
cious repast with as much gusto, as he at present evinces while discussing
the mysterious compounds served at the St. Charles or the St. Nicholas—
not one of which, in most instances, he would be able properly to translate
into his own vernacular. (pp. 186–87)

Hundley held nothing back in his indictment of these parvenus, except to concede that they sometimes treated their slaves well because
it was the fashion to do so. All things considered, the Cotton Snob
was the vilest of creatures—"not only the slave of passion and vanity,
but the slave of Satan also" (p. 181)—and Hundley dismissed him
with the rankest sarcasm. "Cotton *is* king," James H. Hammond had
declared in 1858 on the floor of the U.S. Senate. "No power on earth
dares to make war upon it." [50] Hundley seemed to mock Hammond's
boast: "Stand in awe, O Nations, and hide your little heads, ye Isles of
the Sea, for verily Cotton is King, and the New Order of Chivalry is
the Cotton Snob" (p. 175).

This was more nearly the voice of the irreverent George Fitzhugh
than of the high-minded Hundley, but Hundley had directed his satire at Southerners rather than Yankees. He continued his indictment

50. James H. Hammond, speech, March 4, 1858, in Wilson (ed.), *Selections*, 317.

of Southern society by focusing first on the Southern Bully and then the Poor White Trash. The Bully, found most frequently in the cotton states, also sprang from the middle classes. "A swearing, tobacco-chewing, brandy drinking" man (p. 223), he used foul language, fought chicken cocks, played Old Sledge—and usually had red or sandy hair. The Southern poor whites, like the Georgia Yankees, were nearly a species unto themselves, "about the laziest two-legged animals that walk erect on the face of the Earth" (p. 262). "We contend there is a great deal in *blood*" (p. 251), insisted Hundley, who hardly needed to—and who, like Fitzhugh, was fascinated by theories of racial superiority.[51] Southern poor whites were the descendants of paupers, convicts, and indentured servants from England. "Lank, lean, angular, and bony, with flaming red, or flaxen, or sandy, or carroty-colored hair" (p. 264), the poor white drank to excess. Hundley hoped the United States would seize Mexico or Cuba and export its poor whites.

Hundley concluded his *Social Relations* with a discussion of Negro slavery, and after some hundred fifty pages of iconoclasm—interrupted only by a short chapter in praise of the yeoman farmer—he seemed eager to return to orthodoxy. His case for slavery as a positive good was familiar enough: slavery had brought the Negro out of the savagery of Africa and into the light of Christianity and, besides, had made the American South bear fruit. "The finger of God" directed "so marvellous a development!" (p. 299). The cause of the South was part of a larger mission to "civilize" the darker peoples, and that mission was worldwide. "We firmly believe that South Central Africa will in time come under English domination," Hundley wrote. "We think this thing has been fore-ordained—predestinated from the foundation of the world" (p. 319). The American South would shoulder its share of the white man's burden; its history had been part of the divine plan. "We honestly believe, therefore, God had a design in permitting the old Slave-trade—a design to bless and benefit the human race" (p. 288). "The Almighty" in his goodness had snatched "the poor naked heathen from the burning plains of Africa—clothing them in the habiliments worn by civilized men—enlightening gradually their benighted minds, and rendering their labor . . . so productive as to fill all the ports of commerce with activity . . . giving

51. For a discussion of Hundley's interest in racial superiority, see Cooper, "Daniel R. Hundley," xxxiii–xxxv, xlii–xliv.

thereby bread and life to the toiling millions of God's poor, who would else be left to perish succorless and friendless" (p. 299).

Thus on more comfortable ground, in defense of the South's peculiar institution, Daniel Hundley concluded his book. It was in the climate of 1860—the year of such extreme works as *Anticipations of the Future* and the *Compendium of The Impending Crisis*—a rather strange book, neither friend nor foe to the South (or, rather, both) and certainly not friend to the North. Neither had its author acknowledged that war was imminent, or even possible, as nearly every other writer on the sectional conflict had in 1860. It was as close to being a reflective book as one could find on the eve of the Civil War, and it must have seemed a confusing, contradictory work to those few who read it at the time, as it does to those few who have read it since. Why— aside from an attempt to escape obscurity that had also driven Ruffin and Helper—had Hundley written such a book? Why, in particular, had he leveled his harshest criticism at those people closest to him, the Cotton Snobs who by 1860 had gained ascendancy in the Deep South, including his own state Alabama? The answer is not simply that Hundley had a youthful impulse to be heard: if so, he would have shouted like Helper, stridently and frantically. It was something more fundamental than that, something related closely to Hundley's idea of himself. What we see in *Social Relations* is nothing less than the condescension of the spiritual Virginian toward the Far South, of the older, coastal South toward the new Cotton Kingdom, of the true gentleman toward the nouveau riche imitator. Hundley claimed in *Social Relations* that he himself was "half a gentleman," but only a fleeting and uncharacteristic modesty prevented him from acknowledging what was clear throughout the book: in fact he considered himself the compleat gentleman. Why else would his portrait of the Southern Gentleman—tall, handsome, brave, chivalrous, fond of hunting, fishing, and riding—have been virtually a self-portrait?

To be a gentleman was as important to Daniel Hundley as to any Elizabethan or to any Virginian—indeed more important, because he felt that he was an inhabitant of a land in which true gentlemen were far less numerous than in the Old Dominion. Thus he was intensely concerned, as Henry James later put it, with distinguishing a spurious gentleman from a real one. It was not enough that the Cotton Snob, when visiting in the North, rendered "himself both ridiculous and contemptible"; what was "more and worse" was that he brought "a reproach upon the true Gentlemen of the South" (p. 170). Not really to defend the South, then, or even to criticize it, but rather to express an ideal of the gentleman was Hundley's principal mission in *Social Relations in Our Southern States*. "Alas!" he exclaimed, "how unfortunate is it that true gentility is so little understood or appreciated in this great country" (p. 173). That the North was also guilty of offenses against taste, honor, and chivalry Hundley accepted. But the South—the land, according to Hundley, settled by aristocrats and sons of aristocrats—was, as Fitzhugh had also believed, civilization's last chance. Seen in this light, Hundley's criticism of what the South had become in 1860 was, in large part, a product of his envisioning an ideal South, a South of the mind. The criticism served the larger purpose of the defense of that Southern ideal. He sought to define the true gentleman by showing what that gentleman was not—that is, a Cotton Snob. Hundley wanted, perhaps more than anything else, to inform his Northern readers that the planter swaggering and boasting and flaunting his wealth at Saratoga was not the true aristocrat. Hundley realized that he had to unmask the counterfeit gentleman before he could convincingly defend the real one.

But this the North, in 1860, did not really care to know, and thus Hundley's book, as Ruffin's *Anticipations of the Future* in the same year, changed few minds on any subject. It was simply too late. But it did serve to make him suspect among his fellow Southerners, at least those few who read and acknowledged his book. An Alabamian writing a lengthy essay in *De Bow's Review* praised Hundley's defense of slavery but decried his "gossipy descriptions of society." "We cannot admit his classification of snob and gentleman, or the justness of his satire," J. T. Wiswall insisted. "We . . . cannot sanction this fierce declamation against the upper society."[52] Hundley was a critic of Southern aristocracy, Wiswall charged, and although the charge was erroneous—it was the *pretenders* to aristocracy he had attacked, and his reviewer's failure to realize the difference only proved his point—Wiswall's reaction was probably not unrepresentative of the reaction of those few Southerners who read the book. In 1860 the inhabitants of the Cotton Kingdom knew largely North and South, black and white. Hundley was too complex not only for Northerners but for

52. J. T. Wiswall, "Causes of Aristocracy," *De Bow's Review*, XXVIII (May, 1860), 552, 554, 555. Only *De Bow's Review* of the major periodicals of 1860 published a review of *Social Relations*. See Cooper, "Daniel R. Hundley," xxiv–xxv.

many Southerners as well. Or if not too complex, it was just that the fine distinctions he drew were irrelevant to a South facing war. Hundley's loyalty to the South was questioned, particularly since he had written most of the book while living in Chicago; and his return to Alabama in November, 1860, for his annual winter visit did not allay Southern suspicions. The Cotton Kingdom on the eve of the Civil War was not receptive to critical examination, even, or especially, by one of its own.

Once back in Alabama, however, Hundley set about to prove his critics wrong. If he had not felt, or at least not expressed, the threat of war before, now he was overwhelmed by it. "The heavens are dark and portentous," he wrote in his diary on New Year's Day, 1861, "and war, famine and pestilence may all be looked for during the next twelve months." On January 12 he learned that Alabama had seceded from the Union, and with its secession Hundley was a Unionist no more. For the next three months he alternated between despair and hope, on January 19 writing in his diary that "civil war is inevitable" if "the North does not back down," but two months later writing that "the war fever seems to be abating in the North, and civil war does not seem to be as imminent now as it did a while back. I think it very probable that Lincoln will *back out* of his brave words in his Inaugural" (March 21).

Hundley did not write for publication during these early months of 1861, but confined his observations and opinions to his diary. He hunted, fished, attended church, and looked after family responsibilities, but all the while anticipating war. "I am getting tired to death of fishing and hunting, and general idling, and I long for some active calling," he wrote on March 28. Two weeks later, a day after Edmund Ruffin fired his shot in Charleston Harbor, Hundley found it. "War! War! War!" he recorded on April 13. "Fort Sumpter [*sic*] was attacked yesterday . . . God defend the Right!" On April 19 came word that Virginia had seceded. "Glorious News! It rejoices the hearts of the true Southrons everywhere," Hundley wrote, and thereupon left Alabama for Chicago to dispose of his property. He reached Chicago, but barely escaped a mob which tried to prevent his return to Alabama. When at last he returned in May he drew up papers for a proposed rifle company, began to drill with cadets in order to "learn something of the art of war" (May 15), made speeches in Huntsville urging enlistment, and joined a vigilance committee to administer justice to participants in a "most hellish insurrectionary plot among the slaves" (May 18), which resulted in the execution of several Negroes. The author of *Social Relations* was trying to prove through his actions the loyalty which had been doubted in his written work. He wanted, above all, to expose "the numerous falsehoods in circulation in regard to my being an abolitionist" (July 19).

On July 20, 1861, Hundley received his vindication: his company in Huntsville elected him captain by acclamation. He became increasingly possessed by the war spirit, rejoicing as the news of Confederate successes in northern Virginia reached Alabama and announcing in his diary that he would not be surprised if "the Yankees . . . tucked their tails and run before six weeks" (July 2). Hundley's diary, like Edmund Ruffin's, suggests the extent to which the war overshadowed all personal concerns. On July 21 he wrote, "Reached home again this morning. Found that wife had given birth to a very fine boy. We expect to name him Walter Harris. I leave tonight for Memphis." Never before had Hundley mentioned his wife's pregnancy, and this was the only time he mentioned his son's birth. Despite responsibilities at home, he had written earlier, "I feel that duty calls, honor calls, my country calls, and I must obey" (May 14).

Hundley's diary for the year 1861 (unpublished and now in the possession of his descendants) is a remarkable record of the adjustment of a man of leisure to a life of hardship and privation. It also suggests certain qualities in Hundley that explain further his antipathy to the Cotton Snobs. In those parts of the diary in which he discusses life in camp, he emerges as an intensely moral man who prizes high thinking and plain living, and disapproves strongly of drink, gambling, and sexual indulgence. He was "sad at heart" when he considered "all the wickedness" around him, and he complained in particular of those times when the soldiers were paid: "War, oh the demoralizing effects thereof! . . . There is in camp nothing but gambling, drinking, swearing, and quarrelling. It is a sad spectacle" (December 7). We see Hundley as a contemplative man with an assurance of personal superiority and a certain aloofness from his soldiers. He preferred the company of nature and of his own thoughts to that of his comrades. On one "beautiful—beautiful October day," he elected "to hold communion with Nature," rather than "remaining in camp and listening to the blasphemy usual there" (October 20). "Just at sundown," he wrote a month later, "the skies showed the most beautiful sight I almost ever beheld. I could not help recalling Keats' lines—'A thing of beauty is a joy forever'" (November 21).

He also appears in his 1861 diary as the sort of man who would later be called a "muscular Christian"—strong of body and soul, earnest and courageous, a man disturbed by the lack of religious commitment in others and convinced of God's role in human affairs. We see in Hundley the Southern Calvinist, a firm believer in the total sovereignty of God. When spring rains brought promise of a bountiful Southern harvest he rejoiced, "God is manifestly on the side of the South at the present time. May we by our acts in future still keep Him with us" (July 1). When he heard of further Confederate victories in Virginia and Missouri, he wrote, "When God is for us, who is against us?" (August 19).

These expressions were consistent with the high-minded author of *Social Relations in Our Southern States* who scorned the materialism, gaudiness, and dissipation of the Cotton Snobs. The preference for simplicity, Hundley maintained, was another sign of the true aristocrat—a view not uncommon for a Virginian of the mid-nineteenth century. The diary entries are also consistent with the Hundley who, in *Social Relations*, expressed a belief in God's determination, a divine pattern of human history. A Southern Puritan in this respect as well as in his view of mankind, he wrote that man, "when unregenerate," was "essentially a bestial sort of animal, grovelling in ignorance and vice, and influenced at all times by such sentiments only as are inspired either through fear or self-interest" (p. 284). "The fault," Hundley wrote, "is not in cities, nor yet in slavery, nor in marriage, nor religion; it is in MAN. The old Adam is large as life to this day, and boasts a roomy and well-swept apartment in every human heart, until through faith in Christ and practical godliness we all learn to 'put off the old man and his deeds;' hence, although you were to abolish every institution under the sun, so long as the human race continues mortal and frail as at present there will be no lack of sin and shame, sorrow and suffering" (p. 149).

To be Calvinist and aristocrat, Puritan and Cavalier, at one and the same time was not as difficult in the Old South as it might now seem, and Hundley was among the finest specimens of such a synthesis. It was a combination that prepared him well for the years ahead in which he fought in east Tennessee, was wounded at Port Gibson,

Mississippi, on May 1, 1863, captured near Kennesaw Mountain, Georgia, on June 15, 1864, and imprisoned at Johnson's Island in Lake Erie for the remainder of the war. After he adjusted to camp life, Hundley made a resourceful and successful soldier, and his diary for 1864 shows a confidence as well as a philosophical resignation not always seen in the 1861 entries. The 1864 diary is much more detailed than the earlier record, and for a reason Hundley acknowledged in April, 1864. After the war was over, he wrote, "I shall take my pen to write a book on the subject of this great struggle. For I may as well confess to myself that such an idea has been haunting me for a long time" (April 12).

The diary itself was apparently to be part of the raw material for Hundley's great book about South and North, a book he continued to contemplate long after the war. Although he failed to produce quite the book he intended, and thus never shared the best segments of his diary with a wider audience, it is obvious that he had such an audience in mind as he made some of the entries of 1864. Other entries, such as his expressions of grief at his brother's death, his father's illness, and his family's general misfortune in north Alabama, were personal but equally revealing. Hundley, thirty-two years of age and a colonel attached to Hood's Corps stationed near Dalton, Georgia, had learned to endure: "It is very hard to have to spend so many years of one's prime in this kind of life, but since it seems to be the will of God I shall not complain" (February 7). God and nature remained his refuge. "The woods are now robed in the Spring fashions," he wrote on April 30, "the birds are singing among the green leaves, the air is soft and balmy, all things animate and inanimate except man, breathe of sweet Peace. Alas! how sad the thought that man, the head of all God's creatures in this little orb, should man the same with the fruits of wicked passions." On another occasion, he cursed the war, then added, "And yet, I cannot deny to myself, that it is all God's doing, and that we are justly punished for our sins as a people" (March 30). Not the sins of the South—not slavery—Hundley meant, but the depravity of mankind. Indeed, he was still confident in the spring of 1864 that God was on the side of the Confederacy and that the South would win the war. The Yankees he still saw as a "most despicable race," and not even a very clever one. When he heard that Ulysses S. Grant had been appointed head of the Union army in March, 1864, he wrote, "I am glad of all this. I think Grant one of their inferior officers, have always thought so, and shall confidently expect to see him prove his incompetency before the war is over" (March 18).

Hundley was as mistaken about the abilities of Ulysses S. Grant as he was about eventual Confederate success. By his standards, Grant was not a gentleman; but to be a gentleman was not enough in the spring of 1864. Three months after he prophesied Southern victory, Daniel Hundley was captured while fighting in north Georgia and sent to Johnson's Island. From his standpoint, however, confinement was not all bad. Indeed, if he had made a resourceful soldier, he made an even more resourceful prisoner, and it was because of his enforced leisure that his only other book, *Prison Echoes of the Late Rebellion*, came to be written. *Prison Echoes* consisted largely of entries he made in his diary during the first half of his imprisonment, from June to December, 1864. He took the diary with him when he escaped from Johnson's Island on January 2, 1865, and had it confiscated by Federal officers when he was recaptured nearly a week later. He did not see the diary again until 1874, when he received a letter from a man in New York who offered to sell it to him. After Hundley pleaded poverty, but insisted he was "thoroughly reconstructed," the diary was returned to him. He published it along with his later reflections on the war.

The prison diary, as Hundley himself acknowledged in his 1874 introduction, was a "thorough rebel production" (p. 5) which had been intended for future publication all the while he kept it. Thus on several occasions in the diary he addressed his "readers" familiarly. For Hundley, the Southern gentleman committed to the cult of experience, even life in prison had a value, and that value was precisely the education it provided. Experience was for the recording, and the record was nearly as important as the experience itself. If Hundley took risks in keeping the diary, those risks made living all the more meaningful. Thus he filled the diary with scurrilous remarks about the Yankees in general and Abraham Lincoln in particular. "Never was there before," he wrote on August 1, 1864, "as arrant a nation of hypocrites and cowards as these North men" (p. 107). The Yankees were, as they had been to Fitzhugh, a race apart with a religion apart. "[Henry Ward] Beecher's Gospel of Murder" was "the only orthodox faith" in the North (p. 155), and "bigoted infidels and sacrilegious Goths" (p. 184) shaped the Yankee faith. "The transcendentalism of New-England" had "fast leavened the whole Yankee religion with a mystic creed not very dissimilar to the doctrine of the Buddhists of Hindo-stan" (p. 109). At one point Hundley vowed to cease hating Yankees and, instead, pray for them, but later decided that prayer could be of little value: "God in His own good time will yet bring the people of these Northern states to judgment, and woe be unto them when that day comes!" (p. 153). After Hundley learned of the deaths of several friends, of Yankee atrocities, and of the ransacking of his father's house, he expressed his growing belief that God would wreak his vengeance on the North: "what pen can describe the horrors of that punishment which awaits the vandals who have proven themselves to be as truly the 'scourge of God' as was Attila or Alaric" (p. 166).

Hundley's only refuge besides God was his assurance that he was a gentleman, as many of the others in camp, Yankee soldiers and Southern prisoners, he believed were not. His strength of body, intel-lectual curiosity, and ability to transcend physical hardship would save him. He read, studied German and French, and continued to ex-press confidence that God would work his will. Although he declared in September, 1864, that "it is a very hollow world, a very cruel world, a very shallow world, a very deceitful world, a very vain and selfish world" (p. 141), he still found beauty and honor in it. And although the cause of the South was hopeless by the end of 1864, he wrote in his diary on December 27, "The Confederacy is sore pressed just now, but victory awaits her in the end" (p. 195).

Six days later Hundley escaped from Johnson's Island by acquiring a Federal uniform, posing as a roll-caller, and walking out of camp across the ice of Lake Erie to Sandusky, Ohio. The escape story in-cluded in *Prison Echoes* he told in 1874 after the diary had been re-turned to him, and it was, in its fashion, a suspenseful narrative. His plan was to circle the western shore of Lake Erie and cross from De-troit into Canada. He traveled by night and slept in barns by day, fighting hunger and freezing cold until he became ill and was cap-tured in Fremont, Ohio. He was returned to Johnson's Island, where he remained until July 25, 1865. But the exhilaration Hundley had felt in his escape gave him a new appreciation of the plight of the South-ern Negro. As he crossed the ice of Lake Erie, south to Ohio for the moment but only to turn north toward Canada, he realized that fugi-tive slaves had once gone in the same direction to freedom. When he knew he was indeed free, he cried out, *"Lord God Omnipotent, if it is this to be free, strike when thou wilt the shackles from the slaves of the South!"*

(p. 204). God had predestined this too, he believed; for the moment, the slave and the slaveholder were one.

After the war Hundley returned to Alabama and, despite the loss of much of his diary, intended to write his book "on the subject of this great struggle." As it turned out, he never did. He farmed, practiced law, served as solicitor of Lawrence County, Alabama, briefly edited the *North Alabama Reporter* of Huntsville, lived in relative obscurity his last few years, and died, as befitted a stern Victorian moralist, five days short of the twentieth century. (It was also Hinton Helper's seventieth birthday.) As he suffered through Reconstruction, Hundley believed, "with blind old Milton," that his land had indeed fallen "on evil days and evil tongues." These were "the days of the success of wicked men, of small men, of mean men, of men who are lost to all sense of shame or regard for honor" (p. 14). But Hundley, although sometimes in ill health, was happier in his later years than his fellow Southern interpreters, Fitzhugh, Ruffin, and Helper, had been. He rested his faith in a divine view of Southern history, a belief in God's Providence, in which Fitzhugh and Ruffin, although they occasionally voiced such a belief, could never rest assured. "Jehovah hath spoken the word," Hundley had written just after the fall of Atlanta and after his own capture in 1864, "and it will stand fast. The South will surely triumph in the end. She is fighting for the correct principles of civil and religious freedom, and panoplied thus in the armor of divine truth and justice, she can never be conquered" (p. 44).

Hundley would not have changed his words even if he had foreseen the verdict of the war. It was not military so much as spiritual victory he meant. His was a sentiment that would be echoed by numerous other Southerners, more vindictive than he, in the years ahead. The providential view of Southern history would become increasingly prevalent as Southerners, realizing they had lost the war and had lost control of their society, asked why, and turned to God and to prophecy for answers. The Southerners of the 1850s—Fitzhugh, Ruffin, Helper, and Hundley—had looked to the future, Fitzhugh and Ruffin toward Southern nationhood, Helper to an all-white paradise, and Hundley to whatever Providence ordained. They had written with a confidence in themselves and an appeal to man to solve Southern problems. With the exception of Hundley, they had very rarely appealed to Divine Providence. But the Southern apologists of the late 1860s and 1870s would have nowhere to look but back.

Their cause was lost, their nation dead and gone, and the nation of the spirit had taken its place. God, in the era between Appomattox and Henry Grady, would come to play an increasingly important role in Southern affairs. Southern apologists, many of them Calvinists, could see no reason for their military defeat, save the inscrutable will of a sovereign God. But most of them would remain convinced, as Hundley had been in 1864, that the South would "surely triumph in the end."

PART II

After Appomattox

CHAPTER 1

The Rage of the Righteous:
The War Generation and the Lost Cause

The Confederates have gone out of this war, with the proud,
secret, deathless, *dangerous* consciousness that they are THE
BETTER MEN, and that there was nothing wanting but a change
in a set of circumstances and a firmer resolve to make them
the victors.
> Edward A. Pollard,
> *The Lost Cause*, 1866

And I rage internally when I see our Southern people—my
brothers and yours—meekly admitting the Yankees' claim to
have all the culture, all the talent, all the genius of the country. . . . And I rage tenfold when I see our people—aye, our
women and maidens—taught to hanker after the works of
Mrs. Stowe, that Pythoness of foulness; Lowell, the twice-
branded hypocrite; Whittier, the narrow bitter Puritan; Alger,
the dish-washer of maudlin mysticism, and the rest of that
shabby crew.
> William Hand Browne to
> Paul Hamilton Hayne, September 11, 1871

History will some day bring present events before her impar-
tial bar; and then her ministers will recall my obscure little
book, and will recognize in it the words of truth and righteousness, attested by the signatures of time and events.
> Robert Lewis Dabney,
> *A Defence of Virginia and Through Her of the South*, 1867

In the spring of 1862, not long after Federal troops had occupied
Nashville, the Reverend Samuel Davies Baldwin, minister of the
Methodist Episcopal Church South and author of *Armageddon, or the
United States in Prophecy* (1845), rose before the Yankee conquerors to
speak. He took as his text the thirty-eighth and thirty-ninth chapters
of Ezekiel. The Southern Confederacy, he declared, was the true Israel, and the North was Gog, the destructive invading force. The
South, although destined to be laid waste as prophecy had foretold,
would yet triumph in the end.

For his words Dr. Baldwin was thrown into the Nashville peniten-
tiary and had already been transferred to a Northern prison in 1864
when Daniel Hundley, shortly before passing through Nashville as a

85

northbound prisoner himself, recorded the story in his diary.[1] Samuel Davies Baldwin was to die in 1866 at the age of forty-seven, and would soon be forgotten even by the citizens of Nashville. But the sentiments he expressed in 1862 would resound across the South for the next three years as other parts of Dixie fell to the enemy—and, finally, throughout the entire Confederacy in 1865. As the South was falling the Southern righteous raged. If before the war Southerners had used the word of God to justify slavery, after four years of suffering and privation they took to religion in a more desperate, tormented fashion. Never had the South been so truly haunted by God as in the years just after Appomattox, and it has not been since.

The South was indeed a latter-day Israel, Robert Lewis Dabney and other apologists believed, and Southerners were God's Chosen. But why had they been defeated? Why had they fallen? The Southern mind, shaped by the Calvinist doctrines of God's sovereignty and God's determination, agonized over the question. Not only the divines agonized, particularly the Presbyterians among them, but teachers and editors, generals and common soldiers as well. They had been convinced—at least if we are to judge by their war diaries and journals—that God would ensure their victory. Why had God failed them? Indeed, many of them finally reasoned, God had not failed them at all; rather, they had failed God. "A righteous God, for our sins towards Him," wrote Robert Lewis Dabney, "has permitted us to be overthrown by our enemies and His."[2] Those sins Dabney did not enumerate, but in his mind they most assuredly did not include slavery. They did include such wartime offenses as speculation and profiteering, and they included other, more grievous sins. The Southerner had been overly proud and overly confident. He had not been sufficiently determined. He had not placed his faith wholly in God. He had not stated his case, and thus God's case, to the world with sufficient commitment and fervor. He had not *believed* in the rightness of his cause as strongly as the New England abolitionists had believed in theirs. Finally, the defeat came to be seen as *felix culpa*: the South had fallen *because* it was God's Chosen. It needed to be taught to fail and to suffer, and it would profit from the lesson in the end. Had not God's Chosen, earlier, spent a season in captivity?

1. Hundley, *Prison Echoes*, 40–41.
2. Robert Lewis Dabney, *A Defence of Virginia and Through Her of the South* (New York, 1867), 356.

Thus for the first time in the Southern apologia, God came into the center of the picture. He had been peripheral in the writings of the antebellum apologists Ruffin, Hammond, and Fitzhugh. Man, with his honor, chivalry, and visions of nationhood, had stood at the center of their dreams. What Ruffin saw around and above him was more nearly fate than God's determination, and Fitzhugh did not begin to lean on Providence until his writings of 1861, the time when war was at hand and the need most desperate. But the Southerner after Appomattox, having seen what man had wrought, had nowhere else to turn. "Our best hope," wrote Dabney, "is in the fact that the cause of our defence is the cause of God's Word, and of its supreme authority over the human conscience. For, as we shall evince, that Word is on our side." But *whose* side? That of which South? Dixie, even after Appomattox, was not monolithic. The apologist—Dabney or Alfred Taylor Bledsoe—was apologist for the conservative Southern order, he professed, because of his religious conviction. But that rare Southerner—Atticus G. Haygood or George W. Cable—who turned his back on the Lost Cause and urged Southern social reform grounded his argument as well in religion: social hierarchy and racial inequality were "not Christian." "The faithful servants of the Lord Jesus Christ dare not cease to oppose and unmask Northern radicalism," wrote Dabney in 1867. "We are just as completely dedicated to God's service as though we were Chinese missionaries," wrote Cable in 1884.[3] Dabney and Cable, both loyal Southerners, veterans, and pious Presbyterians with Calvinist upbringings, were as far apart in matters Southern as two men could have been.

The Southern rage to explain, then, took a decidedly different turn in the years after Appomattox. The apologists wrote for reasons different from those of their predecessors, and they spoke to a different audience. If many of the writers of the 1850s—Fitzhugh and Hundley in particular—had written in large part to convince Northerners of the justice of their position, virtually all the postbellum apologists wrote to reassure and persuade their fellow Southerners—and themselves. And they spoke not out of pride so much as pain and suffering. If before the war the apologist had written with the anticipation of a Southern nation, now he wrote only with the bitterness and despair of failure. The military defeat had been a fall from innocence,

3. *Ibid.*, 6, 21; George Washington Cable to Louise Cable, December 31, 1884, quoted in Arlin Turner, *George W. Cable: A Biography* (1956; rpr. Baton Rouge, 1966), 206.

and the world the Southerner entered was a world not of his own making. The Old South he had believed to be civilization itself, the inheritor of the best of Western tradition; and the Yankees, the barbarians, had destroyed it. They had conquered by might, not right. Or *had* the Yankees won yet? That was the unresolved and radical question. As Edward A. Pollard of Virginia wrote, the Confederates after 1865 still believed that they were the better men, theirs the better cause, and that nothing but circumstance had kept them from military victory. It was, Pollard insisted, "a *dangerous* consciousness," and it was dangerous because it meant that Appomattox had not really settled the issue. When the war of arms ceased in April, 1865, the war of ideas—as Pollard announced in *The Lost Cause* (1866)—had just begun. A clerical friend of Robert Lewis Dabney's referred to it as "the second war of independence," and in many ways the Southern states united in this second war as they had not in the first.[4] In 1861 Dabney had thought and written as a Virginian; after 1865 he wrote as a Southerner.

The apologists began to state their case almost as soon as the guns fell silent. Alfred Taylor Bledsoe, an earlier Southern spokesman in his *Essay on Liberty and Slavery* (1856), turned immediately after the war—in "white heat," Richard M. Weaver has written—to the writing of *Is Davis a Traitor, or Was Secession a Constitutional Right Previous to 1861?* (1866). A native of Kentucky who had been educated at Transylvania College and at West Point, Bledsoe for a time had practiced law in Springfield, Illinois, where he had known Abraham Lincoln. From 1854 to 1861 he was professor of mathematics at the University of Virginia, and from 1861 to 1865 he served as undersecretary of war for the Confederacy. In *Is Davis a Traitor?*, Bledsoe, an eloquent, impulsive man, defended the Southern leaders, justified the Confederate cause from a constitutional point of view, and attempted to "vindicate the character of the South for loyalty." Bledsoe was joined by Alexander Stephens of Georgia, the former vice-president of the Confederacy, who also justified the South from a constitutional position, and stated a classic defense of states' rights, in *A Constitutional View of the Late War Between the States* (1868–1870). But the tone of Stephens' work was different from Bledsoe's. A former Unionist and moderate who dem-

---

4. Edward A. Pollard, *The Lost Cause* (New York, 1866), 729; Francis Butler Simkins, "Robert Lewis Dabney, Southern Conservative," *Georgia Review*, XVIII (Winter, 1964), 402.

onstrated little bitterness even after the war, Stephens wrote a lofty and abstract defense of the Southern position, a treatise with four speakers expressing conflicting theories of government.[5]

But perhaps the most intriguing addition to the Southern apologia of the 1860s was Edward A. Pollard's *Lost Cause*, largely because Pollard tried to convince his readers, and himself, that the South had not yet been truly defeated. It had only lost the military phase of a much larger struggle. A former writer for the Richmond *Daily Examiner*, historian of the war, and one of the leading critics of the Jefferson Davis administration, Pollard had been confined in Northern prisons in 1864 and 1865, and upon his release he was burning to tell the "true" story about the war. His 750-page book was subtitled in part, *A New Southern History of the War of the Confederates . . . The Most Gigantic Struggle of the World's History*, and the subtitle suggested something of the grandeur of his vision. *The Lost Cause* was, for the most part, a chronological account of the war, highly colored by the Southern point of view but possessing the pretense of control and objectivity. The truth, Pollard believed, needed little embellishment.

Behind this façade of dispassionate reporting, however, lay a great need to state the South's case—to affirm that it was more valiant, honorable, and courteous in warfare than the North, that it possessed a superior civilization. Pollard's thesis was that the North waged war because it was "coarse and inferiour in comparison with the aristocracy and chivalry of the South" (p. 51), was conscious of its inferiority, and thus was jealous of the South. The "Puritan exiles who established themselves upon the cold and rugged and cheerless soil of New England" were vastly different from "the Cavaliers who sought the brighter climate of the South, and drank in their baronical halls in Virginia confusion to roundheads and regicides" (p. 49). Because the Yankees recognized the difference, and realized that Southern civilization rested on slavery, they began the war to end slavery. But they won in battle not because of their military brilliance and valor, not

5. Bledsoe, *An Essay on Liberty and Slavery*; Alfred Taylor Bledsoe, *Is Davis a Traitor, or Was Secession a Constitutional Right Previous to 1861?* (Baltimore, 1866), vii; Alexander Stephens, *A Constitutional View of the Late War Between the States* (2 vols.; Philadelphia, 1868–1870). For a more complete discussion of Bledsoe's and Stephens' books, as well as Pollard's *Lost Cause*, see Weaver, *The Southern Tradition at Bay*, an excellent study of the works of the Southern apologia written shortly after the war. See also, for a more recent study of many of the Southern writers of the Lost Cause, Charles Reagan Wilson, *Baptized in Blood: The Religion of the Lost Cause, 1865–1920* (Athens, Ga., 1980), and Jack P. Maddex, Jr., *The Reconstruction of Edward A. Pollard* (Chapel Hill, 1974).

even because of superior arms and men, but rather because of the faulty leadership of President Jefferson Davis of the Confederacy. Davis, however, was not the only cause. Southerners in general tended to be vain, overconfident, inefficient, lacking in "commercial tact" and "business knowledge," overly insistent on chivalry and incapable of analysis—traits which were not always shortcomings in themselves but which cost the Confederacy dearly in the war. But the Yankees—such was Pollard's consolation—had won only on the battlefield. The war of ideas would continue.

Thus Edward Pollard, who in 1866 had entitled his book *The Lost Cause*, shortly afterward reconsidered and in 1868 issued a second book, *The Lost Cause Regained*. In between the two books he had changed considerably. At first, he had become even more militant, suggesting in 1867 that the South might still resort to guerrilla warfare to win its independence. But the next year he had decided that reconciliation and cooperation with Northern conservatives was the better course of action. Although in *The Lost Cause Regained*, a campaign tract written against the Radical Republicans, he threatened that Southerners might again resort to arms if they were accorded further harsh treatment—and maintained that the South, even after 1865, could have continued to wage a defensive war if its will had not faltered—now the emphasis had changed. Whether the South rearmed or not, he now insisted, its cause would triumph, for he now identified that cause as white supremacy, a cause not only for Southerners but for white men everywhere. If the South succeeded "to the extent of securing the supremacy of the white man, and the traditional liberties of the country . . . she really triumphs in the true cause of the war."[6] In so writing, Pollard seemed to leave the narrow and provincial ground of most other apologists of the immediate postwar period, who were concerned only with the *South*, and return to the broader vision of Fitzhugh and other antebellum writers: the South as savior for the world. The cause had been redefined—white supremacy, rather than Western civilization—but Pollard would have said that the latter rested on the former. In the concluding section of *The Lost Cause Regained*, he became almost Whitmanesque in his vision of an

---

6. Edward A. Pollard, *The Lost Cause Regained* (1868; rpr. Freeport, N.Y., 1970), 14. See also Maddex, *The Reconstruction of Edward A. Pollard*, 50–84; and Jack P. Maddex, Jr., "Pollard's *Lost Cause Regained*: A Mask for Southern Accommodation," *Journal of Southern History*, XL (November, 1974), 595–612.

America united Atlantic to Pacific by the railroad—but a white America in which the Southern cause had triumphed. It was a vision simultaneously shared by the "Hated Helper" and later articulated by Thomas Dixon.

After Edward Pollard had demonstrated to his satisfaction that the South had won the larger war, he could live in peace. The old bitterness gone, he became a Unionist and, in his *Life of Jefferson Davis* (1869), even a critic of the Old South—and finally, in his last years, an apostle of the New South. It was an ideal prescription for peace of mind and soul—that is, convincing oneself that the South had won after all. But it was not a prescription many other Southerners could accept. Defeat and desolation were all too real in the burned cities, the wasted countryside, and it was to ensure that the Southern cause, though lost, would not be forgotten that numerous polemical magazines sprang up in the years immediately after Appomattox—among them the *Southern Review* of Baltimore founded by Bledsoe in 1867, the *Eclectic* of Richmond begun in 1868 and transferred to Baltimore (as the *New Eclectic*) in 1869, the *Southern Magazine* of Baltimore (a successor to the *New Eclectic*), and *The Land We Love* begun in Charlotte, North Carolina, in 1866. The magazines followed a similar pattern: they began as moderate publications, pro-Southern but preaching reconciliation, but by 1870, as Radical Reconstruction became entrenched, they became noticeably anti-Yankee. In May, 1866, *The Land We Love*, edited by General Daniel H. Hill, advocated adjustment and moderation, announcing that Southerners "must yet of necessity change our minds upon many subjects." But by 1868 Hill was comparing the Yankees to the Huns and, by February, 1869, charging that the North had sent "emissaries of Satan" to ruin the South. William Hand Browne, editor of the *Southern Magazine*, responded similarly to Reconstruction. Not only did his journal adopt a more militant stance in 1870, but Browne raged in private to Paul Hamilton Hayne of South Carolina: "I look forward to the threatening *Yankeeisation* of the South with unspeakable dread and abhorrence. It would not matter so much if the prospect was that of being Anglicised, Gallicised, Teutonised, or Feejeeised; but to be infected with the Yankee soul—the Yankee spirit—great heavens!"[7]

7. Daniel H. Hill, "Education," *The Land We Love*, I (May, 1866), 2; Daniel H. Hill, editorial, *The Land We Love*, VI (February, 1869), 345; Browne to Hayne, July 30, 1870, quoted in Hubbell, *The South in American Literature*, 751.

Of all the polemical journals, Bledsoe's *Southern Review* was perhaps the most militant. After writing his book *Is Davis a Traitor?*, Bledsoe supported the Lost Cause in his *Review* from 1868 until 1877. He continued to defend slavery and secession, and to attack science and industrialism, with religious fervor and conviction. The essays of outside contributors to the *Southern Review* were not particularly angry—in many cases not even Southern—but Bledsoe's own editorials, often edged with sarcasm, were strongly committed to the Southern cause. "Our most gracious, benevolent, and loving fellow-citizens of the North," he wrote in July, 1869, "are striving to accomplish for the South, the same result the French philosophers accomplished for their country—a thorough depravation of character and morals, and by the same means." He returned to the argument of Fitzhugh and other earlier Southern apologists: there existed a "difference in character" between North and South, a difference responsible for the war itself. The North was "of the earth, earthy; and ignores the spirituality of our nature." Its great defect was its "materiality," its God "Mammon." The civilization of the South was "defective, doubtless," but it was "a civilisation seeking a spiritual elevation over matter and money." The North represented barbarism and chaos, the South "decorum" and order, and the ruin the North had wrought had historical precedents: "The civil war in Rome, carried on by Marius and Sylla, in which the slaves were emancipated and made citizens, destroyed the liberties of Rome. The same means . . . must produce the same results in the United States." Thus, Bledsoe still insisted in the year 1869, "the Southern States constitute no part of the United States."[8]

ALFRED TAYLOR BLEDSOE lived until 1877, just long enough to see Northern troops removed from Southern soil. Edward Pollard died in 1872, Alexander Stephens in 1883, and many of the other apologists who survived Reconstruction had also fallen silent by the mid-1880s. The Southern magazines faded one by one as the Lost Cause ceased to be a bitter, exclusively Southern preoccupation and became instead a romantic part of the *national* mythology—the wish for a pastoral neverland to which Americans North and South returned in their

---

8. Alfred Taylor Bledsoe, "Chivalrous Southrons," *Southern Review*, VI (July, 1869), 96, 110, 111, 127.

dreams. Two decades after Appomattox the cause was indeed lost and, except in the nostalgic fiction produced by Southerners as much for Northerners as for themselves, never to be regained. It had become sentimental, even saccharine—something it could never have been for Edward Pollard and Alfred Taylor Bledsoe.

Nor could it have been for Robert Lewis Dabney of Virginia, a Southern partisan who was, more than any other apologist, the last holdout. Dabney was a man whose hostility toward the Yankees and bitterness toward fate, whose rage to proclaim the supremacy of the Old South, were as strong in the year of his death, 1898, as they had been in the year of Appomattox. If the postbellum South produced an equivalent of Edmund Ruffin, it was surely Dabney. He wrote, indeed, what Ruffin might have written if, by some machination of a cruel deity, he had lived thirty years longer, and he wrote in the manner of Edmund Ruffin—indignant, bitter, sometimes furious. He was harsh enough in his middle years when he wrote his *Defence of Virginia and Through Her of the South* (1867) and numerous pro-Southern essays and speeches. But in his later years, with strong face and white hair, completely blind and wracked by pain for which physicians could provide little relief, Dabney seemed a prophet of old come to preach God's wrath against the heathen and to defend and vindicate His Chosen. "I am the Cassandra of Yankeedom predestined to prophesy truth and never to be believed . . . until too late," he lamented in 1894. "I shall die with the reputation," he wrote two years later, "of being a hot, resentful, and imperious man."[9]

No man could have better foreseen his fate. Dabney was indeed a resentful man, a self-proclaimed hater whose hatred extended to anyone and anything foreign to himself or his nature. He was also that most provincial of men, unable to identify with or approve of anything outside his own limited background or experience. He hated— at least before 1861—not only the North but the Deep South as well, and his hatred was not simply the traditional condescension of the older South toward the new. A "dirty, slave-trading, filibustering, proslavery, cotton league," he called the Deep South in 1860, with "a

9. Robert Lewis Dabney to Thomas Cary Johnson, July 1, 1894, and Dabney, unpublished autobiography, both quoted in David Henry Overy, "Robert Lewis Dabney: Apostle of the Old South" (Ph.D. dissertation, University of Wisconsin, 1967), 311. Overy's is by far the best account of Dabney's life. I also draw on Thomas Cary Johnson, *The Life and Letters of Robert Lewis Dabney* (Richmond, 1903).

selfishness so arrogant, so mean, so hypocritical, so fully equal to all
the wickedness of abolitionism." [10] And he hated not only much of the
rest of the South but much of Virginia as well. The wealthy, hedonis-
tic students he met at the University of Virginia, the Scotch-Irish
"peasantry" of the Shenandoah Valley who belonged to a separate
"race," the Richmond city-dwellers who by virtue of residence departed from the agrarian ideal: all deeply offended Dabney. Nowhere
can a better example be found of how far the liberal Jeffersonian
spirit—the breadth of vision and tolerance that characterized an earlier Virginia—had fallen in the mid-nineteenth century than in Robert
Lewis Dabney of Louisa County. Although distantly related to Jefferson and born into the same world, the planter gentry of Piedmont Virginia, Dabney was born three-quarters of a century later, in 1820, and
therein lay a great part of the difference. By the 1830s and 1840s, when
he was intellectually coming of age, Virginia had already slipped from
the spirit of Jeffersonian liberalism into a narrower, more limited society which committed its intellect to a defense and justification of
slavery.

The age was not entirely to blame. Dabney's family shaped him as
well. The Virginia Presbyterians from whom he sprang were a strict,
uncompromising lot; it was they who had opposed the efforts of Jefferson and others to initiate widespread public education in Virginia.
Dabney's father was a particularly pious Presbyterian who, in prepa-
ration for the Sabbath, often spent two days locked in his room studying the Bible. It was hardly coincidental that young Robert Dabney
developed a high moral seriousness, or that the seriousness was intensified at age thirteen when his father died, leaving him responsible
for a plantation and some two dozen slaves. Three years later, at sixteen, he went sixty miles away to Hampden-Sydney, a Presbyterian
college, and later continued his studies at the University of Virginia
and Union Seminary at Hampden-Sydney. What Dabney learned in
seminary only reinforced beliefs he already possessed: in God's absolute sovereignty, predestination, human depravity, and the truth
of an inerrant Bible. This basic Calvinism was to be the force that
informed everything he was to think and write for the next half-
century, the source to which he would always return. He became per-

10. Dabney, quoted in Overy, "Robert Lewis Dabney," 97.

haps the greatest teacher of scholastic Calvinism in the latter half of the nineteenth century, and his Calvinism became as well the justification for his social and political beliefs. "For, unfortunately, the human race is a fallen race—depraved, selfish, unrighteous," he wrote in 1867.[11] It followed that mankind was not to be trusted, democracy was a radical experiment, hierarchy and slavery justified.

During the ten years before the war, while serving as a Presbyterian minister in the Shenandoah Valley and then as a professor at Union Seminary, Dabney had written essays defending slavery from the biblical point of view. But in national politics in the 1850s he tended to be a moderate whose hatred was directed less toward the Yankees than toward the South Carolina firebrands. By the late 1850s he had come to believe that the South had angered God by its defiant pronouncements and rash acts—such as the attack of Preston Brooks, congressman from South Carolina, on Senator Charles Sumner of Massachusetts in 1856—and he believed God would visit His wrath upon His people. Only when Virginia seceded in April, 1861, did he cease to be a Unionist. Once Dabney decided on his course, however, he never turned back. In June, 1861, he volunteered for the Confederate army as a chaplain and in April, 1862, joined Stonewall Jackson in the Valley of Virginia as chief of staff. But the theologian did not take to camp life as easily as Daniel Hundley had; it lacked the physical comfort he took for granted. Thus in July, 1862, ill and aware that he would never make a military man, he went back to Hampden-Sydney determined to fight with his pen. His resolve was strengthened, not diminished, by family misfortune in 1862: the death, first, of a beloved sister and the death shortly afterward of his five-year-old son Tom. Like Ruffin, who had lost three daughters in the single summer of 1855, Dabney had long been plagued by family tragedy. In November, 1855, he had lost his two older sons to diphtheria, a tragedy which left him "paralyzed & stunned . . . almost without hope." Now in 1862, ill himself with typhoid, he saw a third son die. "How fearful it is to live and love in such a world!" he lamented, and, as Edmund Ruffin had responded to death, sought some cause to occupy his mind.[12] Like Ruffin, he turned his thoughts to a defense of his endan-

---

11. *Ibid.*, iii–iv; Dabney, *A Defence of Virginia*, 24.
12. Dabney, quoted in Overy, "Robert Lewis Dabney," 88; and quoted in Johnson, *Robert Lewis Dabney*, 169.

gered South. Stricken with grief and suffering, Ruffin in 1860 had begun to write *Anticipations of the Future*. In his sickbed and still despondent, Dabney in the autumn of 1862 began the work which would in 1867 appear as one of the most heartfelt contributions to the Southern apologia, *A Defence of Virginia and Through Her of the South*.

Dabney at first intended his *Defence* for an English audience. He hoped through it to persuade Great Britain to aid the Confederacy. But he was no more successful as propagandist than he had been as soldier. His defense of slavery and his attack on abolitionists were too absolute, too unrestrained, and his attack on self-government, Confederate officials feared, would offend the English. After determining that such a book would harm the Southern cause more than aid it, they declined to publish it. At the same time Dabney, unaware until later of the fate of his *Defence*, began a biography of Stonewall Jackson authorized by Jackson's widow, a work which also turned into a vehement defense of the South and was poorly received, even by Mrs. Jackson. Having recovered his health, Dabney late in 1864 returned to the army as a chaplain, preached to Lee's soldiers at Petersburg, rejoined Lee's army at Appomattox, and saw the war end. After hiding for a few days to escape imprisonment, he returned to Hampden-Sydney to find his family safe but his house ransacked and most of his livestock driven off. More resolute than ever, he vowed to continue the war in print. As his friend and biographer Thomas Cary Johnson later wrote, in 1865 Dabney became a "grimmer man, with less in the world to love." The iron "had entered his soul." [13]

If we are to judge by his words, Robert Lewis Dabney, his home vandalized, his cause lost, was as angry and bitter as Edmund Ruffin in the summer of 1865. "The Yankees have literally killed that which made the South the South," he wrote to a friend. [14] But Dabney was twenty-six years younger than Ruffin and still had a life to live, one he vowed would be devoted to preserving the Southern way. First he considered planting a new Southern nation in Latin America or Australia, and he gave up the idea only when he realized the hardship of such a life. Dabney the uncomfortable soldier was an unlikely pio-

13. Robert Lewis Dabney, *The Life and Campaigns of Lieut.-Gen. Thomas J. Jackson* (New York, 1866); Johnson, *Robert Lewis Dabney*, 294.
14. Robert Lewis Dabney to Moses Drury Hoge, August 16, 1865, quoted in Johnson, *Robert Lewis Dabney*, 305.

neer. So he resolved to remain in Virginia and write. He republished in 1866 through a New York company the biography of Jackson, to which he added a preface defending the "certain polemic tone" of his book but adding that "the truth, manfully spoken, can never be unwholesome" (p. viii). After the Jackson biography he returned to the defense of the South he had written and seen rejected in 1862. He wrote a new preface, then issued in 1867, two years after Appomattox and four after the Emancipation Proclamation, a book defending slavery as if it still existed. If he had failed in war, both as soldier and propagandist, now he would redeem himself. The South, he wrote in the *Defence*, had "been condemned unheard" (p. 15). So had Dabney.

Thus in June, 1867, when Dabney sat down in his study at Hampden-Sydney, he was determined to redeem not only the South but himself. And if in the charged and furious manner of his new preface he resembled Edmund Ruffin, in his profession of a larger mission he was more nearly a descendant of Fitzhugh. For his message in the *Defence* was not so much Ruffin's defensive and vengeful one as Fitzhugh's idea of the South as conservative check for a world gone mad, savior for a fragmented and atheistic Western civilization. If the North won, he had written in his Jackson biography, Jacobinism would again be loosed in Europe. The South was "bleeding for the common behoof of mankind" (p. 161). In 1867 he reiterated: the cause of the South was "practically the cause of truth and order" (p. 22). The fury unleashed by the abolitionists and then by the Radical Republicans had been a "revolution" against order, property, and religion—an American version of the French Revolution. Thus in the *Defence* he spoke not only to Southerners but to men everywhere "whom Providence will call forth from their seclusion, when the fury of fanaticism shall have done its worst, to repair its mischiefs, and save America [and, elsewhere he insisted, mankind] from chronic anarchy and barbarism; if indeed, any rescue is designed for us. It is this audience, 'fit but few,' with whom I would chiefly commune" (p. 8).

Dabney began his *Defence* by acknowledging that many might judge it foolish that he now came forth to justify "a social order totally overthrown, and never to be restored here" (p. 5). But he wrote because he felt compelled to "lay this pious and filial defence upon the tomb of my murdered mother, Virginia" (p. 5), and "in defending her, I have virtually defended the whole South, of which she was the type" (p. 7). The "last and only office" that remained for sons of the South was "to leave their testimony for her righteous fame" (p. 6). Dabney was obsessed with the verdict of history, expressing no fewer than three times in the early pages of his book his concern about how future scholars would view slavery, the Southern cause—and his book. He needed to write to ensure that posterity knew the truth— and because Southerners before him had not written well enough. "While the swords of our people were fighting the battles of a neces- sary self-defence, the pens of our statesmen should have been no less diligent in defending us against the adverse opinion of a prejudiced world" (pp. 20–21). The North had won the war of opinion as well as arms, and now, "in order to be free we must be respected: and to this end we must defend our good name" (p. 20). Most subjugated na- tions developed "a depraved, cringing, and cowardly spirit," and Dabney wanted to ensure that the South would not succumb to the "degrading and debauching of [its] moral sensibilities and principles" (p. 7). Finally, like Pollard, he believed the cause was not truly lost, the war in its larger meaning not over. Neither was slavery a dead is- sue: "Instead, therefore, of regarding the discussion of the rightful- ness of African slavery as henceforth antiquated, we believe that it as- sumes, at this era, a new and wider importance" (p. 20). "Because we believe that God intends to vindicate His Divine Word, and to make all nations honour it . . . we confidently expect that the world will yet do justice to Southern slaveholders" (p. 22).

In the preface and introduction to the 1867 *Defence* Dabney clearly saw himself as prophet, as a voice from the wilderness the Yankees had made, crying to save Christian civilization in America and the Western world. He was earnest, humorless, noncompromising—the morally superior Southern Calvinist lashing out at the descendants of morally superior New England Calvinists. But the body of the book assumed a less intense tone. In it Dabney justified slavery from vir- tually every point of view, biblical, ethical, and economic. He used the 1860 census to "prove" the South wealthier than the North, just as Helper had used the 1850 census to prove precisely the opposite. Just as Fitzhugh, he stressed the "organic" nature of Southern society, the family resemblance of the master-slave relationship, and the moral superiority of slavery to free labor. Indeed, he was one of very few Southerners who were not afraid to defend "the abstract righteousness" of slavery. Slavery had made Southerners a nobler, more courteous and chivalrous people, unlike the New Englanders who among the middle classes were "mean, inhospitable," and penurious, and among the upper, combined a "domestic scantiness and stinginess with external ostentation and profusion" (p. 325). Just as God had ordained and sanctioned slavery, Dabney insisted in his conclusion, God would now provide for his people in their suffering:

> Although our people are now oppressed with present sufferings and a prospective destiny more cruel and disastrous than has been visited on any civilized people of modern ages, they suffer silently, disclaiming to complain, and only raising to the chastening heavens, the cry, "How long, O Lord?" Their appeal is to history, and to Him. They well know, that in due time, they, although powerless themselves, will be avenged through the same disorganizing heresies under which they now suffer, and through the anarchy and woes which they will bring upon the North. Meantime, let the arrogant and successful wrongdoers flout our defence with disdain; we will meet them with it again, when it will be heard; in the day of their calamity, in the pages of impartial history, and in the Day of Judgment. (p. 356)

Although Dabney's *Defence* was spoken in thunder, his voice, as before, was not widely heeded. The author remained bitter and frustrated, and now doubly so—full of anger both toward the Yankees who had ruined him and toward the Southerners who had neglected him. He attributed the fate of his *Defence* to an "ocean of abolition lies and slanders," and then plunged back into his crusade against the Yankees. If older Southerners would not listen to him, he would appeal to Southern youth. In a speech at Davidson College in 1868— reprinted in General Hill's *The Land We Love*—he expressed fear that young Southerners would "succumb to an apathetic despair": "The danger may be expressed by *the fearful force of conquest and despotism to degrade the spirit of the victims*" (p. 109). Southerners dared not follow the course of Rome, that other civilization sacked by barbarians, and turn to pleasure and idleness. The following year, writing in the *New Eclectic*, Dabney carried his campaign even further: he issued a defense of anger and hatred. Believing that Virginians and other Southerners were accepting too easily Federal dictates, he declared that men from the past—Augustine, Luther, Calvin, Knox—had refused to be "on terms of politeness with sin." No "innocent, little piping," he added, would ever "effect the work of the trumpet blast, which rouses a slumbering nation and shakes the mask off its assailants." "The times," he concluded, "demand 'good haters.'"[15]

Dabney continued to rage as Reconstruction tightened its grip upon the South. "I hear brethren say it is time to forgive," he shouted before the General Assembly of the Southern Presbyterian church in 1870, in response to Northern Presbyterians in attendance who had urged reunion between the churches. "I do not forgive," he cried. "I do not try to forgive. What! Forgive those people, who have invaded our country, burned our cities, destroyed our homes, slain our young men, and spread desolation and ruin all over the land!" "The only choice we have," he wrote three years later to Daniel Hill, "is to teach the Southern people to hate the Yankees, or else, to be all Yankees together." Dabney had been overwhelmed by suffering and loss, and, not unlike one of Melville's *misérables*, after once sensing and experiencing evil in the world, could sense little else. "The day is pleasant and the sun is shining cheerfully," he wrote in 1868, "but to me everything looks as gloomy as if it were clothed in the pall of death."[16]

Throughout the 1870s, Dabney's greatest fear was that the South, particularly the young South, would capitulate to Yankee ways. Talk of regional reconciliation and even cooperation abounded. In 1875 a young Northern journalist, Edward King, published *The Great South*, based on articles he had written for *Scribner's Monthly* on a trip through the Southern states in 1873. King described a South rich in natural resources and ripe for industrial development and commercial progress. Dabney also heard from his fellow Southerners talk of a "New South" of industrialization and commerce, and this talk alarmed him all the more. In 1869, William Lee Trenholm told the Charleston Board of Trade that the South should pursue the "Northern ideal" of industrial development. A year later Edwin DeLeon in an essay in *Putnam's Magazine* entitled "The New South" also advocated industrial progress. The following year Benjamin H. Hill in a speech before a University of Georgia alumni group joined in the call for a New South of

15. Dabney, quoted in Overy, "Robert Lewis Dabney," 163; Robert Lewis Dabney, "The Duty of the Hour," *The Land We Love*, VI (December, 1868), 114; Robert Lewis Dabney, "Laus Iracundiæ," *New Eclectic*, V (July-December, 1869), 529. See also Robert Lewis Dabney, "The Crimes of Philanthropy" (II [December, 1866], 81–93), and "Industrial Combinations" (V [May, 1868], 25–34), in *The Land We Love*.

16. Dabney, quoted in Simkins, "Robert Lewis Dabney," 401, 403; Robert Lewis Dabney to Daniel Hill, December 1, 1873, quoted in Overy, "Robert Lewis Dabney," 161.

manufacturing and commerce. In 1874, DeLeon published a series of articles on Southern industrial progress, which were widely read and discussed. And the same year twenty-four-year-old Henry Grady of Atlanta himself used the term *New South* in an editorial in the Atlanta *Daily Herald.*[17] These and other Southern voices of the 1870s were harsh to Dabney's ear.

Dabney's hatred of industrial civilization was intensified in 1880 when he went to Germany to visit his son. He saw the future and was repelled. German industry, bureaucracy, and universal education all reminded him of what he found in the American North and what he feared for the American South. He returned home more convinced than ever that the Southern way was the only way to save Western civilization. But Southerners themselves, who had fought the Yankees and died at their hands, were now forfeiting the values they had fought to preserve and were embracing those values they had fought against. Such, according to Dabney, was infinitely worse than military defeat.

Again he felt compelled to speak out, but the time and place of his speaking came almost by accident. He was asked to deliver the commencement address at Hampden-Sydney College on June 15, 1882, only because the college could not find a more suitable speaker. His reputation for controversy preceding him, he was asked to give the president of the college some indication of what he would say before he was allowed on the platform. He spoke in the late afternoon before an audience not wholly sympathetic; one of his colleagues left his seat in protest as Dabney began to speak. "The speech was *extempore*," Dabney later said, "none of its verbal dress thought out and nothing written, except some heads on one sheet of note-paper."[18] But however spontaneous, the message was one Dabney had considered for a long time. His 1882 address became his most famous attack on the New South.

In the speech Dabney not only was responding to the Southern industrial boosters and indicting the kind of industrial civilization he had found in Germany but also was responding at least indirectly to

17. William Lee Trenholm, Benjamin H. Hill, and Henry Grady, all quoted in Gaston, *The New South Creed*, 18, 31–33; E. Merton Coulter, "The New South: Benjamin H. Hill's Speech Before the Alumni of the University of Georgia, 1871," *Georgia Historical Quarterly*, LVII (Summer, 1973), 179–99. See also Gaston, *The New South Creed*, 34–36.
18. Dabney, quoted in Johnson, *Robert Lewis Dabney*, 401.

an address given eighteen months before by another Southern Protestant divine at another struggling Southern denominational institution. On Thanksgiving Day, 1880, Atticus G. Haygood, the president of Emory College in Oxford, Georgia, had stood in a Methodist pulpit and proclaimed, "My hope is, that in twenty years from now, the words 'The South' shall have only a geographical significance." Atticus Haygood had much in common with Dabney: he too was a rural Southerner, deeply religious, afraid of scientific encroachments upon the faith of his fathers, and formerly a chaplain in the Confederate army. But what Haygood had said in 1880 Dabney could never have said: he had urged that the past be forgotten and the present faced honestly and critically. The South, Haygood had maintained, was far better off in 1880 than it had been twenty years before, and the reason for its improved fortunes was the death of a civilization based on slavery. But that earlier civilization had left as its legacy a host of problems: "our intense provincialism," a "vast mass of illiteracy," "our want of a literature," "our want of educational facilities," and an inadequate industrial development. The South was undeservedly self-satisfied: "We think better of ourselves than the facts of our history and our present state of progress justify." Haygood had concluded his 1880 speech by predicting that he would be criticized, but had insisted, "I have spoken what I solemnly believe to be the truth."[19] The Thanksgiving Day sermon had attracted widespread attention: although many Southerners had indeed criticized Haygood, a Northern financier had published and distributed ten thousand copies in pamphlet form. The pamphlet had been entitled *The New South*.

It had been bad enough in the eyes of Robert L. Dabney when Southern editors and businessmen preached the New South gospel; it was still more serious when a fellow Southern clergyman, pious though Methodist, declared himself in the camp of the enemy—and, further, when that clergyman, Haygood, compounded his wrongdoing the following year by publishing a book, *Our Brothers in Black* (1881), which challenged the theory of Negro inferiority and advocated education of the Southern Negro. Dabney certainly had Haygood in mind when he stepped to the rostrum on June 15, 1882. He also entitled his address "The New South."[20]

19. Haygood, *The New South*, 10, 12.
20. Robert Lewis Dabney, *The New South* (Raleigh, 1883).

His tone in the speech to the Hampden-Sydney graduating class was at first apologetic: his generation had not left to his young listeners "the heritage of freedom which our fathers left us" (p. 1). Rather, Virginia and the South were "deflowered by subjugation," were "virtually governed by the votes of an alien and barbarous horde" (p. 2)—and, worse, the new generation was not even ashamed. Dabney, the Calvinist theologian, could not neglect the role of a sovereign God in human affairs. A "strange permission of Providence" let defeat come to the Old South, the representative of the "civilized world" (p. 2). But, upon reflection, God's will was not strange at all: the righteous always suffered, and their suffering was for a purpose. Thus, "the task which duty and Providence assigned us was, to demonstrate by our own defeat, after intensest struggle, the unfitness of the age for that blessing we would fain have preserved for them" (p. 3). Southern history was cosmic drama, and "we have now seen but the first act of the drama, and it has been a tragedy. The curtain has fallen for the time to the music of a *miserere*, whose jarring chords have fretted the heartstrings of such as Lee and his comrades into death. It may well happen after the fashion of the mimic stage, the next rise of the curtain may be accompanied by the garish lights of a deceitful joy, the blood stains of the recent tragedy covered with fresh saw dust, and the new actors ushered in with a burst of gay melody. But the other acts are to follow. May they not be tragic also?" (p. 9).

The "other acts" were the coming days of the New South, and Dabney feared what he saw in the new society: greed, materialism, cultural fragmentation, expanded suffrage, centralization of finance, art, and culture, and accumulation of wealth in the hands of the few. Anticipating Donald Davidson by half a century, he lashed out at "Leviathan," the power state. "Canst thou draw out Leviathan with a hook?" he asked, quoting from Job 41:5, "or his tongue with a cord which thou lettest down? Canst thou put a hook into his nose?" (p. 11). A New South was inevitable, he now acknowledged, but "what manner of thing shall it be?" (p. 11). As for himself, he could not understand the new age sufficiently to answer; he himself could never enter it. As one "who fell with the Old South," he would "claim our prerogatives forever of defending our own principles, which a decadent country has pronounced too elevated for it to tolerate" (p. 11). But Dabney cautioned those young Southerners to whom he spoke to enter the new age with trepidation, armed with "truth and righteousness" and on guard against three temptations: to "BECOME LIKE THE CONQUERORS" and succumb to the lust for wealth (p. 12); to fall prey to "moral disgust" and thus relinquish any role in public affairs; and to forget the past or, worse, believe the version of that past handed down by the Yankee conquerors (p. 13). Dabney already saw "ominous signs of yielding," particularly the Southern predisposition toward making "wealth the idol, the all in all of sectional greatness": "I hear our young men quote to each other the advice of the wily diplomat Gorstchacoff [*sic*], to the beaten French: 'Be strong,' they exclaim: 'Let us develope! develope! develope! Let us have, like our conquerors, great cities, great capitalists, great factories and commerce and great populations; then we shall cope with them'" (p. 12). "These be thy gods, O Israel," and they were false gods.

It was not into a new age so much as into battle that Dabney sent the Hampden-Sydney students that June afternoon in 1882. And to those students—a large number of whom were in tears when he finished, if we are to believe Dabney—it must have seemed less a new age than a new land to which he sent them, a strange country which he himself could envision but could not enter. Despite his prophetic bearing, he was no Moses and theirs was not a promised land, but rather one of corruption and shame in which the Philistines rather than God's Chosen would surely triumph. Dabney, sixty-two years old, was defeated and weary, finally resigned to change. The rage had not quite gone out of his voice, but it had become subdued. The cause, finally, was nearly lost. "I have but the dregs of a life to live anyhow," Dabney wrote to his son the following year.[21]

But he had fifteen more years to live, and he never completely gave up. He did have to make severe compromises with life. The summer of 1882, even as he gave his commencement address, Dabney was very insecure about his position in Union Seminary of Hampden-Sydney. Although he had gained in the 1870s a great reputation as scholar and theologian—partly through the publication in 1871 of his *Systematic Theology*—he had made enemies within the seminary as he had elsewhere. His obsessive fear throughout the 1870s was that the Southern Presbyterian church would reunite with the Northern and thus fall under the influence of the Northern body. If that reunion

21. Johnson, *Robert Lewis Dabney*, 201; Robert Lewis Dabney to Charles Dabney, August 14, 1883, quoted in Overy, "Robert Lewis Dabney," 263.

should occur, his position at Union Seminary would become intolerable. Indeed, many of the Virginia Presbyterians, he believed, already were in league with the North. Thus, he had long considered leaving, and in the fall of 1882 he received what he believed was a providential sign. He fell seriously ill with bronchitis, pleurisy, and pneumonia, and he believed the climate of southside Virginia largely responsible for his illness. When the University of Texas offered him the chair of mental and moral philosophy the next spring, he departed for the Southwest.

Thus Dabney, that most provincial of Virginians who in 1860 had nothing but disdain for the Far South, in 1883 transported himself to a land even more remote than that Deep South of his earlier imagination. Like George Fitzhugh before him, he left Virginia and went to Texas to die, and like Fitzhugh he came to miss Virginia. Dabney's last years were even more bitter than his middle ones. Added to his hatred of Yankees and of industrialization, and the continuing fear that the Southern church would join with the Northern, were physical problems from which he found no relief. In the 1880s he learned that he had glaucoma; by 1889—like Fitzhugh in his last year in Texas—he was blind. Still he continued to teach, memorizing his lectures. In 1887 he had stated his creed for the last time in a book, *Sensualistic Philosophy of the Nineteenth Century*, in which he had attacked various manifestations of modernism. For the next ten years, blind and suffering, he continued to preach that creed. He continued, as well, to rage against whatever and whomever offended him—against the University of Texas, in which he had made enemies and which demanded his resignation in 1894; against Union Seminary, which angered him in 1895 by moving to Richmond; and most of all against the Yankees. Until the end he traveled and spoke, continuing to be, as he urged the postbellum Southerner to be, a good hater. On January 3, 1898, he died, and his body was returned to Virginia for burial in the old seminary graveyard at Hampden-Sydney. He had lived long enough: the year of his death Southern soldiers once again wore blue and fought for the Union.

WHY DID only certain of the righteous rage? Why did other Southerners, who apparently suffered more in the War Between the States, express little bitterness in defeat? Why did Alfred Taylor Bledsoe strike out in anger—and Alexander Stephens, though imprisoned and humiliated, express little personal bitterness toward the Yankees? Why did Paul Hamilton Hayne rage, particularly in his letters and essays— and Sidney Lanier, his health permanently impaired from his experience in a Union prison, bear so little personal resentment? Why did Dabney, the pious Virginia Presbyterian who had escaped injury at war, devote his life to revenge upon the Yankees—and George W. Cable, the pious Louisiana Presbyterian twice wounded in battle, not rage at all, at least not against the North?

The answer, of course, is that many factors besides the war itself went into the making of angry Southerners. The "good haters" of whom Dabney spoke were not produced in a single four-year span. But the case of George W. Cable as Southerner was a somewhat special one. Indeed, by the exacting standards of Robert Lewis Dabney, he would not have been considered Southern at all. He had been born in New Orleans in 1844, but his parents were hardly Southern in a manner Dabney would have approved. His mother, of New England stock, was a native of Indiana. His father had been born in Virginia, but had left in 1830 when his father had freed his slaves and moved to Pennsylvania. Even Cable's Virginia origins would have been suspect to a purist such as Dabney. The Cable family had come from Germany in the eighteenth century and had settled near Winchester in the Shenandoah Valley.[22] Dabney, who had served a church for six years in the valley, had decided that its inhabitants were nothing more than "Southern Yankees"—shrewd, industrious, thrifty, and petty. Further, like Fitzhugh, he had no use for Germans. It was not from Dabney's Virginia that Cable's father came.

So the assumption that Cable was not quite fully "Southern," or at least not in the right way, seems at first to have some basis in fact. In any case, it has been an assumption shared both by Cable's Southern contemporaries and by numerous writers since. Cable was a "true Yankee," wrote Creole historian Charles Gayarré, and was besides a "sneak, miserable in the utmost degree as a writer . . . indubitably a prodigious humbug, a phenomenal fraud," a "dollar scraper," an "insect." Gayarré, it must be noted, resented Cable's portrait of the Loui-

22. For biographical information about Cable I rely principally on Turner, *George W. Cable*; Louis D. Rubin, Jr., *George W. Cable: The Life and Times of a Southern Heretic* (New York, 1969); and Kimball King, "George Washington Cable and Thomas Nelson Page: Two Literary Approaches to the New South" (Ph.D. dissertation, University of Wisconsin, 1964).

siana Creoles and also, one suspects, was jealous of the man who had usurped his own territory and had become acclaimed as the Creole authority that Gayarré considered himself. But Gayarré was not alone. Many were the Southern editors who referred to Cable as a "Yankee Puritan"; because of his New England blood, Henry Grady wrote, Cable had never really identified with the South. His was a view expressed more recently by Edmund Wilson, who in *Patriotic Gore* attributed Cable's morality and objectivity to "the New England blood which was mingled in him with that of Virginia" (p. 559).[23]

Wilson believed in blood: it was he who attributed Hinton Helper's violent racism to his "lower-class German blood" (p. 377). But we can find better support for Cable's New England temper in his own words. Indeed, he *was* a sort of spiritual New Englander if we define the New England spirit—and the Southern—as Fitzhugh, Ruffin, Dabney, and later the Southern Agrarians did. If the Southerner indeed had an aversion to abstraction, science, reform, and humanitarian religion—and the New Englander (particularly that extreme New Englander, the abolitionist) embraced all these—surely Cable was a spiritual Yankee. Further, according not only to Fitzhugh, Ruffin, and Dabney, those believers in hierarchy, but according to Cable, the democrat, the Southern temper was aristocratic, the New England democratic. The Southern system, he wrote in 1909, was "frankly and conscientiously designed to promote the elevation of one part of [the] community by purposely massing another part beneath it and by reserving the very name of public society, as well as private, to the upper element alone"; the New England system, by contrast, was "designed for the larger task of uplifting and advancing its entire people as one politically undivided mass." Finally, Cable would be, at least in the eyes of a Southern Agrarian such as Donald Davidson, something other than a "true" Southerner precisely because he approached his homeland analytically and critically and focused on a "problem South"—and in doing so became the first im-

23. Charles Gayarré, quoted in Hubbell, *The South in American Literature*, 656–57; Arlin Turner (ed.), *The Negro Question: A Selection of Writings on Civil Rights in the South by George W. Cable* (New York, 1958), 76. Wilson might have focused more on Cable's German ancestry (as he had on Helper's) than his "New England blood." It is indeed interesting that perhaps the two most notable Southern self-critics of the nineteenth century came from German stock, whereas nearly all of the Southern apologists came from English or Scotch-Irish stock. This is explained, of course, not by "blood" but rather by the relatively late arrival in America of Cable's and Helper's ancestors, as well as their relative detachment from Southern power.

portant postbellum spokesman in a tradition of criticism and reform
that would gain momentum in the twentieth century. It was not Cable's primary purpose—at least after 1880—to remember, defend, preserve, or even appreciate the South. His purpose was to improve it.
"This country of ours," he wrote in 1890, "is a giant with one arm in a
sling. That arm is the South. The whole country knows that because
of something wrong in the South, the whole country, great, rich, free,
and progressive as it is, is immeasurably less than it ought to be. . . .
Half the thought given to the betterment of the economic and civic
conditions of our country is taken up with the problem how to establish a full share of our national vigor, freedom, enlightenment, and
wealth in this crippled, bleeding, and aching arm."[24] Howard W.
Odum, leader of the reform forces in the 1920s, could hardly have
stated better his own view of the South in the national picture.

The reformist bent, the moralism, the focus on a South wounded
not by the Yankees so much as by Southerners themselves—all this,
and not just the Negro question, lay at the core of Cable's quarrel with
the South. And it was precisely Cable's moralism and penchant for
uplift—attributes of the New England Puritans, after all, and particularly their descendants, the abolitionists—that earned Cable a
reputation as a spiritual New Englander long before he was a New
Englander in fact. Cable himself recognized his kinship with the Yankees. "To be in New England would be enough for me," he wrote in
1882 on the occasion of Harriet Beecher Stowe's birthday. "I was there
once—a year ago—and it seemed as though I had never been home
till then." If, as Arlin Turner writes, Cable's words were in part a manner of speaking, they also contained truth. It is clear by the early 1880s
that he was greatly attracted to New England, and in 1885 when he
and his family permanently left the South it was to Northampton,
Massachusetts, they moved. "I must admit," he wrote of the South
that year in a letter to his wife, "I shall not from choice bring up my
daughters in that state of society. The more carefully I study it the less
I expect of it." And, once securely settled in New England, he wrote
in 1887: "Henceforth, more than ever before, my home is in New England. This South may be a free country one of these days; it is not so

24. George W. Cable, "Thomas Nelson Page: A Study in Reminiscence and Appreciation," *Book-News Monthly*, XXVIII (November, 1909), quoted in Turner, *George W. Cable*, 344; George W. Cable, "What the Negro Must Learn," in Turner (ed.), *The Negro
Question*, 206.

now." [25] So Cable made his home the last forty years of his life in Massachusetts, that most odious even of New England states to Fitzhugh and Ruffin—and, further, in Northampton, the seat of Pope Stoddard and Jonathan Edwards, the center of the moral fervor associated with the Great Awakening. Cable even taught Sunday school at the Edwards Congregational Church.

Thus it seemed to his detractors that when Cable left the South in 1884, he had not so much left home as gone home. But, in reality, he had once been very much at home in the South, and what disturbed him in the 1870s and 1880s was what he believed the South had become. He was not, at first, nearly so alienated from the South temperamentally and spiritually as his adversaries claimed. If he was a Puritan, there was after all a tradition of Southern Puritanism (or at least Calvinism)—and traditions of democracy, reform, and social criticism as well. If he had inherited from his mother a deep sense of personal morality and social responsibility, so had many another Southern son. Indeed, Cable had lived very compatibly and happily in the South and with his fellow Southerners for his first forty years. Not only was he charmed by New Orleans and devoted to it, but he had possessed in his youth the conventional Southern sentiments: he had supported slavery and a white man's government, he was loyal to the Confederacy, he hated Ben Butler and the Northern troops who occupied New Orleans in May, 1862. He had joined the Confederate cavalry in 1863 and had been wounded while serving the Southern cause. Even in the late 1860s his beliefs were those of many other Southerners. Perhaps the reformist impulse lay dormant all the while, but if so even Cable himself was not particularly aware of it, and it did not surface publicly until the mid-1870s, and not to any noticeable degree until the 1880s. In the early 1870s, Cable later said, he had no views which departed from the Southern line, and his writing for the New Orleans *Picayune* supports his claim. [26]

Most of Cable's early literary work was also orthodox enough. He had begun to write sketches and stories in the early seventies and when Edward King of *Scribner's Monthly* came to New Orleans in 1873 Cable had sent several stories back with him. Although Cable later

25. George W. Cable, letter printed in *Boston Evening Transcript*, June 15, 1882, quoted in Turner, *George W. Cable*, 222; George W. Cable to Louise Cable, January 31, 1885, Cable, letter of June 8, 1887, both quoted in Lawrence J. Friedman, *The White Savage: Racial Fantasies in the Postbellum South* (Englewood Cliffs, N.J., 1970), 115, 116.

26. Turner, *George W. Cable*, 41.

said that he began to write fiction after reading of the injustice of Louisiana's early Black Code—and indeed one of the early stories, "Bibi," was very critical of slavery and racial prejudice, and consequently was first rejected for publication—most of the other early stories pictured a romantic and charming New Orleans. His were the kind of stories favored by Richard Watson Gilder of *Scribner's Monthly* and other Northern editors in an era of local color, and Cable published seven such stories in *Scribner's* between 1873 and 1876, stories later collected in 1879 in *Old Creole Days*. Although he did suggest racial injustice in stories such as "Tite Poulette," and was not as flattering to the Creoles as he might have been, whatever serious disapproval of the older or contemporary South he might have wanted to express Gilder kept from reaching print.[27]

Cable first spoke out publicly on social injustice in 1875, in a letter to the New Orleans *Bulletin* in which he advocated integrated schools and fair treatment of the Negro. Although his was a moderate statement, it drew a heated editorial response. But the letter, and a second one to the *Bulletin* which the editor refused to print, represented his only outburst until the early eighties. After the 1875 letter he turned his efforts back to fiction, beginning in 1876 or 1877 to work on *The Grandissimes*, a novel of Creole life set in New Orleans in 1803 but also intended, Cable later said, as a commentary on contemporary life in Louisiana. The Grandissimes in Cable's novel are a proud Creole family who have had to adjust to life in a city just acquired by the United States in the Louisiana Purchase. Although in early drafts of the novel the characters discussed slavery and Cable himself offered antislavery asides, in the final version the dialogue about slavery was greatly reduced and the authorial comment largely missing. Still, Frowenfeld, the Northerner recently arrived in New Orleans, provides Cable a voice to condemn slavery, Southern indolence, and the closed Southern mind; and occasionally Honoré Grandissime, sensitive to the problems of the slaves and quadroons his family has wronged, expresses Cable's pleas for racial justice. The Bras Coupé story (Cable's earlier "Bibi," previously unpublished) is a powerful indictment of racial injustice as well. Although Cable's editors at Scribner's urged him to remove contemporary social and political comment from the novel, some of the preaching of the indignant moralist remains. At one point

27. See Rubin, *George W. Cable*, especially 62–76, 145–48, and 218–24, for a discussion of the relationship between Cable and Gilder.

the author interrupts the narrative to observe that a characteristic of tyranny is "a pusillanimous fear of its victim." Then, pursuing his point, he relates the difficult time "our South" had had "casting off a certain apprehensive tremor, generally latent, but at the slightest provocation active, and now and then violent, concerning her 'blacks.' This fear, like others similar elsewhere in the world, has always been met by the same one antidote—terrific cruelty to the tyrant's victims." "Ah!" Cable concluded, "what atrocities are we unconsciously perpetrating North and South now, in the name of mercy or defence, which the advancing light of progressive thought will presently show out in their enormity." [28]

But Southern reviewers of *The Grandissimes* largely overlooked Cable's occasional authorial intrusions. Even the reaction in New Orleans was favorable, except for that of the Creole newspaper *L'Abeille* and of a Creole reviewer, Adrien Rouquette, who charged—anonymously—that Cable had been prompted by a "disguised puritanism, assuming the fanatical mission of radical reform and universal enlightenment." [29] Rouquette's remarks in 1880 anticipated the direction of Southern criticism of Cable during the following decade.

However, the criticism was premature. In 1880 Cable was still a cautious critic, and the novel which he began in 1881—published in 1884 as *Dr. Sevier*—although more realistic than *The Grandissimes*, still concealed his social criticism behind a romantic plot. *Dr. Sevier* did not deal principally with the Creoles, but rather with an outsider, John Richling, who comes with his wife to New Orleans from Milwaukee in 1856. The son of a Kentucky planter, Richling has been disinherited for marrying a Northerner beneath his class. In New Orleans he meets Dr. Sevier, a physician committed to helping the poor. An idealist, Richling sacrifices his health and eventually his life for his work among the downtrodden and the ill.

In *Dr. Sevier*, far more than *The Grandissimes*, Cable had the opportunity for social criticism. Indeed, he had first conceived the novel as an exposé of prison conditions. The story takes place not in the French Quarter in 1803 but in New Orleans from 1856 to 1866, a period not twenty years past as Cable wrote; and in his depiction of social

28. George W. Cable, "Segregation in the Schools," New Orleans *Bulletin*, September 26, 1875, in Turner (ed.), *The Negro Question*, 27–29; George W. Cable, *The Grandissimes: A Story of Creole Life* (1880; rpr. New York, 1957), 315.

29. [Adrien Rouquette], *Critical Dialogue Between Aboo and Caboo on a New Book, or, a Grandissime Ascension*, quoted in Turner, *George W. Cable*, 102.

and economic forces, Cable was the realist he had not been before—
on occasion nearly the naturalist. But even at this early stage it is evident that Cable's fiction followed a pattern of originating as social
criticism and ending as defused romance. In the early 1870s he had
been inspired to write because of his indignation over Louisiana's earlier Black Code; but the stories that resulted and appeared in *Scribner's*
and *Old Creole Days* showed little of that indignation. Similarly, he had
begun *The Grandissimes* with social criticism in mind, but the criticism
that survived was partly obscured by romance. Now, in *Dr. Sevier*,
what began as an exposé of prison abuses became a novel in which a
prison figures only briefly, when John Richling is sentenced to serve
thirty days. Most significantly, the story steers clear of the issue the
author had come to see as the dominant Southern problem—racial
injustice.

Why did Cable avoid race? Louis D. Rubin, Jr., writes that he
avoided it because he did not want, at this point, to jeopardize his
position in New Orleans, which he surely would have done if he had
boldly condemned racial injustice. John Richling would have been the
obvious character to utter such criticism but, as Rubin notes, Richling
was too much the author's self-portrait: he was a bookkeeper as Cable
had been, he was a humanitarian as Cable was, and he came, as Cable's parents had come, from outside Louisiana. Finally, Rubin believes, Cable did not explore race in *Dr. Sevier* because at the time he
wrote the book he did not fully understand himself; he "did not recognize the contradictions within his own personality—the desire for
social approval in New Orleans as contrasted with the desire to protest the injustice being done to the Negro." [30] He could not fully understand the paradoxes in his own nature—the influence of Presbyterian Calvinists but his attraction to the exotic Creoles, his desire to be
at once the social realist and the romantic writer working within the
Genteel Tradition.

As Rubin observes, Cable gave Richling the author's own estrangement from Southern society without making clear the reason for that
estrangement—his disapproval of Southern racial attitudes. Underlying the Negro issue may have been other factors—Cable's belief that
the South was not sufficiently democratic, that it was smug, proud,
and complacent. But Cable himself in the early 1880s was not dis-

30. Rubin, *George W. Cable*, 133—51, especially 144.

turbed by these other factors as he was by race. It was the Negro question that most concerned him, and the Negro he did not feel free to discuss. Thus in *Dr. Sevier* he dealt with less explosive issues, poverty and prison reform, and otherwise wrote a sentimental melodrama. At the end of the book Dr. Sevier and Mary Richling remember their departed loves and cannot forget the past; and perhaps, in their retrospective glance, they represent the South as it existed after Appomattox—looking backward even while working for the future, still gracious and noble, full of high sentiment, but without energy, filled with melancholy. It was a safe ending to a safe novel in which Cable never really took his stand. And this time it was not primarily his editors in New York who were responsible but Cable himself. He was prevented from telling the truth by that force which W. J. Cash would later identify as the savage ideal, that spirit which suppressed dissent and required intellectual conformity. The irony, as Rubin has noted, is that Cable was criticized anyway, and for a passage in *Dr. Sevier* that should have been innocuous. He described soldiers marching through New York City singing "John Brown's Body," and added: " 'Go marching on,' saviors of the Union; your cause is just. Lo, now, since nigh twenty-five years have passed, we of the South can say it!" And although Cable quickly added, " 'and yet—and yet, we cannot forget'—and we would not," the words had been spoken, and not by a character but in the author's own voice.[31]

Cable drew criticism in 1884, however, not for the single slip in *Dr. Sevier* but for the general tenor of his remarks about the South during the previous two years. If as novelist he had continued to be timid, in several speeches and essays in 1882 and 1883 he had become bolder. But even on those occasions he had not spoken out boldly on race. What he had attacked was nearly everything else he found objectionable in Southern life—poor education, intellectual and cultural sterility, inadequate prisons and asylums, and the entire Southern system of justice. In a commencement address at the University of Mississippi in June, 1882, he had fired the first salvo in his new Southern offensive, and although his manner in the Mississippi speech had been cautious, even humble, his words had been charged: "When the whole intellectual energy of the [antebellum] Southern states flew to the defense of that one institution [slavery] which made us the South,

31. George W. Cable, *Dr. Sevier* (Boston, 1884), 377.

we broke with human progress. We broke with the world's thought." Cable had urged his listeners to reunite with the "world's thought" and "human progress": "When we have done so we shall know it by this—there will be no South. . . . We shall no more be Southerners than we shall be Northerners"; and this, Cable added, was precisely what he desired. Not the "New South" but "what we want—what we ought to have in view—is the No South!"[32]

Cable made his "No South" speech to the graduating class at Oxford on June 28, 1882, just thirteen days after Robert Lewis Dabney had made his "New South" speech at Hampden-Sydney. What the one speech affirmed, the other denied. But remarkably, there was little negative response to Cable's speech. Although a minister on the speaker's platform leaped up at one point and accused Cable of heresy, the audience and the Southern press were not particularly critical. The reason they were not is that, again, Cable had not touched on race. Even proclaiming a "No South" was preferable to critically examining the South's peculiar institution. Similarly Cable avoided race, while speaking freely on the other matters, in another commencement address a year later at the University of Louisiana. He defended the privilege of a writer to think freely and speak openly, to "assert rights" and to "present and defend truth" even if what he said shook "the established order of things like an earthquake." Southerners needed to "throw our society, our section, our institutions, ourselves, wide open to their criticism and correction."[33] But he did not specifically mention race.

Cable was still cautious, still speaking abstractly. He was only asserting the *right* of the writer to criticize and attack, not engaging in direct and forceful criticism himself. What he was also doing, however, though it could hardly have been evident to his audience in Mississippi, was justifying himself and perhaps even preparing Southern listeners for the criticism he was about to launch. The moment for such criticism came in June, 1884, at still another commencement address, this one at the University of Alabama. This time Cable did not avoid race, and although the complete text of the speech has not survived, it is clear that he indicted white Southerners for racial injustice

32. George W. Cable, "Literature in the Southern States," in Turner (ed.), *The Negro Question*, 43–44.
33. George W. Cable, "The Due Restraints and Liberties of Literature," quoted in Turner, *George W. Cable*, 142.

and advocated fairer treatment for the Negro. Cable believed he could speak more freely in Alabama because of the state's touted material progress, but even in Tuscaloosa, he later wrote, "I took great pains throughout to use a tone not of superior censure but of confession." Such caution did not disguise his views, and for weeks afterward Alabama newspapers attacked the "New England Puritan." But despite public condemnation, Cable wrote later, "for private expressions of approval and accord I had no lack, and I left Alabama more deeply impressed than ever before with the fact that behind all the fierce and resentful conservatism of the South there was a progressive though silent South which needed to be urged to speak and act. To this end someone must speak first, and as I was not out in the storm, and as one may say, wet to the skin, why should it not be I?" [34]

If in the Alabama speech Cable finally defied the savage ideal and spoke his mind, the next year he published two even more controversial works, "The Freedman's Case in Equity" in the February *Century* and, in part to answer critics of "The Freedman's Case," a second essay, "The Silent South." [35] "The Freedman's Case," first given as an address in Saratoga, New York, to the American Social Science Association, included much of the material of the Alabama speech. Cable spoke, as usual, in a conciliatory voice, identifying himself as "the son and grandson of slave-holders" (p. 410) and insisting that antebellum Southerners had been good men. But they had possessed a great flaw, as Southerners still did: they had believed the Negro inferior and had treated him unjustly. The freedman was still not truly free: he received inadequate justice and inferior education, experiencing discrimination at every turn. Cable spoke of a well-dressed Negro woman and her daughter he had seen who were forced to sit in the same train car as Negro convicts because of Jim Crow laws. Throughout "The Freedman's Case" he was appealing to the white Southern conscience. Only the South could provide an answer to the "Negro problem," he concluded, and he expressed confidence that a "moral and intellectual intelligence" in the South (p. 418) would accept his challenge.

34. George W. Cable, "My Politics," in Turner (ed.), *The Negro Question*, 19–20; Turner, *George W. Cable*, 159; for reaction to the speech at the University of Alabama, see also Rubin, *George W. Cable*, 158–59.

35. George W. Cable, "The Freedman's Case in Equity," *Century*, XXIX (February, 1885), 409–418; George W. Cable, "The Silent South," *Century*, XXX (September, 1885), 674–91.

Cable must have known he spoke too optimistically; he must also have known that Southerners would react angrily to his *Century* essay. In February, 1885, newspapers across the South attacked him, New Orleans papers prominent among them. In "The Freedman's Case" he had advocated only civil equality for the Negro, but most editors assumed he meant social equality as well. "Mr. Cable," wrote Cable's old nemesis Gayarré, "seems to wish to bring together, by every possible means, the blacks and whites in the most familiar and closest friction everywhere, in every imaginable place of resort, save the private parlor and the private bedchamber." "You can form no idea," Cable's friend Marion Baker wrote him from New Orleans, "of how bitter the feeling is against you, as bitter as it used to be against [William Lloyd] Garrison & men of his way of thinking in ante-bellum times." Those spokesmen identified with the New South movement were no more sympathetic than traditional Southerners. Speaking for other Southern editors as well, Henry Grady responded to Cable's views in an article, "In Plain Black and White: A Reply to Mr. Cable," in the April, 1885, *Century*. Cable was a New Englander in spirit, Grady charged, and the South would "never adopt [his] suggestion of the social intermingling of the races."[36] Cable had not suggested that at all.

It was partly to answer Grady and partly to appeal to Southerners of conscience that Cable reentered the controversy in September, 1885, with the publication of the second *Century* essay. In "The Silent South" he was as moderate and conciliatory as before, but he was forced to clarify the positions which had been questioned by his critics. Again, he assured Southerners that he possessed "an admirable affection for the South, that for justice and sincerity yield to none" (p. 674). As if to prove his loyalty and devotion, he eulogized Robert E. Lee and described the statue of Lee in New Orleans, a monument which symbolized "our whole South's better self: that finer part which the world not always sees; unaggressive, but brave, calm, thoughtful, broad-minded, dispassionate, sincere, and, in the din of the boisterous error round about it, all too mute" (p. 674). But the "finer part" of the South, like the statue of Lee, had been silent, and it was to the silent Southerner that Cable appealed. First, he sought to disarm his

36. Gayarré, quoted in Hubbell, *The South in American Literature*, 816; Marion Baker, quoted in Turner, *George W. Cable*, 198; Henry Grady, "In Plain Black and White: A Reply to Mr. Cable," *Century*, XXIX (April, 1885), 910.

critics—"social equality is a fool's dream" (p. 676)—and then he explained and defended positions he had taken in "The Freedman's Case." But he would not compromise his basic stand. Rather, he appealed to Southerners to reject the misguided rule of their leaders and embrace a position of fairness. In believing that the majority of Southerners would follow him, he was greatly mistaken. He had again overestimated the good will of the Silent South.

Because Cable had at least reassured his readers that he did not favor social equality, the Southern response to "The Silent South" was not quite so hostile as to "The Freedman's Case." But Robert Lewis Dabney, now exiled to Texas and nearly blind, read the essay and accused Cable of being a traitor to the South, claiming that he had written for profit and that only "a predestined slave and born dolt" could share Cable's view that slavery caused the Civil War.[37] Numerous other Southerners took up the charge that Cable was out to stir up controversy. They could not have been further from the truth, for if anything was certain about the author of "The Freedman's Case" and "The Silent South" it was that he wanted more than anything else to *avoid* controversy. He was that most reluctant of social critics, unqualified by temperament for his task, and he had taken ten years to bolster his courage to the point that he would speak out boldly. And when finally he did speak, he was in tone the most tactful and sympathetic of critics, proclaiming his own Southern heritage, confessing his own racial sins, and filling his essays with praise for the South— all in an attempt *not* to offend. No Hinton Helper was he, no Daniel Hundley even—large imposing figures who commanded attention. Cable was slight of stature—five feet, five inches—and mild of manner; he demonstrated no youthful enthusiasm, little glee in his indictment. But earnestness and moral conviction he possessed in abundance, and a compulsion to be heard and understood—traits not exclusively Puritan but likely to be interpreted as such.

Cable and his family moved to New England during the height of the Southern controversy. He had taken his wife and daughters to Connecticut in the summer of 1884, two weeks after the Alabama speech, and had decided to leave them there over the fall and winter while he toured and read with Mark Twain—whose own statement on cowardice, courage, and racial injustice, *Huckleberry Finn*, ap-

37. Dabney, quoted in Turner, *George W. Cable*, 218.

peared the same year as "The Silent South" and "The Freedman's Case." There the Cables remained through the "Freedman's Case" controversy and until the summer of 1885 when Cable decided to make Northampton his home. He later wrote that he had moved to New England in 1884 because of "the ill health of [his] family," and that he decided in 1885 to remain because "it was . . . idle to retain my residence in New Orleans, more than fifteen hundred miles from my publishers and the center of the lecture field." He was sensitive to charges that he hated the South and, on the other hand, that he was abandoning the cause of Southern enlightenment. Thus, he never ceased to insist, publicly, that he was a loyal Southerner. "I felt," he wrote in 1898 for publication, "that I belonged still peculiarly to the South." But privately he had written the year before, "Henceforth, more than ever before, my home is in New England." His was an exile he did not welcome, but his South, he added, was not "a free country." [38]

Thus Cable entered a new phase in his career the summer of 1885—expatriate Southerner and critic from afar. He was forty-one years old, and he would remain in New England until his death forty years later. But he would continue to visit the South nearly every year and, more important, would continue to write about it. In the spring of 1887 he took a trip through the Deep South and up through Nashville, where he gave a commencement address at Vanderbilt University entitled "The Faith of Our Fathers." [39] The fathers of his spirit were Washington and Jefferson, and it was to their broad, tolerant vision he wished the South to return. Again, he decried Jim Crow discrimination on Southern railroads, though acknowledging that the racial problem was national, not exclusively Southern. Cable's message was still critical, but again his tone was moderate. He still believed that the majority of Southerners would set things right—or at least he said he did.

In the late 1880s and early 1890s Cable produced numerous speeches and essays on Southern problems. In fact, he was more active as Southern commentator the seven years after leaving Louisiana than he had been at any time before. But now he spoke less to the South and more to the North, and to the Negro himself. [40] In these speeches

38. Cable, "My Politics," 21; Cable, quoted in Friedman, *The White Savage*, 116.
39. See Turner, *George W. Cable*, 250–52; and Rubin, *George W. Cable*, 196–200.
40. See, for example, "What Shall the Negro Do?," given to a Negro audience in

and essays he insisted that the South was in need of drastic change: that it was damaged by one-party politics; that the "natural advantages" that "God [had] given" it were "unsurpassed if not unequalled" but had been used unwisely; that education was vital to any positive change that might come; that the highly touted New South of commerce and industry was suspect but that a new South of the spirit was sorely needed. By 1890, however, Cable had become less confident that the Silent South would ever speak. In a speech given to the Massachusetts Club in Boston he expressed doubt that Southerners could solve their own problems and for the first time suggested federal intervention in Southern affairs.

We find in 1890, then, an expatriate Southerner who prided himself on writing "most of all" for Southern readers but who in fact spoke principally to Northern audiences, and was not really heeded by either. He spoke in Boston and Northampton, Chicago and Cleveland; he had become the North's resident expert on Southern affairs, the man to be summoned when the South needed to be explained. But he was, in a very real sense, irrelevant. The nation as well as the South was moving into an era of white supremacy and segregation, and Cable could do little to reverse the movement. He did try to keep channels open to the South, helping to form in 1888 an Open Letter Club for the free exchange of ideas among liberal Southerners, but the club failed because of the sensitivity of its members to Southern criticism. The savage ideal asserted itself in the early 1890s as it had not since the 1850s. Cable realized his helplessness, and also his special responsibility in the eyes of his fellow Southerners. It was in part to explain and justify himself that in 1888 and 1889 he wrote a revealing essay describing the making of the kind of Southerner he had become. In his apologia, "My Politics," he denied a Puritan influence, stressed his Southern origins and his youthful attitudes and prejudices, and traced the controversy in which he had found himself embroiled in 1884 and 1885. He intended his treatise to serve as an introduction to a new edition of his Southern essays to be published in 1889. His editors decided, however, that he had been too frank and that his apologia should be published only posthumously. That was to be its fate.

Boston, April 13, 1888, and "What the Negro Must Learn," given as a speech at Howard University, May 16, 1890, both in Turner (ed.), *The Negro Question*. See *The Negro Question*, 119–24, for speeches and essays of the late 1880s and early 1890s. See also Turner, *George W. Cable*, 251–61, and Rubin, *George W. Cable*, 201–211.

Such, again, was the power of the savage ideal—even above the Potomac.

If Cable could not publish his apologia in 1889, he would write a novel which would be, in its own right, an attempt to explain his feelings about the South. *John March, Southerner*, written between 1890 and 1893 and published in 1895, was in many ways his most self-consciously Southern work of fiction. Cable wrote his most outspoken and most realistic novel, that is, not only after he had moved north but after he had been effectively silenced as a social critic. Before he began to write he traveled to Cartersville, Georgia, in the spring of 1890 and took careful notes on the model for his fictional town of Suez "in the State of Dixie." The story he wrote was a Southern *bildungsroman*, the kind of work transplanted Southerners from Walter Hines Page to Thomas Wolfe would later attempt—the coming of age of a sensitive Southerner who seeks to escape the clutches of tradition. John March, seven years old when the novel begins, grows up in Suez witnessing the corruption of Reconstruction politics, attends a provincial college, and in his twenties begins to teach in a mountain school. He is seized with a passion for industrial progress, becomes involved in land development schemes, but, lacking all business sense, is exploited by his associates. Financially humbled, he determines to devote himself to the betterment of Suez and, rejecting suggestions that he go north, vows to remain and work at home.

Cable's story, as well as depicting the coming of age of a particular Southerner, is a social history of the South in Reconstruction and post-Reconstruction years. The picture he paints, full of corruption and violence, is not an attractive one. Some of his Southerners are deceitful, others simply pompous, still others committed to an outworn code of honor and chivalry which the author views satirically. The protagonist, March, is himself a creature of forms and poses, a captive of codes of chivalry, honor, and ancestor-worship. His mother, whom he greatly admires, is the worst kind of Southern poetaster. Nor is Cable's South redeemed by Negro virtue; his only significant black character, a Reconstruction politician, is as opportunistic and corrupt as his white counterparts. Cable's most ambitious attempt at critical realism, *John March, Southerner* was also an attempt to capture what the author called the representative South. Both *The Grandissimes* and *Dr. Sevier* had taken place in New Orleans, a city Southern but at the same time, with its French Catholic population, outside the

Southern mainstream. *John March* was located in the upland Protestant country of northwest Georgia, an area more typically Southern. The setting was more nearly contemporary as well. Cable had set *The Grandissimes* eighty years in the past, *Dr. Sevier* twenty-five. In *John March* he looked at the South of his own time.

But despite his criticism of Southern vices and foibles, Cable could hardly be called anti-Southern in this novel; in any case he was not *un*-Southern as his detractors charged. If anything, *John March, Southerner* supports his contention in the late 1880s that he was still very much a Southerner at heart. The point of view of the novel is distinctly Southern: the South, despite its inadequacies, is home to John, and the North is a strange, distant land. Nowhere is this strangeness illustrated better than on the train trip which John and his friend Barbara Garnet make to the Northeast, John in search of capital for land development and a publisher for his mother's poetry, Barbara to attend college. They come out of the warm Southern spring into the cold North. Cable pictures the industrial Northeast: "Long lines of suburban street-lamps were swinging by. Ranks of coke-furnaces were blazing like necklaces of fire. Foundries and machine-shops glowed." [41] At a point south of New York City, but north of the Potomac, John leaves the train and goes into an unnamed city. There his money, his father's watch, and his ticket to New York are stolen. Granted, it is Cable's protagonist, not Cable himself, who finds the Northeast inhospitable, and in depicting the North as an alien land Cable is but reflecting the view of his protagonist. March—man and season—is warm in the South, cold in the North. There is much, however, of Cable himself in March, as the author himself recognized, and nowhere more than on the trip north. "What is it in the South that we Southerners love so?" Barbara asks John as they travel through the upper South. She had told a Northern friend that "it was simply something a North-ern-er can't un-der-stand." "They *can't* understand it!" March agrees. "Our South isn't a matter of boundaries, or skies, or landscapes" (p. 326).

"You cant understand it. You would have to be born there," Quentin Compson declared in Faulkner's *Absalom, Absalom!* (p. 361), and John March, himself heading out of the Deep South into that same iron-cold North, says essentially the same thing. And not only March

41. Cable, *John March, Southerner* (New York, 1895), 343.

but George W. Cable, writing in the same Puritan Massachusetts from which Quentin later speaks, looking back, trying to explain the South. The author's deep-seated affection for the South is reflected in March's "They *can't* understand it," in Barbara's affirmation of a "certain ungeographical South-within-the-South—as portable and intangible as"—and John completes the sentence—"as our souls in our bodies" (p. 327), and in Cable's own description, later in the novel, of John March, now back in the Southern spring, "writing a description of the glorious Southern night to a friend in New England who was still surrounded by frozen hills and streams" (p. 409). The iron chill of New England and the luxuriance and warmth of the South were a contrast Cable found artistically stimulating long before Faulkner and Thomas Wolfe would. And when he betrayed an affection for the South in *John March*, it was more the Old South than the New that captured his imagination. For all of the satire in *John March* at the expense of honor, chivalry, and ancestor-worship, the earlier South looks better than its successor, or at least that part of it located in John March's Suez, the later South of greed, exploitation, and desire for the Yankee dollar. If Robert Lewis Dabney had believed in novels, he would have found in *John March* an indictment of New South materialism as powerful as his own.

John March, Southerner was first serialized, then published in book form in February, 1895, ten years to the month after the publication of the essay, "The Freedman's Case in Equity," that had first brought down upon Cable the full wrath of his fellow Southerners. This time there was little reaction at all. Artistically the book was at best a qualified success; for all the ways in which Cable's work anticipated Faulkner's, in *John March* he more closely resembled Faulkner's less talented contemporary, T. S. Stribling, who also wrote of Southern hill people, corruption, and violence. Those reviewers were indeed correct who said that Cable was artistically more successful when he treated a South removed in time, as in *The Grandissimes*, than when he treated the South of his own time.

But *John March* was a novel Cable had to write, and March was a character he had to create. If his protagonist was in part representative Southerner—he was John March, "Southerner," and he lived in "the State of Dixie"—he was also a projection of the author himself, coming of age in a South different from Cable's own but possessed finally of the same sense of mission and uplift that motivated his creator. In his own town of Suez, John tells a Northern friend, "truth and justice are lying wounded and half-dead, and the public conscience is being drugged! We Southerners . . . don't believe one man's as good as another. . . . My place is here!" (p. 483). When he wrote these words Cable had been in New England a decade, but those ten years, if anything, had made him more self-consciously Southern than ever and had also given him a greater freedom to explain the South. He still could not tell the whole truth because Gilder, the genteel Northerner, had demanded that he cut much of the critical commentary from the first draft of *John March*. But Cable no longer restricted and censored *himself* as he once had—unless his disinclination to place in New Orleans his harsh portrait of contemporary Southern life was itself a form of censorship or restraint. Granted, north Georgia was more "representative," but it was also at a safe distance, geographically and emotionally, from the Louisiana of which he had been a part. In any case, in *John March, Southerner* he had said most of what he had to say for the moment about the South.

Perhaps that is why he returned to writing romances after 1895. More likely, he simply recognized that his realistic fiction pleased neither reviewers nor reading public, and further, that his concern for the Negro, manifest in his essays if not so much in *John March*, was not shared by the rest of America. In any case, after the mid-nineties Cable retreated both from social commentary in essays and speeches and from critical realism in fiction. In fact, he wrote little fiction at all in the late nineties. He served as lecturer and editor, founded Home Culture Clubs to improve the lives of shopgirls and factory workers, and developed a serious interest in gardening; but he stayed away from Southern affairs. And when, at the turn of the century, he did return to the South in fiction it was not to write of problems but of romance and glory—in *The Cavalier* (1901), *Kincaid's Battery* (1908), *Gideon's Band* (1914), the stories in *The Flower of the Chapdelaines* (1918), and *Lovers of Louisiana* (1918). He also wrote a psychological novel, *Bylow Hill* (1902), set outside the South. The first two novels were particularly innocuous, although *The Cavalier*, a romance drawing on Cable's own experience in the Civil War, sold better than any previous Cable book. *Kincaid's Battery* followed the same formula for Civil War romance. Not only had Cable joined the ranks of the Southern romancers, but he also turned to praise their leader. In a 1909 sketch, "Thomas Nelson Page: A Study in Reminiscence and Appreciation," he spoke kindly of the man whose mission it was to defend the very Southern system Cable had attacked and to hold in subjugation the Negro Cable had crusaded to liberate.[42] In praising his traditional adversary, Cable had not changed so much as he had simply tired of battle. His tribute to the South's great defender showed the extent to which the once outspoken Southerner had retreated in the year 1909—the same year crazed old Hinton Helper, half-a-century forgotten, committed suicide in a Washington rooming house.

Cable's final Southern novels did return in some measure to social commentary. *Gideon's Band*, although an antebellum romance of the Mississippi, dealt with Southern race relations in the story of a near-white woman who was classified as a Negro. The stories in *The Flower of the Chapdelaines*, also set in the antebellum South, included discussions of slavery as well. But it was Cable's final novel, *Lovers of Louisiana*, which most nearly returned to the old spirit of social criticism. Here Cable did what he had declined to do in *John March*: he wrote a novel of contemporary Southern life *and* set it in New Orleans, although his portrait was not nearly so harsh as that in *John March*.

His protagonist in *Lovers of Louisiana*, Philip Castleton, the well-to-do son of a New Orleans family and a reformer cast in the mold of the young Cable, falls in love with a woman whose proud Creole father objects to Castleton because of Philip's liberal politics—and also because the father himself had been rejected as an acceptable suitor for Philip's mother twenty-eight years before. Much of the story deals with Philip's efforts to initiate social reform in New Orleans, efforts which closely resemble Cable's own. Castleton writes "high-minded" essays on what Cable calls "The Southern question," essays well received in the North but criticized in Southern newspapers. In a speech to a Negro audience he says virtually what Cable had said thirty years before: "By use of the splendid rights you now enjoy . . . make yourselves privately so estimable and publicly so valuable that the few rights yet denied you will come by natural gravitation if not to you to your children's children!"[43] Castleton is accused of advocating social equality for Negroes, as Cable had been, and he expresses opinions reminiscent of the younger Cable: he is "tired of the South's isolation" (p. 48); he believes "Southerners ought to welcome outside criticism" (p. 47) and ought "to be glad to be studied" (p. 52); and he

42. Cable, "Thomas Nelson Page," quoted in Turner, *George W. Cable*, 354.
43. George W. Cable, *Lovers of Louisiana* (New York, 1918), 107.

believes "our old Dixie, and our old New Orleans as well, are passing, going, have got to go" (p. 264). A true son of New Orleans, Philip insists, cannot improve matters "by echoing the provincial flatteries of her office-seekers and her press. It can't be done . . . by keeping her the mother city of an antiquated Dixie out of step with the nation and the world" (p. 275). Moreover, Philip's father had also pondered the problem South and had once planned "a small, terse book interesting only to the very earnest" which would have presented "a clear, detailed plan of what the South wants to do, socially, politically, in order to fill her place in the world's and America's progress" (p. 53).

At the end of Cable's final novel Philip Castleton, like John March, vows to remain in the South and reform it from within. Is Cable, more than thirty years after moving north, regretting his move? Hardly— and he should not. For the times were different in 1885 when Cable moved than they were in 1917 when young Philip Castleton remains. The South in the eighties was preparing to enter its darkest age of segregation; in 1917 it had not yet emerged from that darkness but it was beginning to stir. More important, George W. Cable was different from his protagonist: Castleton was not the young Cable so much as what Cable might wish to have been—bold and assertive. In fact, the author of *Lovers of Louisiana* more clearly resembled the elder Castleton—a man of Cable's own generation who had conceived a book of social commentary intended for "the very earnest"—than the younger. The young Cable could not have challenged New Orleans head-on and remained, at least peaceably. Indeed, he became more outspoken as a critic *because* he did not try to remain. For Cable, a reluctant disturber of the peace highly sensitive to local criticism, might himself have become part of the Silent South if he had stayed in New Orleans. Going to New England gave him not only perspective but also the freedom to continue what he had just begun. A less reluctant critic—a Philip Castleton—might have remained and fought, and would have been more effective because he remained; but if Cable had stayed he might not have fought at all, or at least not in the single-minded manner he did from 1884 to 1894. That he remained a committed Southerner we might conclude by the title of his final novel: for Philip Castleton and Rosalie Durel are not only lovers of—that is, from, belonging to— Louisiana; they are lovers *of* Louisiana itself. "I see," Rosalie says to Castleton, "that in all your politics, right or wrong, you are a— a lover—of truth—of justice—and of Louisiana, and for me that's enough" (p. 348). Although Cable wrote these words as a citizen of Massachusetts, and he must have realized just how sentimental they were, for him they were also enough.

In 1889, four years after George W. Cable had moved to New England, a book was published in Richmond under the title *The Prosperity of the South Dependent Upon the Elevation of the Negro*. The author, like Cable, attacked the myths of both Old South and New and urged fair treatment for the Negro—suffrage, equal justice, equal education in integrated schools, "free access to all hotels and other places of public entertainment . . . free admittance to all theatres," churches, and public receptions.[44] "Oligarchy, caste, vassalage, are the regnant spirit in the greater portion of the South," he wrote, "and no country can prosper under their weight" (p. 160). Indeed, if the South should refuse to give the Negro his rights, it would be cut off from the civilized world altogether. *The Prosperity of the South* seems at first a book George W. Cable might have written. It was perhaps even bolder than anything he ever wrote.

The author of the book was Lewis Harvie Blair, a Richmond merchant in his mid-fifties and a man like Cable who had come from a strong Presbyterian background and had served as a private in the Confederate army. Like Cable, as well, he was rather late coming to his calling as social prophet: Blair did not begin to write his iconoclastic articles on the South until the mid-1880s, and he wrote them only until the late 1890s. After that—perhaps because he married a woman of more conventional Southern racial views, perhaps because he saw the direction of Southern racial change and knew the fight was lost—Blair abruptly changed. At his death in 1916 he left a 270-page undated manuscript in which he completely reversed his position of 1889. In it he preached white supremacy, the Negro's "absolute subordination to the whites."[45]

Just why Lewis Blair recanted his earlier views is an intriguing question. Just why he chose to criticize the South in the first place is another. C. Vann Woodward, one of very few scholars who have

44. Lewis H. Blair, *The Prosperity of the South Dependent Upon the Elevation of the Negro*, ed. C. Vann Woodward (1889; rpr. Boston, 1964, as *A Southern Prophecy*), 88.
45. C. Vann Woodward, "Lewis H. Blair: Prophet Without Honor," introduction to *A Southern Prophecy*, xlv.

given much attention to Blair, explores both questions in an excellent introduction to a reprint edition of Blair's *Prosperity* which appeared in 1964.[46] But an even more important question for our purpose—and for the case of George W. Cable—is how Blair was able to attack the South for a decade, a period slightly later and even more racially charged than Cable's decade of harshest criticism, and not incur the wrath of his fellow Southerners as Cable had done. Why was he tolerated when Cable was not, particularly when his attacks on segregation were even bolder than Cable's and his calls for reform more radical? The answer reveals a great deal about the nature of Southern social criticism in the late nineteenth century.

First, despite a superficial resemblance to Cable—an urban Southerner of Presbyterian background, a businessman, and a veteran— Blair was vastly different in ways that would make him more acceptable as a critic of the South. Only part of the difference lies in the fact that he lived and wrote in Richmond rather than New Orleans, and that Virginia historically has been more tolerant of criticism than has Louisiana. In fact, by the 1890s Richmond had retreated into patterns of segregation more rigid than those of New Orleans when Cable lived there. More important, Blair *belonged* to his city in a way Cable did not and could not. Since he came from an established Virginia family—his grandfather had been a prominent Presbyterian minister in Richmond—no charges of outsider could be brought against him. The product of a family which included statesmen, generals, editors, and college presidents, Blair himself was wealthy and influential and lived in a mansion on Richmond's Grace Street. He possessed a sense of security Cable never had. But that was not all: the answer to why Blair was tolerated and Cable was not lies as well in the nature of Blair's critical and reformist writing. Quite simply, he was a better strategist than Cable; he appealed to economics rather than morality. The "prosperity" of the South, as his title read, *depended* on "the elevation of the Negro." As Woodward has shown, Blair possessed an ethical idealism and moral indignation as fierce as Cable's. But he

---

46. *Ibid.*, xi–xlvi. See also, on Blair, Charles E. Wynes (ed.), *Forgotten Voices: Dissenting Southerners in an Age of Conformity* (Baton Rouge, 1967), 3–10, 71–72. Wynes also reprints Blair's 1893 essay, "The Southern Problem and Its Solution" (pp. 73–87), as well as essays by other "forgotten voices" of the period 1885 to 1917. Notable among these are essays by two Episcopal ministers, Thomas Underwood Dudley of Kentucky and Quincy Ewing of Louisiana, whose approach to the Southern race problem was closer to Cable's than to Blair's.

shrewdly realized that these were not qualities appreciated by his Southern readers, and thus he based his argument "on Economic Grounds, not on the Grounds of Justice or Religion" (p. 25). Finally, Blair's *tone* was different from Cable's, above all not so earnest. Blair had a slight reputation for iconoclasm anyway—he rather liked the reputation—and, unlike Cable, he may rather have welcomed any attention, even notoriety within bounds, his work brought him.

Blair, thus, possessed a confidence born of old family, wealth, and position—assets that would be valuable for the native Southern critic in any time and place but especially so in the late nineteenth century. Cable's character Philip Castleton may have possessed such traits, but Cable himself did not. The author of "The Freedman's Case" was too earnest, overly zealous, too much the preacher. He *meant* it all too much, as Lewis Blair in the long run really perhaps did not. And high seriousness—moral rectitude on the subject of Negro rights—the South and the nation in the 1880s were not yet ready to accept.

CHAPTER 2

A Page of Virginia
and a Page from Lubberland

We are not a race to pass and leave no memorial on our time.
We live with more than Grecian energy. We must either leave
our history to be written by those who do not understand it,
or we must write it ourselves.

Thomas Nelson Page,
The Old South, 1892

Our sacred past we felt to be safe in your keeping.

Mrs. Paul Hamilton Hayne to
Thomas Nelson Page, May 10, 1888

The Confederacy,—the horrid tragedy of it and the myths
that were already growing over it, its heroes, its Colonels, its
Daughters.

Walter Hines Page,
"Autobiography," 1906

Robert Lewis Dabney wrote until the final decade of the nineteenth
century, George W. Cable two decades into the twentieth. But they
were hardly the only Confederates to take their stand long after Appomattox. Charles Colcock Jones, Jr., son of a proud Georgia family
and a cavalry officer in the war, president of the Confederate Survivors Association of Augusta from 1880 to 1891, and, like Dabney, a
stern Presbyterian, yielded to no one in his praise of the Old South.
And, in certain of his annual Memorial Day addresses to the Confederate survivors, he surpassed even Dabney in the ferocity of his attacks on the New. Another diehard, H. M. Hamill—"born in and of
the old South," a soldier at fifteen under General Lee who had returned home from war at sixteen to "look upon the ruins of the . . .
South"—published in 1913 *The Old South*, celebrating an antebellum
plantation life "arcadian in its simplicity and well-nigh ideal in its conditions." Like Dabney before him, Hamill eulogized the honor, courage, and religious temper of the earlier South and contrasted it to the
corruption and materialism of the new America. Four years later, on
the eve of America's entry into World War I, still another book appeared arguing the virtue of the Southern cause in the "War of Abolition" half a century earlier. Thomas Manson Norwood, an eighty-

year-old veteran and former U.S. senator from Georgia, wrote *A True Vindication of the South* in order to "establish the justice of the South's action before, during and after the War," and to demonstrate that "in 1865 the Northern and Southern colonies were two distinct peoples, of different origins, although from the same island; that in temperament, education, opinions on government—political and ecclesiastical, habits, training, mental and moral, tastes and conduct, they were antipodal."[1] It was clear, fifty years after Appomattox, that Thomas Norwood had not yet traveled the road to reunion.

The books of Hamill and Norwood were representative of many others protesting Southern defeat and decrying Yankee ways on into the twentieth century; but perhaps the most eloquent of all the late works of apologia by Confederate veterans was a book not bitter or vindictive at all—*The Creed of the Old South* by Basil Gildersleeve, the renowned classicist of Johns Hopkins University. A Charlestonian who had fought and suffered a crippling leg wound in the Valley Campaign, Gildersleeve wrote in the 1890s, and published as a book in 1915, a retrospective appreciation of the grace and manner of the *ancien régime*, a tribute which suggested that the author, while not angry, was certainly proud. "Self-respect is everything," he wrote, "and it is something to have belonged in deed and in truth to an heroic generation, to have shared in a measure its perils and privations."[2] Gildersleeve attempted to make others as well as himself understand "what it was to accept with the whole heart the creed of the Old South" (p. 15). Even long after the war he chose not to question Southern principles: "That the cause we fought for and our brothers died for was the cause of civil liberty, and not the cause of human slavery, is a thesis which we feel ourselves bound to maintain whenever our motives are challenged or misunderstood, if only for our children's sake" (p. 51). *If only for our children's sake*: Gildersleeve, unlike Hamill, Norwood, and many other of the old soldiers, was a man with perspective, one who knew why he must suspend critical judg-

---

1. Charles Colcock Jones, Jr., *Annual Addresses to the Confederate Survivors Association* (Augusta, 1881–1892). Those speeches of 1887 and 1889 were particularly heated attacks on the New South. See also Michael M. Cass, "Charles C. Jones, Jr., and the 'Lost Cause,'" *Georgia Historical Quarterly*, LV (Summer, 1971), 222–33. See also H. M. Hamill, *The Old South* (Nashville, 1913), and Thomas Manson Norwood, *A True Vindication of the South* (Savannah, 1917).

2. Basil Gildersleeve, *The Creed of the Old South, 1865–1915* (Baltimore, 1915), 8. First published in the *Atlantic Monthly*, LXIX (January, 1892), 75–87.

ment. In "The Creed of the Old South" and a second essay, "A Southerner in the Peloponnesian War"—in which he compared the American Civil War to the Peloponnesian War, the North being identified with Athens, the conservative Southern Confederacy with Sparta— he well understood that the American South was not the center of the universe, or even always the focus of his own thought.[3] But to this student of antiquity, looking backward from Baltimore, it seemed to embody a nobility and heroism as pure and as remote as the classical age.

The Southern cause, thus, would not truly be lost until all the old soldiers had died, and as a group they lived long and died hard. But after 1890, no longer were theirs the dominant Southern voices. The new age belonged to a generation of younger Southerners born too late to fight but not too late to witness the war and its aftermath. If the apologists of the war generation had taken as their task the perpetuation of the Southern cause, they had succeeded; and if those few critics and reformers of that same generation had, like Cable, seen as their task keeping alive the Jeffersonian spirit of free inquiry and liberal dissent, they had also, if not so well, done their duty. Now, before the century turned, they gave way to new men. Thomas Nelson Page of Virginia would emerge as principal heir to the tradition of Dabney, Pollard, and Gildersleeve, the leading spokesman of the school of remembrance (though more receptive to the New South creed than were his predecessors); Walter Hines Page of North Carolina as principal spokesman for the Silent South after Cable had grown mute—although speaking chiefly, like Cable, from a position far north of the Potomac.

The two Pages, cousins distant if at all,[4] form another pair of those

3. Basil Gildersleeve, "A Southerner in the Peloponnesian War," in *The Creed of the Old South*. First published in the *Atlantic Monthly*, LXXX (September, 1897), 330–42.

4. Walter Hines Page's first biographer, Burton J. Hendrick, writes that the two Pages in their later years frequently discussed their "possible relationship" and even addressed each other as "cousin," but could find no proof of kinship. See Hendrick, *The Training of an American: The Earlier Life and Letters of Walter H. Page, 1855–1913* (Boston, 1928), 5. In discussing the life of Walter Hines Page I draw on details from Hendrick's book and also from Hendrick, *The Life and Letters of Walter H. Page* (2 vols.; Garden City, N.Y., 1922); Charles Grier Sellers, Jr., "Walter Hines Page and the Spirit of the New South," *North Carolina Historical Review*, XXIX (October, 1952), 481–99; and, particularly, from an excellent recent biography, John Milton Cooper, *Walter Hines Page: The Southerner as American, 1855–1918*, (Chapel Hill, 1977). In discussing the life of Thomas Nelson Page, I rely on two very helpful dissertations—Harriet Holman, "The Literary

curiously linked antagonists not uncommon in Southern history. Born only two years apart—Thomas Nelson Page in 1853, Walter Hines Page in 1855—they died within four years of each other. Both grew up in strongly religious homes, had fathers who were Whigs, and early absorbed large doses of Sir Walter Scott. Both came of age not only at the time of but in the midst of the Civil War: Thomas Nelson Page's Hanover County was the site of McClellan's campaign of 1862 and Grant's of 1864, and young Walter Hines Page's house near Raleigh was actually ransacked and occupied by Union soldiers in the final days of the war. Both Pages were educated at small private colleges in Virginia, both aspired early to be creative writers (the one who did not notably succeed in that area, Walter Hines Page, more seriously than the one who did), they had in common a similar mission—reconciliation between North and South—and a desire to speak for the South to the nation. Each was very conscious that he was a product of the upper South—each betraying an attitude of superiority toward and sometimes disdain for the Deep South, the old Cotton Kingdom, as being too extreme or, in any case, not sufficiently civilized—and each moved north and spent the last half of his life outside his native South. Each in his late forties began to write a work of semi-autobiographical fiction. Walter Hines Page's *Southerner* (1909) was serialized in the *Atlantic Monthly* when he was fifty and published as a book three years later. Thomas Nelson Page's *Gordon Keith*, less directly autobiographical, was also published when its author was fifty. The books stemmed from a common impulse: to instruct the young, to set forth a formula for an exemplary life, to tell not only about the South but about the author as well. Finally, both Pages, having virtually given up the profession of letters, were appointed in 1913 to diplomatic posts by their fellow Southerner Woodrow Wilson—Thomas Nelson Page as ambassador to Italy, Walter Hines Page as ambassador to Great Britain.

Linked, then, the two Pages were in numerous ways, but they were antagonists all the same, albeit friendly ones. Despite the parallels in their lives, they were substantially different as men and as Southerners. Thomas Nelson Page, small and courtly, was the aristocrat, the Episcopalian, the Virginian; Walter Hines Page, large and rawboned,

Career of Thomas Nelson Page, 1884–1910" (Ph.D. dissertation, Duke University, 1947), and King, "Cable and Page"—as well as Theodore Gross, *Thomas Nelson Page* (New York, 1967).

the democrat, the Methodist, the North Carolinian. Although the North Carolina Pages had originated in Virginia, Walter Hines Page's great-grandfather had come to North Carolina in the late eighteenth century, possibly because his Methodism made him suspect to his Anglican relatives, more likely because opportunity lay in that region south of the border William Byrd had called Lubberland. One should not exaggerate Walter Hines Page's plebeian origins, as Edd Winfield Parks did when he wrote that Page's family was "beyond even [the] outermost circle" of Southern tradition.[5] In fact Page's grandfather owned a plantation of a thousand acres near Raleigh, and both he and Page's father owned slaves. But Page's father, a progressive who in fact disliked slavery and had little affection for the Old South, made his own way as a prosperous lumberman and businessman. If the Pages of Virginia had declined by the time of Thomas Nelson's birth in 1853, and economically they surely had, the Pages of North Carolina were in the ascendancy.

IN DECLINE or not, Thomas Nelson Page hailed from the Old Dominion, descended from the Nelsons as well as the Pages, and, first and foremost, proclaimed himself a gentleman. To be a gentleman: such was Page's creed, as it had been the creed of earlier Virginians. Fitzhugh and Ruffin—and Daniel Hundley, that Virginian in spirit—had declared *themselves*, above all, gentlemen. So had Alfred Taylor Bledsoe, who had written in 1856 that certain Northern writers were "unworthy of notice" because they were not gentlemen, and their writing "no educated gentleman will tolerate." So did the fictional heroes of Page's own stories and novels: "Gordon Keith was the son of a gentleman," Page began his most nearly autobiographical novel. "And this fact . . . was his only patrimony." The word *gentleman* carried with it a sort of code in Page's fiction: that was all he need say about a character, and everything else was understood. *Gentleman* came through repetition and association to signify certain qualities—a sense of honor and duty, a certain decorum, a devotion to truth, most of all a chivalrous attitude toward women. Woman-worship—gyneolatry, W. J. Cash later called it—had not been an integral part of the creed of the earlier Southern defenders, Fitzhugh and Ruffin, Pollard and Dab-

5. Edd Winfield Parks, "Walter Hines Page and the South," *Segments of Southern Thought* (Athens, Ga., 1938), 273.

ney; and thus Page, although he did not actually introduce the idealization of woman, certainly placed her on an even higher pedestal than she had occupied before. The Southern gentleman, Page wrote, stood before his wife "in dumb, half-amazed admiration, as he might before the inscrutable vision of a superior being. What she really was, was known only to God."[6] Page so wrote in 1891, not long after his own wife's death at an early age; but in fact he was capable of such sentiments at any time. A certain sweetness and light existed in Thomas Nelson Page, a softness not seen in the earlier apologists. It is fitting that when he came to write about a Civil War general he chose not Stonewall Jackson, the stern Calvinist to whom Dabney was drawn, but rather Robert E. Lee—the gentleman.

His insistence on being a gentleman explains much about Page, including the manner in which he went about his defense of the South. He was calm and deliberate, not shrill and angry as Ruffin and Dabney often were. He considered himself first of all a moderate, tolerant man who had "never wittingly written a line," he said in 1906, which he "did not hope might tend to bring about a better understanding between the North and the South, and finally lead to a more perfect Union."[7] If Page wanted a "more perfect Union" only on his own terms—a measure of national respect for the South and, especially, white supremacy—those terms in large measure were granted him. For by 1906 the South's cause, white supremacy, that "lost cause regained" of which Edward Pollard had written, had also become the nation's. The Old South of which Page wrote—a society simple, stable, and endowed with grace and charm—had become a romantic neverland for Americans North as well as South. It was no accident that in the year 1898 Page's novel *Red Rock* sold over 100,000 copies, and that Page in 1900 was one of the most popular American novelists. He was devoted to the South in his fiction, but as his biographer Harriet Holman has observed, the heroes of his novels had objected to secession, the Union officers were often kind gentlemen, and love stories uniting Northerner and Southerner were not uncommon.

Thomas Nelson Page was not the uncritical admirer of the Old South he is sometimes depicted as having been. Nor was he, as Dab-

6. Bledsoe, *An Essay on Liberty and Slavery*, 6; Thomas Nelson Page, *Gordon Keith* (New York, 1903), 3; T. N. Page, "Social Life in Old Virginia Before the War," *The Old South: Essays Social and Political* (1892; rpr. New York, 1968), 155.
7. T. N. Page, introduction [1906] to *In Ole Virginia* (Rev. ed.; New York, 1912), xi.

ney and Charles Colcock Jones and most of the other immediate post-bellum apologists had been, a harsh critic of the New. It is certainly misleading to contend, as Theodore Gross does, that Page "offered a complete defense of Southern life before the war." In his book *The Old South*, as we shall see, Page was a very severe critic of some things Southern, antebellum intellectual life and literature in particular, and he questioned the wisdom of slavery itself. And although Page certainly belongs to the romantic school of plantation fiction—and as such was influenced by his reading of Sir Walter Scott—he was critical of the earlier Virginia novelist John Esten Cooke for seeing "the life of the South as reflected through the lenses of Scott, and his imitators."[8] But Thomas Nelson Page criticizing an earlier Virginia was like Nathaniel Hawthorne criticizing Puritan New England: it was in-family criticism. Page had license to find fault because he was of Virginia.

And the criticism was always in the service of a larger affection and devotion. It was precisely Page's close, almost proprietary relationship to the South that convinced him that he was called to be its defender. Whatever his devotion to the Union—and it was genuine as long as the Union acknowledged his terms—he felt that Northern writers in the quarter-century after Appomattox had distorted Southern life, and their distortions he felt obliged to correct. As Holman writes, he "was under a semi-messianic compulsion to justify the South to the nation." Because the South in the late nineteenth century was unjustly accused, Page, the attorney by profession, would become its advocate. But his task was different from that of its earlier advocates: Page and his generation of apologists were defending a civilization they had not truly known, as Dabney and Jones and Gildersleeve had, and they were describing a war in which—no matter how real to them—they had not actually fought. To them, the Old South had already assumed a romantic and sentimental, almost legendary quality it rarely assumed even in the work of those most committed Confederates Dabney and Jones. It was, Page insisted, a civilization "more unique than any other since the dawn of history."[9] He could describe it thus, in part, because he had barely seen it; but such

8. Gross, *Thomas Nelson Page*, 151; T. N. Page, "A Virginia Realist," preface to *The Old Virginia Gentleman*, by George W. Bagby (New York, 1910), quoted in Holman, "The Literary Career," 187.

9. Holman, "The Literary Career," 56; T. N. Page, "The Want of a History," *The Old South*, 257.

idealization won him praise from a generation of Southerners, particularly Southern women who came to revere Page almost as they loved and revered Lee. Mrs. Paul Hamilton Hayne, wife of the unreconstructed South Carolina poet, saw Page as the keeper of the Southern past, and Mrs. T. P. O'Connor, an equally loyal Southerner, dedicated her book, *My Beloved South* (1913), to him. If Page worshipped woman, woman reciprocated.

To appreciate just how completely Thomas Nelson Page belonged to Virginia and the South, one must first consider his progenitors. The first Page in America had built Rosewell, for a time the largest mansion in Virginia; two great-grandfathers had been governors of Virginia and numerous other Nelsons and Pages had been prominent men in the colony and the state; and Page's own father had served on General Lee's staff in the Civil War. But Rosewell had been sold in 1808, and by the mid-nineteenth century Thomas Nelson Page's branch of the family, while owning a plantation and fifty slaves, was no longer truly wealthy. Page himself was eight when the war came, and "the recollection of the great Civil War," he later wrote, "was the most vital thing" within his knowledge. He grew up reading the classics and eighteenth-century English writers, glorifying the Old South, and, as Kimball King shows, absorbing the Episcopalian ideas of paternalism, hierarchy, and the great chain of being.[10]

At age sixteen Page entered Washington College, of which Robert E. Lee was president; in his early twenties he studied law at the University of Virginia and at twenty-three moved to Richmond, where he began to practice law. In Richmond he also began to write, first dialect poetry, then short stories. "Marse Chan," his first published story, he wrote after being shown a love letter taken from the body of a Georgia private killed in action near Richmond. In the letter the soldier's sweetheart had said she wanted him to come back to marry her, but not without a furlough: "If you don't come honorable, I won't marry you."[11] Moved by the letter, Page went to his office one morning and began to write; he finished the story in a week. It was published in the *Century* in 1884 and was included with five later stories in *In Ole Virginia* in 1887.

10. T. N. Page, introduction to *In Ole Virginia*, viii–ix. For intellectual influences on Page, see King, "Cable and Page," especially 186–92.
11. T. N. Page, introduction to *In Ole Virginia*, ix.

In "Marse Chan," Edmund Wilson writes, Page did for the editors of the *Century* what the editors at Scribner's had urged George W. Cable to do: depict the Old South romantically. Wilson is correct, but only to a point. Most of Page's early stories were indeed placed in antebellum days, and as a freedman, looking backward, says in "Marse Chan," "Dem wuz good ole times, marster—de bes' Sam ever see!" Page recalled, often through his Negro characters, a land of bounty and charm, a people of grace and virtue. But, like Cable, he also had a political intent. His heroes in "Marse Chan" and "Unc' Edinburg's Drowndin'" are Whigs, and his villains are often Democrats. Despite his devotion to the Old South, Page was from the first a writer committed to national harmony and reunion, and "Meh Lady," in which the pure Southern girl marries the Yankee officer, is a story of reconciliation. And Page was already, in ways not so obvious, a critic of the Old South. In "No Haid Pawn," as Louis Rubin has observed, he shows us a brutal, frightening side of slavery in antebellum Virginia.[12] In this story the gracious Southern society is vulnerable: Page speaks in particular of the agitation occasioned "by the discovery of the mere presence of such characters as Abolitionists. It was as if the foundations of the whole social fabric were undermined. It was the sudden darkening of a shadow that always hung in the horizon. The slaves were in a large majority, and had they risen, though the final issue could not be doubted, the lives of every white on the plantation must have paid the forfeit" (pp. 173–74).

For all its charm, a certain sadness characterizes *In Ole Virginia*, a sadness resulting both from the tone of the author writing long after the fall of the old order and from the realization that the old order was flawed in any case. The same mixture of romance and melancholy, and the recognition of underlying tensions, is found in Page's first novel, *On Newfound River* (1891)—a story in which the author first describes the time before the war when "peace and plenty" characterized that part of eastern Virginia through which the Newfound River flowed, then proceeds to tell a story of rivalry and love. Bruce Landon, the impulsive son of a proud and wealthy planter, falls in love with Margaret Reid, the granddaughter of an old navy surgeon who now owns the Landons' ancestral estate. Major Landon hates the sur-

---

12. Wilson, *Patriotic Gore*, 604–616; T. N. Page, "Marse Chan," *In Ole Virginia*, 10; Louis D. Rubin, Jr., "The Other Side of Slavery: Thomas Nelson Page's 'No Haid Pawn,'" *Studies in the Literary Imagination*, VII (Spring, 1974), 95–99.

geon, Browne, and disapproves of his son's courtship. But, as in most Page stories, there is reconciliation. Browne reveals that he is Major Landon's long-lost brother, Bruce proposes marriage and Margaret accepts. All ends happily—but only if one ignores the social and political tensions which lie beneath the apparent harmony. Landon, an aristocratic Whig, strongly disapproves of his son's Democratic allegiance. Further, a strong sense of community—a positive quality in much Southern fiction—operates here to isolate Browne, the outsider who does not share fully the values of the community. Finally, social distinction is divisive: whatever the merits of social rank as Page saw it, here it becomes an abstraction violating the integrity of individual experience. The major condemns Browne and his granddaughter, and forbids Bruce to associate with them because "they are low, and worthless, and unfit associates for a gentleman."[13] The code of the gentleman here becomes the worst kind of intolerance: the major consents to his son's marriage to Margaret only after he discovers she is a lady—Bruce's first cousin, too close for marriage in later Virginia, but nonetheless a lady.

Page may not have fully comprehended, or wanted to comprehend, all the tensions operating within *On Newfound River*—the cost of being a gentleman, in particular—but that he understood to some extent is seen in the collection of essays he published the following year, *The Old South* (1892). In this volume he emerged as the most eloquent champion of the antebellum South—and one of its most perceptive critics. Primarily, he cast himself in the role of defender, and in bringing together several speeches and essays in what was perhaps his most important book, he entered the Southern debate and responded to various Southern progressives from Henry Grady to George W. Cable. In particular his title essay, "The Old South," first given as a commencement address at Washington and Lee in 1887, was a response to Grady's "New South" address to the New England Club of New York in December, 1886.

The New South advocate, Grady, and the Old South's champion, Page, although historically placed in opposing camps, were in fact not so far apart as is often presumed. Both revered the traditional South, and Page did not strenuously object to the New—although he insisted in the early 1890s that "it is to the Old South that the New

13. T. N. Page, *On Newfound River* (New York, 1891), 50. *On Newfound River* was expanded for the Plantation Edition (1912).

South owes all that is best and noblest in its being."[14] The difference in the two men was in large part merely a difference of emphasis: Grady, who valued the Old South, preferred to dwell on the New; and Page, who in many ways admired the New, accentuated the Old. Page was not nearly so opposed to Southern industrialization as were most other Southern traditionalists—in fact, he later came to embrace industry and business as good for the South—and both he and Grady were conservatives on matters racial and religious. Page himself could hardly have issued a more fervent plea for white supremacy and "Anglo-Saxon" blood than Grady's speech, "The South and Her Problems," delivered in Dallas in October, 1887; he could not have made a better case for Negro disfranchisement than the case Grady made before the Boston Merchants Association in December, 1889; and he would not have disapproved substantially of Grady's famous speech a few days later which described a Southern funeral in which the tombstone, pine coffin, shovel to dig the grave, nails in the coffin—all but the corpse himself and the hole in the ground—were imported from the North.[15] He must also have been touched by the irony—and all the more since he was a sentimentalist—that the thirty-nine-year-old Grady was himself the recipient of such a funeral less than two weeks after he made his famous speech: the New South's standard-bearer had caught pneumonia on the trip he had taken to New England for the purpose of explaining the South and had died on December 23, 1889, only six days after returning to Atlanta. Henry Grady had said little on that trip with which Page could not have agreed; and Grady himself, in many respects, was closer in spirit to Thomas Nelson Page than to his fellow New South advocate, Walter Hines Page.

Despite agreement in many areas, however, Page and Grady did look in different directions—the one backward, the other forward—and since the mid-1880s had been clearly placed in differing schools of Southern thought. Thus when Grady had given a speech entitled "The New South," though there was little in the speech itself to which Page might object, he felt obliged to respond. "The Old South" was that response, and it was perhaps the most important speech—and one of the most personally revealing—Page ever made. As he revised it slightly for the 1892 volume, the address was even more revealing.

He began by depicting a South crucified then risen:

14. T. N. Page, "The Want of a History," *The Old South*, 268.
15. See these three speeches in *The New South and Other Addresses*.

Two-and-twenty years ago there fell upon the South a blow for which there is no metaphor among the casualties which may befall a man. It was not simply paralysis; it was death. It was destruction under the euphemism of reconstruction. She was crucified; bound hand and foot; wrapped in the cerements of the grave; laid away in the sepulchre of the departed; the mouth of the sepulchre was stopped, was sealed with the seal of government, and a watch was set. The South was dead, and buried, and yet she rose again. The voice of God called her forth; she came clad in her grave-clothes, but living, and with her face uplifted to the heavens from which had sounded the call of her resurrection. (p. 4)

In so writing, Page went to lengths Robert Lewis Dabney had never approached: the South not merely as savior of Christian civilization, but actually as a type of Christ. As Lewis P. Simpson has written, "The image of the redemptive South" becomes for Page an image "primarily derived from Christian eschatology. The South represents a truth of man and society that God will not allow to remain dead but summons back to fulfill its divine mission in history." In his speech at Washington and Lee, Page had used the word *destroyed* rather than *crucified*, and in later editions of *The Old South* he omitted altogether references to a South "crucified" and to "the cerements of the grave," "the sepulchre," and "her resurrection."[16] One wonders why he decided to delete these references to crucifixion and resurrection in later editions—particularly when these were virtually the only changes he made in "The Old South." Perhaps he realized he had carried Southern mythmaking too far. In any case, in 1892 his message was clear: the South was God's Chosen, meant for a special mission.

Page continued in "The Old South" to eulogize an earlier society that "combined elements of the three great civilizations which since the dawn of history had enlightened the world. It partook of the philosophic tone of the Grecian, of the dominant spirit of the Roman, and of the guardfulness of individual rights of the Saxon civilization. And over all brooded a softness and beauty, the joint product of Chivalry and Christianity" (p. 5). The citizens of the Old South had been

16. Simpson, *The Man of Letters in New England and the South*, 224. See, for example, editions of *The Old South* reissued in 1897, 1912 (vol. XII of the Plantation Edition), and 1927, none of which refers to the South's crucifixion and resurrection. Indeed, it is instructive to compare the rough handwritten manuscript of Page's speech at Washington and Lee (located in the manuscript collection of the Alderman Library at the University of Virginia) with later versions of "The Old South." The language was actually somewhat milder in the 1887 speech than in the 1892 version, but more charged than in the versions of "The Old South" printed after 1897.

devoted not to wealth but to principle; in 1775 they had given up "wealth and ease and security" to fight "for the sake of those principles, of those rights and liberties, which they believed were theirs of right" (p. 21). The Old South had been committed to democracy, but its was assuredly a gentleman's democracy, "distinctly and avowedly anti-radical . . . a steadfast bulwark against all novelties and aggressions. . . . No dangerous isms flourished in that placid atmosphere" (p. 43). Above all, Page asserted, the "final defence [of the South] is this: The men were honorable and the women pure" (p. 48).

Page's tone in "The Old South," tolerant and forgiving, was radically different from that of Dabney and Charles Colcock Jones. It was much closer to Basil Gildersleeve's. Ever the reconciler, Page called Grant a "great general" and Lincoln a "still greater President" (p. 42). But he differed most from the other apologists in his severe criticism of certain aspects of the Old South and the peculiar institution on which it had rested. Slavery, he maintained, was the "curse" of the antebellum South, beneficial for the Negro but detrimental for the Southern white. It was the "great barrier which kept out the light" (p. 51), the "spring of woes unnumbered . . . which clogged the wheels of progress and withdrew the South from sympathy with the outer world" (p. 43). "The greatest evil that ever befell this country," slavery "kept the sections divided and finally plunged the nation into a devastating civil war." It made the South a closed society, an intolerant, sometimes petty civilization:

> The world was moving with quicker strides than the Southern planter knew, and slavery was banishing from his land all the elements of that life which was keeping stride with progress without. Thus, before the Southerner knew it, the temper of the time had changed, slavery was become a horror, and he himself was left behind and was in the opposition.
>
> Changes came, but they did not affect the South—it remained as before or changed in less ratio; progress was made; the rest of the world fell into the universal movement; but the South advanced more slowly. It held by its old tenets when they were no longer tenable, by its ancient customs when, perhaps, they were no longer defensible. All interference from the outside was repelled as officious and inimical, and all intervention was instantly met with hostility and indignation. It believed itself the home of liberality when it was, in fact, necessarily intolerant;—of enlightenment, of progress, when it had been so far distanced that it knew not that the world had passed by.
>
> The cause of this was African slavery. (pp. 25–26)

Thus spoke Thomas Nelson Page, the man to whom the United Daughters of the Confederacy entrusted the defense of old order, who was revered in the South as much as any man since Lee—but what he said was as critical of the Old South as anything George W. Cable had written. What he said—that the South had been injured morally, economically, culturally, and intellectually by slavery—was precisely what, thirty years before, the "Hated Helper" had had to flee the South to say. His charges that the South was "intolerant," that "all interference from the outside was repelled as officious and inimical, and all intervention was instantly met with hostility and indignation" anticipated Cash's savage ideal by half a century. And not only slavery did Page find objectionable in the antebellum order but much more. The South had erred in not producing more material wealth. So committed had it been—strange words for Page—to "the reduction of everything to principles" that it dared not "disturb them by experiment": "in this way there was an enormous waste" (p. 49). The South did not produce and value a significant literature: "It was to this that the South owed her final defeat. It was for lack of a literature that she was left behind in the great race for outside support, and that in the supreme moment of her existence she found herself arraigned at the bar of the world without an advocate and without a defence" (p. 50).

Such was Page's indictment of the Old South, but it was an indictment of a very special kind—criticism of the South as a cultural and political unit whose leaders had been *strategically* in error, but not of the Southerners who had lived under such a regime. For in his "Old South" address Page envisioned a heroic race trapped within a faulty system, a noble people captured by their institutions. Antebellum Southerners were no less worthy than Page had maintained all along; they were victims of circumstance, victims more specifically of non-Southerners who had brought slaves to them in the first place: "We have seen how [slavery] was brought upon the South without its fault, and continued to be forced upon her against her protests" (p. 31). The South had been scapegoat, bearing the nation's burden and suffering—had been "crucified," to use Page's metaphor—for the nation's sins. Indeed, Southerners, being just and honorable men, had tried to resolve the problem themselves: "the very men who fought to prevent external interference with [slavery] had spent their lives endeavoring to solve the problem of its proper abolition" (p. 26).

Here, as elsewhere, Page defended a bit too vigorously. In fact, after 1840 nearly all Southerners who protested outside interference did not themselves seek ways to abolish slavery. But the South's advocate was making his best case.

Despite his censure of certain Southern institutions, then, Page was hardly a member of the school of shame and guilt. He felt no contrition toward the Negro. Indeed, as he saw it, only the Negro had benefited from slavery, had been civilized and Christianized. The white Southerner, honorable and sacrificial as always, had only suffered. Such was Page's message in numerous other speeches in the late 1880s and early 1890s, several of which were published in *The Old South*. A "rhetoric . . . insensibly crept into" these speeches, Page explained, but he reprinted them "in the hope that they may serve to help awaken inquiry into the true history of the Southern people and may aid in dispelling the misapprehension under which the Old South has lain so long" (p. vii).

In most of these other essays he was far less critical of the old regime than he had been in "The Old South." "Social Life in Old Virginia Before the War," in particular, was almost pure idyll, the author describing a comfortable but unpretentious Virginia plantation: bountiful nature, happy children and Negroes, "the infectious music of the banjos," and, presiding over all, the mistress of the house whose "life was one long act of devotion—devotion to God, devotion to her husband, devotion to her children" (p. 155). The master of the house was strong and kind and—Page seemed to believe as fully as Daniel Hundley—possessed a certain physiognomy: "there were nearly always the firm mouth with its strong lines, the calm, placid, direct gaze . . . absolute self-confidence. . . . His opinions were convictions. . . . To be a Virginia gentleman was the first duty" (pp. 157–58). The master's daughter Page romanticized most: "born a lady" with "perfect manners" and "indefinable charm," she was delicate, dainty, pure, and brave. "To appreciate her one must have seen her, have known her, have adored her" (p. 165). The servants were faithful, the mammy warm and tender. "Truly it was a charming life," Page continued. "There was not wealth in the base sense in which we know it and strive for it and trample down others for it now" (pp. 183–84). But there was plenty and abundance. "That the social life of the Old South had its faults," Page concluded, "I am far from denying. What civilization has not? But its virtues far outweighed them; its graces were never equalled. For all its faults, it was, I believe, the purest, sweetest life ever lived. . . . It made men noble, gentle, and brave, and women tender and pure and true" (pp. 184–85).

This is the Thomas Nelson Page of popular reputation, not the social critic of "The Old South." Despite his hints at "faults," hardly a note of disharmony crept into the entire sketch—no malaria and diphtheria, no slave-beating and fear of abolitionists, no Nat Turners scheming in the quarters. This was Page's purest tribute to the antebellum South, written partly, he explained, to "correct [the] erroneous idea of the Old South" given in *Uncle Tom's Cabin* and other abolitionist works, but "mainly [written] from sheer affection."[17] It was a tribute to the moderately well-off planter, not the extremely wealthy one—to the boyhood Thomas Nelson Page himself had known, not the splendid world of his fathers. It was left for another essay, "Two Colonial Places: Old Yorktown and Old Rosewell," to depict this earlier world of the eighteenth-century Nelsons and Pages, and despite Page's depreciation of wealth in much of his writing—his preference for simplicity and comfort—he did not hesitate here to announce that Thomas Nelson, who founded Yorktown, had been "one of the wealthiest men in the colony" (p. 192); that the Nelsons of Yorktown had entertained Lees and Carters, Randolphs and Byrds—and Pages; that Washington and Jefferson and Lafayette had slept there; that General Thomas Nelson, "signer of the Declaration of Independence," had been governor of Virginia and "one of the most brilliant of that body of great men who stand, a splendid galaxy, in the firmament of our nation's history" (p. 195); and that the tombstone in Yorktown of an earlier Thomas Nelson—"Scotch Tom"—bore an inscription and heraldic insignia declaring he had been "a gentleman." The Pages were no less notable. Rosewell, their ancestral home built on the land on which Powhatan lived and Pocahontas saved Captain John Smith, was "the largest mansion in Virginia" when constructed in the early eighteenth century "and continued" to be so "for many years" (p. 215). The first of the family in Virginia, John Page, had been a "literary man" (p. 217); a later John Page, friend of Thomas Jefferson, had been governor of Virginia.

There was nothing of Quentin Compson in this son of aristocracy,

17. T. N. Page, preface to *Social Life in Old Virginia Before the War* (New York, 1897), 5. This essay by Page, which was one of the longer essays in *The Old South*, was issued as a separate book in 1897 with a new preface by the author.

no shame tainting his pride in family, no burden of Southern history. At least there was not in "Two Colonial Places." But in still another *Old South* essay, "Authorship in the South Before the War," Page returned to a theme previously explored in "The Old South"—the want of a distinguished Southern literature and the lack of appreciation of ideas in the antebellum South. And the final two essays in the volume, "The Want of a History" and "The Negro Question," were neither critical nor nostalgic, but rather addressed what Page saw as problems for the contemporary South. In the early essays of *The Old South* Page was the gentle author with a kind, reflective voice; in these last essays, particularly "The Want of a History," his tone became fervent, even hortatory. In a speech delivered earlier in 1892 to the Confederate veterans of Virginia—an address very similar to the speeches Charles Colcock Jones had delivered to Georgia veterans each Memorial Day during the previous decade—Page had complained that Southerners, though they had made history, had failed to write it, thus had not captured life in the Old South as it had been—"the sweetest and purest life which has been lived since the beginning of history."[18] Now in *The Old South* he expounded on the same theme: "By the world at large we are held to have been an ignorant, illiterate, cruel, semi-barbarous section of the American people, sunk in brutality and vice, who have contributed nothing to the advancement of mankind: a race of slave-drivers, who, to perpetuate human slavery, conspired to destroy the Union, and plunged the country into war" (p. 254). Southern history had been written by Northerners, and "it rests with the South whether she shall go down to posterity as they have pictured her—the breeder of tyrants, the defender of slavery, the fomenter of treason" (p. 268). The South needed a prophet and a spokesman, Page concluded: "He must know and tell the truth, the whole truth, and nothing but the truth, so help him, God!" (p. 273).

But truth was perhaps less important to Page than commitment, and he certainly recognized by 1892 that he himself was the Southern champion for whom he called. The Southern writer—belletrist, polemicist, historian—had failed the South before the war, and now if ever he must succeed in stating the Southern case. Thus Southern writers, as Lewis Simpson has written, became in Page's view the priests of a Southern resurrection and Page set up "an image

18. T. N. Page, *Necessity for a History of the South* [Roanoke, 1892], 17.

of the South as a redemptive nation."[19] Nowhere in *The Old South* was the idea of the South as nation's salvation more pronounced than in the final essay, "The Negro Question," for in this essay Page saw the future of the nation, indeed Western civilization, dependent upon the white South's resolution of its racial problem. He professed, as Fitzhugh and Dabney had before him, that the South was the guardian of Anglo-Saxon civilization, and thus of the well-being and survival of the nation. If the Negro won equality and enfranchisement in the South, he would win in the North as well, and Anglo-Saxon civilization would be doomed. Such was the thesis of "The Negro Question." It was his "sense of duty," Page insisted, that drove him to write, and he spoke "with the hope and in the belief" that his essay might "serve to call attention to the real facts in the case" (p. 324). To that end he demonstrated the ways Negroes and whites differed "scientifically," insisted that the Negro had "improved" very little since emancipation, and then turned to censure another Southerner whom he refused to recognize as fully Southern—George W. Cable. "Perhaps no clearer or more authoritative exposition of the views held by the North on this question can be found than that set forth by Mr. G. W. Cable delivered before the Massachusetts Club of Boston on the 22nd of February, 1890" (pp. 286–87). "Now what is the question?" Page asked. "Is it merely the question, as stated by Mr. Cable, 'whether the Negro shall not have the right to choose his own rulers'; or is it a great race issue between the negro and the white?" (p. 306). The latter, Page maintained, and it is obvious that the fear of Negro domination principally motivated him: "We are ready to continue our aid [to the Negro]; but we will not be dominated by him. When we shall be, it is our settled conviction that we shall deserve the degradation into which we shall have sunk" (p. 344).

What Page was saying was nothing more or less than what most other prominent Southerners were saying in the year 1892—his fellow Richmond aristocrat Lewis Blair excepted—but he later realized that his heated words broke with the calm, retrospective spirit of *The Old South*. "The Negro Question" was the only essay he chose to omit when he reissued the book in 1912. He substituted for it another essay, "The Old-Time Negro." It was a subject with which Page was more comfortable.

But he had emerged in *The Old South* as the leading spokesman for

19. Simpson, *The Man of Letters in New England and the South*, 225.

traditional Southern values. He had stated clearly and forcefully, and in his own voice, views only suggested in his fiction. The year after the book appeared he gave up his law practice, remarried, and moved to Washington. He would never return to Virginia to live. But Virginia and the South continued to occupy his imagination. In 1894 he wrote "The Burial of the Guns" and "Little Darby," stories treating the Civil War and its aftermath, as well as one of his most popular tales, "The Old Gentleman of the Black Stock," set in the postbellum South. He also brought together in 1894 a number of light sketches and tales into a volume, *Pastime Stories*, and he republished "The Gray Jacket of 'No. 4'" (first published in the *Century* in 1892), a sentimental story of loyalty to the old Confederacy. The same year, his first full year in Washington, he also began work in earnest on revising *Red Rock*, the ambitious novel of Reconstruction he had begun much earlier.[20]

In *Red Rock* Page presumed to strive for objectivity and historical accuracy, but it was obvious when the book appeared in 1898 that he had missed his mark. If it was truth he sought, it was the kind of truth he had recommended in "The Want of a History"—truth from the Southern point of view. *Red Rock* was not set in Virginia as Page's earlier fiction had been, but rather, Page wrote in his preface, somewhere else "in the South, somewhere in that vague region partly in one of the old Southern States and partly in the yet vaguer land of Memory" (p. vii). Why was it not set in Virginia? Partly, one suspects, because Page, like many Virginians who owed their loyalty principally to the Old Dominion when they considered antebellum times, felt an allegiance to a larger South after Appomattox: Reconstruction had united the Southern states as the war itself had not. Further, Virginia would have been an unlikely setting for a novel in which Page wanted to describe the horrors of Reconstruction, simply because the worst abuses had not taken place there. In Virginia, not scalawags alone—as in *Red Rock*—but old George Fitzhugh worked for the Freedman's Bureau. White Southerners had fared much worse in Louisiana and South Carolina, and when Page undertook research for *Red Rock* the two books on which he relied dealt with Reconstruction in South Carolina.[21]

20. T. N. Page, *Red Rock* (New York, 1898). Holman shows that *Red Rock* had been written and revised at least once before 1885.

21. Gross, *Thomas Nelson Page*, 88. See John A. Leland, *A Voice From South Carolina* (Charleston, 1879), and James S. Pike, *The Prostrate South: South Carolina Under Negro Government* (1874; rpr. New York, 1968).

Despite his initial intention to be objective, Page realized his partisanship in *Red Rock*, his departure from the moderation of his earlier fiction. As he wrote Arthur Hobson Quinn:

> It may interest you to know that when I first undertook to write "Red Rock," after having written a third or more of the novel I discovered that I had drifted into the production of a political tract. I bodily discarded what I had written, and going back beyond the War, in order to secure a background and a point of departure which would enable me to take a more serene path, I rewrote it entirely. I had discovered that the real facts in the Reconstruction period were so terrible that I was unable to describe them fully, without subjecting myself to the charge of gross exaggeration.[22]

But even after his rewriting, Page did not achieve the "more serene path" he professed to follow. Although he did begin with his customary picture of a "goodly land," a nearly idyllic South before the war, he soon turned to the political tensions of the 1850s. The war itself Page virtually ignored—the war he would have had to make heroic and glorious for *both* sides, and that, in 1898, he did not care to do— but rather he proceeded to the ugly aftermath of war. At that point his story became flat, became nearly the tract Page said he was trying to avoid. In Reconstruction, Southerners had been "subjected to the greatest humiliation of modern times," Page wrote in his preface. "Their slaves were put over them—they reconquered their section and preserved the civilization of the Anglo-Saxon" (p. viii). Such was precisely the story Page told. He presented unredeemed villains—the carpetbagger Jonadab Leech, the scalawag Hiram Still—and corrupt freedmen, and he countered them with faithful former slaves and pure Southern ladies. Most of all, he created gentlemen.

To be a gentleman: such was the sine qua non in *Red Rock*. And there could be Northern gentlemen—although, as we shall see, of a special variety—as well as Southern ones. The dispute in *Red Rock*, indeed, is not so much between North and South as it is between gentlemen and scoundrels. As one of Page's Southern gentlemen says of the transplanted Northerner Major Welch, he is a "gentleman" and "gentlemen are the same the world over in matters of honor" (p. 421). But the great majority of Page's gentlemen are Southern—Dr. Cary, Mr. Gray, and those apprentice gentlemen, Steve Allen and the younger Jacquelin Gray. Their certainty of their rank, and of their ulti-

---

22. T. N. Page to Arthur Hobson Quinn, [n.d.], quoted in Quinn, *American Fiction* (New York, 1936), 360.

mate triumph, sustains these men no matter how harsh their immediate circumstances. Such confidence ensures their superiority to those who might be materially above them. Dr. Cary, a Whig, a Unionist, and the epitome of a gentleman, serves as a spokesman for the author. When secession comes, he protests, "We are at war now—with the greatest power on earth: the power of universal progress. It is not the North that we shall have to fight, but the world. Go home and make ready. If we have talked like fools, we shall at least fight like men" (p. 41). Cary similarly expresses Page's view of Reconstruction: "It is the greatest Revolution since the time of Poland. . . . They have thrown down the men of intelligence, character, and property, and have set up the slave and the miscreant" (p. 200).

But even in this most partisan of Page's novels, a work in which he is as militantly Southern as he was ever to be, he did not paint an altogether flattering picture of the South. Certain qualities of the Southerner which Page views favorably do not strike the modern reader as praiseworthy at all. If there is nobility in Page's gentlemen, there is also a serious blindness: Dr. Cary at first is deceived by Hiram Still, whom he takes to be a "kind-hearted man" (p. 197). The Southerner's apparent generosity toward Northerners of good breeding may also be deceptive: those Yankees such as Welch whom the Grays and Carys accept are Northerners who embrace Southern values. Even Steve Allen, the hero of the book, has many of the worst traits of the Southern aristocrat—in particular, an exaggerated insistence on honor and pride. After the war he is too proud to hoe, and too proud not to ride with the Klan. His shortcomings may seem relatively harmless—as harmless as the insistence of Mr. Langstaff, the rector, that the Garden of Eden was located near Red Rock plantation—but they betray a provincialism and insularity all too common in Page's gentlemen. Even more serious is the class snobbery of the Carys and the Grays toward commoners such as Hiram Still. Still's rage against the planters, his desire to acquire their plantations, is partly justified; it is at least understandable at that point in the story when Dr. Cary deems Still's son, who has become a physician, an unworthy candidate for the hand of his daughter. Still's son is rejected in part because his father is a scalawag. But it is more basic than that: he is not a gentleman.

The year of *Red Rock*'s publication, 1898, was a time of great racial unrest and upheaval in the South, a moment so tense that Page's mother felt God had ordained the time the book should appear. Although Northern reviewers believed, this time, Page had overstated the Southern case, and produced a melodramatic, artistically flawed work, Southerners praised the novel. "I honestly believe you have done more to set the South right in the eyes of the world and to correct the misrepresentation of fanatics, fools & scoundrels," wrote one reader, "than all the other stories put together." [23] Page's more militant approach to Southern problems was also evident in other stories written just after *Red Rock*, particularly "The Spectre in the Cart," a tale of racial violence and brutality. But his primary interest, now that his Reconstruction novel was written and the new century approached, was not so much the Old South, or even Reconstruction, but rather the New South—in particular, the question of how a gentleman, reared in the Old South, applied its values and principles in the New. It was a story he told in different ways in his next two novels, *Gordon Keith* (1903) and *John Marvel, Assistant* (1909). It was, in many ways, his own story.

Gordon Keith, as we have seen, comes nearer to being autobiographical than any other character in Page's fiction. Like Page, he was born on a Virginia plantation in the decade just before the war—born to a Whig and, Page tells us in the first sentence, a "gentleman." [24] After the war, despite poverty and lost opportunity, he was, like his creator, bent on restoring the family name and recovering the old family place. After college, like the young Page, Keith worked to "secure the success with which he would burst forth on an astonished world" (p. 133). Like Page, he taught school for a time, returned for further study, and eventually achieved that success he sought—in Keith's case, as a mining engineer and businessman. He valued the old, rural South but by middle age preferred to live outside it. Just as Page, after 1893, chose to be a Southerner in Washington, Keith preferred for a time to be a Southerner in New York. But, unlike Page, in the end he returns to Virginia, though not to the plantation.

Gordon Keith is a novel in which Page dramatized many of his own early hopes and dreams. But it is a story not so much in the Southern as in the American grain—a retelling of the tale told by writers as

23. Thomas H. Carter to T. N. Page, December 1, 1898, quoted in Holman, "The Literary Career," 78.
24. T. N. Page, *Gordon Keith*, 3. For an excellent discussion of *Gordon Keith*, see Wayne Mixon, *Southern Writers and the New South Movement, 1865–1913* (Chapel Hill, 1980), 37–41.

early as Hawthorne of the innocent and honorable young man from the country coming to the city to make his fortune. Even more basic, it is the story of the pilgrim, the knight of virtue, encountering Vanity Fair and surviving—but only after a struggle. Page's young hero moves from one world to another entirely different. Indeed *Gordon Keith*, although it takes place at roughly the same time as *Red Rock*, seems ages removed from the Old South. "When in after times," Page wrote at the beginning of the novel, "in the swift rush of life in a great city, amid other scenes and new manners, Gordon Keith looked back to the old life on the Keith plantation, it appeared to him as if he had lived then in another world" (p. 4). But it was not a matter of time so much as place. A non-Southerner visiting the plantation, Elphinstone, even before the war "would have departed with a feeling of mystification, as though he had been drifting in a counter-current and had discovered a part of the world shattered and to some extent secluded from the general movement and progress of life" (p. 5). The impression of an earlier time is further enhanced by the mythic tone of the early pages, at times the biblical cadences: "Yet it came to pass that within a few years an invading army marched through the plantation, camped on the lawn, and cut down the trees"; Gordon Keith and his father were "thrown out on the world" (p. 5).

The world before the fall from the Eden that was Elphinstone was a world, most of all, of gentlemen, and if the creed of the gentleman was important in *Red Rock*, it virtually dominates this novel. At the beginning of the book the word is used repeatedly. Gordon Keith "was the son of a gentleman"; his father "was a gentleman of the old kind," whose "one standard was that of a gentleman" (p. 3). If this were Mark Twain, that son of a transplanted Virginian, rather than Thomas Nelson Page, one might suspect the author was ridiculing the whole idea of the Southern gentleman. But this was Page and no irony was intended. Indeed, *Gordon Keith* could well have been entitled "The Education of a Gentleman," for in it Page sought to explore as he really had not before the essence and meaning of *gentleman*. What was assumed in *Red Rock* was here examined and defined: "Gordon Keith, when a boy, thought being a gentleman a very easy and commonplace thing. He had known gentlemen all his life—had been bred among them. It was only later on, after he got out into the world, that he saw how fine and noble that old man [his father] was, sitting unmoved amid the wreck not only of his life and fortunes, but of his world" (p. 34). A gentleman was one who scorned wealth for its own sake and preferred unpretentious comfort, who scorned fashion and preferred simplicity, who always viewed the present in light of the past. Gentlemen are noticeably missing in the world Gordon Keith discovers in New York, a world of cultural fragmentation and unhappiness.

If *Gordon Keith* is the story of an old-school Southerner who successfully makes the transition into the larger postbellum world, Page's next novel, *John Marvel, Assistant* (1909), tells the story of another such Southerner, Harvey Glave, who fails to do so. Glave, like Keith, superficially resembles Page himself:

> My family was an old and distinguished one; that is, it could be traced back about two hundred years, and several of my ancestors had accomplished enough to be known in the history of the State. . . . We had formerly been well off; we had, indeed, at one time prior to the Revolutionary War, owned large estates. . . . My childhood was spent on an old plantation, so far removed from anything I have since known that it might almost have been in another planet.[25]

Such was precisely the history of Thomas Nelson Page, and as the story unfolds we see other ways in which Glave resembles the young Page. He is short of funds in college, but he becomes a lawyer, and as a young lawyer, like Page in Richmond, is "taken into the best social set in the city" and finds himself "quite a favorite among them" (p. 45). He writes articles for a "leading monthly magazine" (p. 47) and, like Page, feels a superiority to those who deem themselves "upper class" because they possess wealth: "My soul revolted at the thought of this man standing as the type of our upper class" (p. 207).

Clearly, as in *Gordon Keith*, Page identified with his protagonist. But the situation is not quite the same. Here, as Kimball King points out, Page has a perspective he had lacked before: he depicts, and *intends* to depict, a Southerner of aristocratic heritage in something less than a favorable light.[26] Glave is proud and bigoted and, even more damaging in Page's eyes, indecisive and ineffectual. At college he refuses to room with a Jew, Leo Wolffert, and at first joins his classmates in keeping his distance from Wolffert. As a student—he later acknowledges—he is shallow, snobbish, and affected. Later, after moving to a

25. T. N. Page, *John Marvel, Assistant* (New York, 1909), 1–2.
26. King, "Cable and Page," 336.

Western city—also the residence of Wolffert and John Marvel, a backwoods idealist who had been Glave's good friend in college—Glave acquires what appears to be a social conscience, although it is a small, limited one. He sympathizes with the plight of the workers to whom Marvel and Wolffert are dedicated, but his understanding of their condition is superficial and his commitment to their cause halfhearted. Glave is one old-school Southerner who cannot come to terms with the modern world, cannot apply the gentlemanly code of the Old South in a different time and place. One wonders if he could have even *in* the Old South. In any case, he fails where Gordon Keith had succeeded.

John Marvel, Assistant was Page's one attempt to write a nearly contemporary "problem" novel—as *John March, Southerner* had been Cable's—and Page was even less equipped for his task than was Cable. He had been, even more than Cable, primarily a local colorist, and by 1909 local color had given way to the naturalism of Dreiser, Norris, and Crane. Page had been aware of changing critical tastes long before 1909 and, shortly after the publication of *Red Rock*, had turned to works of social commentary and reminiscence to express his ideas. Between 1904 and 1908 he had published three nonfiction books—*The Negro: The Southerner's Problem* (1904), *The Old Dominion* (1908), and *Robert E. Lee: The Southerner* (1908)—in which he took his case for the South directly to his readers.

The Negro was, in part, a response to Southerners such as Cable and Lewis Blair, and it was Page's most comprehensive discussion of the race question. Conditions had changed since 1892, when he had included "The Negro Question" in *The Old South*: segregation had become firmly entrenched in the South, and even such earlier critics as Cable and Blair had ceased to protest. Page's own position was basically unchanged. He favored segregation and disfranchisement of Negroes, as he had before—except that in 1904 he was even more insistent that white supremacy was "not due to any mere adventitious circumstances, such as superior educational and other advantages during some centuries, but an inherent and essential superiority, based on superior intellect, virtue, and constancy."[27] In *The Negro* Page drew a more severe indictment of the black American than any

27. T. N. Page, *The Negro: The Southerner's Problem* (New York, 1904), 292–93.

he had drawn before: the Negro had become less productive since emancipation, his moral values had declined, and he was responsible for more crimes—including rape, for which lynching, if not exactly justified, Page explained, was at least understandable. Page blamed these changes in the Negro on Northern philanthropists and reformers, and echoed the antebellum apologists in his criticism of abstract theorists who did not really understand the Negro and the South.

This basic argument Page sustained in seven of the eight essays in *The Negro*. But it is the eighth, "The Old-Time Negro," that is most interesting. For here we see what Page truly missed in the new Negro—his faithfulness and his affection. It was not so much that the Negro in 1904, as Page described him, was lazy, immoral, and criminal; it was that he no longer seemed so kind and good-natured as Page remembered him, that he no longer devoted his entire being to the welfare of the planter and his family. Page did not openly make such a diagnosis, but it is evident in various parts of the essay, most noticeably perhaps in his fond recollection of his mammy: "After forty-five years, I recall with mingled affection and awe my mammy's dignity, force, and kindness; her snowy bed, where I was put to sleep in the little up-stairs room" (pp. 177–78). A half-century before, well-bred Southerners, including young Thomas Nelson Page of Oakland, had been loved, protected, pampered, and petted by the black Southerner. In 1900, or so Page believed, the love had disappeared.

The Old Dominion, published four years later, was a less intense book than *The Negro*. In it Page collected nine essays, most of which he had originally given as speeches and many of which were variations on themes in *The Old South*. But absent was the self-criticism that had characterized parts of *The Old South*. Although Page still condemned slavery and the insularity it brought—antebellum Southerners "knew little more of the modern outside foreign world than they knew of Assyria and Babylon"[28]—he did not dwell on the subject. Rather, in sketches on topics from Jamestown to Reconstruction, he stressed the civilized quality of life in Virginia, the extent to which it resembled English country life. The "race" of early Virginians had been heroic, "clearly patterning their lives on Plutarch's characters, with a tempering of Christianity" (p. 339). Even the Negroes of Vir-

---

28. T. N. Page, *The Old Dominion* (New York, 1908), 238.

ginia appeared "to be of a higher grade generally than those of States further South" (p. 324).

With *The Old Dominion* Page had come full circle. When he had begun to write in the 1880s it had been with a deep affection for old Virginia. In the 1890s and through 1904 he turned—in *The Old South, Red Rock,* and *The Negro*—to the larger South, and with a tone often less nostalgic, more urgent. But in 1908 in *The Old Dominion,* and in his biography of Robert E. Lee the same year, he returned to his native state and to his original voice. The Lee biography, in particular, is important as an index to Page's thought. Just as Dabney's *Jackson* had been a tribute to a tradition and a cause as well as a man, so was Page's *Lee*: the subject was the embodiment of the best qualities of the antebellum South, and Page subtitled his book simply *The Southerner.* "It is a law of Nature," he wrote, "that character is a result largely of surrounding conditions, previous or present." [29] Great as Lee was, "I believe that in character, he was but the type of his order, and noble as was his [*sic*], ten thousand gentlemen marched behind him who, in all the elements of private character, were his peers" (p. 289). His subject was not to be described, Page insisted, "in the language of eulogy" (p. ix), but it was a language he himself could hardly avoid, particularly at the end when he described Lee, defeated, in the mountains at Washington College. "History may be searched in vain," he wrote, "to find Lee's superior, and only once or twice in its long course will be found his equal" (p. 285). After the war his character was examined by "hostile prosecutors," and "from this inquisition he came forth as unsoiled as the mystic White Knight of the Round Table" (p. 286). The best response to those who attacked the Old South was that "it produced such a character as Robert E. Lee" (p. 289).

The Lee biography was Thomas Nelson Page's last full-length tribute to the Old South. It was, in many respects, the culmination of his work. [30] After 1909, comfortably situated in Washington, he became less the writer, more the man of affairs. Although the eighteen-

29. T. N. Page, *Robert E. Lee: The Southerner* (New York, 1908), 288. Page's *Lee* was issued first in a smaller edition in 1908, then rewritten in two volumes for the Plantation Edition in 1911 and 1912.

30. *The Red Riders,* left uncompleted at Page's death, was completed by his brother Rosewell and published in 1924. A Reconstruction novel set in South Carolina, it resembles *Red Rock* in many ways, including the celebration of a group similar to the Ku Klux Klan and a marriage of Northerner and Southerner in the end.

volume Plantation Edition of his work appeared between 1910 and 1912, by that time Page's primary interests lay elsewhere: in 1913 he was appointed ambassador to Italy. He lived until 1922, and the year after his death his brother Rosewell said he had led an "ideal" life.[31]

It is a word of which Page himself would have approved, not so much in the sense that his life had been unmarred by hardship—the death of his first wife in 1888 had brought him deep sorrow—but in the manner in which he preferred to view the world. He viewed it in terms of truth and righteousness, of ladies and gentlemen. Indeed Page, perhaps more than anyone else, disproves the assumption that the Southern writer always possesses a fury against abstraction. He created a *world* of abstractions: his fictional characters lived, as he himself lived, by codes and creeds. The rules by which a gentleman conducted himself, distinctions of birth and station, hierarchy and social rank, all rested on abstractions, on rigid formulas for human conduct. All denied or at least greatly modified genuine human interaction—between white and Negro, gentleman and commoner, man and woman—thus all limited and constricted human experience. And it was those grandest of abstractions—honor, courage, purity, patriotism—to which Page was chiefly devoted.

The Old South itself very nearly became an abstraction in his mind. His defense of that South was not the visceral defense of a Ruffin or a Dabney, or (save perhaps after his first wife's death) an antidote to sorrow. It was rather a reasoned response, motivated he believed by a higher instinct and undertaken, except in some few cases, calmly— or, what was more important, with the appearance of calm. Late in his life Page was to be criticized by a new generation of Southerners and parodied by his fellow Richmond aristocrat James Branch Cabell, but in his own time he was acknowledged to be the South's champion even by philosophical opponents such as Cable. Never had there been, nor would there be, such an effective *public* defender of the South. Fitzhugh was too eccentric, Ruffin and Dabney too frantic and self-absorbed, and twentieth-century apologists Donald Davidson and William Alexander Percy would be too narrow in their appeal. But Page rested in that same calm assurance, felt himself motivated by that same sense of responsibility, first to his state, then to his sec-

31. Rosewell Page, *Thomas Nelson Page: A Memoir of a Virginia Gentleman* (New York, 1923), 205.

tion, that had motivated his hero Lee in 1861. Not so much a rage to explain did Page possess—a gentleman did not rage—but rather an obligation, a considered duty.

"IT OCCURS TO me that I am for the first time in my life doing what I have always wished to do," Walter Hines Page at age fifty-seven wrote in his notebook. "I recall that I set out to write: that was what I have always wished to do." The year before, 1911, he had made a similar note, this time stating his intention to write a "Novel of Present So. Life." But not long after these entries, in March, 1913, Walter Hines Page was named ambassador to the Court of St. James's. He never wrote the projected novel. At his death in 1918 he had produced only one work of fiction, the semi-autobiographical novel *The Southerner* (1909). It had been written in 1905 during a rare break in his busy life, when he was in Florida recuperating from a streetcar accident. It was in part a product of enforced idleness, but another factor may have inspired Page. In January, 1905, two months before he began to write, he had met Thomas Nelson Page for the first time. They had discussed, among other matters, Southern history and the Negro.[32]

It is remarkable in itself that the two Pages did not first meet until they were fifty. Both had been prominent in Southern affairs for two decades, and certainly each knew of the other. Walter Hines Page was particularly aware of Thomas Nelson Page, to whom he had long been compared, to his disadvantage. On one occasion in 1902 the *Presbyterian Standard* of North Carolina, one of his early foes, had drawn such a comparison. Thomas Nelson Page had created literature, the *Standard* insisted; Walter Hines Page had created only trouble for the South, and thus was "a page that needs to be turned down." Such was the attitude of many other Southerners of the day. As Edd Winfield Parks later wrote, "At the turn of the century, southern men in abundance called Walter Hines Page traitor and yellow dog." He was "damned as a modern Judas."[33]

In fact, Page was not treated quite so harshly as that. He was never scorned almost universally in the South as was George W. Cable, and

---

32. W. H. Page, notebook entries, 1911 and December, 1912, quoted in Cooper, *Walter Hines Page*, 204 (see also 197–98).

33. *Presbyterian Standard*, quoted in Cooper, *Walter Hines Page*, 198; Parks, *Segments of Southern Thought*, 273.

certainly he was never hated like Hinton Helper. It was not necessarily that Page spoke less boldly than Cable and Helper, it was just that he knew when and where to speak and, later, how to smooth over his words, pacify at least some of his enemies. He was by nature a diplomat, and his bitter criticism of the South surfaced only when he let down his diplomatic guard or, in one notable instance, when he wrote under a pseudonym. He was from 1913 to 1918 United States ambassador to Great Britain, but his entire adult life, as John Milton Cooper has shown in his excellent biography, he was an ambassador from the New South to the nation. He was, however, an ambassador different from those other apostles of the New South, Henry Grady and Richard Edmonds. Like Grady he advocated material progress and envisioned the South in the national picture, but he did not, like Grady, pay homage to the Old South and he was not an uncritical industrial booster. As Paul Gaston has written in *The New South Creed* (p. 51), Page was easily the most gifted and complex of the New South spokesmen, and the most critical as well. What he saw when he looked at Dixie was a problem South, the same South that Howard W. Odum and the social scientists would see and seek to remake thirty or forty years later. Yet his concerns were not precisely those of Odum. Although he did anticipate the Chapel Hill sociologist in his crusade for Southern education and public welfare, he did not focus on race as Odum was to, and as Cable and Blair already had. Rather, he believed, or at least declared, that intellectual poverty and cultural barrenness were responsible for the Southern condition, and those problems, particularly in his early years, were his targets. Further, for one sometimes identified in the twentieth century as the father of modern Southern liberalism, Page was not even much of a liberal: he was antipopulist, antilabor, and rather conservative on race; he supported Theodore Roosevelt and William Howard Taft; and he came to identify himself with the business interests of the East.

Walter Hines Page is a very hard Southerner to classify, much harder than Cable, Odum, and other native Southern critics. If he was by nature a diplomat, he was also—openly in his early years, more guardedly later—an iconoclast; and in fact in his writing of the 1880s, his attacks on the Mummies of North Carolina, "ignorant and provincial men," he anticipated not the somber Southern problem-solvers such as Odum but rather Gerald W. Johnson, W. J. Cash, and the gleeful Southern rebel-journalists of the 1920s and 1930s. In these early writings he was more the reckless critic than the politic man of affairs, less given to the "patient uplift" of which Cooper writes than to venting his personal wrath against the South. But he was that only at first. After 1890 the iconoclast and the diplomat were at war in Page, and the diplomat usually won. His underlying attitude toward the South, as his private letters show, did not change substantially: it remained deeply critical. But the depth of his critical feeling emerged publicly only rarely—in his early years, in the series of letters he wrote to the Raleigh *State Chronicle* in 1885 and 1886; later, in 1906 and 1909, in the two versions of his autobiographical novel, *The Southerner*. The first occasion came just after Page had left the South for good but had not yet become established in New York—and thus was free to speak his mind as he had never been before and would never be again. The second came when he had already achieved success and wealth and had little to fear, and even at that, in *The Southerner*, he wrote under a pseudonym. Many other times he spoke and wrote about the South, and critically enough to be attacked for his views, but rarely did he let his audience know how strongly he objected to the old order and how truly critical he considered the condition of the contemporary South.

He told enough of the truth, however, even after 1890, to come down to Southern traditionalists of the twentieth century as their leading ideological foe. There was no Southerner except perhaps Gerald W. Johnson against whom the Southern Agrarians railed more. To Donald Davidson, Page was a facile thinker, "a journalist and promoter . . . a man of his day" against whom "the greatest charge [that could be brought] . . . is the foolhardiness, amounting at times to a kind of liberal bigotry, with which he used his influence." Page taught that "Southerners must repudiate the quarter-century of history from 1850 to 1875," and in so teaching he "brought the [Southern] tradition into a discredit that it never deserved." Page's case, Davidson charged, was "the tragedy of the progressive who cannot rise above his origins without becoming an exile or a snob." If he had possessed any love for the South, that love "was philanthropic rather than comradely." Davidson's fellow Agrarian, John Donald Wade, agreed. After Page moved north, he wrote, his attitude toward the South was like that toward "a highly esteemed sister . . . to straighten her out by voluminous correspondence." Agrarian Frank Owsley was more blunt:

Page was "the man who was first ashamed that he was a Southerner." [34]

Just what kind of Southerner was Page, this expatriate who, Davidson charged, had rejected that part of Southern history from 1850 to 1875? He identified himself as a man faithful to an earlier Southern tradition than the one Davidson described, the Jeffersonian tradition of democratic liberalism and free inquiry. Indeed, Cooper suggests that Page—with his versatility, optimism, and faith in science and technology—resembles no other American, North or South, so much as he resembles Jefferson. Perhaps; and yet one might see Page as not so much a latter-day Jefferson as a latter-day Southern version of Benjamin Franklin. Practical, energetic, materialistic, opportunistic, embodying the Protestant work ethic and the impulse to do good—even to the point of naming his magazine *World's Work*—Page was as close to the Yankee Franklin as any Southerner could be. Like Franklin, as a child he was destined for the ministry, then rejected a religious vocation and made his name in journalism; like Franklin, he engaged in self-improvement projects, founded clubs, and worked for civic betterment; like Franklin, he made money (even, like Franklin, investing his time and money in a better kind of stove), and, once secure professionally and financially, wrote an autobiography and closed his career as a wartime diplomat across the Atlantic. Those Southern traditionalists who set their sights on George W. Cable as Southern Puritan missed the mark: it was not Cable but Walter Hines Page who was the Southern Puritan, albeit a Puritan like Franklin of the secular, work-ethic variety.

But to suggest that Page resembled the industrious Yankee Franklin, and that he rejected the Southern leisure ethic, is not to say that he was not also Southern. His origins, unlike Cable's, cannot be questioned. Descended from Virginians and Carolinians, he was born near Raleigh in 1855, at age ten saw his house occupied by Union soldiers, and then grew up surrounded by the heroism, military glory, and sentimentality of the Lost Cause. He came from a family of fervent Southern Methodists, attended a military school in which the cadets wore gray uniforms, and loved the novels of Scott and the poetry

---

34. Donald Davidson, "Dilemma of the Southern Liberals," *The Attack on Leviathan: Regionalism and Nationalism in the United States* (Chapel Hill, 1938), 276–78; John Donald Wade, "Old Wine in New Bottles," *Selected Essays and Other Writings of John Donald Wade*, ed. Donald Davidson (Athens, Ga., 1966), 159; Frank L. Owsley, "A Key to Southern Liberalism," *Southern Review*, III (Summer, 1937), 31.

of Timrod—all qualities, H. L. Mencken later said, which ensured Southern orthodoxy. Yet there was a side to Page's background which was not orthodox at all. His father had been an antisecessionist Whig whose political hero was Henry Clay, not Calhoun, and the elder Page had not fought in the Civil War, a fact that embarrassed the young cadet Walter Page in the late 1860s. But Frank Page was more interested in business than the Lost Cause, and the son inherited the father's progressive spirit.

Yet Page did not seriously question his Southern heritage until age twenty-one, when, after receiving his undergraduate education at Methodist colleges in North Carolina and Virginia, he crossed the Potomac going north. He studied Greek for two years under Basil Gildersleeve at Johns Hopkins University, but neither Gildersleeve's love of the classics nor of the Old South exerted much influence on his young student. Page spent the summer of 1877 in Bismarck's Germany, and what he found was vastly different from what Robert Lewis Dabney found on a similar trip at about the same time. In letters sent back to the Raleigh *Observer*—his first published work—he praised German energy and efficiency, and contrasted them with the lethargy and waste he found in North Carolina. In other letters he wrote to the *Observer* upon his return to Johns Hopkins he urged the adoption of German methods.

But that Page in Baltimore was still in many ways the provincial Southerner is suggested by his letters home, in one of which he referred to "the Southern race (I say race intentionally: Yankeedom is the home of another race from us)." [35] After leaving Baltimore without having completed his degree, he taught briefly in North Carolina and Kentucky and in 1880 took a newspaper job in St. Joseph, Missouri, where he again had a chance to ponder the South from afar. In May, 1881, he published in the *Atlantic Monthly* his first major essay, "Study of an Old Southern Borough," [36] an article he had written two or three years before and in which he probably had in mind his hometown of Cary and the neighboring town of Hillsborough. His "Old Southern Borough" was a curious study, on the one hand suggesting an admiration for the sleepy town where the old order still reigned, where women were "purer" and "tenderer" than those elsewhere (p. 658)

35. Hendrick, *The Life and Letters of Walter H. Page*, I, 28.
36. W. H. Page, "Study of an Old Southern Borough," *Atlantic Monthly*, XLVII (May, 1881), 648–58.

and old men remote from the present still read Scott and quoted Virgil; on the other hand depicting a dull, stagnant town resembling nothing so much as the drowsy Mississippi River village described by Mark Twain shortly before in the pages of the *Atlantic*. "There is little animation in man or beast," Page wrote. "The very dogs look lazy. . . . The streets are neglected, and in places almost impassable; the paint is worn from most of the houses; the people are slow in their movements . . . inert and stagnant men" (pp. 652–53). The industry and vigor of Germany and the American North still sharp in his mind, Page undoubtedly considered his own position when he added, "Sometimes a lad from an old borough, in the first dawning of his thought, discovers for himself the mental stagnation of his surroundings, sees the stupid way that is open for him at home, and rebels against it. The only successful rebellion, however, is an immediate departure. For, if he begins to deliberate, he is apt to be caught by the spell of inertness, and live out his life and die before he decides whether to go away or not" (p. 654).

At the time he wrote, Page had not yet made that final decision. He had resolved, however, to work to change the South, particularly its literature. "By heavens! It is a chance!" he wrote a friend the same year his "Old Southern Borough" appeared. "I mean to live and die trying it. There is no second ambition in my soul." In the spring of 1881 he left St. Joseph and traveled across the Deep South for the first time, recording his observations in articles for the New York *World*, the Boston *Post*, and other Northern newspapers. The trip was a valuable stage in the apprenticeship of the young Southerner: he called on tired, old Jefferson Davis in his home on the Mississippi Gulf Coast and found the president of the late Confederacy lying on a lounge, Mrs. Davis fanning him. The energetic New Southerner met the Old and was both shocked and moved. "The dead stillness of everything is almost oppressive," he wrote, "and the countryless gentleman, who must be among the most lonely men of the world, doubtless adds much to the feeling of solitude."[37] He also visited Cable in New Orleans and Joel Chandler Harris in Atlanta and later in 1881, when he returned to Atlanta to cover the International Cotton Exposition, he met Henry Grady, new editor of the Atlanta *Constitution*. Page's travels in the Deep South had confirmed earlier beliefs that

37. W. H. Page to John B. Wardlaw, [1881], quoted in Cooper, *Walter Hines Page*, 60; W. H. Page, quoted in Hendrick, *The Training of an American*, 144.

slavery had had a disastrous effect on the South, that the Far South was inferior to Virginia and Carolina, and that industry, agricultural improvement, and education were the keys to an enlightened region.

Page would have remained in the South in 1881 if Grady had offered him a position on the *Constitution,* but when no offer came he took a job with the New York *World.* All the while he was in New York, however, he thought of returning to North Carolina, and he made his decision to return in 1883 when Joseph Pulitzer bought the *World.* Page, who did not approve of Pulitzer's sensationalist journalism, returned to Raleigh to begin his own newspaper, the *State Chronicle.* He was to remain in Raleigh a little more than a year and in that year, his first biographer Burton J. Hendrick writes, he sought to "revolutionize" North Carolina: the state had never been "so angered, so jarred, so instructed, so entertained."[38] In fact, most of Page's irreverence and most of the angry response of Tar Heels came after he had left the newspaper and had returned to New York, from which he sent back caustic dispatches. While in Raleigh he was a rather courageous but not a particularly iconoclastic editor.

He left North Carolina in February, 1885, partly because the newspaper had not been a financial success but principally because he despaired of ever finding a congenial political and intellectual climate in the South. In 1880 he had written that he would hesitate to live anywhere else, that he felt at home in Dixie "in a sense that I can be at home nowhere else. Anywhere in the South, I should be at home; anywhere out of the South, I shall be a stranger. And I had much rather labour & live among my own people." But in that same letter he had added that he saw little hope of prevailing against the "strong Southern conservatism," and now, five years later, he realized just how right he had been. As he boarded the train north he felt mainly relief,[39] and also the anticipation of reaching an environment receptive to critical thinking. He had found intellectual companionship in Raleigh only among a small group of progressives who called themselves the Watauga Club, which included among its members such unlikely reformers as Charles W. Dabney, the son of Robert Lewis Dabney, and Thomas Dixon, later to become famous as the racist author of *The Clansman.* But except for his Watauga associates Page felt

38. Hendrick, *The Training of an American,* 168.
39. W. H. Page to Edward Everett Hale, January, 1880, quoted in Cooper, *Walter Hines Page,* 49 (see 81 for Page's mood).

isolated and stifled, and although he did not leave North Carolina under the same shadow that George W. Cable, that same year, left Louisiana, he was just as certain as Cable that he would never come back. Like Cable, he found a certain freedom in the Northeast. There he was able to turn his thoughts to the true condition of the South in a manner not possible before. Now he could write openly what before he had only thought and expressed privately.

Page had only enough money to pay his fare to New York, and he had no definite job awaiting him. According to Hendrick, however, he began a book on the South shortly after he arrived in New York. He also began to write articles on the South to submit to the *Atlantic Monthly*, *Harper's*, the *Century*, and the *Independent*. But his most outspoken work of this period, the product of the pent-up frustration of the previous year, he sent back to his old newspaper in Raleigh. From mid-1885 to late 1886 Page dispatched essays for his successor, Josephus Daniels, to print, and the words of the youthful Page, particularly in February and March, 1886, belie his later image as moderate and mediator. But they present in some respects the essential Page, the man who felt after arriving in New York a freedom he had not felt as an editor in Raleigh and was not to feel later as a respected and responsible editor, publisher, and regional ambassador in New York and Boston.

His most famous letter to the *State Chronicle*, dated February 1, 1886, was occasioned in part by the refusal of North Carolina political leaders to support a state industrial school, a project which Page and the Watauga Club had proposed. But Page's disappointment prompted him to go beyond the subject at hand, and led to an outright attack on Tar Heel reactionaries, the Mummies who controlled the state: "They don't want an industrial school. That means a new idea and a new idea is death to the supremacy of the Mummies. Let 'em alone. The world must have some corner in it where men can sleep and sleep and dream and dream, and North Carolina is as good a spot for that as any." He grew even more critical:

> There is not a man whose residence is in the State who is recognized by the world as an authority on anything. Since time began, no man or woman who lived there has ever written a book that has taken a place in the permanent literature of the country. Not a man has ever lived and worked there who fills twenty-five pages in any history of the United States. Not a scientific discovery has been made and worked out and kept its home in

North Carolina that has ever become famous for the good it did the world. It is the laughing stock among the States.[40]

Henry Louis Mencken of Baltimore was five years of age when these words appeared, and the mature Mencken probably never read them. But the resemblance of Page's attack to parts of Mencken's famous indictment of the South, "The Sahara of the Bozart" (1920), is so remarkable—in language, tone, speech cadences, and catalogue of inadequacies—that one wonders at first if Page did not serve as model for the South's arch-critic himself. As Mencken wrote thirty years later:

> Once you have counted James Branch Cabell . . . you will not find a single southern prose writer who can actually write. And once you have—but when you come to critics, musical composers, painters, sculptors, architects and the like, you will have to give it up, for there is not even a bad one between the Potomac mud-flats and the Gulf. Nor a historian. Nor a sociologist. Nor a philosopher. Nor a theologian. Nor a scientist. In all these fields the south is an awe-inspiring blank—a brother to Portugal, Serbia and Esthonia [sic].[41]

Mencken would have disliked being scooped by Walter Hines Page. He was critical of Page because of Page's partisanship toward England during the First World War, and because of his devotion to uplift. Besides, he sprang from that breed which Mencken despised, the Southern Methodist. And Page himself in his later years would hardly have been drawn to Mencken, who helped to shatter that American Genteel Tradition of which he himself was a part. But the younger Page, as he stood in New York in 1886, was precisely that postbellum Southerner that Mencken later described, that Southerner of talent and ambition who, finding nothing for himself in his own land, had come north "with no baggage save good manners and empty [belly]."[42] The author of the Mummy letters of 1886 was hardly genteel, and his intent in the letter of February 1 was far from "patient uplift." He was angry at the Mummies, angrier that he himself had had to leave home

40. W. H. Page, "Letter from New York," Raleigh *State Chronicle*, February 4, 1886. Although the dateline for Page's "Letter" was February 1, it appeared in the newspaper on February 4.

41. H. L. Mencken, "The Sahara of the Bozart," *Prejudices, Second Series* (New York, 1920), 138–39.

42. See H. L. Mencken, "The Calamity of Appomattox," *American Mercury*, XXI (September, 1930), 29.

to achieve reward and recognition. He obviously had himself in mind as he continued his February 1 letter: "When every intellectual aspiration is discouraged, when all the avenues that lead to independent thought and to mental growth are closed, when every effort to broaden the people into a great commonwealth that shall lead in the Union—every movement—is balked by the dead weight of these provincial and ignorant men, who are suffered to rule by heredity and by their general respectability in private life—there is absolutely no chance for ambitious men of ability, proportionate to their ability. . . . It is the fault of the insufferable narrowness and mediocrity that balks everything."

Page was not through. In rhetoric again anticipating Mencken's, he elaborated: "Count on your fingers the five men who fill the highest places or have the greatest influence on education in North Carolina. Not one of them is a scholar. Count the five most influential editors in the State. Not one of them could earn in the great centres of journalism $10 a week as a reporter."[43] Those were bold words, especially for a newspaperman who still had no regular job in New York, one who, despite his self-confidence, could not be entirely sure that at some point he would not have to go home and seek employment from those same five editors he had condemned. The words were bolder than anything George W. Cable, recently arrived in New England, had spoken—except that Page in his entire Mummy letter of February 1 did not ever mention race.

But Page did, like Cable, bemoan a Silent South: "Of the thousands of men who know I am writing the truth, not one in ten will say so publicly." This passion for truth-telling continued to hold him in the weeks that followed. "The men and forces who rule society," he wrote in the *State Chronicle* of February 11, his letter datelined February 8, "are opposed to intellectual progress"; the "presumptuous powers of ignorance, heredity, decayed respectability and stagnation that control public action and public expression are absolutely leading us backward intellectually." "If any is offended," he added, "then him have I described." The criticism Page drew from these letters surpassed anything he had seen before, but he continued to attack. He

43. Again, compare the speech cadences to Mencken's in "The Sahara": "Once you have counted Robert Loveman . . . and John McClure . . . you will not find a single southern poet above the rank of a neighborhood rhymester. Once you have counted James Branch Cabell . . . you will not find a single southern prose writer. . . . And once you have . . . ."

tried, however, to enhance his credibility by identifying himself with his readers. "I am a citizen of North Carolina," he wrote in the *State Chronicle* of February 18. "I expect to spend the greater part of the next fifty years in the State at an editorial desk playing the same cheerful tune." It was a lie, and Page knew it. Three months later he wrote his father that the North was home: "Here is the place that we must live." [44]

He really could not have gone home again after the Mummy letters. But he rose rapidly in the Northeast—as talented Southerners, according to Mencken, always did. In 1891 he became editor of the *Forum*, in 1895 moved to Boston and the following year assumed control of the *Atlantic Monthly* (becoming the first *Atlantic* editor besides William Dean Howells from outside New England), and in 1899 returned to New York to begin his own publishing house, Doubleday, Page & Company, and his own magazine, *World's Work*. But the South, a problem South, continued to occupy a part of his mind. According to Charles Sellers, the fifty issues of the *Forum* published while Page was editor contained thirteen articles on the South, the twenty-one issues of the *Atlantic* contained eight, and the one hundred fifty-one issues of *World's Work* he edited included eighty-two such articles. Doubleday, Page became the nation's leading publisher of notable Southern books, including those of Ellen Glasgow, Sidney Lanier, Page's old friend Thomas Dixon, and Booker T. Washington. In the early 1890s Page acquired control of the *Manufacturer's Record* of Baltimore, that voice of the industrial New South, although he lost money in the venture and relinquished control to Richard Edmonds shortly afterward. He also worked with the Southern Education Board, the hookworm commission, and numerous other agencies of uplift and improvement. And through all these channels, particularly his editorial posts and work with Southern education, he became acquainted with virtually every notable Southern leader and intellectual of the progressive stripe. William P. Trent, Edwin Alderman, Edgar Gardner Murphy, William Garrott Brown, William Dodd, C. Alphonso Smith, Edwin Mims, John Spencer Bassett: all Page knew and most he corresponded with. They constituted, in one sense, a more effective version of the Open Letter Club that George W. Cable had conceived in the late 1880s. Page had disagreements with some of

44. W. H. Page to Frank Page, May, 1886, quoted in Cooper, *Walter Hines Page*, 80.

these men, notably Murphy, an Episcopal priest from Alabama and a leading proponent of child labor legislation. The two men spoke from different points of view, Murphy representing social Christianity and Page democratic liberalism. In others of the group—Trent, Mims, and Bassett in particular—Page showed a proprietary interest. Trent, a pioneer in Southern literary study and founder of the *Sewanee Review*, contributed on Southern subjects to the *Atlantic* when Page was editor. Like Page, he had studied at Johns Hopkins, was a Jeffersonian and a severe critic of the Old South, and, like Page, he eventually came to New York to live and work. Mims, an English professor at Page's old college, Trinity, in North Carolina, he encouraged to write boldly on Southern subjects. Indeed, Mims may have benefited most from Page's support, since he possessed a certain timidity Page attempted to exorcise. Mims's Trinity colleague Bassett was anything but timid, and when he wrote in 1903 in the *South Atlantic Quarterly* that Booker T. Washington was "the greatest man, save General Lee, born in the South in a hundred years"—and drew the ire of Josephus Daniels, editor of the Raleigh *News and Observer* and Page's former colleague and friend—Page sprang vigorously to Bassett's defense. Bassett also wound up in the Northeast, not in Page's New York but in Cable's Northampton. "I merely wanted a peaceful atmosphere," he wrote a friend.[45]

Throughout the 1890s and into the twentieth century Page pondered the South in public and in private, and as usual his private expressions were more critical than were his public statements. In his letters around the turn of the century he came to identify two reasons for Southern social and cultural poverty, the poor white and the hold of fundamentalist Southern religion—precisely the factors to which Mencken later attributed the critical state of Southern health. "I tell you," Page wrote to his wife in 1899, "the sorry white man in the South is the real curse of the land. He is the fellow for whom South-

---

45. Sellers, "Walter Hines Page," 492; [John Spencer Bassett], "Stirring Up the Fires of Race Antipathy," *South Atlantic Quarterly*, II (October, 1903), 299; to William K. Boyd, January 2, 1912, quoted in Bruce Clayton, *The Savage Ideal: Intolerance and Intellectual Leadership in the South, 1890–1914* (Baltimore, 1972), 101. Clayton's work contains the fullest treatment of Southern progressives at the turn of the century, as well as a good discussion of Page's relationship with Mims (pp. 58–62). For an example of Edgar Gardner Murphy's concerns, see *Problems of the Present South: A Discussion of Certain of the Educational, Industrial, and Political Issues of the Southern States* (New York, 1904) and *The Basis of Ascendancy: A Discussion of Certain Principles of Public Policy Involved in the Development of Southern States* (New York, 1909).

ern civilization sacrifices itself." But Page, who had once considered the Methodist, then the Unitarian ministry, found religious intolerance even more responsible. "Any discussion of religious influence in the South," he wrote Trent, "which does not say strictly, point-blank and with emphasis, that the intellectual life of the people has been hindered unspeakably by the narrowness of religious opinion falls short of the most important fact that needs to be said about the South." Page urged that Trent emphasize in his writing "the effect of [Southern] religious dogma upon intolerance of liberal opinion in general." He offered the same analysis in a letter to Robert C. Ogden of the Southern Education Board: "I doubt if there had come a week in twenty years but some Southern man has told me or written to me of his sense of suffocation—his longing for fresh air; and their troubles have come oftener from church parties than from political parties." On another occasion, when Edwin Mims asked his advice about a move from the University of North Carolina (for which Mims had left Trinity) to take the English department chairmanship at Vanderbilt, Page warned, "If those Bishops should get the lead or even if their influence should continue to be great I should almost despair of the accomplishment of any broad thing at Nashville. They are a pestiferous lot, they are persistent and vindictive. Unless they are knocked out completely they will come again." [46]

Page was one of very few influential Southerners of his generation to place on religion so much of the blame for Southern shortcomings. In this respect, too, he had far more in common with later Southern critics such as Mencken and Cash than with most of his own Southern contemporaries. Yet he did not express strongly in speeches and in print his antipathy to Southern religion; in fact, most of his public comments on Southern shortcomings, religious and otherwise, in the 1890s and the following decade were rather mild. In an 1893 *Forum* article, "The Last Hold of the Southern Bully," he lashed out at that Southerner he had privately identified to Mrs. Page as "the sorry white man," and which he now called "the race bully," "the romantic bully." The "Southern bully" (Daniel Hundley had used the term long before) he particularly blamed for the rise in Southern lynchings. But

---

46. W. H. Page to Alice Wilson Page, March 2, 1899, quoted in Hendrick, *The Training of an American*, 393; Page to William P. Trent, October 6, 1896, and Page to Robert C. Ogden, December 17, 1903, both quoted in Cooper, *Walter Hines Page*, 145, 213; Page to Edwin Mims, January 5, 1911, quoted in Clayton, *The Savage Ideal*, 59.

the "brute" among Negroes was responsible as well: the two united "against civilization." In other essays and speeches Page stressed public education as the most effective way out of the Southern dilemma. In May, 1897, in Greensboro, North Carolina, he attacked those Southerners who took an elitist view of education, pointed to examples of Southern ignorance, and urged above all the development of the "forgotten man" and "forgotten woman." In a second speech, "The School That Built a Town," given in December, 1901, at Georgia State Normal College, Page described a mythical Southern town which built a public school which, in turn, brought progress to the community. A third article, "The Rebuilding of Old Commonwealths," initially promised to be bolder than either of the earlier discussions. A trip through the South in 1899—his first extended trip since 1881—had depressed him, particularly in the area of race relations. He returned to Boston intending to write his impressions for the *Atlantic*. But because of illness and his departure from the *Atlantic* later in 1899, he did not complete the essay until 1902, and the tone was not so critical as it might have been. Page did depict a South beset by problems, and repeated his thesis that slavery had retarded Southern progress and diverted the Southern people from their natural inclination toward democracy. He also reiterated that public education and industry were the keys to Southern enlightenment. But he added, "No man who knows the gentleness and the dignity and the leisure of the old Southern life would like to see these qualities blunted by too rude a growth of sheer industrialism." "How in the march of industrialism [may] these qualities of fellowship and leisure . . . be retained in the mass of the people; and how [might they] be transplanted to corresponding towns in other parts of the Union?" [47] At the same time, 1902, Old South advocate Thomas Nelson Page was embracing industrialism, the New Southerner Walter Hines Page was questioning it.

His *Atlantic* essay Page combined with the two earlier speeches, "The Forgotten Man" and "The School That Built a Town," and issued his first book, *The Rebuilding of Old Commonwealths*, in 1902. He also continued to write editorials on Southern topics and to recruit South-

47. W. H. Page, "The Last Hold of the Southern Bully," *Forum* XVI (November, 1893), 303; W. H. Page, "The Forgotten Man," "The School That Built a Town," and "The Rebuilding of Old Commonwealths," all in *The Rebuilding of Old Commonwealths* (New York, 1902), 1–47, 51–103, 107–153 (see, in particular, 114, 141).

ern contributors for *World's Work*. But at the same time he was speaking publicly about Southern progress, encouraging Southern writers, serving on education and hookworm commissions—in general devoting himself to uplift—he was contemplating a darker and more personal statement on the South. That statement took the form of a book, *The Autobiography of a Southerner Since the Civil War*, which was published in four installments in the *Atlantic* in 1906 under the pseudonym Nicholas Worth—and, revised and expanded, was issued in 1909, the pseudonym intact, as *The Southerner: A Novel, Being the Autobiography of Nicholas Worth*. The publisher was Doubleday, Page & Company.

The 425-page book was Page's clearest exploration of his identity as Southerner, although it has received relatively little attention from Page scholars.[48] In the book he attempted in several ways to dissociate himself from his character Nicholas Worth, by making the second half of the story much less autobiographical than the first and by expressly labeling the 1909 version *A Novel* after failing to designate it so in 1906. But the book remained highly autobiographical. It was not only an "autobiography of the spirit" as one of Page's detractors, Edd Winfield Parks, wrote,[49] but in many respects autobiography in fact. The story begins in a village a few miles from the capital city of an Atlantic coast state bordering Virginia: that is, Page's birthplace, Cary, just outside Raleigh in North Carolina. Young Nicholas Worth, like his creator, is the son of a Whig and a pioneer Southern industrialist, and he grows up in a country house near the railroad. He sees the coffins come home from the Civil War and watches as the Yankees occupy his own house. As a boy, he is destined for the Methodist ministry, attends a military academy which venerates the Confederate cause, and feels most comfortable when he retreats to "the Old Place," his grandfather's plantation. Also like Page, he first attends a small Southern college, then goes north for university instruction and begins to question the Southern tradition and write letters back to the newspaper in his state capital. Like Page, Nicholas Worth—in the 1906 version, although not the 1909—also considers becoming a Uni-

48. Hendrick, who devotes three volumes to Page, mentions *The Southerner* on only one page. Cooper, whose study is specifically of Page as Southerner, devotes but four pages to the novel and generally understates its importance as a key to Page's feelings about the South.
49. Parks, *Segments of Southern Thought*, 285. Page references are to the 1909 version of *The Southerner*.

tarian minister. These and other parallels link the lives of Nicholas Worth and Walter Page. The ways in which Worth's life differed—his father runs a cotton mill rather than a lumber mill, and the Northern university he attends is Harvard, not Johns Hopkins—are incidental. The one major departure from Page's early life—the death of Nicholas Worth's father at the hands of a thief just after the war—was included either to provide drama or to distance the author from his protagonist. One suspects the latter.

There are greater departures from Page's own life in the second half of the novel. Although Worth, like Page, returns to his native state after receiving his university education, unlike Page he remains at home. He accepts a position as county superintendent of schools, works for industrial education, and receives the praise of many of his neighbors. But his advocacy of better Negro schools, in addition to his Northern education and his suspected agnosticism, leads to his dismissal. He then teaches history at the state university (Page had taught briefly at Chapel Hill) and campaigns along with Professor Billy Bain (modeled on Page's friend Charles D. McIver) for state education for women. He joins a progressive group called "the Club" (or "the Sunrise Club" in the *Atlantic* version), clearly the Watauga Club of Page's days in Raleigh, and with its backing runs for state superintendent of schools. Despite the opposition of Colonel Stringweather and a newspaper, *The White Man* (whose editor may have been modeled on Page's *State Chronicle* successor, Josephus Daniels), Worth apparently wins the popular vote, only to lose because of vote fraud. Despite such corruption—or, indeed, to fight it—he decides to remain in his native state. In the *Atlantic* version he assumes control of the family cotton mill after his brother's death; in the 1909 novel his future is not specified. But it is clear in each version, particularly the 1909, which contains a postscript "Twenty-five Years Afterwards," that Nicholas Worth is home to stay.

That Worth stays home while his creator had not may not be so significant as it at first seems, for although Page did feel a measure of guilt in leaving the South in 1885 he also continued, like Nicholas Worth, to work for Southern betterment. Indeed, whatever guilt Page felt may have actually motivated him to produce, among other things, a book such as *The Southerner*. It is a curious book, tinged at time with regret and even self-deprecation, in certain ways a Southern version of *The Education of Henry Adams*. Like Adams, who wrote the bulk of his spiritual autobiography the same year Page wrote his, Page creates a certain character, an alter ego, and has this character examine his past and his tradition in a quest for order. As a youth, like Adams, he finds that order largely in the reassuring peace and stability of his paternal grandfather's home, and when his grandfather dies an era ends: "It seemed to me that the history of the world fell into two periods—one that had gone before and the other that now began; for, when we buried him, we seemed to be burying a standard of judgment, a social order, an epoch" (p. 86). Later, like Adams, having failed as a man of action Nicholas Worth expresses a certain awe at those members of his family who have succeeded in the nineteenth-century world of commerce and public affairs.

But Page's book, deficient in a sustained irony and in a larger grasp of history, falls far short of Adams' autobiography; it would fall to a later writer, as we shall see, to write the Southern *Education*. In ways more immediate and more tangible, the story of Nicholas Worth resembled Cable's *bildungsroman* of the previous decade, *John March, Southerner*. Not only are the characters Nicholas Worth and John March similar—both about the same age, growing up in the Piedmont South during Reconstruction, both given to questioning their Southern heritage but finally devoting themselves to Southern reform—but the reasons the two books were written are similar. Both Cable and Page, having left the South in 1885 for intellectual freedom, found themselves in late middle age in the Northeast with little prospect of ever returning south to live. Neither had yet written his apprenticeship novel. That is precisely what *The Southerner* was for Page, *John March, Southerner* to a lesser extent for Cable. In each case the author has his protagonist remain in the South even though he himself had not.

But Page's novel was more than the Education of Nicholas Worth. It was also his harshest criticism of the South since the Mummy letters, his second strongest ever. "The audacity of the thing at least is splendid," Page wrote his wife after completing most of the 1906 version.[50] It was in *The Southerner* that he issued his famous indictment of the "ghosts" which haunted Dixie after Appomattox—the Negro, religious orthodoxy, and the Confederate dead. The presence of the first ghost Nicholas Worth sensed from early childhood. The second, "an

50. Page to Alice Wilson Page, March, 1905, quoted in Cooper, *Walter Hines Page*, 198.

indescribable terror in this violent religion," he discovers after attending a religious revival: "The terror and the gloom . . . I can recall now. I had an impulse to run from home till it should end" (pp. 21–22). The last of the ghosts, the Confederate dead (or what was worse, the Confederate living), he discovers at the Gresham School. The war had paralyzed its participants: "It gave every one of them the intensest experience of his life [as Page's old teacher, Basil Gildersleeve, had also maintained], and ever afterwards he referred every other experience to this. Thus it stopped the thought of most of them as an earthquake stops a clock. . . . Their speech was in a vocabulary of war; their loyalties were loyalties, not to living ideas or duties, but to old commanders and to distorted traditions. They were dead men, most of them, moving among the living as ghosts; and yet, as ghosts in a play, they held the stage" (p. 46). Freedom of expression in the South was virtually dead. In the small sectarian college Worth attends, "formulas so took the place of thought as to forbid inquiry" (p. 68).

When Worth travels north to Harvard he encounters a Northern roommate, Cooley, who is fascinated by the South and urges his Southern friend to explain it. The situation is not unlike that Faulkner later creates in *Absalom, Absalom!*: in their rooms in Cambridge, Cooley—the name suggests an outsider with the detachment of Faulkner's Shreve McCannon—pursues his questioning with "logical simplicity" (p. 90). Worth, no Quentin Compson but the self-conscious Southerner at Harvard nonetheless, is forced to face the meaning of the South as he had not before. But Worth emerges whole, no longer so painfully Southern. As he travels home by train after two years in Massachusetts, he declares, "I was now at home at Harvard; free, too, as I had not before been. Could I ever be free in the South?" (p. 106). Only the women of his own family and the Southern spring now draw him home. As he crosses the Potomac, he later recalls, "I was aware that I was coming into another world. A feeling of homelessness came over me and I felt a doubt whether I really knew either of these worlds" (p. 108).

What Worth sees as he passes through Virginia discourages him further: not the "neat villages and well-kept lawns and painted fences" of New England (p. 109) but mudholes and shacks and squalor. Despite his misgivings, and compelled by his sense of duty, he remains in the South, but what he learns confirms his doubts. He is dismissed as school superintendent "in the Name of Our Holy Religion . . . in the

Name of our History and our Honoured Dead . . . [and] in the Name of our Anglo-Saxon Civilerzation. . . . Against the Church, and the ex-Confederates and the Pious Lady and our Honoured Dead and Anglo-Saxon 'Civilerzation' nothing could prevail" (p. 181). In the 1906 *Atlantic* version Page went further: "The Church, the race question, and the hands of dead men . . . together made the ghost called Public Opinion. . . . Many a Southern man has been banished from the land that he loved and would proudly have served by this simple process of invoking these forces against him." "The Confederacy,— the horrid tragedy of it," he had written in the *Atlantic* (but not the 1909 version), "and the myths that were already growing over it, its heroes, its Colonels, its Daughters." He bemoaned "the suppression of one's self, the arrest of one's growth, the intellectual loneliness, and the personal inconvenience of living under conditions like these" and "this was not the worst of it": the old order, the worship of the Confederate dead, "held back the country almost in the same economic and social state in which slavery had left it. . . . The very land suffered."[51]

Thus Page wrote in 1906—but not in 1909, at which point, having had time to reflect, he had modified his indictment. But only to a degree: the criticism of the ghosts and their paralyzing effect remained. As was his custom, however, Page was careful not to completely alienate his Southern readers. He ended his spiritual autobiography with a celebration of his grandfather and the Old Place, virtually the only remnants of the Southern past he venerated, and then added in a "Leave-Taking": "If any reader of what I have written shall find anywhere a single word of bitterness, I pray him to rub it out. For I have not meant to write such a word" (p. 425). But Page had indeed written parts of his book if not in bitterness at least in gleeful mockery, and he knew it. He had also written, far more than he was willing to admit in 1909, from his own heart. "It is a story," he insisted then, "and not a history." In 1906 he had not been so hesitant to acknowledge the autobiographical nature of his work. In the beginning of the *Atlantic* version he had announced with the false modesty of Franklin at the beginning of his *Autobiography*: "Since my own life, and its somewhat exciting small struggle for light and freedom and a proper perspective, have happened to fall in the cotton belt, and illustrate, by small

51. W. H. Page, "The Autobiography of a Southerner Since the Civil War," *Atlantic Monthly*, XCVIII (August, 1906), 163, 165–66.

deeds and adventures, this great story of a freedom of a people, partly achieved and now rapidly coming, I have determined to write the story of it. . . . I have changed names and places in the story, and disguised some incidents, *not essential facts*, only because it is unfair to give publicity to some old deeds and opinions of former enemies that we are all willing to forget" [italics mine].[52]

Page should have known the pseudonym Nicholas Worth would not conceal his identity for long. According to Hendrick, the identification of the author was "immediate and accurate." But, in fact, several reviewers, even of the 1909 version, did not guess the author, and as late as 1910 such a close observer of the South as Harvard historian A. B. Hart admitted in his book, *The Southern South*, that he did not know who had written *The Autobiography of Nicholas Worth*. But North Carolinians knew better. Page was identified as soon as the first *Atlantic* installment reached Raleigh, and Daniels' *News and Observer* ran a withering review of the book. More objective outside reviewers, only some of whom knew Page's identity, pointed to the many artistic shortcomings in the novel—a didactic tone and poor characterization among them. A writer in the *Nation* called the author "a critic and would-be reformer and transformer" possessed of "steady and strong and at times passionate rebellion." "There is too much of the spirit of the combatant," he added, "and something, we fear, of the bitterness of unpicturesque repulses." Another reviewer, a Southern woman writing in the *Independent*, could not identify the author but charged that he had written "an indictment of a whole people" in a "cold, sneering manner." Mrs. L. N. Harris continued in a statement that described Page's own position, and the dilemma of the Southern social critic, perhaps better than she knew:

> There is a certain terrifying power in the South that makes a Southerner, such as the author of this book must be or have been, willing to sacrifice the credit for his good deed by failing to sign his name to an enlightening criticism of his section like this. This is not because he fears the sword, but the heart of his people. They do not merely turn their back upon the perpetrators of such a wrong as this author has committed; they have a power of contempt that is not intellectual or reasonable, but sincere, definite, personal, and with a kind of invincible blood-righteousness in it. And the

52. W. H. Page, promotional pamphlet for *The Southerner*, 1909, quoted in Cooper, *Walter Hines Page*, 203. The cotton belt, in broad terms, did extend to Page's part of North Carolina. His grandfather grew cotton and had a gin. W. H. Page, "The Autobiography of a Southerner," 2.

victims of it declare that it is the most lasting, embarrassing and painful experience a man can have in this life. This accounts for a good many excommunicated Southerners who no longer make their home in this section. They have told the truth about their own people in a manner which gives a false impression as well as a true one.[53]

Page was precisely that Southerner, expatriate though never excommunicated, pulled by conflicting desires: to tell the truth about the South and, at the same time, to retain the admiration and affection of his fellow Southerners. He could not do both, but he *attempted* to do both, and as a result there existed a certain confusion in his attitude toward the South. In 1885 he could announce in a newspaper column that he fully expected to live and work in his native state, but three months later would confide that he had no intention of living there. In 1909 he could write, or rewrite, a book which depicted a poor, benighted, even savage South, but then publish it under a pseudonym. Shortly afterward, as the editor of *World's Work*, he demonstrated the same basic caution when he advised Edwin Mims, who was preparing a series of articles for him (and certainly needed no such advice): "Do not take up the race problem as a separate subject. Do no more with it than you are obliged to do. . . . In general, do not open up (certainly do not dwell on) any violently controversial matter." And he said this despite his earlier suggestion that Mims boldly attack Southern shortcomings, and despite a letter to Mims only six months later in which he insisted that the South was "100 years behind in intellectual curiosity" and possessed "the oratorical habit of speech which means lying (almost comically) about Religion, Woman, and Reading."[54]

There was, at last, a certain failure of nerve in Walter Hines Page. No all-or-nothing man was he, no Helper or Ruffin or Dabney. Unlike them, he almost always kept in mind the consequences of his truth-telling. There is solid evidence in the Mummy letters, *The Southerner*, and his private letters that what the Agrarians later charged was in fact partly true: that Page actually disliked the South as it was, or,

53. Hendrick, *The Life and Letters of Walter H. Page*, I, 92; A. B. Hart, *The Southern South* (New York, 1910), 18; Raleigh *News and Observer* review by J. G. de Roulhac Hamilton, quoted in Cooper, *Walter Hines Page*, 203; H. M. Stanley, review of *The Southerner, Nation*, November 25, 1909, p. 512; Mrs. L. N. Harris, "A Southern's [*sic*] View of 'The Southerner,'" *Independent*, November 11, 1909, pp. 1090–91.

54. W. H. Page to Edwin Mims, [spring, 1911], quoted in Edwin Mims, *The Advancing South* (Garden City, N.Y., 1926), 42; Page to Mims, October 25, 1911, quoted in Clayton, *The Savage Ideal*, 60.

rather, focused so completely on its flaws that he could not easily see its virtues. Certainly he demonstrated less affection for the traditional South than any other prominent white Southern spokesman of his generation, including Cable, who, even after he left the South, continued to be taken with its charm; and certainly less than such native critics of a later generation as Odum and Cash. Yet Page was openly critical less frequently than they were. He was, more than any of them, a public figure, a genial and politic man who valued his role as Southern spokesman in the North, who relished the frequent invitations to speak in the South, and welcomed the kind of public exposure North and South that led to his appointment in 1913 to the Court of St. James's. Indeed, those very qualities which made Page a successful man of affairs in the North—his practicality, his love of the spotlight, his ability to win and influence people—might have served him well if he had stayed at home and had spoken out more. Unlike Cable, he might have been very effective as a critic in residence; he had the personality and, at least at first, the stamina for it. Although he was affable, even charming, he could also be vigorous and combative; temperamentally he was not unlike his friend Theodore Roosevelt. Or rather, he would have liked to be. In fact, he was but an apprentice to the Roosevelt code, prevented from achieving exemplar status by his occasional failure of nerve and constant awareness of consequences.

And one other quality Page lacked, one possessed in abundance by Ruffin and Dabney before him and by Cash and William Alexander Percy after him: the tragic vision. Or perhaps it was, rather, that he refused to give in to it. Above all the product of mid-nineteenth-century optimism, he preferred to deny the darkness in life, or at least chose to flee from it as soon as his conscience would permit. Nowhere is this seen more clearly than in the area of race, and in no particular instance more than in the long trip through the South he took in 1899, presumably to write about Southern race relations for the *Atlantic*. As Cooper shows, he was profoundly moved on this trip by the plight of the Negro; and as Morton Sosna writes, he confided to a friend in 1899 that in twenty years of thinking he had not been able to forget the race problem, that its pathos was eternal.[55] But Page suggested little of this pathos in his editorials and essays after the 1899 trip, and

55. Cooper, *Walter Hines Page*, 147–49; Morton Sosna, *In Search of the Silent South: Southern Liberals and the Race Issue* (New York, 1977), 12.

by the time "The Rebuilding of Old Commonwealths" appeared in the *Atlantic* in 1902 his rage to explain publicly had waned. The concern still burned within. He expressed it in letters to his wife, and he acknowledged in *The Southerner* the power of the Negro over the white Southerner: "We have permitted ourselves in fact to be ruled— in our minds and actions and emotions and characters and fears—by the One Subject. We had for three long generations been really ruled by the Negro" (p. 269). But he did not ever speak boldly, in public address or in print, of the pathos and tragedy of the black American.

In this one respect Page himself was one of those Southerners "ruled" by the Negro, silenced or at least subdued by that "ghost" of the freedman he himself identified. He was a more effective critic of Southern sloth, poverty, and intellectual and cultural sterility than any other Southerner of his generation, and he was among the most perceptive and most truthful of commentators on the limitations of the industrial New South. But he never allowed himself to speak fully and truthfully about the Negro. Perhaps, in an age of Jim Crow, he believed it futile to speak too loudly. Perhaps he understood that to probe too deeply would lead only to despair. Unlike the absolutists Helper and Ruffin and Dabney, he refused to examine too closely what he once called "the tragic possibilities always beneath the surface." [56] But, unlike them, he survived and prospered.

56. W. H. Page to Alice Wilson Page, [1899], quoted in Cooper, *Walter Hines Page*, 148.

CHAPTER 3

Odum, Davidson, and the Sociological Proteus

> The sociological truth-seeker is like the man in the old Greek
> fable who comes to ask questions of Proteus. He must know
> what grip to use, and must hold on firmly through all manner
> of transformations. Then at last he may come upon some Pro-
> tean wisdom, ancient as the sea.
>
> Donald Davidson,
> "Howard Odum and the Sociological Proteus," 1937

> The sociologists, some quite unwillingly, others with obvious
> unction and high hope, have inherited the leadership formerly
> held by William Lloyd Garrison, Wendell Phillips, Charles
> Sumner, Thad Stevens, and Company.
>
> Donald Davidson,
> "Preface to Decision," 1945

> It has long been suspected that sociologists and poets have
> little confidence in one another.
>
> Richard M. Weaver,
> *The Ethics of Rhetoric*, 1953

It is not unusual for men to hate and attack other men, other sections
and nations, other political and economic systems—the Southern
apologists of the nineteenth century did all this and more—but rarely
has a man planned and executed a crusade against a particular academic discipline as Donald Davidson of Nashville did in the early and
mid-twentieth century. That discipline was sociology, and his war on
sociology, Davidson believed, was just another phase in the larger
Southern war against abstraction, that old and bitter struggle fought
in the nineteenth century by George Fitzhugh, Edmund Ruffin, James
Hammond, and a host of other Southern apologists. Sociology, as Davidson saw it, was the most abstract of disciplines and, because it
studied people in the mass, the most dangerous. It was particularly
hazardous to Southerners because, in his view, it was committed to
changing and reforming them, to taking the color and vitality out of
their lives and reshaping them in the standardized American mold.
That was not precisely what Howard W. Odum and the sociologists at
Chapel Hill had in mind, but Davidson feared they had. Thus, his indictment against sociology went something like this: The sociologist

was the twentieth-century successor to the nineteenth-century abolitionist. A disturber of the peace and the status quo, he abhorred the
concrete, the organic, and the religious, and preferred the abstract,
the theoretical, and the scientific. Indeed, so blinded by charts, tables,
and statistics was he that he could not see the flesh and blood individual. He not only described and analyzed, he also prescribed and recommended and then called on the centralized state—"Leviathan"—
to help him implement his recommendations and systems. Most of
all, he viewed the South from a vantage point outside the Southern
tradition—which was conservative, religious, possessed of a historical sense, and given to the sacredness of the individual and a sense
of place. And that tradition was segregationist. The sociologist, even
if a Southerner by birth, was by trade progressive, scientific, and
ahistorical, and he held little regard for the integrity of place or of the
individual. And he was an integrationist. Given his way, the Southern
sociologist of the 1920s and 1930s would transform the entire South
into a gigantic laboratory for social experimentation. And his spiritual
brother, the Southern writer who had fallen under the "sociological
influence," had already portrayed for the nation a South filled with
grotesque poor whites, decadent aristocrats, and religious fanatics.
Such were the contentions of Donald Davidson.

The South had had sociologists before 1920, or at least those who
called themselves sociologists. George Fitzhugh had proclaimed himself one of them. But Fitzhugh's *Sociology for the South* was hardly the
same brand of social science as that emanating from Chapel Hill in the
twenties and thirties. The "Hated Helper," Davidson would have
said—with his tables, charts, statistics, and emphasis on a problem
South—was the true ancestor of the accursed modern breed. But the
man who, in fact, presided over the sociological empire which Davidson attacked was as different from Helper as he could have been—
although both possessed a fondness for statistics and both were, either by birth or adoption, North Carolinians and thus identified with
the "agitating and crusading spirit" which Davidson believed "animated many of the North Carolinians."[1] But in other respects Howard W. Odum of Chapel Hill could hardly be identified with the
sociologist-as-demon Davidson depicted, as Davidson himself acknowledged at times.

1. Donald Davidson, "Howard Odum and the Sociological Proteus," *The Attack on
Leviathan,* 388.

One Southerner with whom Odum did have something in common, insofar as his background was concerned, was Donald Davidson himself, although neither man acknowledged the resemblance. Certainly the public roles the two men assumed in Southern intellectual life were vastly different: Davidson, the staunchest, least compromising, and longest enduring of the Southern Agrarians, the most eloquent or in any case the most persistent Southern defender in the twentieth century; and Odum, a leading critic of the Agrarians and the Southern "sectionalism" many of them espoused, one of the most committed and certainly the most earnest of Southern reformers in the twentieth century. Few other Southerners after 1900 took the South so *seriously* as Davidson and Odum did, and few others identified their lives and work with it so completely.

Indeed Davidson and Odum constitute, although not so dramatically as the two Pages, another in that series of Southern antagonists, similar in many respects but vastly different in outlook. Both were born in the rural South—Davidson in Tennessee, Odum in Georgia—of pious Methodist families of plain stock, both attended Methodist colleges (Vanderbilt and Emory), had extensive instruction in the classics (Odum, the eventual social scientist, writing his M.A. thesis on the religion of Sophocles), and became university professors. Both were collectors of homespun ballads and tales, romantic lovers of the folk who believed that culture was an organic outgrowth of the people rather than a sort of polish applied from without. Both were personally committed to the soil (Odum the sociologist at least as much as Davidson the Agrarian) and were, after their early years, rather provincial men, culturally self-sufficient Americans who felt little need to visit Europe. Indeed Davidson, particularly in later life, may have had more personally in common with his adversary Odum than he did with his close friends among the Fugitive-Agrarians, John Crowe Ransom and Allen Tate. Both Ransom and Tate were elitists, as Davidson never really was. Both were intellectually sophisticated in a sense Davidson was not. Both eventually left the South, while Davidson—like Odum—remained. And both Ransom and Tate had by the 1940s gained great reputations as men of letters, while the reputation and influence of Davidson, like that of Odum, had begun to decline. Davidson and Odum were undeniably nineteenth-century men, the sociologist as fully as the poet, and by the mid-twentieth century the times had passed them by.

But it was the times, particularly events in the South of the 1920s to which Odum and Davidson responded in a markedly different fashion, that made them the adversaries they became and led to the development of the two broad "schools" of Southern thought with which they were associated: the Regionalists of Chapel Hill and the Vanderbilt Agrarians. Indeed, one must first consider the events before considering the adversaries. For the decade of the 1920s was in many regards the most crucial decade for Southerners since the 1870s, one characterized by the same uncertainty and fear of change, and by the same clash of ideas and forces of that earlier decade; and as a result of that change, the South inhabited by Odum and Davidson in 1930 was as different from that described in 1910 by Thomas Nelson Page and Walter Hines Page as the world of the Pages had been from Reconstruction. As Davidson himself later wrote, the great Northern offensive of the 1920s had come in between:

> The new attack . . . upon Southern life and its characteristic institutions [began] . . . during the Harding Administration. . . . This attack [was] more abusive and unrelenting than anything the Southern states have experienced since the last Federal soldier was withdrawn from their soil. In the nineteen-twenties there was no single institution, like slavery, upon which attacks could be centered. They had a vaguer objective in the so-called backwardness, or "cultural lag," of the South. The Northern press, with all of the Southern press that takes its cue from New York . . . unanimously agreed that the South [was] guilty of numerous crimes against progress.

Northern journalists and social scientists "wherever they went on their missions of social justice . . . carried with them a legend of the future, more dangerously abstract than the legend of the past, and sternly demanded that the local arrangements be made to correspond with it, at whatever cost."[2]

The result of the Northern offensive of the 1920s, as George B. Tindall has observed, was the creation of an image of the benighted South, a savage South of racial hatred and religious fanaticism—an image created in part by the *Nation*, the *New Republic*, the *Century*, and other Eastern magazines. Individual Yankees also made forays into the South, scavenging for salable material and returning north to

2. Donald Davidson, "Expedients vs. Principles—Cross-Purposes in the South," *The Attack on Leviathan*, 315; Donald Davidson, "Still Rebels, Still Yankees," *American Review*, II (November, 1933), 62.

put it in print. Frank Tannenbaum, a Columbia University professor described by one Southerner as "a charming young foreigner with a slick tongue," traveled through Dixie gathering information, sent back his discoveries to the *Century*, and upon his safe return collected the essays in his highly critical *Darker Phases of the South* (1924).[3] The war against the South in the 1920s was conducted on several fronts: H. L. Mencken in general command, his special domain being intellectual and cultural sterility; Tannenbaum and his fellow social scientists concentrating on social ills; Oswald Garrison Villard and the *Nation* crusading against lynching; and W. E. B. Du Bois filling the pages of the NAACP journal, the *Crisis*, with a bitter indictment of Southern racial attitudes and practices.

The result was that the South of the twenties became a land of ridicule, a region of belts—the Bible Belt, Hookworm Belt, Malaria Belt, Chastity Belt—most of which were provided by Mencken. And the Yankee offensive, as Mencken said, "knocked the potential [Southern] critics out of their shells." As Tindall has written, "a fifth column of native Menckens and Tannenbaums" emerged in the South, and by exposing Southern savageries those Southerners, mainly journalists, "found an almost ridiculously simple formula for fame."[4] Crusading Southern newspapers captured five Pulitzer Prizes between 1923 and 1929, and new journalistic stars such as Gerald W. Johnson of North Carolina rose to national attention. Other Southerners who had long chafed under the restrictions against Southern dissent, and many of whom had left the South, burst forth in the new climate of freedom. William H. Skaggs, an embittered Alabamian in New York, serves as a case in point. A former mayor of Talladega, Alabama, a populist who had been defeated and rejected in the 1890s by the planters and industrialists of his native state, he had left Alabama in the late nineties soured by his experience, had largely restrained his anger for

3. Frank Tannenbaum's essays are: "The Ku Klux Klan—Its Social Origins in the South" (*Century*, CV [April, 1923], 873–82), "The South Buries Its Anglo-Saxons" (*Century*, CVI [June, 1923], 205–215), "Southern Prisons" (*Century*, CVI [July, 1923], 387–98), and "A Shortage of Scapegoats" (*Century*, CVII [December, 1923], 210–19), all in *Darker Phases of the South* (New York, 1924).
4. H. L. Mencken to Howard W. Odum, October 4, 1924, in Howard W. Odum Papers, Southern Historical Collection, University of North Carolina, Chapel Hill [all letters to and from Odum are in the Odum Papers, unless otherwise noted]; George B. Tindall, "The Benighted South: Origins of a Modern Image," *Virginia Quarterly Review*, XL (Spring, 1964), 289.

more than two decades, and had then burst forth in 1924 with a book entitled *The Southern Oligarchy*, which he subtitled *An Appeal in Behalf of the Silent Masses of Our Country Against the Despotic Rule of the Few*. Skaggs decried "the corrupt practices and criminal lawlessness of a provincial Oligarchy" and appealed to "the patriotism and sober judgment of the American people in behalf of the great mass of white and colored citizens of the Southern States, who are held in political subjection and economic serfdom." A latter-day (though nonracist) Hinton Helper come to pass judgment, he blasted an "Oligarchy" of moneyed interests "that rules the South in almost a complete replica of the radical and reactionary leaders of the Slave Oligarchy before the Civil War." It was clear that Skaggs saw himself in the tradition of Helper, whose term *oligarchy* he had borrowed and whom he described in his book as "a respectable citizen of North Carolina, who had the courage to tell the plain truth and to give the people of his section patriotic and faithful warning," and whose writing "could just as well be applied to the situation as it actually exists at the present writing."[5]

William Skaggs, whose pent-up fury found release after a quarter-century, was perhaps the most extreme of native white Southerners of the 1920s who turned a critical eye on their homeland. But he was not alone. And he and others accused by Davidson of fouling their own nests did not write without reason. The dramatic rise in lynchings in 1919 and 1920, the Scopes evolution trial of 1925, the anti-Catholicism engendered by the Al Smith campaign of 1928, the textile mill violence of Gastonia and Marion and Elizabethton in 1929: in all these the South called attention to its ignorance, violence, and religious bigotry. The Scopes trial as an influence on the views of Odum, Davidson, and other Southerners of their generation deserved special consideration. For in many ways the trial at Dayton, Tennessee, in July, 1925, was a prototypic event, one that brought to the surface all the forces and tensions that characterized the South after World War I, drama-

5. William H. Skaggs, *The Southern Oligarchy: An Appeal in Behalf of the Silent Masses of Our Country Against the Despotic Rule of the Few* (New York, 1924), vii, x, 98, 279. For a discussion of Skaggs's troubles with the "oligarchy" of his native state, see Terence Hunt Nolan, "William Henry Skaggs and the Reform Challenge of 1894," *Alabama Historical Quarterly*, XXXIII (Summer, 1971), 117–34. Skaggs had not been completely silent between 1900 and 1924. While living in Chicago in 1909 and 1910, he had written occasional letters on Southern education to the Birmingham *Age-Herald*.

tized most forcefully the struggle between the provincial, religious South and the modern, secular world, and caused—forced—Southerners such as Odum and Davidson to face squarely the matter of the South and themselves as Southerners. More than one hundred reporters attended the trial of John Thomas Scopes—whose crime was that he had taught evolution in the public schools of Tennessee—and witnessed the battle between Clarence Darrow and William Jennings Bryan. Virtually every thinking Southerner had some response to the occurrences at Dayton, and, indeed, it may not be claiming too much to say that three broad schools of Southern thought were defined, even partially created, by their reaction and response to Dayton.

The progressive school, typified by Edwin Mims of Vanderbilt, saw the trial as a problem in public relations—poor public relations. Mims's response was simply to say it wasn't so, that Dayton was not representative of the South but was rather an aberration. Since Dayton was an embarrassment to Mims, he urged enlightened Southerners to join him in showing the nation that the South could do better. Howard Odum saw the trial altogether differently: it was real, it was all too representative, and it was tragic—not for what it let the nation see about the South (not, that is, as a public relations failure), but for what it revealed to the South about itself. Odum the sociologist immediately diagnosed the problem and set about collecting hard data with which he could document Southern social and intellectual inferiority in order to initiate action to correct it. A third group, of which Davidson was a part, reacted in a still different manner. If Mims had denied the South's backwardness, and if Odum had admitted a backward South and had set out to remedy it, some of Mims's colleagues in the English department of Vanderbilt University said, in effect, the South is guilty as charged, and not only is it guilty of fundamentalism and general backwardness but we hope it remains so. Thus when Mims asked John Crowe Ransom if he, Davidson, and Allen Tate would join the campaign to create a better Southern image, they refused. Instead Ransom, Davidson, and Tate turned to a defense of Southern provincialism, fundamentalism, and supernaturalism, those very qualities that Mencken and the Northern journalists had labeled "barbaric": in short, not the best the South had to offer but apparently the worst. In the context of advanced Southern thinking of the twenties, such a position was not simply courageous. It was unimaginable.

But the position of Ransom and Davidson, and that of Odum, would not be fully developed and articulated until 1930. Mims had his say first, and it came shortly after Dayton. He immediately wrote letters and articles—"Intellectual Progress in the South" and "The South Pleads for Just Criticism"—explaining that "papers, magazines, and books vie with each other in emphasizing the things that show the South at its worst" and insisting that the South was not really as bad as Dayton had suggested. A year after Dayton he expanded his essays into a book, *The Advancing South*, which is both one of the most important works written by a Southerner in the 1920s and a prime study in the Southerner's capacity for self-deception. Mims, the former protégé of Walter Hines Page, still identified himself with the Page school of Southern thought at the time he wrote *The Advancing South*. But he had apparently forgotten Page's advice—the early advice, not the later—to write boldly and truthfully. He was, in *The Advancing South*, too much the booster, not sufficiently the critic. At the time he wrote the book, there had indeed been Southern progress on several fronts: education had improved, lynching (the incidence of which had risen just after the First World War) had declined, journalism had become more realistic, and self-criticism had crossed the Potomac heading south. Something approaching a "war of liberation," as Mims contended, had begun "in the Southern states." Mims was not precisely a conscientious objector in this war, but neither was he on the front lines. Eager to praise those "liberal leaders who are fighting against the conservatism, the sensitiveness to criticism, the lack of freedom that have too long impeded Southern progress," he was at the same time all too willing to accept as true progress anything that masqueraded as it. In characteristic Mims fashion, he insisted, "And yet it is my contention in this volume that the situation, bad as it is, is not as bad as it seems." And he ended the book on a similarly upbeat note: "Conditions are rapidly changing, the tide has turned."[6]

Mims's book was a cultural equivalent of *The Blue Book of Southern Progress*, that booster of Southern economic fortunes published in Baltimore. It was in most regards a romanticizing of the New South

6. Edwin Mims, "The South Pleads for Just Criticism," *Independent*, November 20, 1926, p. 589. See also Edwin Mims, "Intellectual Progress in the South," *Review of Reviews*, LXXIII (April, 1926), 367–69; "Why the South Is Anti-Evolution," *World's Work*, L (September, 1925), 548–52; and *The Advancing South*, vii, 12, 313.

just as surely as Thomas Nelson Page's work was a romanticizing of the Old. Although *The Advancing South* was received favorably by a majority of Southern editors and reviewers, it failed to please the Southerners Mims most wanted to please, those "liberal leaders" of Southern thought who he said were "fighting for emancipation from outworn tradition" (p. viii). Gerald Johnson of North Carolina, Mencken's lieutenant in the Southern war of liberation and a prime recipient of Mims's praise, wrote, "One cannot avoid the feeling that the shattering battleaxe might do more real good to the South than the trumpet and cymbals, seductively as they are used." Liberal Tennesseans Joseph Wood Krutch and T. S. Stribling also charged that Mims had been too moderate, and other South-watchers from Mencken to Allen Tate criticized the book. Mims was "the worst sort of academic jackass," Mencken wrote a Southern friend, and then charged in a lengthy review in the *American Mercury* that Mims was guilty of the worst kind of self-deception. Instead of romanticizing a New South, he should have attacked the Southern clergy "vigorously and with clubs." Tate, Mims's former student, was even more severe. Mims's work, he wrote Davidson, was "probably the worst book ever written on any subject."[7]

The Advancing South, in truth, was not nearly that bad, and neither was its author. It was simply that Mims, although only fifty-four when his book appeared, had already outlived his time. He serves as a study in Southern timidity, or more precisely in the fate of the genteel Victorian critic who ventured into the harsher world of the post-Dayton American South in which lines were more firmly drawn and sides more vigorously chosen. Perhaps the nearest figure to an 1890s

7. Gerald W. Johnson, "The Advancing South," *Virginia Quarterly Review,* II (October, 1926), 596; H. L. Mencken to Julia Harris, July 31, 1926, in H. L. Mencken Microfilm Collection, Princeton University Library, Princeton; H. L. Mencken, "The South Looks Ahead," *American Mercury,* VIII (August, 1926), 508; Allen Tate to Donald Davidson, July 29, 1926, in Donald Davidson Papers, Special Collections, Vanderbilt University Library, Nashville [all letters to and from Davidson are in the Davidson Papers, unless otherwise noted]. For further reaction to *The Advancing South* and the best account of Mims's life, see Leah Marie Park, "Edwin Mims and the Advancing South, 1894–1926: Study of a Southern Liberal" (M.A. thesis, Vanderbilt University, 1964). See also, for an excellent analysis of Mims's thought, Michael O'Brien, "Edwin Mims: An Aspect of the Mind of the New South Considered," *South Atlantic Quarterly,* LXXIII (Spring, 1974), 199–212, and (Summer, 1974), 324–34; and of a discussion of Mims's relationship with Davidson, Michael O'Brien, "Edwin Mims and Donald Davidson: A Correspondence, 1923–1958," *Southern Review,* New Ser., X (Autumn, 1974), 904–922.

New South intellectual still operating in the 1920s, he was a moderate man, a master of compromise, in an age when moderation and compromise alone no longer would suffice.

HOWARD ODUM at times showed signs of being a Mimsian progressive: his private correspondence, even with adversaries, demonstrates just how much he too desired compromise and good will. But he was a man born later than Mims, one who genuinely believed that the South needed radical change and who, if the occasion arose, was capable of summoning a fire, a love of combat, that the genteel professor lacked. Thus when Odum had been called to Chapel Hill in 1920 he had come, at age thirty-six, as a man with a mission. He had seen the worst of Southern poverty and ignorance, both from his own upbringing—in "the ruralest of the rural South," he wrote, among people "from which is [sic] recruited our fundamentalists and often our Ku Klux folk"—and from two years of teaching in rural Mississippi. But Ph.D.s in psychology from Clark University and sociology from Columbia had convinced him that poverty could be attacked and attitudes changed. After teaching for eight years in his native Georgia, he had become head of the new School of Public Welfare (later the School of Social Work) at the University of North Carolina. Two years later, in 1922, he had founded the *Journal of Social Forces*, a dynamic and outspoken publication which Mencken called the most important journal the South had produced, and two years after that, in 1924, he had established in Chapel Hill the Institute for Research in Social Science. By the mid-1920s, the time of the Scopes trial, Odum had already given the South, as Mencken wrote, "a whiff of the true scientific spirit."[8] Later, in the 1930s, he became the acknowledged leader of Southern progressive forces, the man who kept in touch with virtually all other Southerners in the critical movement and directed a program for Southern change.

Despite his accomplishments early and late, Howard W. Odum is a somewhat enigmatic figure in twentieth-century Southern history—a man George B. Tindall has called "the most perceptive observer of

8. Howard W. Odum to Josephus Daniels, February 12, 1925 (copy); H. L. Mencken, "Beneath the Magnolias," Baltimore *Evening Sun*, October 20, 1924; H. L. Mencken, "The South Rebels Again," Chicago *Tribune*, December 7, 1924.

the Southern scene during the first half of the century,"[9] one who conceived plans for the South on a gigantic scale, but a man whose hopes and plans ultimately were not completely realized. He was that most versatile of Southerners, both social scientist and humanist, realist and romantic, author of dry sociological textbook and moving personal memoir, committed at once to the laboratory and to the soil. Even as a sociologist he seemed multidimensional: as a graduate student he had been influenced both by William Graham Sumner—particularly Sumner's belief in unyielding folkways—and by his mentor at Columbia, Franklin Giddings, who held a much more optimistic view of man's capacity for change and reform. Later, at Chapel Hill, he counted among his correspondents both harsh Southern critics such as Mencken and staunch Southern defenders such as Davidson. It is significant that Mencken among others saw the beginning of the Southern *literary* renascence in the arrival of a sociologist, Odum, at Chapel Hill—because, Mencken contended and Donald Davidson reluctantly agreed, the new critical spirit, the sociological impulse, strongly influenced Southern literature of the 1920s. And, in 1929, when twenty-nine-year-old W. J. Cash of Charlotte began seriously to contemplate a book on the Southern mind, it was Odum to whom he wrote a lengthy letter outlining the plans for such a book and asking for advice.[10]

Odum considered himself, then, not the South's press agent, as Mims ultimately did, but rather its diagnostician and healer. "The South needs criticism, and severe criticism," he wrote in the 1920s, and it needed in particular the kind of treatment Odum would dispense. In the *Journal of Social Forces* he first wrote his prescription for Southern ills. Although *Social Forces* was, in fact, a thoroughly respectable, often dry, sociological publication, it contained a sociology for the South. And if it looked like a "government report," Mencken wrote, "inside it is full of dynamite, for what it presumes to do is to

9. George B. Tindall, "The Significance of Howard W. Odum to Southern History: A Preliminary Estimate," *Journal of Southern History*, XXIV (August, 1958), 307. For excellent discussions of Odum's role in twentieth-century Southern affairs, see also Sosna, *In Search of the Silent South*; Michael O'Brien, *The Idea of the American South, 1920–1941* (Baltimore, 1979), 31–93; Richard H. King, *A Southern Renaissance: The Cultural Awakening of the American South, 1930–1955* (New York, 1980), 39–51. For biographical information about Odum, I rely principally on Wayne D. Brazil, "Howard W. Odum: The Building Years, 1884–1930" (Ph.D. dissertation, Harvard University, 1975).
10. H. L. Mencken, "The South Astir," *Virginia Quarterly Review*, XI (January, 1935), 50; W. J. Cash to Howard W. Odum, November 13, 1929.

upset all the assumptions upon which the thinking of North Carolina, and indeed of the whole South, has been grounded since the civil war, and to set up a new theory of the true, the good, and the beautiful upon a foundation of known and provable facts."[11]

Such was a radical goal, and Odum's commitment to it—his determination, he wrote in 1923, to present "dynamic stuff," to discover "what constitutes our present day 'poor white trash,'" and especially to look critically at the Southern clergy—earned him the scorn of many Tar Heels. "Such teaching might be indorsed [sic] in Nihilistic Russia," wrote a North Carolina minister after Odum printed two articles dealing critically with Christianity, but "finds no place in Christian North Carolina." Odum's *Journal of Social Forces* was being used, wrote another, "for what is, to all intents and purposes . . . infidel propaganda by Northern writers." Odum, the rural Southerner of Methodist stock, was genuinely disturbed by such criticism: "If . . . the methods [Southern ministers] have used with all untruths and threats . . . is Christianity," he wrote in 1925, "I don't think I can be either a Southerner or a Christian."[12]

Odum attacked Southern ills not only in *Social Forces* but also, beginning in 1925, in a series of books. In *Southern Pioneers in Social Interpretation* (1925) he brought together a collection of essays in praise of Woodrow Wilson, Walter Hines Page, and other progressive Southerners and wrote a forceful introduction, "A Southern Promise," in which he accused the South of being, on the one hand, "hot-headed, emotional, unthinking in its attitude toward many questions and toward those who do not agree with its opinions or traditions, or those who do not approve of its conduct" and, on the other, "boastful and superficial with reference to its achievements." The South was virtually a closed society, he maintained, "afraid, not of negro domination, but of itself, of each other, afraid to speak the truth or act justly because of what the folks will say." The South denied "freedom of speech": "Restrictions encompass the simple, sincere, courageous

11. Howard W. Odum, "A More Articulate South," *Journal of Social Forces*, II (September, 1924), 730; Mencken, "The South Rebels Again."

12. Odum to H. L. Mencken, September 12, 1923, in H. L. Mencken Papers, New York Public Library, New York; J. L. Guthrie to the Raleigh *Times*, March 4, 1925; Odum to J. S. Foster, March 7, 1925 (copy). For an account of Odum's problems with North Carolina ministers, see Willard B. Gatewood, Jr., "Embattled Scholar: Howard W. Odum and the Fundamentalists, 1925–1927," *Journal of Southern History*, XXXI (November, 1965), 375–92.

telling of the truth about the South, its people, its history, its tasks,"
and an "atmosphere of fear . . . permeates the whole [Southern] body
politic."[13] In so writing, Odum both recognized the Silent South
which Cable had earlier identified and described the savage ideal before Cash gave it a name.

Despite his protestations, Odum at times rather enjoyed his role as
disturber of the peace, not only stirring up North Carolina ministers
but, as Gerald Johnson wrote, driving textile manufacturers "into
spasms of terror." By 1926, however, as he wrote a friend, he had
come to sympathize with those Southerners "who feel that propaganda on the South is one of the chief indoor sports of unstable folk
in other climes" and was himself "provoke[d]" by "the North's attitude towards the South . . . its wild opinions and judgements about
us." One factor in Odum's reassessment, just as it had been in Davidson's, was the Scopes trial. He could share none of his friend Mencken's glee—"On to Dayton," Mencken had written him, "The greatest
trial since that before Pilate!"—and after the trial he wrote in *Social
Forces*, "What I found at Dayton was more pathos than joke, more
futility than fighting, more tragedy than comedy." His more compassionate attitude toward the South was reflected as well in a semi-
autobiographical work, *An American Epoch* (1930), which expressed
more clearly than anything to that time his deepest feelings about the
South.[14]

An American Epoch spans four generations, from the early nineteenth century to the early twentieth, and the first of the four generations was represented by "the old Major" and "Uncle John," thinly
veiled portraits of Odum's own grandfathers—his mother's father, a
slaveholding planter, and his father's father, a nearly illiterate farmer.
Their sons and daughters had been the architects and builders of the
post-Reconstruction South, their grandchildren—Odum's generation—"the leaders and workers of the first third of the twentieth century" (p. x), and their great-grandchildren the future Southern leaders, the "Next Generation" to which Odum dedicated his book. The

13. Howard W. Odum (ed.), *Southern Pioneers in Social Interpretation* (Chapel Hill,
1925), 16, 17, 21.
14. Gerald W. Johnson in the Baltimore *Evening Sun*, September 24, 1926, quoted in
Tindall, "Howard W. Odum," 291; Howard W. Odum to Julia Harris, January 31, 1926
(copy); H. L. Mencken to Howard W. Odum [June, 1925]; Howard W. Odum, "The
Duel to the Death," *Journal of Social Forces*, IV (September, 1925), 189; Howard W. Odum,
An American Epoch: Southern Portraiture in the National Picture (New York, 1930).

book drew roughly on Odum's family history, at one point referring to "a grandson of the old Major" who went north "for his advanced degree" (p. 68) and turned to pondering the South. But interwoven in his story of the two families is a social history of the South. Uncle John looked to the future and his sons prospered after the war; the Major lost three sons in the war and his daughters married Uncle John's sons who were in the ascendancy. In telling the story of the families, Odum described Southern religion, politics, education, agriculture, industry, and folk life of the middle and late nineteenth and early twentieth centuries. Only in his remarks on Southern religion and the Southern aversion to honest examination was he deeply critical. He had written Mencken that in parts of his book he had "used considerable of the Menckeniana [and] toned it down," and undoubtedly he referred to his remarks on Southern evangelical sects. Religious revivals, he wrote, "often joined hands with the Ku Klux Klan. . . . The revivals came also to be a fanning breeze for the fires of bigotry and intolerance, and the revivalists used a powerful mob psychology to warp the minds and souls of thousands of children and youth who were never to recover." Odum had become hostile to militant Southern religion not only because of his own encounters with ministers over *Social Forces* but also because of Dayton and, equally disturbing to him, the anti-Catholicism manifest in the campaign against Al Smith in 1928. His chapter on religion in *An American Epoch*, Gerald Johnson wrote him, was "more damaging" than Mencken's irreverent *Treatise on the Gods*.[15]

But in most other respects, *An American Epoch* was a book Donald Davidson could have written. For the sturdy plain white, the "middle Southerner" Odum called him, was the hero of his epic, and his portrait of Uncle John, illiterate yet happy and heroic, differed little from the portraits drawn in the late 1920s and early 1930s by Davidson and his fellow Agrarians Frank Owsley and Andrew Lytle. Uncle John loved hymns and ballads and fiddling, and if he felt superior to the Negro he also treated him kindly. Uncle John was Owsley's proud yeoman farmer brought to life, the creation of the folk society, the representative man of the Old South.

But a writer whose work Odum's *American Epoch* more closely resembled, whose efforts he anticipated, was his young acquaintance

15. Howard W. Odum to H. L. Mencken, May 13, 1930 (copy); Gerald W. Johnson to Howard W. Odum, April 5, 1930.

Wilbur Cash. It was while Odum was writing *An American Epoch* that he had received Cash's lengthy letter outlining a book on the "Southern mind" and discussing, among other subjects, Southern cultural barrenness and the disproportionate power of the "holy men." Odum had replied within a week, advising Cash to go ahead with the book, but wondering whether he could make his book dramatically interesting and at the same time avoid generalization—a problem Odum was facing in his own book. In his letter Odum had also stressed the humble origins of most Southern "aristocrats": "Many of the southerners who were reputed to have a plantation and leisure still ate dinner in their shirt-sleeves and washed on the back porch and let the chickens roost in the top of the trees in the yard. Or did they? . . . Many of the beautiful old homes and great families grew up from log cabins in the pioneer wilderness, enlarged and then rebuilt and then entirely transcended by the big house."[16] It is possible that Cash had already planned to emphasize these points before Odum wrote him—and before Odum's description in his book of the prospective Southern planter who had come into the Cotton Kingdom and had built "first the log house, then the wings to it in the back and on the side. Then . . . boards and columns and paint and its gradual evolution into the 'big house' and of the farm into the plantation" (p. 19). In any case, one finds this same insistence on the humble origins of the aristocrat and the growth of the big house out of the log cabin in the book that Cash published in 1941 as *The Mind of the South*.

Odum also anticipated Cash in his narrative informality, his method of relating Southern history by focusing on representative characters (particularly his "middle" Southerner who suggested Cash's "man at the center"), his emphasis on the paternalistic nature of textile mill owners of the late nineteenth century, and his indictment of Southern religious excess, self-deception, and intolerance of self-criticism. He treated the same time period as Cash, the early nineteenth century through the first third of the twentieth, and although, like Cash, he insisted that "there were many Souths, yet *the* South" (p. 330), he also, like Cash, was concerned largely with the heavily Protestant, cotton-growing Piedmont. Tidewater, mountains, the old Southwest, Catholic southern Louisiana: all are virtually ignored by both Odum and Cash.

16. W. J. Cash to Howard W. Odum, November 13, 1929; Odum to Cash, November 20, 1929 (copy).

An American Epoch is hardly *The Mind of the South*. Odum lacked Cash's vision and imagination, stylistic resources, and single-minded devotion to a task. But one does not venture far in suggesting that, in many respects, *The Mind of the South* is the kind of book Odum wanted to write when he undertook *An American Epoch*—a book exploring and explaining the meaning of the South and the author's own relationship to it. Odum would not tell about the South with the relentless honesty of Cash because Odum was a Southern leader and public figure as well as a writer, and telling the entire truth might have jeopardized his other work. There was, to repeat, something of Edwin Mims in him, the desire to please all Southerners, and if one is to judge by the reviews of *An American Epoch* he did precisely that in 1930. Historian Holland Thompson called it "the most important book which has come out of the South in many years," and other Southern scholars and journalists joined in the praise. Almost alone in his disapproval was Stringfellow Barr, editor of the *Virginia Quarterly Review*, who wrote that "Southerners like Mr. Odum believe and hope [the South] is catching up. Southerners like myself don't believe the parade is worth catching up with." Odum's genuine bafflement at Barr's "absurd misinterpretation" anticipated his attitude for the decade to come. "How one section can keep on trying to build a wall around itself and be different from the rest of the world is more than I can yet see," he wrote a friend. However, "I am mighty glad the discussion will get started, because it will be of the essence of current interest and discussion."[17] Odum was correct about the discussion, but he had not identified the foe. For one month after *An American Epoch* appeared, the Southern Agrarian manifesto, *I'll Take My Stand*, was published. The North Carolinian was to discover that the enemy lay not across the Dividing Line but across the Appalachians.

Odum had described his method in *An American Epoch* as a "new romantic realism" (p. x), which was no more of a paradox than many other of his concepts. He had intended to write a "critical analysis based upon sympathetic understanding of facts" (p. x). He had wanted, as well, to write a book which stressed the "national" quality of the Southern experience, and he had concluded by insisting that "the story of Uncle John, the old Major, and their descendants was, first of all, an American story" (p. 328). To underscore the fact, he had

17. Stringfellow Barr, "Catching Up with America," New York *Herald Tribune*, October 26, 1930; Howard W. Odum to Sydnor Alexander, October 27, 1930 (copy).

called his story an "American" epoch and had given it the subtitle *Southern Portraiture in the National Picture.* Two chapters had dealt specifically with North-South relations and images, and a third, "Regional Range and Power," had also treated the South in a national context. Clearly, Odum was moving away from the old Southern sectionalism and toward the movement with which he was to be associated the remainder of his life—Southern regionalism.

He formulated his ideas just before Frederick Jackson Turner published his monumental work, *The Significance of Sections in American History* (1932), and although he acknowledged the historical significance of sections as Turner described them, he also believed sectionalism in the twentieth century to be an antiquated, even dangerous concept. It viewed "the region first and the nation afterwards," whereas Odum's regionalism placed "the nation first, making the national culture and welfare the final arbiter." Regionalism was of more interest to the sociologist, as sectionalism was to the historian; and although Odum had distrusted the regional approach to Southern problems in the 1920s, preferring a state by state approach, by the early 1930s he had become committed to it.[18] Rigorous planning, he believed, was necessary to lift the South out of its social and economic morass, but first it was necessary to document the depth of its problem.

This Odum did in his most ambitious work, *Southern Regions of the United States* (1936), the product of a comprehensive regional study which he had directed—and a work in which the author was addicted to the table and the chart just as fully as the "Hated Helper" had been three-quarters of a century before. Odum measured Southern per capita income, agricultural production, industrial output, welfare expenditures, highway construction, and some six hundred other categories and found the South deficient in nearly every one—except homicide. On a map labeled "Rank of States Based on Twenty-three Cultural Tables" every Southern state wore black, indicating the lowest classification; only two non-Southern states, West Virginia and New Mexico, were also black. The picture Odum painted with statistics was a dismal one: the South as impoverished and troubled land. But it was also a land blessed with natural resources—rivers, plentiful

18. Howard W. Odum to the Southern Regional Commission, February 13, 1934 (copy). See also "From Sectionalism to Regionalism," in Howard W. Odum and Harry Estill Moore, *American Regionalism* (New York, 1938), x, 35, 39, 43; and O'Brien, *The Idea of the American South,* 47–48, 60–68.

rainfall, minerals, forests—and its task was to use those resources wisely. The key to its success was industrial and agricultural planning, social planning, even "planning strategy in the field of cultural relations."[19] "Reconstruction" was the word Odum chose to describe his master plan to reshape the South, an ill-chosen word and a strange one for a man with a sense of Southern history. He outlined two "six-year priority schedules" which emphasized land utilization, industrial experimentation, and legislative processes. Only on race would he make haste slowly: "It is too big a burden to place upon one or two generations the task of changing the powerful folkways of the centuries at one stroke" (p. 483). But if folkways were powerful, so potentially were "technic ways," revised attitudes brought about by changes in society. Thus the South must carefully utilize "social planning" to ensure the Negro "a greater participation in the social control of the region" (p. 485). In the following two decades, as he became a cautious integrationist, Odum would increasingly consider the power of technic ways. But in 1936 he still advocated a social system that would be separate and truly equal.

Odum recognized that Southerners were "not ready for social planning," were "always skeptical of too much theorizing and experimentation" (p. 577). Yet his book, which recommended such planning, was received surprisingly well. It was not the planning itself that upset some Southern readers so much as Odum's pronouncement that there no longer existed "a regional area or culture which, when analyzed, can be measured in terms of what is currently called 'the South'" (p. ix). That is, regionally, there was a Southeast and a Southwest—but there was no South. Even one Southern progressive who usually supported Odum, Nell Battle Lewis of the Raleigh *News and Observer*, angrily responded, "The South continues to exist for me. . . . Dr. Odum can keep his 'social science' and be damned, and I shall keep the half-mystical tenderness of October in North Carolina." But on the whole *Southern Regions* was received as a relatively objective compendium of useful facts and statistics chronicling the Southern condition. Only Donald Davidson recognized that so apparently moderate and rational a book was motivated by a deeper impulse. "The pages of this book are calm," he wrote, "but it takes only a little reading between the lines to sense an air of tension and indeed

19. Howard W. Odum, *Southern Regions of the United States* (Chapel Hill, 1936), 199.

desperation."[20] Davidson was correct. Odum feared the South in the mid-1930s would retreat from his cooperative regionalism into divisive sectionalism, and he believed that only a book which brought the facts into the open would awaken Southerners to the need for careful regional planning.

In many respects Odum reached his peak of influence with *Southern Regions*. He would live another eighteen years, would continue to espouse his theory of regionalism, but he would steadily lose influence after the late thirties. The Council on Southern Regional Development, which he had conceived in the early thirties to study and attack Southern social problems, failed to materialize, and its failure was perhaps his greatest disappointment.[21] He also lost the deft touch he had earlier possessed for attracting Northern foundation money. Most discouraging, he lost the support of some Southerners who had earlier been in his camp, partly because he sometimes found it difficult to share leadership. Although he continued to hold significant positions—president of the Interracial Commission in 1937 and first president of the Southern Regional Council in 1943—he was reluctant to support like-minded organizations which he perceived as rivals. He refused to attend the Southern Conference for Human Welfare in Birmingham in 1938, allegedly because he thought Communists were behind the meeting, although many of his fellow Southern liberals did attend and Frank Porter Graham of Chapel Hill was named president of the group. He was also critical of the NAACP, of Negro leaders Walter F. White and A. Philip Randolph, and of Gunnar Myrdal, whose *American Dilemma* (1944) had looked askance at liberal Southerners and had ignored Odum's *Southern Regions*.

The optimist of *An American Epoch* had grown increasingly pessimistic about the South. "As I see it," Odum wrote Will W. Alexander in 1934, "we are on the eve of undoing practically all that we have tried to do. . . . These are not merely academic distinctions, but they lie at the very heart of the South's parting of the ways again." In the early 1940s he became even gloomier. World War II, he believed, further revived sectionalism and increased racial tension to the extent that the South of the 1940s was even less open and tolerant than

---

20. Nell Battle Lewis, quoted in John C. McKinney and Linda Brookover Bourque, "The Changing South: National Incorporation of a Region," *American Sociological Review*, XXXVI (June, 1971), 410; Davidson, *The Attack on Leviathan*, 287–88.

21. See Tindall, "Howard W. Odum," 299–300.

the South of the 1920s. The Southern racial situation during the war years, he wrote, constituted the greatest domestic crisis "since the period a hundred years earlier, which led to the War between the States," but in his book on the subject, *Race and Rumors of Race* (1943), Odum suggested no clear way out.[22] Although he reported and in many cases attempted to defuse rumors about racial tension and violence in the South, and was sympathetic to the plight of the Negro, he took no firm stand. Rather he exhibited an excess of moderation, a lack of resolution, a surprising failure of nerve for a Southerner who had boldly challenged Southern orthodoxy in the 1920s.

But in the midst of his pessimism of the 1940s, in his retreat from the public prominence he had enjoyed during the previous two decades, Odum wrote a book which, although little known, reveals perhaps more than any other his deepest feelings about the South. *The Way of the South* (1947) seems at first a curious way for a social scientist to end his career. Containing few blueprints for Southern progress, it was rather a lyrical celebration of the Southern folk. But, in fact, in *The Way of the South* Odum's career had simply come full circle: he had begun as a romantic, a rather unscientific celebrator of the folk, black and white, and he ended the same way. The hard social science had come in between. Odum's initial interest had been in the classics, then in the folk songs of the Mississippi Negroes among whom he lived from 1904 to 1908. His first published article in 1909 had been "Religious Folk-Songs of the Southern Negro," and his first dissertation, in psychology at Clark University, had also been on Negro folk songs. Even during his period of hard-hitting social criticism in the 1920s, he had helped compile the volume *Negro Workaday Songs* and had written a folk trilogy based on the experiences of an itinerant black laborer he had met. The books *Rainbow Round My Shoulder (1928)*, *Wings on My Feet* (1929), and *Cold Blue Moon* (1931) depicted the wanderings of Odum's "Black Ulysses"; a seeming departure from romantic portrayal of the Negro, it was nevertheless in its way a romanticizing of the Negro's condition. In the books Ulysses told his own story in his own words and through his own songs, recalling his childhood, war experiences, drinking, gambling, and women, all a part of a rootless and violent life. Mencken in the *American Mercury*

22. Howard W. Odum to Will W. Alexander, February 8, 1934 (copy); Howard W. Odum, *Race and Rumors of Race* (Chapel Hill, 1943), 165. See also Howard W. Odum, "Social Changes in the South," *Journal of Politics*, X (May, 1948), 242–58.

called *Rainbow Round My Shoulder* "an epic in the grand manner and one of the most eloquent ever produced in America." *Wings on My Feet* he believed even better, and after reading *Cold Blue Moon* he exclaimed, "What a trilogy! It will be read for many years."[23]

The point is that Odum was never exclusively, or perhaps not even first and foremost, a realistic social scientist; and when he wrote *The Way of the South* he was only returning to his initial romanticism. A book originally cast in the mold of *An American Epoch*, a social history of the South, it became as Odum proceeded much more visionary than the earlier work. Its subtitle, *Toward the Regional Balance of America*, and perhaps the discussion of regional planning in the final section, might have suggested the social scientist at work, but not even the most fervent Agrarian could have detected the stench of social science about the rest of it. An unashamed celebration of the Southern land and the Southern folk, *The Way of the South* takes its inspiration not from William Graham Sumner or Franklin Giddings—but rather from Walt Whitman. That the Whitman influence was conscious is demonstrated by the several references to the poet and several quotations from *Leaves of Grass*. Odum's story of Southern black and white, he writes, "needs the hand of a double Walt Whitman"; he refers to "Walt Whitman's dream" and on the final page of the book urges young Americans to take their inspiration from "America's two greatest prophets of understanding and cooperation, Walt Whitman and Abraham Lincoln."[24]

Equally significant, it is Whitman whose speech rhythms and rambling catalogues Odum seeks to duplicate throughout the work. From his first chapter on "Nature"—the very capitalization suggests the sociologist less than the transcendentalist—he is given to Whitmanesque catalogues, the recitation of names particularly of Indian derivation: "Call the long roll of mountains . . . the Alleghenies and the

23. Howard W. Odum, "Religious Folk-Songs of the Southern Negro," *Journal of Religious Psychology and Education*, III (July, 1909), 265–365; Howard W. Odum, and Guy B. Johnson, *Negro Workaday Songs* (Chapel Hill, 1926); Howard W. Odum, *Rainbow Round My Shoulder* (Indianapolis, 1928); Howard W. Odum, *Wings on My Feet* (Indianapolis, 1929); Howard W. Odum, *Cold Blue Moon* (Indianapolis, 1931); H. L. Mencken, "Black Boy," *American Mercury*, XV (September, 1928), 126; H. L. Mencken, quoted in Richard H. Thornton to Odum, May 31, 1929; H. L. Mencken, quoted in Howard W. Odum to D. L. Chambers, November 4, 1930 (copy).

24. Howard W. Odum, *The Way of the South: Toward the Regional Balance of America* (New York, 1947), 45, 11, 341.

Blue Ridge, the Great Smokies . . . the towering tops . . . Chichwal-
nercky, Kissimee, Pakataka and Shandoken, Catacton and Massanu-
ton. . . . And then a thousand rivers rising in the hills . . . the Potomac and the Rappahannock, the York and the James, the Roanoke
and the Santee, the Peedee and the Savannah, the Tennessee and the
Cumberland" (pp. 5–6). Not only mountains and rivers he includes
but trees, flowers, animals, birds, and, whether with Whitman in
mind or not, even varieties of grass, all in the cadences of the poet:
"White oak and red oak, post oak and water oak / Sweet gum and
black gum, sourwood and mulberry, / White spruce and red spruce,
river birch and yellow / . . . And how many hundred species of flow-
ering trees and shrubs? / . . . Riotous blooming rhododendron, thou-
sand-acred gardens of Appalachia" (p. 7). Nor did Whitman's repetition of initial words and sounds escape him: "Of the families of the
Lily and the Heath and the Mint, / Of the crawfoot and the poppy
and the iris" (p. 8). "The orders of the woodpeckers and cuckoos; /
The orders of the cooing pigeons and doves" (p. 10). And at times, as
in Odum's rousing tribute to Southern mineral wealth, the result is
less sublime than ridiculous: "Aluminum and arsenic, barium and be-
ryllium, bismuth and boron" (p. 14). Those of the Fugitive-Agrarians
who bothered to read it were undoubtedly amused: such was the
verse of a sociologist-turned-poet, this Whitman with a clipboard.

But it is not so much the artistic merit as the intent of Odum's venture into verse that is significant: he resorted to his rambling catalogues for the same reason Whitman did—he desired to be inclusive
above all, to speak for Southerners of all ranks and stations. It was not
the first time he had attempted to speak with the bardic voice—*An
American Epoch* contained occasional Whitmanesque flourishes, and
Whitman himself, Mencken once proclaimed, "would have wal-
lowed" in *Rainbow Round My Shoulder*—but it was his boldest such attempt.[25] Falling far short of being a Southern "Song of Myself," *The
Way of the South* nonetheless had at its center a persona who embraced
the entire South, and it also demonstrated the same desire for con-
creteness which had motivated the true Southern poets who were his
adversaries. In the middle part of the book he had returned to the
material of *An American Epoch*, reintroducing Uncle John and the old

25. Mencken, "Black Boy," 126.

Major. Only at the end did he resort to the language of social science, and even then interrupted his discussion of planning with lines from Whitman.

Odum died seven years after the publication of *The Way of the South*. At his death he left two major uncompleted manuscripts, "Mid-Century South," which was to be a "New Southern Regions," and a memoir, an autobiographical novel entitled "White Sands of Bethlehem." The latter work, Odum's daughter later said, was to have been his "magnum opus," the story, told more imaginatively than *An American Epoch*, of the rural middle-class Georgians from whom he had sprung.[26] Odum, thus, was one in that series of Southern interpreters from Edmund Ruffin through Walter Hines Page to W. J. Cash whose place in history is ensured by other successes but whose goal to excel in belles-lettres was never realized. Nor at his death in 1954, just six months after the Supreme Court decision he accepted with ambivalence, was his reputation as an academic sociologist as lofty as it once had been. Like Edwin Mims in the 1920s, he had, at least by the modern standard of his discipline, outlived his time. But if, as Faulkner once suggested, one's greatness is measured by the difficulty of one's undertaking, Odum was among the greatest of Southerners. His design for the South, his plans for land utilization, use of resources, and industrialization were schemes more ambitious and more encompassing than those of any other private Southern citizen in the twentieth century. He did not want to standardize the South and destroy its folk culture, as Donald Davidson sometimes thought and as Odum's own sociological vocabulary—and his occasional tone of condescension toward the "folk"—sometimes suggested. Rather he wanted to purge the South of pettiness and prejudice so that the cherished folk culture, black and white, could flourish. As an essentially nineteenth-century man, a romantic, for a time he actually seemed to believe it could be done.

IF HOWARD ODUM of Chapel Hill was the sociologist who would be poet, Donald Davidson of Nashville was the poet whose concerns during the latter half of his life seemed more sociological and political than poetic. Before Dayton, he had been one of the Fugitive poets of

26. Mary Frances Odum Schinhan to the author, December 2, 1977.

Vanderbilt University who had, as they declared in the first issue of their magazine, wanted to flee "from nothing faster than from the high-caste Brahmins of the Old South." After Dayton, he became more polemicist than poet—an unashamed admirer and defender of the traditional South, the most committed of the Southern Agrarians, the "organizer and energizer" (as Louis Rubin has written) for *I'll Take My Stand* (1930), and a man who in the three decades after the Agrarian manifesto led a Southern assault against social science, reform, abstraction, big government, and racial integration. Davidson was a man of intense loyalties and deep-seated suspicions, given at various times both to exultation and depression. "Don, you have a gift for persecution and martyrdom," Allen Tate once wrote his friend,[27] and he was not far wrong. After Davidson broke with Tate and Ransom— or rather, he believed, they broke with him, for they were the ones in the late 1930s who retreated from the Agrarianism to which Davidson held fast—he became a somewhat lonely and melancholy man, even at times an angry one. As long as he had been a part of an intellectual and spiritual community, he had thrived. It was only in the mid-1930s, when the enthusiasm of his comrades waned and Davidson felt he was fighting nearly alone, that he became most resolute and most outspoken; and in the 1940s and 1950s the resoluteness turned to defiance and sometimes bitterness.

Donald Davidson was not Edmund Ruffin, but he was perhaps the nearest the twentieth century has come to a Ruffin in his wholehearted and lasting commitment to the Southern cause. In several of his essays of the 1930s, particularly "Lands That Were Golden" and "Expedients vs. Principles," he tried to accomplish what Ruffin had attempted in his novel *Anticipations of the Future*—to seize the offensive, turn the tables on the Northern accusers, and align the South with the West and the rest of the American "hinterland" against the

27. "Foreword," *Fugitive*, I (Spring, 1922), 2; Louis D. Rubin, Jr., *The Wary Fugitives: Four Poets and the South* (Baton Rouge, 1978), 137; Allen Tate to Donald Davidson, December 4, 1942, in John Tyree Fain and Thomas Daniel Young (eds.), *The Literary Correspondence of Donald Davidson and Allen Tate* (Athens, Ga., 1974), 328–29. For an excellent discussion of Davidson's life and work, see Rubin, *The Wary Fugitives*, 136–250, 256–66. Other studies of Davidson on which I draw are Thomas Daniel Young and M. Thomas Inge, *Donald Davidson* (New York, 1971); Louise Cowan, *The Fugitive Group* (Baton Rouge, 1959); M. E. Bradford, "A Durable Fire: Donald Davidson and the Profession of Letters," *Southern Review*, New Ser., III (Summer, 1967), 721–41; Richard Gray, *The Literature of Memory: Modern Writers of the American South* (Baltimore, 1977), 94–105; and O'Brien, *The Idea of the American South*, 185–209.

urban Northeast. As Ruffin in his *Anticipations*, Davidson made the urban North the "abnormal" and thus the aberrant society, the South the sane and normal one. Ruffin in his novel had imagined and described a Southern assault on the North Atlantic states. Davidson named his most important book *The Attack on Leviathan*: not a "Defense" or "Vindication" of the South but an "Attack" on the industrial North and on an expanding federal government which drew its values and assumptions from science and technology. Davidson later said that *I'll Take My Stand* itself had been part of a Southern offensive: "In championing the South we were abandoning the defensive attitude. . . . We were rejecting the defeatism of Walter Hines Page and Henry Grady and the servile collaborationism of the modern Southern liberals. For the first time since Lee's invasion of Pennsylvania in 1863 we were taking the South into an offensive movement. We were attacking, not retreating." [28] Although he included his fellow Agrarians in his description, in fact by the late 1930s only he still held the offensive. And even that offensive was somewhat illusory: *Could* he successfully attack a modern American society in which Leviathan had already triumphed? The situation facing him was very different from that confronting the Southern apologist of 1855 or 1860. Ruffin had written with the confidence that the South would indeed triumph, would become a nation not only in spirit but in fact. He had anticipated the *future*. But Davidson, writing at a time when the South had already lost, was forced to look backward. There was no meaningful offensive to seize, and for this reason his attack was largely in vain.

Among the many changes that had occurred in the South of the 1920s was a shift in the balance of power between the Southern apologist and the Southern critic, and by the late 1920s, for the first time, the apologist was outnumbered, or at least overshadowed, in his own intellectual community—that is, among influential Southern scholars, journalists, and shapers of thought. Within that Southern community the critic had formerly been the outnumbered and embattled one. Helper, Cable, Walter Hines Page: each had been at variance with "official" Southern thought (although each progressively less so) and each had left the South for the Northeast. But with the 1920s and the great assault from the North, the situation changed. The majority

28. Donald Davidson, *Southern Writers in the Modern World* (Athens, Ga., 1958), 51.

of that Southern community of "enlightened" writers and thinkers, that body of Southerners who wrote in national journals and in leading Southern newspapers, declared itself on the side of progress and liberalism and turned its back on Southern tradition—as, indeed, even Davidson and his Nashville colleagues had in the early 1920s before they reexamined that tradition. Suddenly, in the 1920s, the traditionalists were the embattled ones—to such a degree that it seemed nearly inconceivable that, in 1930, a group of well-educated Southerners of sound mind, including two Rhodes scholars, would undertake a defense of the traditional South. Davidson's task, thus, was different from that of any Southern apologist before him. Fitzhugh had issued his *Sociology for the South*, and Edward Pollard, Alfred Taylor Bledsoe, Charles Colcock Jones, and Thomas Nelson Page their works, anticipating a largely favorable reception in Southern newspapers and journals—the "official" approval and in some cases the adoration of the Southern community. Davidson, Tate, Ransom, and the other Agrarians took their stand in 1930 knowing they were going *against* that "official" enlightened Southern position, and Davidson, nearly alone after 1936, continued to write with such an understanding. He was doubly rejected—forced on the defensive not only by national opinion, which had been a familiar enough position for the Southern apologist of any time, but also by the very South for which he presumed to speak. The critic was in the ascendancy, the apologist in decline.

If Davidson's beleaguered state stemmed partly from this rejection by the Southern intellectual community, his resentment of sociology and sociologists in particular stemmed from his belief that those infected with the "sociological-journalistic" spirit had by and large assumed leadership in that community. They had followed the lead of the Northern crusaders of the 1920s, those "sociological missionaries" who had arrived "almost daily from the slum-laboratories of Chicago and New York." But Davidson's rage against social science went deeper than that. As he himself once remarked in a letter to John Donald Wade—a letter that wound up in Odum's hands—"natural differences" existed "between sociologist and professor of English." Indeed, there had long been, not only to Davidson but to many other literary humanists, something rather sinister about the social scientist, or the scientist of any variety. One thinks of Hawthorne and his mad scientists, those who cared infinitely more for knowledge than for man. Such a suspicion seemed to be held, in particular, by the twentieth-century Southern writer. Among Faulkner's least attractive characters are those driven by what Davidson called the "sociological impulse"—one thinks of Joanna Burden in *Light in August* with her commitment to righting social wrongs. One also considers Flannery O'Connor's Rayber, in *The Violent Bear It Away*, the epitome of the secularist committed to the analysis of man. Davidson's fellow Agrarian, Ransom, declared himself in 1934 "habitually a little irritated with sociologists" and saw sociology as a "struggling infant science" whose devotees did "not always bother much about a background." Richmond Croom Beatty and George Marion O'Donnell, writing in the *American Review* in 1935, also attacked sociology. But Donald Davidson, both literary humanist and Southern writer in the modern world, feared social science far more than did any of his contemporaries. One imagines him shuddering at the description of Odum and his fellow workers in Chapel Hill given—and intended favorably—by Jonathan Daniels in 1941: "[Odum] took us out into a big central hall where maps and charts showed the results of studies about the people in North Carolina and wide regions around it. . . . All around it, in offices able research [sociologists] were assembling . . . data." [29] Davidson blanched at the prospect. Man, below the Potomac, was not the proper study of mankind.

But Davidson's distaste for social science stemmed as well, one suspects, from the language of social science, the jargon which traditionally has disturbed the sensibilities of the word-conscious humanist. Odum's stylistic bumbling in particular must have grated on the ears of so gifted a stylist as Davidson. "I have a way of not making myself very clear," Odum announced to a friend in 1926, and it was a conclusion his readers had already reached. [30] The spirit of Whitman might have inspired him, but as a stylist he was a close cousin of Theodore Dreiser. The wonder, given Odum's insensitivity to language and, what's more, his *attempt* to use language poetically—as well as his dedication to a reform that went deeply against Davidson's grain and

29. Donald Davidson, "'I'll Take My Stand': A History," *American Review*, V (Summer, 1935), 305; Donald Davidson to John Donald Wade, March 3, 1934, in Odum Papers; John Crowe Ransom, "Sociology and the Black Belt," *American Review*, IV (December, 1934), 148; Richmond Croom Beatty and George Marion O'Donnell, "The Tenant Farmer in the South," *American Review*, V (April, 1935), 82; Jonathan Daniels, *Tar Heels: A Portrait of North Carolina* (New York, 1941), 274.
30. Howard W. Odum to A. C. Barnes, December 6, 1926 (copy).

his acknowledged leadership of a rival school of Southern thought—
is that Davidson did not attack him in the 1930s and 1940s more often
than he did; and the reason Davidson did not—the reason he often focused his attack on Odum's ideas or his colleagues rather than
Odum himself—was, quite simply, that he rather liked the man. One
should not underestimate the power of personal cordiality to Davidson: with him, the personal often took precedence over the ideological. A man who had befriended him, such as Edwin Mims, he could
accept and defend although, as in Mims's case, he disagreed violently
with much of what his friend represented. Odum was not the friend
and mentor Mims was, but Odum did try to maintain a civil relationship with Davidson throughout the 1930s. The two men sniped at
each other in letters to friends and, in print, expressed disagreement
with each other's ideas, but the criticism would have been much more
frequent and damning had not both been committed to a personal
civility.

The surprising fact to one who reads the writings of Fugitive Donald
Davidson in the early 1920s is that he ever became an adversary of the
Chapel Hill group at all. A son of the New South—his middle name
was Grady, after the greatest of New South boosters—he had at-
tended Vanderbilt University and had returned there to teach after
World War I. As a Fugitive poet he had paid little attention to the
South, and in his book column in the Nashville *Tennessean*, "The Spyglass," he had voiced liberal Southern opinions—praising, prior to
July, 1925, such iconoclastic Southern magazines as the *Reviewer* of
Richmond and the *Double Dealer* of New Orleans, outspoken Southern rebels such as Odum, Gerald Johnson, and novelist Frances Newman, and on occasion even Mencken. Also in his February 1, 1925,
column he had called the *Journal of Social Forces* a "force on the side of
liberalism and clear thinking." The next month he had praised the
new Southern "mood of self-analysis and self-criticism" and had declared, "Nothing is more necessary to the South at this stage of its
development than the kind of criticism which men like Gerald Johnson, Addison Hibbard [professor of English at the University of North
Carolina], and Paul Green are beginning in the pages of 'The Reviewer.'" Only a month before the Scopes trial he had expressed a
Mimsian concern that Tennessee might be embarrassed, and the very
week of the trial he had commended Mencken for the number of

Southerners who appeared in the *American Mercury*. His personal correspondence with Tate demonstrated a distaste for Southern conservatism, and his letters to Hibbard and Green hailed the new Southern spirit. He was "tremendously happy to hear," he wrote Hibbard in 1924, that the *Reviewer*, which had moved from Richmond to Chapel Hill in 1924, was "to be continued by you North Carolina live wires," and in February, 1925, he wrote Green praising a *Reviewer* editorial which had criticized Southern traditionalism and called for social criticism.[31] Davidson appeared to be a bona fide liberated Southerner. If he did not actually carry a copy of the *American Mercury* around under his arm, as Tate did, he did send his poetry to Mencken.

Then came Dayton, and, as Davidson later wrote, the Scopes trial, "with its jeering accompaniment of large-scale mockery directed against Tennessee and the South, broke in upon our literary concerns like a midnight alarm." For himself and Ransom "the Dayton episode dramatized, more ominously than any other event easily could, how difficult it was to be a Southerner in the twentieth century, and how much more difficult to be a Southerner and also a writer." "It was not the sole cause of change," he said later, "but from about that time Ransom, Tate, Warren, and I began to remember and haul up for consideration the assumptions that, as members of the Fugitive group, we had not much bothered to examine." The trial "started a boiling controversy, and started a reconsideration."[32]

The change in Davidson's attitude after 1925 is indeed astounding. His earlier praise of the Chapel Hill liberals turned into sneers at "the 'enlightened' North Carolina school." His old friend Hibbard, he wrote John Gould Fletcher, was one of "a new set of 'scalawags' and carpetbaggers," and "the liberals of the South" as a group, he insisted elsewhere, were "men of borrowed ideas." The change in Davidson's tone, particularly toward the North Carolinians, was so drastic that one at first wonders if something other than Dayton played some part in it. Indeed in the months just before the Scopes trial, Davidson had had several poems rejected by Paul Green of the *Reviewer* and had come to believe that the North Carolinians as a group had little regard

31. Donald Davidson, "The Spyglass," Nashville *Tennessean*, February 1, March 1, June 7, and July 5, 1925; Donald Davidson to Paul Green, [February, 1925], and Donald Davidson to Addison Hibbard, December 27, 1924, both in the possession of Mrs. Paul Green, Chapel Hill.

32. Davidson, *Southern Writers in the Modern World*, 30, 40; Davidson, quoted in Rob Roy Purdy (ed.), *Fugitives' Reunion* (Nashville, 1959), 198.

for his work. Similarly, he had earlier received rejection slips from Mencken, whom he now came to see as the inspiration of the Southern liberals with particularly close ties to Chapel Hill. One cannot completely discount such slights, given Davidson's sensitivity to outside criticism and his habit of seeing rejection as personal affront. But far more significant was his deep—if newly acquired—disgust with what he called the "Walter Hines Page school" of Southern thought. To Tate, who had written him that he was through attacking the Old South (except "that in it which produced . . . the New South"), he replied, "You know that I'm with you on the anti-New South stuff. . . . I feel so strongly on these points that I can hardly trust myself to write." The South, he wrote in April, 1927, had "arrived at a crisis": "It has always possessed great individuality which under modern influence it runs a great risk of losing. To retain its spiritual unity the South . . . must become conscious of and not repudiate whatever is worth saving in its traditions." Two months later he wrote Fletcher that he, Ransom, and Tate were "trying to formulate . . . some kind of *modus vivendi* for Southern Americans."[33]

In his poetry and published essays of the late 1920s Davidson's new resolve was evident. His earlier poetry, much of which had been published in *An Outland Piper* (1924), had given little attention to the South and the matter of a traditional society. But shortly after Dayton he began to write the series of poems which became *The Tall Men* (1927)—poems, largely in the heroic vein, which treated Tennessee pioneers, Tennesseans at war in 1861 and 1918, and Tennesseans in a threatening modern world. The book, he later wrote, was "intended to be a dramatic visualization of a modern Southerner, trapped in a distasteful urban environment, subjecting the phenomena of the disordered present to a comparison with the heroic past." Davidson demonstrated a similar concern for the Southern tradition in his polemical writing, particularly his literary column in the *Tennessean*. At first it was not Odum and the sociologists per se he attacked but rather what he called the "sociological spirit" in literature. In August,

33. Donald Davidson to Allen Tate, October 26, 1929, in Allen Tate Papers, Princeton University Library, Princeton; Donald Davidson to John Gould Fletcher, June 13, 1927 (copy); Donald Davidson to E. C. Aswell, October 2, 1927 (copy); correspondence between Davidson and Green, February 18, March 2, 21, 25, and July 6, 1926, all in the possession of Mrs. Green; Tate to Davidson, March 1, 1927, and Davidson to Tate, March 4, 1927, both quoted in Cowan, *The Fugitive Group*, 244; Donald Davidson to R. N. Linscott, April 9, 1927 (copy); Davidson to Fletcher, June 13, 1927 (copy).

1925, a month after Dayton, he denounced those Southern iconoclasts who tagged "at Mr. Mencken's coattails," and in other columns in 1926 and 1927 attacked those Southern writers—Green and Gerald Johnson of North Carolina, James Branch Cabell of Virginia, T. S. Stribling of Tennessee, Clement Wood of Alabama, Frances Newman of Atlanta, Julia Peterkin and DuBose Heyward of South Carolina—whose work was "marred by an irreverent attitude toward the South," a "sociological thesis," an excessive concern with the Negro, or, in some cases, all three. In their excessive concern with "special 'problems' and contemporary manias," Davidson charged, these writers had departed from the "autochthonous ideal," the state of harmony between the writer and his social environment. In fleeing from the Southern tradition, they might find themselves "in a spiritual desert more painful than the Sahara of Mencken's imagination." [34]

Such was the thesis of many of Davidson's "Spyglass" columns in the three years after Dayton, and also the thesis of two longer essays written for a national audience, "The Artist as Southerner" (1926) and "First Fruits of Dayton" (1928). "The liberal cause," he declared, insisted on "purely intellectual things. Look where you will—in politics, religion, literature—liberals fear emotion, as much as Satan himself." But the liberals and critics, Davidson acknowledged, were in charge: it seemed "that any acidic and depreciatory view of Southern life was prima facie evidence of a high-class artistic performance." [35]

By 1927 Davidson had identified another enemy which he considered every bit as dangerous as liberalism and in fact was allied with it: an "industrialism, which in its eternal flux represents a principle not native to this section." He was hardly alone among American writers of the 1920s in protesting the coming of the machine age to the American provinces. Sherwood Anderson, in his novel *Poor White* (1920), had registered his protest. But industrialism as a significant movement came to the South later than to the East and Midwest, arriving in the 1920s at about the same time and with the same force as the boll

---

34. Davidson, *Southern Writers in the Modern World*, 32; Davidson, "The Spyglass," September 18, 1927. See other "Spyglass" columns, 1924–1930, in John Tyree Fain (ed.), *The Spyglass* (Nashville, 1963).

35. Donald Davidson, "The Artist as Southerner," *Saturday Review*, May 15, 1926, pp. 781–83; Donald Davidson, "First Fruits of Dayton," *Forum*, LXXIX (June, 1928), 896–907; Donald Davidson, "Critic's Almanac" (formerly "Spyglass"), Nashville *Tennessean*, November 17, 1929. For a response to "The Artist as Southerner," see Addison Hibbard, "Literary Lantern," Greensboro *Daily News*, May 31, 1926.

weevil coming up from Texas and Yankee criticism coming down from New York. But the machine came disguised as a friend and Southerners welcomed it. Southern industry was a spiritual movement, a speaker told the delegates at a Southern textile conference, "a divine institution": "The pioneers of Southern industry were pioneers of God, they were prophets of God doing what God wanted done. . . . When the first whistles blew the people flocked to the light from barren places." "Industrialism," wrote Johns Hopkins economist Broadus Mitchell, was "the instrument of Southern salvation." Thus Southern towns from Virginia to .Texas advertised themselves in Richard Edmonds' *Blue Book of Southern Progress* as "Southern Cities Seeking Industry." Birmingham called itself the "Next Capital of the Steel Age," Lincoln County, Tennessee, the "Ruhr of America." Birmingham was the Pittsburgh, High Point the Grand Rapids, Atlanta the New York of the South. And with the coming of industry, Southern values were changing. "The dominant culture of the coming South," wrote sociologist E. C. Lindeman in the *New Republic*, "will take its cues from Rotary, Kiwanis, Chamber of Commerce, and the Manufacturers' Association." "Industrialism," wrote Mitchell approvingly, "is precipitating in the South a whole series of imperative new moralities." In a hundred towns from the Potomac to the Rio Grande, observed Gerald Johnson, himself no uncritical booster of the new age, "there is no God but Advertising, and Atlanta is his prophet." [36]

It was precisely this new religion that Davidson recognized and feared. In "First Fruits of Dayton" he questioned the basic concept of progress—"Whose ideal of progress is the South to follow? The ideal of Mr. Mencken, if he has one? Of Mr. Oswald Garrison Villard? Of Mr. Walter Lippmann?" (p. 901)—and defended the same "provincialism" he had attacked four years before. He was also ready, by 1928, to assume more active leadership in a new Southern "movement" that he, Tate, and others had discussed. He was especially enthusiastic about a volume of essays the participants in the movement were planning. Although Davidson was determined, as he wrote Tate, that the

36. Davidson, "The Spyglass," June 19, 1927; industrial promoter, quoted in Stringfellow Barr, "Shall Slavery Come South," *Virginia Quarterly Review*, VI (October, 1930), 489; Broadus Mitchell, "Fleshpots in the South," *Virginia Quarterly Review*, III (April, 1927), 171, 176; E. C. Lindeman, "Notes on the Changing South," *New Republic*, April 28, 1926, p. 299; Gerald W. Johnson, "Greensboro, or What You Will," *Reviewer*, IV (April, 1924), 169.

new movement must go "entirely away from the Mencken–[Sinclair] Lewis trend," he was not certain at first precisely what form it should take and who should be included. The list of suggested contributors to the proposed volume of essays included such Southern liberals as Mitchell, Will W. Alexander, and journalists Johnson, Julian Harris of Georgia, and Grover Hall of Alabama—and, Herman Clarence Nixon wrote, Davidson might "feel [Odum] out," although "I am doubtful of the probability of his chiming in with our concept on the Articles." The range of possible contributors—names suggested to Davidson and Ransom—and the remarks of other Southerners who corresponded with Davidson in 1929 and 1930 show just how greatly the Southern intellectual community misunderstood what the Nashville poets were about. "I wish I knew," Josephine Pinckney of South Carolina wrote, "why it is that the South as a section is so conservative, so slow to accept new ideas along any lines, and why we never promulgate new ideas ourselves." "You are of the south," Howard Mumford Jones of Chapel Hill wrote Davidson, "but not a professional Southerner." [37] The North Carolinians in fact had little idea what was under way in Nashville, so busy were they with their own projects—Jones and Addison Hibbard planning a volume on Southern culture from the progressive point of view, Green working in Europe under a Guggenheim Fellowship, Odum completing *An American Epoch* and operating under the impression that his ideological enemies, if he had any, probably lay in Virginia.

Thus in November, 1930, when a book appeared under the title *I'll Take My Stand: The South and the Agrarian Tradition* Southern liberals were at first less angry than confused. Indeed, the twelve contributors to the volume were themselves far from united in their views toward the South, despite their apparent endorsement of a "Statement of Principles," written largely by Ransom, which announced a preference for an agrarian over an industrial way of life—in which, they contended, religion, manners, the arts, and other amenities suffered, labor became unbearable, and economic evils such as unemployment and overproduction abounded. But in particulars, indeed in the very idea of the South they were espousing, the twelve contributors differed. Ransom in his essay "Reconstructed But Unregenerate" spoke

37. Donald Davidson to Allen Tate, December 29, 1929, in Tate Papers; Herman Clarence Nixon to Donald Davidson, February 21, 1930; Josephine Pinckney to Donald Davidson, June 22, 1930; Howard Mumford Jones to Donald Davidson, June 15, 1929.

of a South which had "founded and defended a culture . . . according to the European principles," stable principles which he contended were vastly different from America's pioneer values. Similarly, Tate had written Davidson in 1929 that the Agrarians must be "the last Europeans."[38] But Davidson defended a South which, he later wrote, was "the best available existing model" of traditional *American* principles, by which he meant the very pioneer values Ransom rejected.

Such disparity demonstrates a problem in the traditional approach to *I'll Take My Stand*: a tendency to get at the meaning of the volume as a whole, rather than to examine the individual essays, which are, in some cases, substantially different from each other. Thus commentators have often debated whether the twelve essayists had in mind the Southern planter or the plain white farmer, whether they were affirming Southern aristocracy or frontier democracy. In fact they—or individuals among them—had in mind both the planter and the farmer, both aristocracy and democracy, which is to say that some of their number were elitist, others democratic. They came from a variety of backgrounds, wrote for widely different reasons, and represented different points of view. Ransom, Davidson, Tate, John Gould Fletcher, and Robert Penn Warren were poets, and Stark Young, John Donald Wade, and Andrew Lytle also were belletrists. But Frank Owsley was a historian, Herman Clarence Nixon a political scientist, Lyle Lanier a psychologist, and Henry Blue Kline an economist and journalist. Nor were all conservative Southerners: Nixon and Kline were soon to become New Dealers. It is important to view the twelve as individual Southerners—nearly all of whom had studied or taught at Vanderbilt University—who came together for a moment in 1930, but had earlier held widely divergent views on certain matters, would later, and in fact did even as they wrote *I'll Take My Stand*.

But one bond the essayists did share—and a significant bond it seems to me—is that they all came from the Deep or Mid-South. Seven were native Tennesseans or Kentuckians, the others from Alabama, Mississippi, Arkansas, and, in one case, Georgia. There was not a Virginian or Carolinian in the group (Tate came closest), not one representative of those states which had traditionally provided Southern intellectual leadership. This was a new Southern movement, a

38. Twelve Southerners, *I'll Take My Stand: The South and the Agrarian Tradition* (1930; rpr. New York, 1962), 3; Allen Tate to Donald Davidson, quoted in Simpson, "The South's Reaction to Modernism," 49.

trans-Appalachian one, and as such it represented a radical departure from the intellectual authority of the older coastal South. It was in some part a reaction to that older South, particularly since the intellectual communities in both Richmond and Chapel Hill seemed to the Agrarians to have fallen under the influence of Mencken and "urban" Eastern thought, and even Charlestonians such as Heyward and Julia Peterkin seemed to write mainly for New York. But the Agrarians came from across the mountains, and most of them were very conscious of it.

Donald Davidson was particularly conscious, and his essay "A Mirror for Artists" was an indictment both of an industrial civilization—which, he maintained, could not properly foster and nurture the literary artist—and of certain Southern writers, mainly Carolinians and Virginians, who followed the lead of the industrial East. The arguments of those who favored industrial civilization—that art prospered in such an environment because of more leisure, more subsidies for artists, and wider distribution of art—were erroneous, he contended, because such a civilization removed the artist from nature, the traditional source of his strength. An industrial society might enshrine art, in museums and galleries and libraries, but did little to produce it. Rather, the artist in an industrial society became critical, abstract, alienated from his tradition. This had already happened to the Southern literary artist who had fallen under the modernist, cosmopolitan influence: "Why does Mr. Cabell seem so much nearer to Paris than to Richmond, to Anatole France than to Lee and Jefferson? Why does Miss Glasgow, self-styled the 'social historian' of Virginia, propagate ideas that would be more quickly approved by Oswald Garrison Villard than by the descendants of the first families? Why are DuBose Heyward's and Paul Green's studies of negro life so palpably tinged with latter-day abolitionism? Why does T. S. Stribling write like a spiritual companion of Harriet Beecher Stowe and Clarence Darrow?" (pp. 58–59). The answer in all cases, Davidson claimed, was the same: "The Southern tradition in which these writers would share had been discredited and made artistically inaccessible; and the ideas, modes, attitudes that discredited it, largely not Southern, have been current and could be used" (p. 59).

Davidson's essay was but one of several in *I'll Take My Stand* going against the progressive Southern grain, and the reaction to the volume, particularly in North Carolina and Virginia, was immediate. Many reviewers assumed that the Agrarians were successors to Thomas Nelson Page, that they celebrated the plantation and the big house. Some few others recognized an allegiance to a simpler folk tradition. But virtually none asked what might be seen in retrospect as a central question: Just how exclusively had the Southern tradition—or, at any rate, the Southern ideal—been agrarian anyway? They would have had cause to ask. Certainly Jefferson and John Taylor of Caroline were often called agrarians and Taylor's book *Arator* had been, in part, a celebration of the agrarian life. But both Jefferson and Taylor had envisioned an agrarian economy which did not necessarily rest on slavery; and Jefferson, in any case, once he was in the White House, had modified his earlier position and declared that the nation's prosperity depended "on a due balance between agriculture, manufactures, and commerce." Certain of the antebellum Southern apologists such as Alfred Taylor Bledsoe had indeed been strongly anti-industrial, but the most notable of their number, Fitzhugh, had advocated industry for the South. There was no greater commercial booster North or South than James D. B. De Bow of New Orleans, and his widely circulated *De Bow's Review*—with its motto "Commerce is King"—was among other things an antebellum *Blue Book of Southern Progress*. Indeed, as we have seen, the term *agrarian* had often been held in disfavor in the nineteenth-century South. Not only had Fitzhugh declared himself against "infidelity, agrarianism, free love, and anarchy," but E. N. Elliott in his influential *Cotton Is King* (1860) had inveighed against "AGRARIANISM," that mixture of socialism, utopianism, and various other isms which came from the North.[39]

But none of the reviewers of *I'll Take My Stand* raised this question. They seemed to grant that the Southern tradition was rather exclusively agrarian, as the twelve essayists had claimed. What they disputed was the claim that the tradition had been a healthful and desirable one. In Chapel Hill, when Odum saw a prepublication copy of the volume—and realized that *An American Epoch* would not be the only notable Southern book of the season—he immediately wrote Mencken urging him to look into this "new Harper book, *I Take My Stand* [*sic*], being by eleven [*sic*] southerners pleading elegantly and artistically for an agrarian society."

39. Thomas Jefferson, quoted in Hubbell, *The South in American Literature*, 125; George Fitzhugh, "The Northern Neck of Virginia," *De Bow's Review*, XXVII (September, 1859), 287–88; Elliott, *Cotton Is King*.

What these brethren do not sense [he added] is the fact that all of the old southern romanticism has been thoroughly interwoven with a realism, which, even though in the long run may develop a fine culture, is at the moment a pretty sordid fact. . . . One may admit with great enthusiasm all the virtues of the southern way of life, developed to its maximum capacity, and still recognize the overwhelming forces which have translated such a dispensation into the merest romanticism. What we have to find now is the product of what was and what is—as a fact and not as an ideal.[40]

Before Odum had a chance to respond publicly, Gerald Johnson issued the opposition statement. He wrote first for the *Virginia Quarterly Review*, a journal the Agrarians had earlier hoped to find sympathetic to their aims, since its editor, Barr, had questioned industrialism. But the *Virginia Quarterly* essay by Johnson was scathing in its criticism: "Have [the Agrarians] never been in the modern South, especially in the sections still completely ruled by agrarianism? Have they been completely oblivious to the Vardamans, the Bleases, the Heflins, the Tom Watsons, who are the delight of Southern agrarianism? Have they never been told that the obscenities and depravities of the most degenerate hole of a cotton-mill town are but pale reflections of the lurid obscenities and depravities of Southern backwoods communities?" "At first blush," Johnson wrote the next month in *Harper's*, "it seems incredible that twelve men, all born and raised in the South, all literate, and all of legal age, could preach such doctrine without once thrusting the tongue in the cheek or winking the other eye. . . . Of such a philosophy one can only say that it smells horribly of the lamp, that it was library-born and library-bred, and will perish miserably if it is ever exposed for ten minutes to the direct rays of the sun out in the daylight of reality." The Agrarians, he insisted, were not facing facts: agrarianism had given the South "a hookworm-infested, pellagra-smitten, poverty-stricken, demagogue-ridden" civilization. Although industrialism had its faults, it had already come south, and "sniveling and excuse-hunting on the part of intelligent Southerners are a worse betrayal of their ancestors than are Gastonia, lynching, demagoguery, and religious fanaticism combined."[41]

Johnson entitled his *Harper's* essay "No More Excuses" and spoke as "a Southerner to Southerners." By the time his reviews appeared,

40. Howard W. Odum to H. L. Mencken, November 3, 1930, in Mencken Papers.
41. Gerald W. Johnson, "The South Faces Itself," *Virginia Quarterly Review*, VII (January, 1931), 157; Gerald W. Johnson, "No More Excuses: A Southerner to Southerners," *Harper's*, CLXII (February, 1931), 333, 334, 337.

other progressive Southerners were clamoring to be heard, and their tone was as urgent as his. The Chattanooga *News* pointed to the "economic absurdities" of "the young Confederates" and the Macon *Telegraph* called them a "socially reactionary band." William S. Knickerbocker, editor of the *Sewanee Review*, and W. B. Hesseltine, a history professor at the University of Chattanooga, also wrote essays attacking the Agrarians, Knickerbocker drawing on Odum and Broadus Mitchell for support.[42] Knickerbocker and Barr debated the Agrarians in Richmond, Atlanta, New Orleans, Chattanooga, and Columbia, Tennessee, Barr's debate with Ransom in Richmond drawing 3,500 people. Thus with the furor occasioned by *I'll Take My Stand*, the tone of the Southern debate changed. Throughout the 1920s, even after Dayton, this debate had been relatively polite. Traditional Southerners had attacked outside critics, particularly Mencken, but except for Davidson they had rarely publicly attacked other Southerners. And the Southern iconoclasts had focused largely on Southerners dead and gone such as Thomas Nelson Page, or on live preachers, politicians, and textile barons. But rarely had the liberals publicly accused other Southern *intellectuals*—perhaps because they could not conceive of any who did not share their point of view. Despite criticism of other Southerners voiced privately among friends—in letters exchanged between Davidson and Tate on the one hand, Odum and Johnson on the other—this criticism had rarely appeared in print. Indeed it seems that liberal and conservative Southerners did not know how far apart they really were: as we have seen, Howard Mumford Jones and Josephine Pinckney had written Davidson in 1929 and 1930 assuming he was a progressive, and the Agrarians had considered asking Odum and actually did ask Johnson to join in their manifesto. But with the publication of *I'll Take My Stand* the peace was shattered. Southerners who heretofore had fired their ammunition largely at Yankees or at long dead Southerners now took aim at each other.

Johnson predicted in his review of *I'll Take My Stand* that the Agrarian philosophy might "echo the voice of the South during the next twenty years," and indeed, throughout the 1930s, the pages of the

---

42. The *News* and the *Telegraph* quoted in Davidson, "'I'll Take My Stand,'" 316; William S. Knickerbocker, "Mr. Ransom and the Old South," *Sewanee Review*, XXXIX (April–June, 1931), 222–39; W. B. Hesseltine, "Look Away, Dixie," *Sewanee Review*, XXXIX (January–March, 1931), 97–103.

Virginia Quarterly Review, the *Sewanee Review,* and (after 1935) the *Southern Review* resounded with discussions of the Agrarian and the Regionalist positions. It was, from Davidson's point of view, the "fanatically liberal North Carolinians" with their "dissociated cynicism," their "agitated and crusading spirit," and their spiritual home in that "center of progressive agitation," Chapel Hill, versus those conservative Southerners who defended traditional values and virtues and whose spiritual home was Nashville. It was, as he saw it, another battle in that old war between those who examined and analyzed— the sociologists and journalists—and those who felt. And it had become clear by 1933 that Davidson himself was the most committed spokesman among the traditionalists. The earlier plans of the Nashville group—for an Agrarian publishing house, bookstore, and magazine or newspaper—had not materialized (although the *American Review,* founded in 1933 by Seward Collins, served in part as an Agrarian journal). Neither had Tate's plan to establish "an academy of Southern *positive* reactionaries" which would propound "a complete social, philosophical, literary, economic and religious system." But despite the absence of such institutional bonds, the Nashville and Chapel Hill groups were soon referring to each other as schools—the North Carolinians were "Odum's school," Davidson wrote—and schools of thought they assuredly were, representing two very different approaches to Southern life. The South had not before seen anything precisely like it—certainly not the discussion between Old South and New South advocates of the late nineteenth century who, for the most part, coexisted harmoniously, Henry Grady paying tribute to the Old South and Thomas Nelson Page to the New; and certainly not before the war when a meaningful debate between proslavery and antislavery forces was impossible. But in the 1930s two conflicting and articulate schools of Southern thought did emerge, and at stake, at least as the participants saw it, was an issue no less important than what the South would become. The difference in the two groups, Odum wrote in 1934, was "not just academic to me, but vital, in fact the most vital single issue that has been involved in what I have been trying to do for the last ten or fifteen years."[43]

At first the liberals gained more recruits: not only Odum and his

43. Johnson, "The South Faces Itself," 156; Allen Tate, quoted in Simpson, "The South's Reaction to Modernism," 49; Howard W. Odum to Benjamin Kendrick, February 8, 1934 (copy).

fellow sociologists in Chapel Hill and Johnson, Cash, and several other Tar Heel journalists but also Barr in Charlottesville and Howard Mumford Jones of Chapel Hill, who wrote Davidson in January, 1931, "I belong to the Barr school of thinking on this topic." Although the South indeed needed "to take stock of itself," Jones told Davidson, he could not "agree that it is possible to return to an agrarian economy." About the same time, Virginius Dabney, editor of the Richmond *Times-Dispatch*, also declared on the side of the Regionalists. Indeed, the progressive party seemed so strong that Odum hoped to win over one of the Agrarians, John Donald Wade. Earlier he had tried to bring Wade to Chapel Hill as a professor of English, partly so he could "center as much of the progressive bunch as possible," and even after Wade joined the Vanderbilt faculty in 1928 he still believed, as he wrote in 1929, that Wade might be "in time . . . a real white hope." Although he was disappointed with Wade's participation in *I'll Take My Stand*, he continued to believe that this particular Agrarian was "essentially interested in the Chapel Hill group as one growing in strength and expression" and was "eager to come to North Carolina as a sort of professor of southern culture." [44] But Wade, who by 1932 had grown close to Davidson, never came to Chapel Hill.

Throughout the early 1930s the ideological side-choosing continued. "The more you write," Frank Owsley told Davidson in 1931, "the clearer the issues seem." The Agrarians, it is clear from Davidson's correspondence, were very conscious of the threat from "the North Carolina school of progressive liberalism," and Davidson was trying to meet that threat in every way possible. Johnson needed "badly to be exposed," he wrote John Gould Fletcher, and it was "up to one of us to hit him good and hard." At the Southern Writers Conference in Charlottesville in 1931, Davidson and Paul Green debated whether the creative mind could function in a machine age. Davidson said it could not. At a later conference Odum took the floor and denied that "regionalism" had anything to do with traditional "sectionalism." "The progressives—or liberals, or socialists, whatever Odum and his school

44. Howard Mumford Jones to Donald Davidson, January 20, 1931, December 8, 1930; Donald Davidson to John Gould Fletcher, March 23, 1931 (copy); Howard W. Odum to Harry Woodburn Chase, May 6, 1925 (copy); Howard W. Odum to H. L. Mencken, July 23, 1929 (copy); Howard W. Odum to Edmund Day, April 4, 1931 (copy). See also Odum to Chase, August 15, 1924 (copy); John Donald Wade to Howard W. Odum, June 5, 1927; Odum to Wade, June 16, 1927 (copy); and Wade to Odum, July 20, 1927.

may be," Davidson wrote Fletcher, "are simply afraid of the word [sectionalism] which for fifty years has been used as an epithet." He liked Odum and Barr, Davidson insisted, but "I don't believe very strongly in the seriousness of their concern about Southern (or other) matters. They look to me like folks who, after being sure of a snug institutional corner, simply keep abreast of the 'advanced' views and bet on the respectable horses." [45]

As Davidson refined his views through correspondence with Fletcher, Owsley, Tate, Wade, and other Agrarians, his confidence in his position increased. That confidence had waned during much of the period from 1929 to 1932, despite the excitement generated by the publication of *I'll Take My Stand*. Davidson had first become depressed over his failure to complete a history of Southern literature which he had undertaken in 1929 for the Oxford University Press, a failure Ransom termed "a tragic experience," and early in 1931, shortly after the publication of *I'll Take My Stand*, his father had died. To add to his troubles, in the spring of 1932 most of his books and letters and many of his other possessions were destroyed by fire. When Wade offered lodging for the academic year 1932–1933 on his estate in Marshallville, Georgia, Davidson accepted. The year in middle Georgia revived his spirits. Although the feelings of loneliness and rejection by many of his fellow Agrarians remained and were even intensified as the 1930s progressed, his commitment to his particular version of the Southern cause increased. Indeed it may be said to have increased because of the rejection and isolation. In 1936 Davidson wrote Robert Penn Warren that he had become an "outsider": "the state of my feelings is so confused and irritated that I cannot tell to my own satisfaction whether I have just stepped outside or been kicked outside." But his writing of the mid-1930s showed little of the confusion: it was his clearest writing, as well as his most committed. His case was not so extreme as those of Edmund Ruffin and Robert Lewis Dabney, whose commitment also was greatest when they felt rejected by their fellow Southerners, but it was not entirely dissimilar. The writing filled a vacuum in his life as it had theirs. As he wrote Wade, "I am thoroughly tired of being servile and merely imitative. I am worn-out and

45. Frank Owsley to Donald Davidson, April 8, 1931; Donald Davidson to John Gould Fletcher, March 23, 1931 (copy); Fletcher to Davidson, April 11, 1933; Davidson to Fletcher, April 16, 1933 (copy). See also Donald Davidson, "A Meeting of Southern Writers," *Bookman*, LXXIV (January-February, 1932), 494–96; and Josephine Pinckney, "Southern Writers Congress," *Saturday Review*, November 7, 1931, p. 266.

sick of seeing the South made an experimental ground for any idea, no matter how half-baked and untested, that happens to originate in a New York or Chicago study."[46] Thus he would write to correct the injustices. Since none of the other Agrarians vigorously supported him after 1934—except Fletcher, the fervor of whose commitment stemmed in part from his own emotional instability—he would fight nearly alone.

Davidson began the most important phase of his career as polemicist shortly after he read Turner's *Significance of Sections in American History*. He responded to Turner in a manner far different than Odum had. In the winter and spring of 1933, sitting in the cottage in Marshallville, he worked out his own theory of sectionalism—at the same time Odum, supported by foundations and grants, worked in Chapel Hill to develop his theory of regionalism. In more than a dozen essays written in the mid-1930s Davidson attacked liberalism, regionalism, sociology, the values of the "metropolitan East," and finally—in 1938—"Leviathan." All of these evils, Davidson charged, valued or were grounded in abstraction. The sociologist and Southern Regionalist, the Eastern journalist, the creators of Leviathan: all denied or abhorred the concrete, the South as it was, and all found their salvation in theory, reform, and social planning. All sought to change the South, to remake it.

There was also another, although less obvious target in several of the essays of the 1930s—not the North or Leviathan but rather the seaboard *South*. In "New York and the Hinterland" and "The Two Old Wests" Davidson celebrated the old Southwest and attacked the coastal South. This older Southeast—Maryland, Virginia, and the Carolinas—had fallen under the Northeastern influence and, as the home of spiritual Yankees with Southern accents, had escaped the worst of the Yankee onslaught. In the 1920s "cities like Baltimore and Charleston, even parts of Virginia and North Carolina, were spared rough treatment; they were conceded a lingering modicum of civilization."[47] They had not suffered as Davidson's trans-Appalachian South had suffered. The Southwesterner more than ever was Davidson's

46. Donald Davidson to Robert Penn Warren, October 21, 1936, quoted in O'Brien, *The Idea of the American South*, 194; Davidson to Wade, March 3, 1934, in Odum Papers. For a discussion of this period in Davidson's life, see O'Brien (pp. 189–95).

47. Donald Davidson, "Lands That Were Golden: New York and the Hinterland," *American Review*, III (October, 1934), 545. This essay also appears in *The Attack on Leviathan* and in Donald Davidson, *Still Rebels, Still Yankees* (Baton Rouge, 1957).

hero; to read the essays of the mid-1930s, one would believe that the Southerner who had crossed the Appalachians into Tennessee or had headed south around them to Alabama and Mississippi—or the descendant of such a Southerner—possessed a special virtue. Like Robert Lewis Dabney, Davidson was doubly provincial: it was not so much the South he prized and defended but the South beyond the mountains, and even more particularly, Tennessee. The one exception was that Eden he had discovered in Wade's middle Georgia.

Davidson's initial concern in the essays of the early and mid-1930s was the effect the "social program" taking root in Chapel Hill was having on the Southern writer. In an essay in *Poetry*, "The Southern Poet and His Tradition," he repeated his charge of the late 1920s: the effect of a "plan" undertaken by Northern philanthropists and Southern liberals to reform the South had "undoubtedly been to dislocate many Southern writers from a proper relation to their own people and their own tradition." At the University of North Carolina in particular, Southern writers were encouraged to be "Southern spokesmen."[48] In a second essay, "The Trend of Literature," Davidson repeated his criticism of the "sociological spirit," and this time on the enemy's home ground—in *Culture in the South*, a collection of essays, largely by progressives, published in 1934 by the University of North Carolina Press. The book was in large part a response to *I'll Take My Stand*, and its editor, W. T. Couch, criticized the Agrarians in his introduction. But at the same time Couch desired inclusiveness: Chapel Hill, unlike Vanderbilt, was forever attempting to embrace the entire South. Couch wanted the opposition represented.

But Davidson's two essays on literature in the early 1930s demonstrated little advancement over his thought of the late 1920s: it was still the Southern *writer* who he feared, as he had in *I'll Take My Stand*, would be damaged by industrialism and its resulting social program. It was primarily after reading Turner in 1933, and observing life in middle Georgia, that his area of concern expanded from the Southern artist to the South and the Southerner in a more general sense. "The idea I wish to develop," he wrote Fletcher, "is that the obvious, but neglected offset to the Leviathanism and omnivorous abstraction of our times may be found in the natural sectionalism that exists in the United States." "Odum is quite wrong," he wrote a week later. "It is

48. Donald Davidson, "The Southern Poet and His Tradition," *Poetry*, XL (May, 1932), 102.

just a quibble to say that regionalism is not sectionalism. . . . They all talk about sectionalism as 'narrow,' but they see the very real tendencies that are driving people away from centralism, and they get up a polite, innocuous sociological-economic word."[49]

Davidson's new emphasis was seen first in the late summer of 1933 in a lengthy essay, "Sectionalism in the United States," in which he insisted that Americans, "worn out with abstraction and novelty," were ready to return to the indigenous virtues upon which he believed sectionalism rested. In this essay he attacked the "apostles of social abstraction" who tried to eradicate sectional differences and "make Americans in the laboratory of abstraction." "We do not really want a scientific society, even if we could get it," he wrote. "We are Rebels, Yankees, Westerners, New Englanders or what you will, bound by ties more generous than abstract institutions can express." Five months later, in an essay prompted by Virginius Dabney's *Liberalism in the South*, he repeated his criticism of Southern progressives. "Dilemma of the Southern Liberals" appeared in an unlikely place, the *American Mercury*—he had sent it to Mencken, who had passed it along to his successor as editor—but Davidson, as he had in "The Trend of Literature," rather relished invading the camp of the enemy. Since the "intellectual pedigree" of Southern liberals "must be traced on the Northern side of the Potomac," he charged, they were outside the Southern tradition. He erred, however, in linking too closely the new Southern liberals with the progessives of the Walter Hines Page school: Odum, Gerald Johnson, and Virginius Dabney had themselves on occasion criticized Southern industrial progress and Babbittry. The contemporary Southerner whom Davidson more nearly described, whether he realized it or not, was his friend Mims—to whom he had sent the essay just before it appeared, apologizing for not "making distinctions that I am quite aware ought to be made" and even weakly identifying himself as "a liberal of some sort, I know not what."[50]

Davidson accelerated his attack on Southern liberalism and "abstraction" during the mid-1930s. In "New York and the Hinterland" (1934) he repeated that the liberals had been unduly influenced by

49. Donald Davidson to John Gould Fletcher, April 7, 16, 1933 (copies).

50. Donald Davidson, "Sectionalism in the United States," *Hound and Horn*, VI (July-September, 1933), 564, 586, 587, 589; Donald Davidson, "Dilemma of the Southern Liberals," *American Mercury*, XXXI (February, 1934), 228; Donald Davidson to Edwin Mims, January 24, 1934, quoted in O'Brien, "Edwin Mims and Donald Davidson, 911, 912.

"the literary, or sociological, or merely journalistic" approach of the Eastern intellectual. If the metropolitan critics had any belief, "it was in the power of science to determine the conditions of human life." In other essays he continued his celebration of the Southern and Western "hinterlands," those regions deprecated by the Eastern intellectuals. The "Southwesterner" was loyal and brave, hated collectivism, abstraction, and "theoretical" schemes. His simple virtues "the social reformer will see . . . as faults," but to the Southwesterner himself "life, liberty, and the pursuit of happiness [cannot] be reduced to such pale equivalences as are represented in statistical tables. . . . What do such abstractions mean when he strides away from office or field, with the sun on his shoulders, and looks at the hills?"[51]

By 1934, as Davidson seized the offensive, Odum for the first time recognized the seriousness of the threat, although at first he sought to understate his concern. "As you know, I very much enjoy the Davidson viewpoint," he wrote John Donald Wade in February, 1934. "I judge, however, from much evidence and from many years of trying to study the situation that there is a great danger in the revivification of the old sectionalism." At the same time, Davidson wrote Wade, who maintained ties with both groups, complaining that Odum was not taking the Agrarians seriously *enough*. In his revealing five-page, single-spaced "Comment on Odum's Criticisms and Proposals," which accompanied a lengthy letter to Wade, he outlined his areas of both agreement and disagreement with Odum. He acknowledged that Odum had "given as close study to regionalism and sectionalism as any living Southerner," but feared that Chapel Hill regionalism was a "very submissive, decent, orderly kind of thing— almost a servile creature." But principally he objected to Odum's impression of the Vanderbilt group. Remarking upon Odum's "silence on 'I'll Take My Stand,'" he concluded, "I think the answer is plain, and I will make bold to state it: The 'I'll Take My Stand' group were and are a sentimental and decorative lot, charming perhaps, but impractical certainly and without influence upon a changing South. One reads such folks, enjoys them, then goes on about the real business of life." And if Odum did grant the Agrarians any influence, it was of a subversive sort: "Underneath it all, I suspect [Odum] of suspecting us as guilty, or about to be guilty, of some heinous indiscretion, such as

51. Davidson, "New York and the Hinterland," 552; Donald Davidson, "Lands That Were Golden: The Two Old Wests," *American Review*, IV (November, 1934), 38, 39, 40.

starting a new Ku Klux Klan, or failing to salute the colors or preferring Dixie to 'America the Beautiful.' Or, more gravely, that we are a
new school of secessionists."[52]

Wade apparently sent Davidson's complaint to Odum, who by this
time had begun to take the Agrarians very seriously indeed. Six
weeks earlier he had received a letter from historian Benjamin Kendrick of the Woman's College of the University of North Carolina, asking his support for a "Southern Council," a new journal to discuss
Southern issues, and a "new regionalism" which would blend the
best of the Old South with the New. Since Odum suspected Kendrick
of Agrarian sympathies, he had refused to give his support. He had
no objection, he replied, if Kendrick wanted "to join the Nashville
group," but he personally found Kendrick's position antithetical "to
all that this particular group here [in Chapel Hill] has been standing
for for the last ten years."[53]

In fact, Odum had overreacted. He had "misread the situation,"
wrote George Fort Milton of Chattanooga, "in resembling Kendrick to
. . . Davidson and the Young Confederates of Nashville." But his response suggests the extent to which he had come to acknowledge
Davidson's challenge, and he responded to that challenge in his accustomed manner: he sought to disarm his adversary through friend-
ship. Shortly after the Kendrick affair he wrote asking Davidson to
state his case in *Social Forces*. Davidson responded that he would welcome the opportunity: "For years I have been wondering about the
polite poaching in which we have all been engaged—with the sociologists becoming literary, and the literary people becoming sociological.
I am glad that it can cease to be poaching and become frank inter-
change of views on a ground where all can meet." Odum maintained
a congenial correspondence with Davidson during the next few
months, even inviting him to participate in an April meeting in Chattanooga of the Tennessee Valley Institute so that Davidson might
"give the Institute the benefit of your enthusiasm, study, and clear
thinking upon the dangers and limitations" of "social Planning." Da-

52. Howard W. Odum to John Donald Wade, February 15, 1934 (copy); Davidson to
Wade, March 3, 1934, in Odum Papers.
53. Benjamin Kendrick to Howard W. Odum, January 27, 1934; Odum to Kendrick,
January 29, 1934 (copy); Kendrick to Odum, January 31, 1934; Howard W. Odum to Alexander, February 8, 1934 (copy). Although it was true that Davidson supported some
of Kendrick's proposals, Kendrick was not about (as Davidson wrote Wade) "to commit some sort of sociological sabotage" (Davidson to Wade, March 3, 1934, in Odum
Papers).

vidson attended, and Odum wrote shortly afterward that he had enjoyed seeing him "in action": "It was pretty clear that you had your audience with you." [54]

At the same time Odum and Davidson were courting each other, it is clear in their letters to their own allies that each felt harmony to be merely the better part of strategy. Each believed that the other represented a well-intentioned but misguided cause and that he would in time come to see matters differently. "The theory now," Odum wrote Will W. Alexander in May, "is that it is better for us to work with that group and pull them along. Davidson is very cordial and very appreciative, and it is perhaps just as well not to criticize them now. My own impression is that they are growing considerably." The University of North Carolina Press, Odum said, was "even considering" publishing a book by Davidson "as a sort of opposite discussion to my *Southern Regions*." Odum had in mind Davidson's correspondence with W. T. Couch, director of the university press, discussing both a book "on sectionalism" and a "second symposium" apparently by Davidson and certain other Agrarians. Davidson, for his part, believed it "good strategy"—he wrote John Gould Fletcher—for the "second symposium" to be published in "that center of progressive liberalism which is N. Carolina. . . . The logic of events is turning them all our way, I am inclined to think." [55]

Davidson believed he had struck twice in the camp of the enemy— he would be published first in *Social Forces* and then by the University of North Carolina Press—and conversion was his aim. Indeed, he wrote Fletcher, he believed Couch was "already nearer to our point of view than he officially 'lets on.'" But all the while, the North Carolinians had a similar strategy: by taking Davidson in, they might modify *his* views. Little change except in tone was evident, however, in the

54. George Fort Milton to Howard W. Odum, February 7, 1934; Howard W. Odum to Donald Davidson, March 16, 1934 (copy), and Davidson to Odum, March 21, 1934, both in Odum Papers; Odum to Davidson, April 4, May 11, 1934. After reassuring Odum that Kendrick's plans were not the same as Davidson's, Milton hastened to add that he himself did "not adhere to any degree to that [view] Donald Davidson so artistically expresses."

55. Howard W. Odum to Will W. Alexander, May 7, 1934 (copy); W. T. Couch to Donald Davidson, October 13, 1933, and May 31, 1934; Donald Davidson to John Gould Fletcher, June 5, 1934 (copy). The "second symposium" to which Davidson refers was never published by the University of North Carolina Press. But Davidson's book "on sectionalism," *The Attack on Leviathan*, was published by North Carolina in 1938.

essay Davidson wrote for the October, 1934, issue of *Social Forces*. He was responding in large part to Odum's essay, "Regionalism vs. Sectionalism in the South's Place in the National Economy" (March, 1934), in which the sociologist had drawn a sharp distinction between regionalism and sectionalism. But in *Social Forces* Davidson was careful not to criticize Odum by name. Rather, in an essay entitled "Where Regionalism and Sectionalism Meet," he stressed the similarities in the two and attempted to defend sectionalism against Odum's charges. Sectionalism was "the political approach" as regionalism was "the economic and cultural approach to an identical set of facts." Regionalism was "cool and abstract," sectionalism personal and emotional, but the two met "at the point where action succeeds the compilation of data." Davidson expressed a fear, which at this point he did not identify as his own, that the Tennessee Valley Authority, as an example of social planning, was "a sort of proving-ground for the social experimentation of the planned society" and that it carried with it the dangers "of an abstract point of view"; but writing in Odum's journal he expressed confidence that Southern Regionalists did not want "a society so rigidly planned that it requires a dictator." [56]

Despite a cordial personal relationship between Odum and Davidson in 1934, it was clear to their allies that their positions had grown even further apart. Writing in the *Sewanee Review*, William Knickerbocker charged the "Apostolic Twelve" of Nashville, and Davidson in particular, with an inadequate understanding of Southern liberalism, a liberalism which "refuse[d] to admit Mr. Davidson's dilemma that there is a choice between two modes of action or of propaganda—between Marxism and Nashville Yeomanism." But Davidson's ire was stirred less by the *Sewanee Review* than by the *Virginia Quarterly Review*, which he hoped, as he wrote Fletcher, "might be coming over to the agrarian [*sic*] side a little." He was incensed when the *Quarterly* published in January, 1935, an attack on the Agrarians, himself in particular, by Mencken. He grew even angrier when the *Quarterly* planned a special Southern issue without first asking him to contribute—and then later, when he finally was asked, rejected his essay, a history of *I'll Take My Stand*. The turn of events led him to propose to

56. Davidson to Fletcher, June 5, 1934; Donald Davidson, "Where Regionalism and Sectionalism Meet," *Journal of Social Forces*, XIII (October, 1934), 25, 27, 28.

Tate, Fletcher, and other Agrarians an attack against the *Quarterly*, going "over the entire career of the magazine and planning a campaign on general grounds."[57]

Although Davidson failed to carry out such a campaign, the conflict with the *Virginia Quarterly Review* during the winter and spring of 1935 serves as an example of his beleaguered state of mind during the mid-1930s. He believed more than ever that Southern intellectuals, particularly those in Chapel Hill and Charlottesville, were out to get him. This feeling was intensified during 1936 and 1937 as Davidson found himself the target of other attacks, particularly by his former correspondent W. T. Couch of Chapel Hill. In an article in the summer, 1936, *South Atlantic Quarterly*, Couch had challenged an assumption by Davidson which had previously gone virtually unchallenged—that the Southern tradition was indeed agrarian and conservative. Four months later, on Davidson's home ground in Nashville, Couch continued his attack. At a meeting of the Southern Historical Association in which Davidson had criticized Chapel Hill sociologists and social planners, he took the platform and dismissed the Agrarian position as romantic mythmaking. Couch published his remarks under the title "The Agrarian Romance" the next fall in the *South Atlantic Quarterly*.[58]

Thus during the mid-1930s, at a time when many of the earlier Agrarians seemed to have abandoned the cause, Davidson operated under a sort of siege mentality, attacking Southern liberals, progressives, and Regionalists who he feared, in their efforts to expose and eradicate Southern ills, might eradicate Southern distinctiveness as well. By 1936 his attack was directed not so much against Southern Regionalists in general as Southern sociologists in particular—a group also headed by Odum and equally guilty, he believed, of abstraction. As before, he was rougher on Odum's lieutenants than on Odum himself. In an essay, "A Sociologist in Eden," written for the *American Review*, he discussed at length *Preface to Peasantry*, a study of two black belt Georgia counties written by a Chapel Hill–trained so-

57. William S. Knickerbocker, "Asides and Soliloquies," *Sewanee Review*, XLII (April–June, 1934), 133–34; Donald Davidson to John Gould Fletcher, March 12, 1935 (copy).

58. W. T. Couch, "Reflections on the Southern Tradition," *South Atlantic Quarterly*, XXXV (July, 1936), 284–97; R. H. Woody, "The Second Annual Meeting of the Southern Historical Association," *Journal of Southern History*, III (February, 1937), 83–84; W. T. Couch, "The Agrarian Romance," *South Atlantic Quarterly*, XXXVII (October, 1937), 419–30.

ciologist, Arthur Raper, and published by the University of North Carolina Press. Raper incurred Davidson's wrath because one of the counties he examined was John Wade's "Eden," which Davidson had celebrated in a *Virginia Quarterly* article in 1934.[59]

But Raper, "one of the younger group of Southern sociologists and economists whose leadership seems to be in the direction of the University of North Carolina" (p. 180), detected problems Davidson never knew—or acknowledged—existed, and presumed to tell him that Macon County, Georgia, was not paradise after all. Davidson resorted to the sarcasm he had come increasingly to use when dealing with sociologists: "How vain was my concern, how feeble my conception of the all-seeing eye of sociology! I now discover that the wise serpent, the Light-Bringer himself, was in that region before and after my visit, not for purposes of temptation so much as to focus upon Eden the central blaze of a high-powered social-scientific investigation" (p. 179). Davidson had found middle Georgia to be in good health, but "a glance through [Raper's] sociological microscope shows the decay germs already busily growing. . . . What differences are there between the (doubtless) inferior alchemical pottering of a humanistic, or literary, interpretation of Eden and the (surely) superior interpretative method of the trained social scientist? It will be most interesting . . . to see what the sociologist has to say about a region somewhat closer than the Fiji Islands" (p. 183). His essay was not "an attack upon sociology in its rightful capacity" (p. 185), Davidson insisted, but it was certainly an attack on the activist sociology preached by Odum and practiced by his colleagues. That sociology, he complained, focused on types rather than individuals. It was overly rational and thus denied the emotions. It could not "examine human ways without indulging in abstractions which to the lay reader seem to dehumanize" (p. 185). It viewed the rural South with "urban eyes." And despite its claims to objectivity, it was not even objective: "sociologists, absorbed in their abstractions, sometimes do not realize how their great structures of fact may be invalidated by wrong assumptions. And that is the moment when sociology becomes dangerous" (p. 197). If a sociologist took "an Eden" such as Macon County and made "it out to be a Hell, then that sociologist had better begin to

59. Donald Davidson, "A Sociologist in Eden," *American Review*, VIII (December, 1936), 177–204. Donald Davidson, "The Sacred Harp in the Land of Eden," *Virginia Quarterly Review*, X (April, 1934), 203–217.

sociologize himself, for there is something wrong with him" (p. 204).

"A Sociologist in Eden" was Davidson's strongest attack yet on social science, but he had just begun. Six months later, again in the *American Review*, he assailed John Dollard's book, *Caste and Class in a Southern Town*.[60] A research associate in sociology at Yale, Dollard had descended into the Mississippi town of Indianola and had written a "sociological *Gulliver's Travels*" (p. 155) which depicted a South that Davidson again insisted he did not recognize: "Familiar things have suddenly taken on a pasty, unreal complexion. The world has assumed a dizzy effervescence, like the nauseous, boiling stir of termites under a lifted plank. Still worse, the perspective has altered sickeningly. All that was big has become little. All that was little has swelled up fantastically" (p. 152). The "grand assumption," he continued, "is that Southerntown is abnormal and queer—otherwise [the sociologist] would not be investigating it. He, the sociologist, is not queer, and sociology is not queer. And what is queer about Southerntown? There are two races in it, white and black, that live together and yet are separate in certain fundamental relationships" (p. 153). In so writing, Davidson had finally articulated his strongest objection to the militant sociologist—a fear that through analysis and reform the sociologist would violate the "racial integrity" (p. 165) of the South. For the first time, the cause that Davidson was to champion the rest of his life surfaced, and when he turned to race Davidson came close to losing control. Dollard's suggestion that white women might be sexually attracted to Negro men was "obscene," he charged, and Dollard's remarks on miscegenation were "at times so revolting and obscene that they could hardly be reprinted here" (p. 165). And if the white Southerner "can be convicted in no other way, he will be convicted on evidence procured from the sewers of Freudian psychology" (p. 167).

Davidson's discussion of Dollard's book did him no credit. He appeared in the light that his enemies often cast him and even some of his fellow Agrarians had come to see him—prudish, narrow, suspicious of modernism in any form, the defender of white supremacy above all else. That essay anticipated the direction of much of his writing for the next quarter-century. But before he turned primarily to racial concerns he produced in 1938 two books which were among his

60. Donald Davidson, "Gulliver With Hay Fever," *American Review*, IX (Summer, 1937), 152–72.

finest: *Lee in the Mountains and Other Poems* and the collection of essays entitled *The Attack on Leviathan.*[61] The volume of poetry contained revisions of the poems published earlier in *The Tall Men* (1927), but the finest of the poems was the more recent "Lee in the Mountains." Centered in the consciousness of Robert E. Lee as he went about his duties as president of Washington College in the late 1860s, the poem achieved an artistic control and composure not always seen in Davidson's post-Fugitive poetry. As Lee awaits the beginning of chapel he walks across campus to his office, where he works on his father's memoirs and reflects on his own Civil War experience, asking himself if he should have prolonged the war, if the peace he had made had been honorable. The ring of the chapel bell calls him back to the present and to his students. It was a moving poem, but also more "modern" than Davidson's previous verse—which is perhaps why Tate liked it much better than the earlier efforts. But at its center was the familiar Davidson theme, the power and value of tradition.

The Attack on Leviathan dealt with a similar theme, but possessed a tone polemical rather than nostalgic. Consisting of essays Davidson had written throughout the 1930s, about two-thirds of which had been published previously, it was his longest single work and also his most important. For this was Davidson's most ambitious defense of sectionalism, his most impassioned attack on centralization in government, in the culture, and in the arts. More than half the essays dealt with the South—Southern art and culture, the debate between the sectionalists and the Regionalists, and the threat of Southern liberals and sociologists. Certain of the essays—"The Diversity of America," "Federation or Disunion," "Regionalism in the Arts," and "Regionalism and Nationalism in American Literature"—were attempts, drawing on Frederick Jackson Turner but going beyond Turner, to establish the preeminence of the sections in American life, and if in these essays Davidson sometimes referred to sections as "regions," it was only, he explained, because "region" was the current term. Other essays—"Still Rebels, Still Yankees," "Social Science Discovers Regionalism," "Expedients vs. Principles," and "Howard Odum and the Sociological Proteus"—were more specifically discussions of the social planner and his proposals for the South.

Of the latter group, "Still Rebels, Still Yankees" is illustrative of Da-

61. Donald Davidson, *Lee in the Mountains and Other Poems* (Boston, 1938).

vidson's continued attack on those who "live in a sociological pickle of statistics and progress" (p. 132):

> They are eternally looking for what they call "social values," but they strangely confine their research to libraries and graduate "projects" at the large universities. They avoid the places where social values may be encountered in the flesh. If they stumble upon a living social value, walking visibly about some spot of earth and drawing its nutriment from a tradition embodied in the houses, speech, crafts, music, folklore, and wisdom of an actual people, their rule is to denounce it as an anachronism and to call for its extermination. For them, nothing must grow according to its nature, but things "develop" by laboratory formulae, which are obtained by inspecting the reactions of the most abnormal and depressed specimens of humankind, too weak to protest against sociological vivisection. (p. 132)

In this essay Davidson described two representative characters, "Brother Jonathan of Vermont and Cousin Roderick of Georgia," who possessed distinctive sectional characteristics and values but whom the sociologist would remold to resemble each other: "The picture of America, as sociologically reformed, does not contemplate any great concessions to Yankee uprightness or Rebel relaxation. Indeed, the sociologist, armed with science, is ready to follow reformation with transformation. In the vast inevitable working of the social forces, sectional differences become irrelevant. With a cold smile the sociologist pronounces a death sentence upon Rebel and Yankee alike" (p. 143).

Davidson's social scientist "with a cold smile" resembled Hawthorne's Dr. Rappaccini more than any flesh and blood sociologist living in Chapel Hill. As in Hawthorne head triumphed over heart: the sociologist conducted his experiments with scientific curiosity but with little regard for the welfare of his subjects. He "connive[d] to put a stigma" upon Brother Jonathan and Cousin Roderick "or destroy them" (p. 154). The Southern social planner, Davidson believed, threatened to do precisely that. Although Odum's studies of Southern life had some value, the "Southern Realists" tended "to narrow their interpretation of history to the single focus of economic determinism." Besides, in racial relations they seemed "to be, though guardedly, amalgamationists" (p. 325). If their plans were executed, they would make the South even more dependent upon "the Federal mechanism" (p. 326). Davidson himself spoke for "principles," he insisted, the agrarian principles of Jefferson and John Taylor of Caroline. But the social planners relied on expedients. As for Odum's "six-year-plans" of economic development for the South, did the new Southerners "really think that six-year plans are preferable to the Jeffersonian way of building for the centuries?" (p. 337).

Despite such criticism of social scientists and planners in *The Attack on Leviathan*, Davidson's view of sociologists was in fact much more complex than before: if he came to censure them, he also came, in his way, to praise them. Focusing on Odum's *Southern Regions*, which had appeared two years before, he shrewdly decided to let the sociologist work for him—to let Odum's charts and statistics support his own contention that the South was different, and vastly different, from the rest of the United States. "Sociology," he wrote, "is indeed in many ways the friend of differentiation" (p. 40). And thus in several essays in this book he spoke not unkindly of Odum.

There were valid reasons, if he searched for them, for Davidson to embrace sociologists as allies. After all, a sociologist, William Graham Sumner, with his belief in the power of folkways, had suggested that Southerners could never be converted from segregation. Still, Davidson's basically favorable appraisal of *Southern Regions* must have appeared curious to readers of *The Attack on Leviathan*. Odum's book, he wrote, was "surprisingly free from the agitating and crusading spirit that has animated some of the North Carolinians" (p. 287) and contained "no sheer fanaticism . . . no special pleading, no carelessness in handling facts" (p. 286). Such praise makes one wonder if Davidson had actually read *Southern Regions* carefully. Although Odum had indeed eschewed a "crusading" tone, he nonetheless represented that rational, scientific approach to truth that Davidson deplored. Any number of things in the book should have offended him, not the least of which were the method and the vocabulary of the social scientist. "The study sought," Odum had written, "to explore the southern regions as a laboratory for regional research and experimentation in social planning" (p. 3). He had "envisaged" the South "in terms of testing grounds of American regionalism" (p. ix), and the "first essential" in the South was the adoption of a "'scientific' and 'theoretical' framework" (p. 598). In particular Odum's attempts to "index" culture and construct a "Rank of States Based on Twenty-three Cultural Tables" were the sorts of efforts for which Davidson had earlier attacked Mencken. Odum had also advocated "the modification of culture" (p. 596), "cultural reconstruction" (p. 209), and "the adequate readjustment of the nation's southern regions to the new America" (p. 211), and he had criticized the agrarian ideal: "The substance of the nostalgic yearnings of this particular group of agrarians [who envision "the glory that was the Old South"] is little more than this: the culture of the Old South, if it had been what it was purported to be, which it was not, would have constituted a magnificent contribution to a richer civilization. . . . Manifestly, there is little realism here" (p. 55). He had been even harsher toward a Southern "sectionalism" which had "constituted a continuous major crisis," a Southern "tragedy . . . conditioning the South to isolation, individualism, ingrowing patriotism, cultural inbreeding, civic immaturity, and social inadequacy" (p. 13).

Almost everything Davidson had championed from 1930 to 1936, agrarianism and sectionalism in particular, Odum had condemned in *Southern Regions;* nearly everything Davidson had attacked—scientific approaches to truth, cultural rank, "cultural reconstruction," and the amalgamation of the South into the nation—Odum had defended. Yet Davidson still commended *Southern Regions* and the reason he did was that he could use the book for his own ends. Odum's researchers had dug up data to document the Southern distinctiveness he himself had long claimed, and had also documented his complaint that "the South's position, relative to the other regions, is one of colonial degradation" (p. 298). Perhaps the South was statistically inferior, but that inferiority in itself constituted a kind of difference. Thus Davidson included in *The Attack on Leviathan* an essay, "Howard Odum and the Sociological Proteus," which was not unfavorable to its subject.

Sociology was protean to Davidson because it was changeable and elusive. But, he concluded in this particular essay, it was not altogether bad. Or, rather, it was not always bad. If there existed in the South a "militant school" of sociology of which Arthur Raper was representative, there also existed a "moderate school" which included Odum and his colleague Rupert Vance. Raper was "an eager missionary, who will take his chances of getting into the cannibal pot if, with the Great White Father's bureaus at his back, he can briskly proselyte the Southern savages" (p. 300). Odum, by contrast, had "met the test which distinguishes statecraft from charlatanry in the application of social science" (p. 298). Although Davidson had not retreated from his distaste for "social planning," it was, he feared, the way of the future. And if it were the way, Odum's "is the best way to go modern under sociological auspices, as Mr. Raper's is the worst possible way" (p. 311).

The Attack on Leviathan represented Davidson's most mature thinking, the product of his reflection since 1930. It was also the work in which he most nearly fit into the tradition of earlier Southern apologists such as Fitzhugh and Robert Lewis Dabney. Like Fitzhugh, he defended provincialism, decried "cosmopolitan institutions and productions," particularly of the Northeast, and attacked the critical spirit in literature—although he disagreed with Fitzhugh as to the perils of industrialism. Dabney he resembled even more closely, particularly the Dabney of the "New South" address who had protested the great accumulation of wealth in an industrial society and the centralization of power in the American Northeast, had warned the South not to adopt the Northern habit of making "wealth the idol, the all in all of sectional greatness," and had anticipated Davidson by fifty years in his reference to centralized federal authority as "Leviathan."[62]

The influence of Robert Lewis Dabney had declined sharply after his 1883 attack on Leviathan. Fifteen years of suffering and misery and feelings of rejection had followed. Davidson's decline was not so drastic, not so marked by physical suffering, but he too became a lonely and sometimes resentful man, one whose view of life became increasingly narrow and limited. He was to live thirty more years, but aside from a book on the Tennessee River which he wrote in the 1940s and a few good poems of the mid-1950s his best work had been done. Jonathan Daniels, visiting him in his spare living room in Nashville in the late 1930s, found him already "a very sad man" filled with "a sense of personal defeat . . . in the failure to make even contact with the imponderable mass of Southern thinking and acting." Daniels' judgment might at first be held suspect—he himself was one of the North Carolina liberals Davidson distrusted—but not Davidson's own assessment. He had become a "lone guerrilla," he wrote Tate in 1937, and three years later he lamented, "It is this intellectual isolation, this lack of communion, which I feel the most. . . . What fault

62. Fitzhugh, Cannibals All!, 58–61; George Fitzhugh, "Uniform Postage, Railroads, Telegraphs, Fashions, Etc.," De Bow's Review, XXVI (June, 1859), 662–64; Dabney, The New South, 11, 12.

was I guilty of? Did I just fail to keep up with the pattern of your thinking, and, though once worthy, thus become unworthy?" A "cloud" had come between Tate, Ransom, Lytle, and himself.[63]

The cloud was created in part by Davidson's own intransigence toward modernism. More and more he sneered not only at Marx and Freud but also Joyce, expressionism, dadaism, and the "infantilism of Gertrude Stein and various Parisian coteries." In 1933 Tate had written him, "If a Southern provincialism cannot assimilate the technique of Joyce and understand it, I am ready to move away," and in 1940 Tate again accused him of provincialism in literary tastes, even of being "contemptuous of art." As a literary artist himself Davidson became static. He continued to defend agrarianism and sectionalism, to attack industrialism, social planning, sociology, socialism, New Dealers, integrationists, the "new ethnic stocks" of the Northeast, and the "North Carolina school." In the autumn of 1939, writing in the *Southern Review*, he issued an eleven-page indictment of a young historian who, armed with a Ph.D. from Chapel Hill, had questioned the sectional approach to Southern problems. Davidson disputed C. Vann Woodward's "class approach" to the South, his "Marxian" interpretation of H. C. Nixon's *Forty Acres and Steel Mules*.[64]

Such were the concerns of Donald Davidson during the last three decades of his life. Increasingly—particularly after 1950—he took his stand for racial segregation and white supremacy, in 1950 joining the Tennessee States Rights Committee and in 1955 becoming chairman of the anti-integrationist Tennessee Federation for Constitutional Government. He continued to write for the *Southern Review*, the *Sewanee Review*, the *Saturday Review*, and other journals, although more and more he found that even his old friends were reluctant to accept his work. In the late 1950s he produced *Still Rebels, Still Yankees* and *Southern Writers in the Modern World*, two more volumes of essays on his

63. Jonathan Daniels, *A Southerner Discovers the South* (New York, 1938), 114; Donald Davidson to Allen Tate, March 27, 1937, quoted in O'Brien, *The Idea of the American South*, 194; Davidson to Tate, February 23, 1940, in Fain and Young (eds.), *The Literary Correspondence of Donald Davidson and Allen Tate*, 323–24. Davidson objected to Daniels' description. He wrote John Gould Fletcher (July 24, 1938) that after a two-hour conversation Daniels "of course deemed himself qualified, a la Count Keyserling, to make a complete report on agrarianism, past, present, and future: the report is, I gather, that we are amicable dreamers, pleasant nostalgics, etc. etc., etc."

64. Davidson, "New York and the Hinterland," 555; Allen Tate to Donald Davidson, February 5, 1933; Davidson to Tate, February 23, 1940, in Fain and Young (eds.), *The Literary Correspondence of Donald Davidson and Allen Tate*, 323; Donald Davidson, "The Class Approach to Southern Problems," *Southern Review*, V (Autumn, 1939), 261–72.

familiar theme, the value of Southern tradition. Two essays, "Preface to Decision" and "Why the Modern South Has a Great Literature," [65] serve to illustrate his dominant concerns in those late years—white supremacy and the condition of Southern literature.

Both essays were, fundamentally, attacks on sociology, the first on the sociologist's role in the area of race relations, the other on his role in culture and literature. The social scientist belonged in neither area, Davidson asserted. To the Southern sociologist, he charged in "Preface to Decision," "the cause of the [Southern racial] problem is race prejudice, which is a kind of social disease afflicting white folks, especially in the South; the sociologist is a kind of doctor, who isolates and describes the disease, and then designates remedy and treatment; apply remedy and treatment through Federal legislation, and you have the cure" (p. 394). But the sociologist, he charged, lacked the historical sense:

> In order to study the Negro problem the sociologist must abstract it. That is always the first act of a science. But in omitting the history of the problem or in treating the history negligently—he always does one or the other— the sociologist throws out of consideration the very data which are of primary importance to the members of the society he is studying. To the conservative white man such a study will seem horribly distorted and partial. But to all who would like for various reasons to avoid and ignore the lessons of history . . . the sociological study is a boon from Heaven. . . . Even then, the abstraction would not be so dangerous, if the final step were not always to advocate remedial legislation. (pp. 396–97)

The modern sociologist, Davidson insisted, was a romantic: "His social survey is his letter to Santa Claus. He expects the politician to be Santa Claus and to bring fulfillment down the chimney" (p. 404). Any good sociologist should regard the folk and should respect "Custom over Law," but the modern sociologist disregarded custom. It was left to the humanist, Davidson, to protest those laws which violated custom: he even went so far as to contend that the Southerner should not be bound by the Fourteenth and Fifteenth Amendments. He warned his fellow Southerners in a voice as urgent as Dabney's half a century before: the "modern liberal, walled up in sociological abstractions" (p. 412), was presiding over the decline and fall of the white South.

Davidson had spared Odum the worst of his criticism in "Preface to

---

65. Donald Davidson, "Preface to Decision," *Sewanee Review*, LIII (July-September, 1945), 394–412; Donald Davidson, "Why the Modern South Has a Great Literature," *Still Rebels, Still Yankees*, 159–79.

Decision." He was merely one of those Southerners "anxious to be 'liberal' but too slothful or sentimental to inspect the full implications of their liberalism (p. 402). But in the later essay, "Why the Modern South Has a Great Literature," he was sharply critical of that tendency in Odum which had long disturbed him but which he had forgiven in *Southern Regions*: assigning cultural rank to states and sections through compilation of statistical evidence. Davidson believed now he had found the perfect refutation of the accuracy of such a practice: William Faulkner of Mississippi. Thus in a speech at Mississippi State College in April, 1950, he insisted that Faulkner proved the sociologists wrong. Otherwise, how could Faulkner, probably the greatest living American writer, arise in the state which finished dead last in most cultural indexes?

Davidson began his speech by declaring sarcastically:

> The official, the really valid answer to my question, "Why does the modern South have a great literature?" ought to come from modern science . . . from the social scientist. . . . I turn hopefully to the sociologist, for he makes it his business to deal with all cultural matters whatsoever. . . . I turn to sociology and ask whether it can account for the appearance in Mississippi, of all places, of William Faulkner, in the three decades between 1920 and 1950. My question has a corollary which I believe I am entitled to state: Can sociology also explain why William Faulkner, or some novelist of comparable stature, did not appear, during this period, somewhere north of the Ohio—say, in Massachusetts or Wisconsin? (pp. 161–62)

Basing his response on the cultural indexes in Odum and Moore's *American Regionalism* (1938), Davidson continued, "I am very sorry to report to you that during William Faulkner's formative period the cultural factors were extremely forbidding in the State of Mississippi. I can hardly see how Mr. Faulkner survived, much less wrote novels. On the evidence of Mr. Odum's tables . . . I would confidently assert, as a devoted follower of sociology, that a William Faulkner in Mississippi would be a theoretical impossibility; and that, if he emerged at all, he would have to originate in, say, Massachusetts, where the cultural factors were favorable to literary interests" (pp. 162–63). But since Faulkner was born and bred in Mississippi, "we must, under the rigorous impulsion of sociology, reach an astounding conclusion: Namely, that the way for a society to produce a William Faulkner is to have him born in a thoroughly backward state like Mississippi" (p. 167). There must then, Davidson continued, "be some cultural factors that [the sociologist] left out; but if he can get a large financial subsidy from the Social Science Research Council, he will assign a squad of graduate students to do the job, and start punching cards and running the calculating machines, and in a few more years he will have some more indexes to round out the picture" (p. 170).

Davidson was uttering a crowd-pleasing sentiment, and he knew it. He was speaking in Mississippi to Mississippians, and he and his audience mutually rejoiced at the "backwardness" Odum had assigned them—the kind of backwardness that produced a novelist such as Faulkner. But Davidson was engaged in something other than crowd pleasing: he was articulating a deeply held belief, that culture was not to be measured by tables and charts, that it did not even have much to do with literacy and sanitation—but rather that it was organic, emanating and drawing its richness from the folk. He was also affirming his allegiance to a "knowledge that possesses the heart rather than a knowledge achieved merely by the head"—and this knowledge of the heart was "the great, all-pervasive 'cultural factor' for which the sociologists have neglected to provide data." Therefore, "they cannot account for William Faulkner and other writers, and their diagnosis of Southern society is untrustworthy" (pp. 171–72).

The South, ultimately, Davidson associated with the heart, the North with the head—and religion with the heart, sociology with the head. The domain of science and industrialism had meant "that the works of the great Northern writers tend to be all head and no heart. Or else they bear the marks of a lamentable conflict between head and heart" (p. 174), resulting in a critical point of view. And not only Northern writers were so afflicted but Southerners who had fallen under the sociological spell. If William Faulkner represented the Southern writer as artist, Thomas Wolfe represented the Southern writer as social critic: "I suggest that his trouble was that he had been taught to misunderstand with his head what he understood with his heart. Thomas Wolfe had a divided sensibility, which very likely resulted from his education at Mr. Howard Odum's citadel, the progressive University of North Carolina, and from his subsequent unfortunate experience at Harvard" (p. 176).

That the University of North Carolina was not yet "Odum's citadel" when Wolfe was a student—that Wolfe left Chapel Hill the year before Odum arrived—was not important to Davidson. Neither was his own earlier charge that Faulkner, along with Erskine Caldwell and

T. S. Stribling, was among the Southern "metropolitans."[66] What was important, as he spoke in Faulkner's Mississippi, was that both Faulkner and Wolfe served his purposes: one wrote with his heart, the other from and with his head, and the "divided sensibility" of the latter was partly a result of Howard Odum's social program.

With this accusation in 1950 Davidson broke the peace—the civility that, despite differences in point of view, had always existed between Odum and himself. Davidson had often resorted to sarcasm in discussing other sociologists, or Odum's *programs*, but rarely—publicly—Odum himself. Odum did not respond immediately to Davidson's remarks, but when Louis Rubin and Robert Jacobs asked him to write such a response for their volume, *Southern Renascence* (1953),[67] he responded in characteristic fashion—in a tone as earnest and straightforward as Davidson's had been sarcastic. Davidson's questions, he maintained, were apparently based on a "general misunderstanding of sociology" and on "the facile assumption that the sociologist would always look for a great literature in an advanced society with a high index of gadget civilization, advanced achievements in the arts and sciences, and in the setting of intellectualism and cultural specialization" (p. 85). Mississippi was indeed the "lowest indexed state" and Massachusetts "the highest indexed" (p. 85), but, Odum contended, Davidson should have known the value that Odum himself placed on the kind of "folk-regional culture" out of which Faulkner emerged. That folk-regional culture was experiencing in the 1920s a "growth stage" (p. 94) that made it possible for a writer to describe his culture with originality and seek to preserve it artistically. Faulkner had come along at a fortunate time.

What the sociologist Odum was saying in the language of social science was not far from what the humanist Allen Tate had already said: the Southern literary renascence resulted in part from a particular transitional period in Southern history which caused the Southern writer to give a "backward glance" as he moved into the modern world, to be "conscious of the past in the present."[68] But Odum went beyond a purely historical or sociological explanation, and in doing so he avoided the trap which Davidson had set for him. Faulkner, he

66. Davidson, "New York and the Hinterland," 559.

67. Howard W. Odum, "On Southern Literature and Southern Culture," in Rubin and Jacobs (eds.), *Southern Renascence*, 84–100.

68. Allen Tate, "The New Provincialism," *Virginia Quarterly Review*, XXI (Spring, 1945), 262–72.

added, could *not* be explained exclusively in sociological terms. Environment did not account for everything, and sociologists had never claimed it did. Heredity explained a great deal, and William Faulkner was a "natural" (p. 100).

Odum's response was milder than it might have been, but Davidson's attack after he had presumed their battle finished must have disappointed him, particularly since it was launched from the state where, half a century before, his own interest in folk culture had begun. *He* certainly did not need to be told that culture was not to be equated with literary, scholarly, or artistic achievement, that all its components could not be measured by charts. He knew Faulkner's people, he believed, better than Davidson ever could: "I remember riding an unbroken colt from Toccopola to Pontotoc, to Tupelo to New Albany in and out across swollen streams and backwoods and pine hills, often reflecting physical reality stranger than fiction. I have been close enough to Faulkner's quicksands to sense something of its [*sic*] terrors and have often imagined, behind the cedars and columned houses, that anything could happen there" (p. 97).

Such was a side of Odum that Davidson hardly imagined, but a side which, as we have seen, became more and more evident as he grew older—and was never far beneath the surface. A preference for the "folk of the countryside" to the "sophisticated urban intellectual," a belief that the nation needed and the South had a chance to offer a "renaissance of intellectual conviction, spiritual rejuvenation and stable morality that does not rattle with superficial verbiage": these were Davidson's sentiments, but they were Odum's words.[69] Davidson hardly noticed. So committed was he to his own idea of the South that he could not conceive of a sociologist, a devotee of tables and charts, who valued the South as much as he did, not even a sociologist such as Odum who had been born and reared a rural Southern Methodist, who wrote folk epics and spent his weekends tending Jersey cows. Davidson's view of life had become increasingly rigid, almost allegorical, with his divisions into North and South, black and white, head-centered and heart-centered writers. He himself, with his devotion to categories, nearly became a victim of the abstraction he loathed. One again is reminded of Hawthorne a full century earlier but in a society similarly undergoing a transition from old agrarian or-

69. Odum, *The Way of the South*, 64; Odum (ed.), *Southern Pioneers in Social Interpretation*, 27.

der to new industrial one—with *his* antipathy to science and reform, his fear of experimentation, his protest against head-centeredness, his fury against abstraction. The protean sociologist was to Davidson as the Giant Transcendentalist had been to Hawthorne—murky, foggy, obscure. Chapel Hill was hardly Brook Farm, but it too was grounded in theory and abstraction, bent on change and reform, violating something deep in human nature—or so Davidson charged.

From this belief that not only the traditional South but man himself was being devalued came Davidson's compulsion to preach. And like Fitzhugh and Dabney before him, he asserted that in speaking for the South he was speaking for right thinkers everywhere. In an essay in 1960, "The New South and the Conservative Tradition," he said what Fitzhugh had said exactly one hundred years before: in a time of turmoil and upheaval, on the brink of a great national crisis, Southern conservatives were fighting their battle not only for the South but for the preservation of the nation. And beyond that, he wrote in 1958, his cause he "might call . . . the cause of civilized society, as we have known it in the Western World, against the new barbarism of science and technology controlled and directed by the modern power state. In this sense, the cause of the South was and is the cause of Western civilization itself."[70]

Davidson insisted that he wrote to free man from the tyranny of science and the "power state." Odum believed, to the contrary, that man's freedom might best be achieved precisely through those two institutions—that science and a compassionate centralized authority might release the South from its fears and prejudices and enable it to realize the potential of its folk. Davidson's vision, although he realized its improbability, was that the South would spiritually expand to alter the nation itself. Odum envisioned not expansion but merger: the South would join in the nation and partake of the national mythology to which it had contributed a great deal in the first place. Davidson, if one follows Odum's logic, could not be free because he was *too* firmly rooted in Southern tradition, and in particular because of his obsessive concern of the 1940s and 1950s—the Negro. The black man cast a shadow over Davidson's South; the Negro "problem"—created, he charged, by sociologists and other liberals—meant the de-

70. Donald Davidson, "The New South and the Conservative Tradition," *National Review*, September 10, 1960, pp. 141–46; Davidson, *Southern Writers in the Modern World*, 45.

struction of that representative Southern Eden he had known in middle Georgia. Nor did Odum escape entirely the shadow of the Negro, but his faith in science and his belief in the basic goodness of man provided him weapons with which he believed he could combat racial and social injustice. His vision, though bolstered by charts and statistics, was essentially, as we have seen, that of the folk poet celebrating the region as it grew with the nation. It was a vision both broader and more generous than Davidson's; for Davidson, despite his insistence that he spoke for Western civilization, when he spoke most truthfully spoke only for the South.

CHAPTER 4

The Meaning of Aristocracy:
Wilbur Cash and William Alexander Percy

I never could see any point when you are born a gentleman in
trying to act as if you were not one.
William Alexander Percy to
Donald Davidson, May 31, 1930

What had really happened here, indeed, was that the gentlemanly idea, driven from England by Cromwell, had taken
refuge in the South and fashioned for itself a world to its
heart's desire: a world singularly polished and mellow and
poised, wholly dominated by ideals of honor and chivalry and
noblesse.
W. J. Cash,
The Mind of the South, 1941

In that particular Southern tradition which demands melodrama and
coincidence of its history, that tradition in which Edmund Ruffin, who
fired the first shot of the Civil War, should at war's end pledge his
hatred to the Yankees and turn his gun upon himself; or, in which the
South's most eloquent defender and its most perceptive critic of the
late nineteenth century should bear the same name and, in some
respects, the same biography—in that tradition it is not inappropriate that the two modern Southern works of interpretation and self-
exploration which come closest to deserving the adjective "classic"
should have been published within a single month of each other in
the same year, 1941, and by the same publisher, Alfred A. Knopf. Or
that the authors of those works, *The Mind of the South* and *Lanterns on
the Levee*, though in middle age when their books appeared—Wilbur
Cash was forty, William Alexander Percy fifty-five—should both be
dead within a year.

Southern history, wrote Richard M. Weaver, was dramatic. It was,
said Shreve to Quentin at Harvard, better than *Ben Hur*. But there
were, as well, quieter similarities in the lives of Wilbur Cash and Will
Percy, two Southerners from vastly different Souths: Cash from the
Carolina Piedmont, Percy from the Mississippi Delta. First, unlike
nearly every other critic and apologist we have encountered in this

study, both Cash and Percy were one-book men,[1] and into his one book each poured the impressions and convictions of a lifetime. Each wrote a book of Southern interpretation which was much more than that. Both *The Mind of the South* and *Lanterns on the Levee* were brilliantly conceived and controlled works of art, triumphs of tone and style, and as deserving of a place in American literature as the works of Faulkner and Wolfe, Warren and Welty. Both men were bachelors (Percy his entire life, Cash until six months before his death) who wrote in the late 1930s with intimations of mortality—Percy in poor health, determined to put on record his convictions while he was still able, Cash in apparently adequate health but shaken and strangely moved by the early death in 1938 of Thomas Wolfe, a fellow Carolinian exactly his age. Neither Cash nor Percy was a stranger to loneliness, melancholy, and feelings of inadequacy, or even to self-destruction. Percy's favorite cousin, whose sons he later adopted, committed suicide; Cash himself—less than five months after his book appeared—took his own life.

If Cash and Percy shared certain qualities, however, the two books they produced in 1941 could hardly have been more different. What the one writer affirmed, the other eloquently denied. Cash's was the voice of the "plain" white Southerner, Percy's of the planter, Cash's of the democrat, Percy's of the aristocrat. In one respect, their books continued the Southern debate of the 1920s and 1930s, Cash belonging to the school of Odum, Percy less precisely to that of Davidson. It was to Odum, as we have seen, that Cash in 1929 had presented, in a five-page letter, his ideas for a book on the South. Though more than a hundred miles away in Charlotte, he shared the spirit of Chapel Hill. Percy corresponded with Davidson during the 1920s and early 1930s and applauded the philosophy of *I'll Take My Stand*, a copy of which Davidson sent him. Indeed, to some extent, Cash and Percy represent a continuation of the counterpoint between two schools of Southern thought going back to Appomattox and before—Cash an heir to the tradition of guilt and shame, Percy to the school of remembrance. It was Southern shortcomings, the burden of Southern history, upon which Cash focused, like Cable and Walter Hines Page and

---

1. Percy also published three volumes of poetry, but *Lanterns on the Levee* was his only work of prose. See *Sappho in Levkas and Other Poems* (New Haven, 1915), *In April Once and Other Poems* (New Haven, 1920), and *Enzio's Kingdom* (New Haven, 1924).

Odum before him. The beauty and glory of that past, or at least his part of that past, attracted Percy. But, in fact, neither Cash nor Percy belonged to any school, and if *The Mind of the South* and *Lanterns on the Levee* were seen by some as a continuation of the verbal war of the 1930s between Regionalists and Agrarians, such was not the intention of either author. Cash possessed a psychological insight, an individual brilliance—finally, an independence of mind—which surpassed that of his predecessors, and Percy differed from the Agrarians both in his subject and in his tone. His South was not theirs: the Mississippi Delta was as different from middle Tennessee as it was from Piedmont Carolina. The planter exclusively, and not the farmer, he had in mind. But most of all, Percy's *voice* was not the defiant voice of Davidson, or of most of his spiritual ancestors of the nineteenth century. "The times demand good haters," Robert Lewis Dabney had written in 1869, and Davidson on occasion would have subscribed to the statement. But Percy possessed a gentleness of manner, a tone of sorrow and finally resignation, an unwillingness, even an inability to rage. "I am not a good hater," he proclaimed in 1941.[2]

THE PROMINENCE of W. J. Cash in Southern intellectual life might be measured by the stature and diversity of his critics. Clement Eaton, C. Vann Woodward, Richard Beale Davis, Louis D. Rubin, Jr., Dewey W. Grantham, Jr., Sheldon Hackney, Eugene Genovese: these and others have taken pains to dissect *The Mind of the South*, all have found it wanting for reasons we shall later see—and most have conceded its brilliance.[3] Such is indeed heady company for an obscure North Carolina newspaperman who wrote only one book and was known as something other than a small-city editorial writer for only

2. William Alexander Percy, *Lanterns on the Levee: Recollections of a Planter's Son* (1941; rpr. Baton Rouge, 1974), 116.
3. See especially, C. Vann Woodward, "White Man, White Mind," *New Republic*, December 9, 1967, pp. 28–30, and "The Elusive Mind of the South," *American Counterpoint*, 261–83; Richard Beale Davis, "Early Southern Literature," in Louis D. Rubin, Jr., and C. Hugh Holman (eds.), *Southern Literary Study* (Chapel Hill, 1975), 23–24; Louis D. Rubin, Jr., "The Mind of the South," *Sewanee Review*, LXII (Autumn, 1954), 683–95; Dewey W. Grantham, Jr., "Mr. Cash Writes a Book," *Progressive*, XXV (December, 1961), 40–42; Hackney, "Southern Violence," 906–925; Genovese, *The World the Slaveholders Made*, 137–45. See also, for two recent discussions of Cash, O'Brien, *The Idea of the American South*, 213–16; and King, *A Southern Renaissance*, 146–72.

five months of his life. Indeed, one suspects, it is as much the audacity of Cash's attempt as his success that has drawn to him such
attention. His undertaking was perhaps the nonfictional equivalent of
Thomas Wolfe's novels: he would surround, encompass, and exhaust
his subject, would do no less than isolate, define, and explain the
"mind" of the South.

Cash gave his entire adult life to the task, produced a *tour de force*,
then less than five months after he produced the work that ensured
him the sort of recognition he had long sought, he committed suicide—a fact which has perhaps contributed to his mystique as brooding, beleaguered Southern prophet, and has certainly done nothing
to discourage interest in his life and work. By the 1960s *The Mind of the
South* had become a sort of Southern testament, the first work on the
South suggested to outsiders, the book Northern civil rights workers
carried with them on their Southern forays. One exaggerates only
mildly in suggesting that Cash became more than an author and *The
Mind of the South* more than a book: together they came to constitute a
school of Southern thought, an intellectual force, to be drawn on,
cited, and contested.

Wilbur Joseph Cash was an unlikely candidate for fame. Born in
May, 1900, in the cotton mill town of Gaffney, South Carolina, where
his father was manager of the company store for Limestone Mills, he
grew up in an orthodox and strict Baptist home. His forebears, of
Scotch-Irish and German stock, had lived in that area along the border between the Carolinas since the early eighteenth century. When
he was twelve the family moved thirteen miles to Boiling Springs,
North Carolina, where his father took a partnership in a general
store. From his youth he was a reader, a dreamer—and a Confederate. He was "reared an intense sentimentalist to the South," he later
recalled, and at age thirty-six his "blood still [leapt] to the band's playing of 'Dixie,' and to such flourishing phrases as 'the sword of Lee.'" [4]
As a child he refought Civil War battles and read Scott, Dickens, Kip-
ling—and Thomas Dixon, author of *The Leopard's Spots* (1902) and *The
Clansman* (1905) and a native of Cleveland County, North Carolina,

4. Joseph L. Morrison, *W. J. Cash: Southern Prophet* (New York, 1967), 6–24; W. J.
Cash, autobiographical sketch written for Alfred A. Knopf, 1936, quoted in Tom Dearmore, "The Enigma of W. J. Cash," in Louis M. Lyons (ed.), *Reporting the News* (Cambridge, Mass., 1965), 383. I rely principally on Morrison's brief biography for details of
Cash's life.

to which the Cashes had moved. Dixon was a local hero—Baptist preacher, novelist, and white supremacist—and as such was regarded highly in the Cash household. Cash attended an academy in Boiling Springs, then at age nineteen—after brief, unhappy stays at Wofford College and Valparaiso University—he enrolled at Thomas Dixon's alma mater, Wake Forest College. There a new phase of his education began. A Baptist school near Raleigh, Wake Forest was surprisingly liberal for its time and place. At least its president, William Louis Poteat, was: he prized free inquiry and encouraged bold expression. At Wake Forest, Cash read Cabell, Sinclair Lewis, and Mencken, wrote for the college newspaper, became an iconoclast, and spoke of someday writing a book about the South. After leaving Wake Forest in 1923, he taught for two years, tried to write a novel, then went to work for the Charlotte *News*. Bothered by hyperthyroidism and extreme irritability, he left his newspaper job in 1927 and bicycled across Europe. Like Henry Adams, he was drawn to Chartres; at the sight of the cathedral he was moved to tears. His health, which had improved in Europe, further declined after he returned to America. For the remainder of his twenties he lived at home, worked on a small newspaper in Cleveland County, and began in earnest his search for the truth about the South.

The first fruits of that search were two essays written for his idol Mencken and published in 1929 in the *American Mercury*. "Jehovah of the Tar Heels" was a mocking treatment of Senator Furnifold Simmons of North Carolina; Cash's style was indisputably Mencken's and so was his vocabulary. Speaking of the "essential sottishness of democracy" and of "Great Moral Ideas," he drew an indictment of Southern religion and insularity. In the second essay Cash offered two theses, neither original: that the mind of the New South was "still basically and essentially the mind of the Old South" and that the typical antebellum Southern planter, outside the Tidewater, was in fact a backwoods "farmer." He also railed in Menckenian language against the Southern "shamans" and "holy men," against Southern leaders, "sworn enemies of the arts, of all ideas dating after 1400, and of common decency." A thinker in the South was "regarded quite logically as an enemy of the people, who, for the common weal, ought to be put down summarily." It was an essay written expressly for Mencken, restating the thesis—and in the tone—of "The Sahara of the

Bozart." The seven-page essay appeared in October, 1929. It was entitled "The Mind of the South."[5]

The young newspaperman's ideas about the South were largely formed by the time he first appeared in the *Mercury*. In the area of belles-lettres he admired Cabell, DuBose Heyward, and Julia Peterkin, in social commentary he was drawn to Odum and the reformers—all of whom, he had written in the *Mercury*, were "not, in any true sense, of the Southern mind," since all were "above and outside any group mind" (p. 192). Shortly afterward he expanded his list to include two other young Southerners who had attracted national attention in 1929: William Faulkner and Thomas Wolfe. In Wolfe particularly he saw a history resembling his own. The author of *Look Homeward, Angel* had also been born in 1900 of plain Scotch-Irish and German stock, and fewer than a hundred miles away from Cash. Like Cash, he had attended college in North Carolina, had become an iconoclast whose patron saint was Mencken, and had come to see religion as the great obstacle to Southern intellectual progress. Like the author of "The Mind of the South," he published his first significant work in October, 1929, and for it drew the wrath of his homefolks. A year later, like Cash, he responded negatively to *I'll Take My Stand*, and soon found himself placed in the Chapel Hill school of Southern thought. It was no wonder, nine years later, that Thomas Wolfe's early death frightened the other Carolinian.

If the 1920s had been for Cash an exciting decade, characterized by a clash of ideas and intellectual ferment, the 1930s were a confusing period, frustrated by ill health, psychological breakdown, and professional insecurity. Throughout the early 1930s, however, he continued to send essays to Mencken, who delighted in his latest Southern find. In "The War in the South" (1930), an account of the textile troubles Cash had witnessed firsthand in Gastonia, North Carolina, in 1929, he subscribed to Mencken's thesis that after the Civil War the cotton mill owner had replaced the "gentleman planter as head of the Southern social order"—a thesis Cash himself would later dispute. In "Paladin of the Drys" (1931), an essay about Senator Cameron Morrison of North Carolina, he reinforced the Menckenian idea of the entire

5. W. J. Cash, "Jehovah of the Tar Heels," *American Mercury*, XVII (July, 1929), 310–18; W. J. Cash, "The Mind of the South," *American Mercury*, XVIII (October, 1929), 185–92.

South as colossal human comedy. "Close View of a Calvinist Lhasa" (1933) was even more spectacularly Menckenian: Cash described his adopted home Charlotte as the center of conservatism in North Carolina, "a citadel of bigotry and obscurantism," "the chief enemy of civilization in the Near South." In "Buck Duke's University" (1933) he pointed to religion as the first cause of Southern anti-intellectualism and saw in "old Buck's Christian purposes" the kind of thinking that could destroy the impressive new university he had erected in Durham. James Buchanan Duke was "a red-headed, shambling Methodist jake . . . which is to say, a sort of peasant out of the Eleventh Century, incredibly ignorant, incredibly obtuse, incredibly grasping and picayune." [6]

The essays were undeniably Menckenian, both in point of view and in vocabulary: "civilized minority," "Shamans," "holy men," "blackamoors," "Ethiops," "that amazing and sulphurous land below the Potomac." Cash's South was populated with the same grotesques that inhabited Mencken's own, and his subjects—cotton mill barons, preachers, demagogues, Negroes, and poor whites—were also Mencken's. It was as if the young newspaperman had read the *Mercury* editor so often and had quoted him so frequently that the same words, the same rhythms, even at times the exact phrases reverberated in his mind. Cash thus served Mencken in the early 1930s in the same way another North Carolinian and Wake Forest alumnus, Gerald W. Johnson, had served him in the 1920s: as chief Southern contributor to the *Mercury*, the dispenser of the Menckenian doctrine of Southern backwardness. In January, 1934, he wrote his final essay for Mencken, "Holy Men Muff a Chance," in which he insisted that Southern preachers were missing an opportunity by not taking advantage of the Great Depression, a time when "the harvest is ripe for the holy men of God." [7] This was Cash's seventh essay for the *Mercury* in a period of four years, and in it the Mencken style had finally become stale. That style, to be purely effective, presupposed a writer's detach-

6. W. J. Cash, "The War in the South," *American Mercury*, XIX (February, 1930), 163–69; W. J. Cash, "Paladin of the Drys," *American Mercury*, XXIV (October, 1931), 139–47; W. J. Cash, "Close View of a Calvinist Lhasa," *American Mercury*, XXVIII (April, 1933), 443–51; W. J. Cash, "Buck Duke's University," *American Mercury*, XXX (September, 1933), 102–110.

7. W. J. Cash, "Holy Men Muff a Chance," *American Mercury*, XXXI (January, 1934), 112–18.

ment from his subject. Cash, as he himself had come to realize, was anything but detached when he contemplated the South, and the wonder is that he had succeeded in a satirical vein as long as he had. Now it was time to find his own voice.

He found that voice in an essay, "Genesis of the Southern Cracker" (also written for the *American Mercury* but after Mencken's departure and no longer in the Mencken style); another essay, "The Reign of the Commonplace," which appeared in Lillian Smith's magazine *Pseudopodia* in the autumn of 1936; and finally in articles he began to contribute to the book page of the Charlotte *News* in the mid-1930s. His *News* essays treated many subjects—one, written a year before his death, was a light piece on suicide (his native South Carolina, it seemed, had the lowest rate in the country)—but many dealt with Southern affairs. In particular, he continued to praise Odum and the other Southern reformers and to decry their ideological adversaries, the Southern Agrarians. As early as 1926 he had expressed disapproval of the poetry of the Fugitives, who he believed were poseurs. Four years later he had railed at *I'll Take My Stand*, and in 1933 he had sent Mencken an article harshly critical of the Agrarians—an article which Mencken believed "a magnificent refutation of the Tate Ransome [*sic*] Company" but which he felt should be published in a Southern journal rather than in the *Mercury*. Later in his *News* column Cash both criticized and parodied the Agrarians. He failed to acknowledge that he himself had previously expressed sentiments similar to theirs. In his 1929 *Mercury* article he had maintained that "the mind of the South" was "a mind . . . of the soil rather than of the mills" and had warned that the cure for Southern provincialism—that is, industrialism— might prove worse than the disease. He had expressed the fear that "we shall merely exchange the Confederate for that dreadful fellow, the go-getter . . . the Hon. John LaFarge Beauregard for George F. Babbitt."[8]

Wilbur Cash as he wrote in the 1930s, then, fell precisely into no

8. W. J. Cash, "Genesis of the Southern Cracker," *American Mercury*, XXXV (May, 1935), 105–108; W. J. Cash, "The Reign of the Commonplace," *Pseudopodia* (Autumn, 1936), in Helen White and Redding S. Sugg, Jr. (eds.), *From the Mountain* (Memphis, 1972), 251–55; W. J. Cash, "Suicide Surge," Charlotte *News*, July 24, 1940, in Morrison, W. J. Cash, 268–69 [see Morrison, pp. 220–94, for other Charlotte *News* essays]; H. L. Mencken to W. J. Cash, August 26, 1933 (copy), in Mencken Papers; W. J. Cash, "Rum, Romanism, and Rebellion," Charlotte *News*, June 12, 1938, in Morrison, *W. J. Cash*, 238–41; Cash, "The Mind of the South," 185, 192.

one school, and most of what he wrote during that decade never saw print in the 1930s. For what preoccupied him during those years was the book on the Southern mind which he had conceived in his student days of the early 1920s, proposed and formulated by 1929, and agonized over for the next eleven years. It was the book that had gained momentum in 1929 when Mencken had shown Cash's essay "The Mind of the South" to his publishers Alfred and Blanche Knopf—and Mrs. Knopf had written Cash asking him to send an outline and sample chapter.

Cash at first apparently intended a more contemporary, less historical work, one espousing the Odum–Gerald Johnson philosophy with a dash of Mencken thrown in. According to Joseph Morrison, in the sample chapter he had planned to attack the Fugitive-Agrarians for romanticizing the Old South and Edwin Mims for glorifying the New. But when he began to work on the book it became something quite other, and more, than that. He worked in fits and starts throughout the 1930s, first announcing in a Guggenheim Fellowship application that he would complete the book by early 1933, then promising the Knopfs he would have the manuscript to them by July, 1936, then 1938, then February, 1939. If, as Dr. Johnson once wrote, a man would turn over half a library to produce a single book, Cash did that and more. He wrote, destroyed, and rewrote, aiming for perfection. At first he sought to document his work, piling up footnotes on every page in an attempt, he wrote later, "to back up some of my statements with references to facts in the books of other men." Then he threw away much of what he had written and started again—without footnotes. The central ideas in the book came gradually. At first, in his 1929 letter to Odum, he had described the Old South as "that static and paternal order with the landowners on the one hand, and the slaves and the poor-whites on the other." But later he obviously heeded the words of Odum, who advised: "I should not draw the lines very closely between the different cultural groups of the South. That is, the lines between your old-time romantic gentleman of the South and other types . . . were not always so closely drawn." Other points of emphasis came later. But during the mid- and late 1930s, as Morrison writes, Cash experienced a writing block. Although he had no trouble producing editorials and reviews for the Charlotte *News*, his long-awaited book was another matter. Perhaps, as Morrison suggests, the block resulted because Cash's interest in the South was, in the late 1930s, partly overshadowed by the war in Europe.[9] But he must have remembered, as well, the unfavorable local response to his earlier *Mercury* essays, particularly "The Mind of the South" and "Close View of a Calvinist Lhasa."

Meanwhile, as Cash found himself unable to complete his book about the South, he must have noticed that any number of his fellow Southern journalists were having no trouble at all. Nearly every prominent Southern newspaperman—Gerald Johnson, Virginius Dabney, Jonathan Daniels, and John Temple Graves among them— seemed to be proposing or writing such a book. Johnson in *The Wasted Land* (1938), which was based on statistics presented in Odum's *Southern Regions*, held that the South was a region of "wasted men, wasted money . . . wasted time, wasted opportunity," but one that could right itself socially and economically through Odum's planning approach. Dabney's *Below the Potomac* (1942) was a portrait of the latest New South from the point of view of a certified Southern liberal. Although the author acknowledged Southern problems, his tone was upbeat, not unlike that of Mims's *Advancing South* (1926). Graves and Daniels were writing more personal books. Daniels' *Southerner Discovers the South* (1938), probably the most charming book of the period, also attracted the most attention.[10] Based on a trip the Raleigh editor had made around the South in 1937, it was a folksy narrative, recording its author's impressions of the South and his fellow Southerners. This was no book of criticism: Daniels came back from the Deep South with an awareness of social and economic problems, but he, like Dabney, painted a basically optimistic picture of the South at the end.

Cash read and absorbed both Johnson and Daniels, fellow North Carolina liberals. Dabney's work he had praised before. But a Southern book of the late 1930s which seemed to interest him even more was one which attracted less attention than any of the others—a work entitled *90° in the Shade* by a thirty-nine-year-old journalism professor at the University of Alabama named Clarence Cason. For Cason's book, published in 1935 by the University of North Carolina Press, at-

9. Morrison, *W. J. Cash*, 49, 66 [quoting Cash]; Cash to Odum, November 13, 1929, and Odum to Cash, November 20, 1929 (copy); Morrison, *W. J. Cash*, 94–100.

10. Gerald W. Johnson, *The Wasted Land* (Chapel Hill, 1938), 7; Virginius Dabney, *Below the Potomac: A Book About the New South* (New York, 1942); John Temple Graves, *The Fighting South* (New York, 1943); Daniels, *A Southerner Discovers the South.* See also Virginius Dabney, *Liberalism in the South* (Chapel Hill, 1932).

tempted to do approximately what Cash was attempting in his book. Cason announced in his foreword that he had tried to isolate and define the "character" of the Southern states. The South was diverse, he acknowledged, but it was "self-conscious enough and sufficiently insulated from the rest of the country to be thought of as a separate province."[11]

Cason was a native Alabamian and, though generally considered a liberal, he announced that he was "not without an intuitive bias on the side of traditionalism and the *status quo*" (p. 130). A "good and hopeful southerner" (p. 172), he possessed "a mind which, for all its faults, is of the South and southern" (p. 130). The son of a physician with a keenly developed sense of noblesse oblige, Cason counted himself among the disinherited of the South, a victim of what William Faulkner a hundred and fifty miles to the west was, at about that time, identifying as Snopesism. As a member of a family which had been economically deprived "for a generation," he resented the new moneyed class: "We had found ourselves in the hazardous position of maintaining a sense of superiority on the basis of a past which grew increasingly shadowy and uncertain" (p. 121). But in his book, he maintained, he intended neither "justification [nor] condemnation of the South. At the risk of exhibiting myself as unmoral, I confess that I am far less interested in administering uplift in the southern states than in simply having the pleasure of talking about the region" (p. x).

That was unlikely. As Faulkner was also writing at about that time, it was impossible for the Southern writer, at least the serious and honest one, to write with "pleasure" about the South, to make writing "any fun." Rather, the Southerner "unconsciously" wrote "into every line and phrase his violent despairs and rages and frustrations or his violent prophesies [*sic*] of still more violent hopes."[12] Such, subsequent events would prove, was particularly true of Cason. On the surface his book was mild enough. Comprised of "ideas [which] have been simmering in the mind of the author for at least half a dozen years" (p. xii), it would attempt a middle course. Although there ex-

11. Clarence Cason, *90° in the Shade* (Chapel Hill, 1935), ix. See also Elvy E. Callaway, *The Other Side of the South* (Chicago, 1934), another book written by an Alabamian at about the same time as Cason's. Callaway, a lawyer and a Republican, is critical of many aspects of the South—its religious orthodoxy, its advocacy of Prohibition, and its treatment of the Negro—but he nonetheless insists that he is a white supremacist. Like Cason, he is but a mild social critic.

12. William Faulkner, unpublished manuscript, August, 1933, quoted in Joseph L. Blotner, *Faulkner: A Biography* (2 vols.; New York, 1974), I, 811.

isted in the South some "physical and mental privation" which could "be attributed only to some gigantic error in philosophy, or to some overwhelming catastrophe" such as the Civil War (p. xi), the South also had much to offer—an appreciation of leisure and a code of manners, a true spirit of paternalism, a tolerant attitude on the part of its "best people," a "wisdom, dignity and self-reliance" (p. xii) which belonged, in any case, to the Old South.

Cason strove throughout to be moderate—he demonstrated a veritable rage for moderation—but it was clear to his readers that he found more to censure than to admire in Dixie: the South as it stood in 1935 was overly sensitive to criticism, inhospitable to outside ideas, given to demagogy, lynching, and a religion which reinforced Southern prejudices. Cason tried to qualify his criticism in numerous ways. He stressed from the beginning that a work such as his was necessarily impressionistic—that what one man observed another might not, that, indeed, he himself might be wrong. He sought, that is, to absolve himself of the role of truth-sayer. At one point, after he had catalogued Southern shortcomings and then offered Wisconsin as an example of a clean, progressive state without such flaws, he hastened to add that he really preferred the South: "I, for one, would far rather live in the South—for all its faults—than in any other part of the world that I have ever seen" (p. 185). Cason played it equally safe at the end of the book. After declaring that the South "would profit from a nice, quiet revolution," he was quick to add, "I do not mean a Communistic revolt, or another Populist uprising, or further developments of Fascism in the South" but rather a "revision of the region's implanted ideas," a realistic examination of social problems, a "redirection of the South's courage and audacity, and a determination that the southern conscience shall be accorded the reverence due a sacred thing" (pp. 185–86). He rested his case on the Southern past: those "who love the South" would be inspired by a vision worthy of that past (p. 186).

Wilbur Cash, reading Cason's book at a time he was struggling to complete his own, would have been interested in the work under any circumstances. But he must have read with particular interest Cason's description of the South as a "separate province" (a conclusion he had also reached) and his remarks on cotton mill owners, and mill villages. Cason had also expressed a compelling interest in fascism, Southern style, that matched Cash's own. "One is almost forced to believe," the

Alabamian wrote, "that a peculiar type of Fascism has been at work below the Potomac" (p. 89). "If one must seek a classification for the Heflins, Bilbos, and [Huey] Longs, it would not be too wide of the mark to term them American Fascists. . . . Their political victories have been won through the mass force of machines built upon every conceivable form of racial, sectional, class, and religious prejudice" (p. 106). Finally, Cash must have noted Cason's remarks on the South's intolerance of criticism—which resembled the savage ideal he himself had just articulated in the last of his *Mercury* articles—and must have seen in Cason himself an example of that savage ideal at work. For Cason, who feared that even his mild criticism would bring a hostile reception from his fellow Alabamians, took his own life just before the book came out. Moved by Cason's death, Cash wrote in his own manuscript: "Poor Clarence Cason, who taught journalism at Alabama, felt compelled to commit suicide, in part at least because of his fear of the fiercely hostile attitude which he knew that both the school authorities and his fellow faculty members would take toward his criticisms of the South in his *90° In The Shade*" (p. 334).

At the end of July, 1940, after waiting for eleven years, Alfred Knopf received a completed manuscript from Cash. "The thing is at last done," the author wrote, "and I am as relieved as I know you are. The history of that book is strange stuff." The last two or three years of writing had been particularly tense. Cash apologized to Knopf for being a "lazy fellow," but in fact it was not sloth so much as his obsession with European affairs and a reluctance to let his book go that had prevented him from finishing. Now, once he had the manuscript, Knopf worked quickly. *The Mind of the South* was published on February 10, 1941, and the reviews which followed were almost unanimously laudatory. Cash's fellow Southern newspapermen Dabney, Gerald Johnson, Graves, George Fort Milton, Mark Ethridge, and others were lavish in their praise—although Dabney was not so glowing as Cash felt he should have been and wrote telling him so.[13]

Readers seemed to realize from the beginning that W. J. Cash had

13. W. J. Cash to Alfred A. Knopf, July 27, 1940, quoted in Morrison, *W. J. Cash*, 100 [see also 112–13]. For reviews of *The Mind of the South*, see Virginius Dabney, in *New York Herald Tribune Books*, February 9, 1941, p. 3; Gerald W. Johnson, "Below the Potomac," *New Republic*, May 12, 1941, p. 673; George Fort Milton, "A Southern Liberal," *Yale Re-*

written a Southern book like no other written before. "Anything written about the South henceforth," wrote an anonymous reviewer in *Time*, "must start where he leaves off."[14] Cash's thesis was hardly unique—the Southern mind possessed a high degree of unity, and Southern history a definite continuity. The South, stretching from Virginia to Texas, was "not quite a nation within a nation, but the next thing to it" (p. viii); it was "a tree with many age rings . . . but with its tap root in the Old South. . . . The mind of the section, that is, is continuous with the past" (p. x). In addition to these themes, Cash stressed the individualism and romanticism of the Old South, the seemingly contradictory strains of hedonism and Puritanism in the Southern character, and the South as an uncultured land: "In general, the intellectual and aesthetic culture of the Old South was a superficial and jejune thing, borrowed from without" (p. 97). He chose as his generic Southern figure, his "man at the center," a simple yeoman who through hard work became a planter and fell into the traps of mythmaking and posturing. Finally, he created original terms to explain certain phenomena in Southern society: the "proto-Dorian" bond was that convention which "elevated" the nonslaveholding white "to a position comparable to that of, say, the Doric knight of ancient Sparta" (p. 40), the "savage ideal . . . that ideal whereunder dissent and variety are completely suppressed and men become, in all their attitudes, professions, and actions, virtual replicas of one another" (pp. 93–94).

Cash, of course, had antecedents. His man at the center, as we have seen, was suggested by the two generic Southerners, Uncle John and the old Major, whom Odum had employed in *An American Epoch*. Cash's representative man was modeled on his great-great-grandfather, as Odum's had been on his two grandfathers. Cash's famous phrase "not quite a nation within a nation" may have been derived from William J. Robertson's reference to the South as "a nation within a nation" in his book, *The Changing South* (1927), which appeared just before Cash began to write and which he almost certainly read. His emphasis on "the frontier the Yankees made" after the Civil War had

---

view, XXX (April, 1941), 831–33; Charles Lee Snyder, "How the South Came to Think and Feel as It Did," *New York Times Book Review*, February 23, 1941, p. 4; David Cohn, "Tissues of Southern Culture," *Saturday Review*, February 22, 1941, pp. 7, 16–17.

14. "Psychoanalysis of a Nation," *Time*, February 24, 1941, p. 97.

been anticipated by Gerald Johnson, who had written in *Harper's* in 1929, "The South after the Civil War was to all intents and purposes a frontier." Indeed, nearly all of the subjects—religious frenzy, the Klan, the poor white, and the subculture of the Southern cotton mill—that Cash treated in *The Mind of the South* Johnson had discussed in the 1920s in the pages of the *American Mercury*, at a time Cash was a devoted reader of the *Mercury*. Johnson had insisted upon the essential romanticism of the Klansman, the role of chivalry in his conduct, he had stressed the extent to which the rise of cotton mills in the post-Reconstruction South was an economic equivalent of war, and had seen the mill as an extension of the plantation, paternalism and noblesse oblige intact.[15] Cash made the same points in *The Mind of the South*. And Cash had been scooped not only by a contemporary Southern liberal but by an earlier conservative as well. George Fitzhugh had anticipated Cash's celebrated proto-Dorian bond eighty years before when he had written in *Cannibals All!* that slavery made nonslaveholding whites "privileged citizens, like Greek and Roman citizens, with a numerous class far beneath them" (p. 320). The Southern white man, like the Roman, could be a "noble and a privileged character," Fitzhugh had contended, and his "high position" would be due to the presence of the Negro. "One free citizen" did not "lord it over another" in the South; hence came "that feeling of independence and equality that distinguishes us; hence that pride of character, that self-respect. . . . It is a distinction to be a Southerner, as it was once to be a Roman citizen."[16]

It was not, then, Cash's originality of concept that accounted for the power of his book. Not only Fitzhugh, Robertson, Odum, and Johnson but numerous other Southerners had stated at least part of his thesis before. It was rather the process of synthesis that distinguished Cash's work: he brought the parts together. It was also his *method*— the same amateur Freudianism that American writers such as Sher-

---

15. William J. Robertson, *The Changing South* (New York, 1927), 1; Gerald W. Johnson, "The Cadets of New Market—A Reminder to Critics of the South," *Harper's*, CLX (December, 1929), 117. See also Gerald W. Johnson's essays in the *American Mercury* "Journalism Below the Potomac" (IX [September, 1926], 77–82); "The Ku Kluxer" (I [February, 1924], 207–211); "Saving Souls" (II [July, 1924], 364–68); "Service in the Cotton Mills" (V [June, 1925], 219–23); and "The South Takes the Offensive" (II [May, 1924], 70–78).

16. Fitzhugh, *Sociology for the South*, 147–48, 255 [see also 93].

wood Anderson and Faulkner had employed in Cash's formative years, the 1920s and early 1930s. The author of *The Mind of the South*, the *Time* reviewer declared, had produced "a psychoanalysis of his own native land" (p. 97). Cash had written that the South suffered from "a sort of social schizophrenia," that it contained a divided "psyche." The Old South had been afflicted by a "guilt complex about slavery": "In its secret heart [it] always carried a powerful and uneasy sense of the essential rightness of the nineteenth century's position on slavery. . . . The Old South, in short, was a society beset by the specters of defeat, of shame, of guilt" (p. 63). Because the Southerner "secretly" believed slavery to be wrong, he had adopted "defense mechanisms" to hide the truth from himself. He had justified slavery as beneficial to Negroes because it "civilized" and Christianized them. He justified it by reasoning that an omnipotent God had predestined it: "Hence slavery, and, indeed, everything that was, was His responsibility, not the South's" (p. 84). He also told himself that he was noble, chivalrous, and kind, and that the Yankee, particularly the critic of slavery, was "low-bred, crass, and money-grubbing" (p. 64). He wrote romantic fiction, casting himself in the role of the heroes of Sir Walter Scott, celebrating his own virtues. And he adored woman, reasoning that she would not be safe if the black man were not kept in subjugation: the "rape complex," in Cash's words. He psychoanalyzed the South Old and New, and finally he analyzed himself. Although he insisted he meant the Southern writers of fiction, Wolfe and Faulkner and Caldwell, more than any of them he was describing himself when he wrote:

> Readers of the *American Mercury* in H. L. Mencken's time as editor will recall that baiting the South in its pages was one of the favorite sports of young Southerners of literary and intellectual pretensions.
>
> In reality they hated the South a good deal less than they said and thought. Rather, so far as their hatred was not mere vain profession designed to invite attention to their own superior perception, they hated it with the exasperated hate of a lover who cannot persuade the object of his affections to his desire. Or, perhaps more accurately, as Narcissus, growing at length analytical, might have suddenly begun to hate his image reflected in the pool.
>
> All these men remained fundamentally Southern in their basic emotions. Intense belief in and love for the Southern legend had been bred into them as children and could not be bred out again simply by taking

thought. . . . And their hate and anger against the South was both a defense mechanism against the inner uneasiness created by that conflict and
a sort of reverse embodiment of the old sentimentality itself. (pp. 386–87)

If Cash was like Wolfe, Faulkner, and the other writers he had described in his relationship to the South, he was also like them in one
other significant way: he wanted first and foremost to be a writer of
imaginative literature. "I want above everything to be a novelist,"
Cash had written in a brief autobiographical sketch for Knopf in 1936,
and it was a desire he had possessed since his early twenties when he
had attempted to write fiction. In 1936 he had applied for a Guggenheim Fellowship with the intent of writing a novel about the Old
South. In another Guggenheim application he had proposed a novel
about the New South: "the story of the character and development of
a certain Andrew Bates, born the son of a wealthy cotton mill family
in piedmont North Carolina in 1900, down until the outbreak of the
second world war in 1939," and "the story of his father and grandfather [and] the rise of an industrial town in the South after the introduction of the idea of Progress after 1880." In his book column in the
Charlotte News he had pointed to the need for the sort of novel he
proposed: "No one has adequately told any part of the story of the
great dream of progress, now ringing slowly to its end—of the rise of
mills and towns in the hill-country of the south and its repercussions
in the lives of men and women."[17]

Cash did not write a novel on the subject, but he did write The Mind
of the South; as he described it in 1940, that book was "creative writing." It contained a plot—as Louis Rubin has written, it's the "Rich
People" against the "Poor People," and the "Rich People" offer the
"Poor People" religion and cotton mill jobs and the "proto-Dorian
Bond" to keep them from becoming "Class Conscious."[18] The book
also possessed a consciously developed persona and a consciously literary style. Cash is familiar with his reader in the manner of the Victorian narrator, referring repeatedly to himself and the way he is telling his story. The author, or his persona, is virtually a participant in
the story, in the sense that Fielding and Thackeray and Trollope are

17. Cash, autobiographical sketch, quoted in Dearmore, "The Enigma of W. J.
Cash," 384; Cash, Guggenheim application, 1940, quoted in Morrison, W. J. Cash, 105;
W. J. Cash, "Southland Turns to Books with Full Vigor," Charlotte News, February 9,
1936, in Morrison, W. J. Cash, 223.
18. Cash, quoted in Joseph L. Morrison, "The Summing Up," South Atlantic Quarterly, LXX (Autumn, 1971), 483; Rubin, "The Mind of the South," 687–89.

participants in theirs. He is master of ceremonies, the man in charge, the reader's guide through the maze of Southern history. He interrupts himself, digresses, questions himself: "But I must pause to explain more fully" (p. 23); "I shall have, indeed, presently to report" (p. 32); "But I am leaping ahead too rapidly?" (p. 41); "I have been taking you deep into the territory of a second great Southern characteristic" (p. 46). He demonstrates a proprietary interest in his story, referring repeatedly to "our Southerner," "my Irishman," "our simple generic figure." The process toward understanding in *The Mind of the South* is a shared one, almost a conversation with the reader, and the author wants to ensure that the reader follows his reasoning at every turn. All he writes rests on what he has said earlier, thus the narrative is filled with "as I have said." Cash is weaving a pattern, creating a design. But he also has the confidence to question his own positions: "I am too easily slurring over that narrow class consciousness" (p. 41). Or "It may be objected that I am assuming too much. . . . Let us grant it" (p. 54); "I have dealt with the mind of the Old South in oversimplified terms" (p. 61); "It seems a flat contradiction, no doubt" (p. 114); "But I have diverged a little" (p. 388). Or, after debunking the Southern love of progress, "But I generalize too easily, I am a little fanciful and maybe a little dubious, and of course I ought not to be so" (p. 225). Cash is not going to let his reader catch him in anything: he anticipates every criticism, setting straight every possible objection of his reader. He is obliged to the reader, he wants to please. No one will leave this show dissatisfied.

Such is assuredly not conventional history, not of the twentieth-century variety anyway. Nor is the *style* conventional. If Cash is no longer the Menckenian showman of the *American Mercury* days, neither is he the measured, understated scholar. The tone is nearly mythic at times, as if Cash were writing about distant times and faraway people: "By 1885 men were arising in the land" (p. 113). At other times, when he goes into the mind of his man at the center, he utilizes a modified stream of consciousness. Throughout he demonstrates the same love of words as Wolfe and Faulkner, the romantic, rhetorical Southern style. And he reveals the same penchant for exaggeration, for superlatives as Wolfe. The Old South was, in some respects, "one of the most remarkable societies which ever existed in the world" (p. 38), Southern individualism the "most intense individualism the world has seen since the Italian Renaissance" (p. 32). Southerners during Reconstruction became "the most sentimental people in history" (p. 130), the Southern poor white was "one of the most complete romantics and one of the most complete hedonists ever recorded" (p. 52).

Although the voice is authoritative, the style is casual and conversational, seeming to move easily from topic to topic. But underlying the casual style are a tight control and organization. And behind the author's seeming generosity and assurance is a great caution. If, as Morrison writes, there is desperation in *The Mind of the South*, Cash surely conceals it. But the way he conceals it is to hide behind his bright, witty, pleasing persona, to serve as gracious narrator to his gentle reader. His repeated qualification of points and his self-questioning suggest insecurity as much as generosity. It is a form of defensiveness—a defense mechanism, Cash might have said. The gracious narrator is not so fully in charge as he might seem.

Indeed, it is the accomplished style of *The Mind of the South*, the authoritative tone and the general flow of the narrative, that is likely to divert the reader from both the author's insecurity and his errors in historical interpretation. Cash tells such an intriguing story, that is, and tells it so well that historical accuracy initially seems secondary: the reader allows himself to be carried along. Cash seems at first, simply through his artistry, to have solved the problem that Howard Odum pointed out in 1929: how he could make his book dramatically interesting and at the same time avoid generalization. He could not, of course, and the wonder is that for nearly a quarter-century few scholars—except Louis Rubin in his essay in 1954—called his hand.

But once the criticism began, it came from various sources—most notably, C. Vann Woodward in an essay, "The Elusive Mind of the South," first published in 1969 and, revised, in *American Counterpoint* (1970). Woodward enumerated Cash's shortcomings: He had not recognized the intellectual life of the Old South, had ignored philosophers such as Fitzhugh, and had barely mentioned Jefferson and Calhoun. He had put too much emphasis on unity and continuity in Southern history; in fact, the "mind" of the South was not so monolithic, nor were the Old South and the New so similar as Cash suggested. He was "confused" about aristocracy, assuming that its members should always be genteel. Finally, his range was limited. He had written of the Carolinas, which he knew; he had ignored the Far

South, which he did not. He had written extensively of the cotton mill, but had ignored most other Southern industries. Cash had written a significant book, Woodward concluded, even a spectacular one, but also one highly flawed.[19]

Other scholars, as well, have disagreed with much in *The Mind of the South*. Paul Gaston in *The New South Creed* (1970) also took issue with Cash's claims for continuity in Southern history. The New South prophets had preached a *new* set of values, he contended. They had found fault with the antebellum ideal of leisure, they had put business above politics and rhetoric, and had advocated a more practical education. Eugene Genovese, one of Cash's severest critics, disagreed with his claim that the Southern slaveholder felt great guilt over slavery, and even more with his contention that the Old South was bourgeois, that it possessed no true aristocracy outside the Tidewater. The Southern planter was acquisitive, Genovese conceded, but he possessed an aristocratic vision. Like Woodward, he insisted that Cash romanticized "aristocracy."[20]

The indictment against Cash could continue. His title was, of course, misleading: it was not the Southern "mind" he depicted—like Henry Adams, he did not recognize that mind—but rather its folk character. And it was not "of the South" he wrote, but, as Woodward pointed out, a limited part of it. His title might well have been, if he had been writing a doctoral dissertation rather than a personal essay, "The Cultural Unity of the White Piedmont South, 1830–1940." Historically, Cash was off base in other particulars. His view of Reconstruction has been invalidated by historians, his understanding of populism was flawed, he omitted the mind of the Negro in his analysis and wrote only of the white mind. His understanding of Puritanism was faulty, distorted no doubt by too much reading of his mentor Mencken. "From the first great revivals onward," he had written, "the official moral philosophy of the South moved steadily toward the position of the Massachusetts Bay Colony" (p. 59). In fact, Southern "Puritanism" was vastly different from the New England variety, less structured, less intellectual, more emotional—raw Calvinism, rather than the cerebral Puritanism of the Massachusetts Bay.

19. Woodward, "The Elusive Mind of the South," 261–83.
20. Gaston, *The New South Creed*, 11–12 especially; Genovese, *The World the Slaveholders Made*, 137–45.

But these were mistakes in interpretation that many professional historians could, and did, make in the 1930s. If Cash misunderstood Reconstruction and populism, so did many other scholars of the period. If he used "mind" as metaphor, so had many previous scholars. And if he insisted on calling Southern Calvinism "Puritanism," so did William Faulkner in *Light in August*, *Absalom, Absalom!*, and other works. In other regards, while Cash was often wrong in detail, he was usually right in general. Although there was not absolute continuity in Southern history, there was indeed a greater degree of continuity between 1830 and 1940 than in the history of New England or the Middle West during the same period, partly because the ethnic makeup of the Southern population remained roughly the same, partly because the South was largely rural and its position of assumed inferiority in relation to the rest of the country did not change. There was, indeed, a "mind" of the South—a popular mind—in 1940 in the sense that there was not a mind of the Middle West or the Far West; and even the New England mind in 1940, because of radical changes in New England society, would have to be discussed largely in the past tense. There is evidence, as well, that the Southern slave owner, at least before 1830, often did experience guilt over slavery. Further, Cash did not really ignore the Negro as some of his detractors have charged: he neglected to explore the Negro *mind*—to do so might indeed have been presumptuous of him—but certainly not the impact of the Negro on the white mind. In that respect, the Negro is at the center of his book—the proto-Dorian bond, the savage ideal, Southern violence, even the worship of woman Cash relates to the presence of the Negro in the South. Finally, one might question Genovese's contention that the Deep South planter was an aristocrat because he adopted an aristocratic outlook and took the Virginian as his model. As Daniel Hundley demonstrated in *Social Relations in Our Southern States*, the Cotton Snob might have thought he possessed an aristocratic vision, that he was imitating the best of Virginia, but in fact he misunderstood what Virginia, at its best, had been—open, tolerant, given to comfort more than ostentation.

As concerns Cash's limited geographical range, it is true that the Mississippi Delta and Catholic Louisiana were as foreign to him as California. But the extent to which he understood the mind of the upland cotton country of the Far South might be suggested by a comparison of his new, raw planter with Faulkner's Mississippi planter,

Thomas Sutpen. Cash's "generic Southerner" was a South Carolinian, not a Mississippian, but except that a generation separated the two, the Mississippi experience as Faulkner depicts it in *Absalom, Absalom!* was not unlike that of upcountry South Carolina. Cash wrote that his man at the center represented "the new order of planters"; he was crude and rough, he started with nothing except energy, determination, and a capacity for hard work. From the beginning, Cash maintained, his primary characteristics were "innocence" and simplicity. He demonstrated, at the same time, the "most intense individualism" the world had seen for four hundred years, "since the Italian Renaissance and its men of terrible fury" (p. 32). He came into the upcountry, made his way on the frontier where shrewdness was more important than refinement (where refinement was, in fact, a handicap), where the admired qualities were "great personal courage, unusual physical prowess, the ability to drink a quart of whiskey" (p. 39). He acquired land and slaves, grew cotton, soon became wealthy, and eventually built a big house which some called a mansion. And he dreamed. Though uneducated and unacquainted with formal culture, he aped Tidewater manners, ways foreign to him, and he made himself an "aristocrat." He wanted education and culture and good marriages for his sons and daughters. He wanted, that is, to found a dynasty.

Not Thomas Sutpen precisely, but very close—the mythic proportions and ruthlessness of Faulkner's character excepted. Sutpen, too, was an upland planter, a shrewd, strong, courageous, and ambitious man who started with nothing, worked hard, acquired wealth and position, built a big house, aped Tidewater manners when he chose, wanted education, culture, and good marriages for his son and daughters—and wanted to found a dynasty. He too dreamed, and his problem, Faulkner wrote, was "innocence." And what else was Thomas Sutpen but the embodiment of the extreme individualism Cash described, himself a man of terrible fury. Again, this was Mississippi, not South Carolina—but it, too, was upcountry, closer in spirit to Cash's South Carolina Piedmont than to Will Percy's Mississippi Delta. The primary difference in Sutpen and Cash's new planter is that with Sutpen the entire process Cash describes in *The Mind of the South* was accelerated. He acquired the slaves *before* he began to grow cotton, and his *first* house was a mansion. He became an "aristocrat" far more rapidly. But Cash, always ready to modify his thesis slightly, would have accounted for the difference this way: "In many parts of the South, as in Mississippi, it even happened, because of the almost unparalleled productivity of the soil, in accelerated tempo, and so went even further" (p. 18).

W. J. Cash did not understand William Faulkner as well as he might have—in 1936 he had written in the Charlotte *News* that Faulkner's view of Southern life was not comprehensive enough, that he did not adequately treat social forces—but Cash did understand the world of Yoknapatawpha, or at least the northern Mississippi on which it was based. What he continued to misunderstand, however, and did not even appreciate as he did Faulkner was that other Southern phenomenon of the 1930s, Agrarianism. In *The Mind of the South* he continued, though modified, the criticism he had voiced throughout the 1930s in the pages of the Charlotte *News*. *I'll Take My Stand*, he wrote, had been "an attempt to revive and fully restore the identification of that Old South with Cloud-Cuckoo Town, or at any rate to render it as a Theocritean idyl" (p. 390). The Southerner had never been totally and consciously devoted to agrarianism, he insisted, "the facile assumptions of Allen Tate and the Southern Agrarians to the contrary notwithstanding" (p. 185). And "nothing could be more unlike the life of the English squire in its fundamental aspect than that native to the South . . . John Crowe Ransom to the contrary notwithstanding" (p. 31). The Agrarians had not acknowledged the faults of the Old South, they had refused to admit that industrialism was not the sole cause of modern Southern ills, their influence had encouraged "smugness and sentimentality in many quarters" (p. 394). Finally, Cash disagreed with Agrarian claims that the Old South had been a "cultured" society, although this disagreement stemmed from the conflicting ideas of culture which Cash and the Agrarians had in mind. Cash did not regard culture, as they did, as an organic expression of the folk. The culture Southerners possessed, he had written Odum in 1929, "did not spring from the South but came in from without." It was "not, in fact," the possession of "the man in the street." [21] In 1941 Cash

21. Cash on William Faulkner, quoted in Morrison, *W. J. Cash*, 158; Cash to Odum, November 13, 1929. Cash wrote of Faulkner's lack of attention to social forces: "The whole fault here is just that he shows us what without in the least telling us how and why."

viewed culture in virtually the same way: it was a commodity to be purchased in museums and galleries.

But despite his disagreements with the Agrarians in *The Mind of the South*, Cash was more charitable toward them than he had previously been, perhaps because, after damning them for a decade and a half, he had come to realize that he shared certain views with them. Allen Tate in his essay in *I'll Take My Stand* had said precisely what Cash was to say eleven years later—that the Southerner was "simple," "simpleminded." Frank Owsley agreed with Cash that Southern planters had usually been of "plebeian origin." And Cash himself in certain of his book columns in the Charlotte *News* had expressed opinions on contemporary Southern literature which could have come from the typewriter of Donald Davidson, particularly the view that Southern literature focused too much on low life. "I'd like to see the country represented as being populated by somebody besides these poor whites and the coons," Cash had written in 1936.[22] And despite his assertion in 1941 that the South had never been consciously devoted to agrarianism, he himself had written in 1929, as we have seen, that the mind of the South was the mind of the soil. For these reasons, perhaps, in *The Mind of the South* Cash did acknowledge some merit in the Agrarians. They had given more emphasis to the simplicity and plainness of the antebellum South than some of their critics had realized, and "the virtues they assigned to the Old South were essentially the virtues which it indubitably possessed . . . much the same virtues I have myself assigned to it at its best: honor, courage, generosity, amiability, courtesy" (p. 392). They had also rendered "services in puncturing the smugness of Progress, in directing attention to the evils of *laissez-faire* industrialism, in their insistence on the necessity of developing a sensible farm program for the region, and in recalling that the South must not be too much weaned away from its ancient leisureliness—the assumption that the first end of life is living itself" (p. 394).

But Cash's remarks on the Southern traditionalists were sufficiently critical that the only negative response to *The Mind of the South* came from Nashville. The Agrarians, indeed, had known what to expect even before the book appeared in February, 1941; two months earlier

22. Allen Tate, "Remarks on the Southern Religion," *I'll Take My Stand*, 171; Cash, "Southland Turns to Books With Full Vigor," 223.

Cash had published an excerpt, "Literature in the South," in the *Saturday Review* in which he had taken the Agrarians to task. As soon as the book appeared, Vanderbilt professor Richmond Croom Beatty answered with a harsh review in the Nashville *Banner* in which he charged Cash with "contradictions and muddleheadedness," "vapid and meaningless" generalizations, and a "sentimental, even irresponsible . . . tone." The book might have more accurately been called "The Mind of North Carolina."[23] Beatty's review was the only immediate response from Nashville. That of the most committed Agrarian would not come until the summer of 1941 when Donald Davidson delivered a twenty-page attack in the *Southern Review*.

Davidson had resented Cash's treatment of the South since the iconoclastic *American Mercury* essays of the late 1920s and early 1930s, and he continued to resent it long after Cash died. A quarter-century later, in 1968, he was still disparaging *The Mind of the South* as "W. J. Cash's piece of Menckenesque journalism." But the only time he really let loose was in the 1941 essay.[24] Cash's sin, he charged, was that found in many other of the North Carolinians: a devotion to abstraction. In his book Cash had tried to "abstract" the Southern "mind" and he could not "after all succeed in abstracting it" (p. 5). Cash's interpretation of Southern history was "deeply colored by the reading he did in the gay, emancipated 1920's, when Gerald Johnson and Broadus Mitchell were still the wonder of our stage" and when young Southerners "learned something they had never known before—the sneer" (p. 12). Cash's citations referred "rather exclusively" to Johnson, Mitchell, and "others of the North Carolina school" (p. 12). In particular, Davidson objected to Cash's use of terms such as *proto-Dorian*—"perhaps the word is Menckenese" (p. 5)—and charged that his treatment of religion was "decidedly Menckenesque . . . a trashy way of discussing the greatest of all issues, indeed the ultimate issue" (p. 8). Evangelical religion was to Cash "a completely vulgar phenomenon" and "vulgar Fundamentalism" a force that interfered with "the march of progress" (p. 8). But even Davidson, predisposed as he was against Cash and all he represented, was forced to admit that *The*

23. W. J. Cash, "Literature in the South," *Saturday Review*, December 28, 1940, pp. 3–4, 18–19; Richmond Croom Beatty, review of *The Mind of the South*, Nashville *Banner*, February 26, 1941.

24. Donald Davidson, foreword to Weaver, *The Southern Tradition at Bay*, 15; Donald Davidson, "Mr. Cash and the Proto-Dorian South," *Southern Review*, VII (Summer, 1941), 1–20.

Mind of the South was "brilliantly executed, abounding in miscellaneous passages full of insight, and enormously instructive even in its errors" (p. 11). At the end of his review he returned to the mocking tone with which he had begun and assumed the role of the night-riding Southerner, driven by the savage ideal, out to lynch Cash: "And now, fellow-Southerners, Proto-Dorians, the moon is setting, and the Fiery Cross is burning low. . . . Shall we use the gun or the rope? Or ride him on a rail? Or just turn him loose?" (p. 19). Since he was a native son, Carolina-born and Baptist-educated, "I say, turn him loose. . . . Mr. Cash wrote that-there book for the Yankees anyway" (p. 20).

If Cash indeed held delusions of persecution in the spring and summer of 1941, Davidson's review would have done nothing to relieve them. But, in fact, he probably never saw the essay. He did see Beatty's earlier review, and in the Charlotte *News* of May 10, 1941, sneered at "the most ill-natured book review" he had ever read, "written by a young man who grades English A at Vanderbilt University, and who belongs to the Agrarian group which loudly professes to be made up of Southern aristocrats." But Cash's mind in May of 1941 was not exclusively on his critics. He had ended his long bachelorhood five months earlier, marrying Mary Ross Northrop of Charlotte. He also was making plans to leave North Carolina. The previous summer he had written Mencken that, although his book was "comparatively mild stuff," "the reaction of the publisher [of the Charlotte *News*] and this town generally may not make me altogether happy." Mencken had suggested the Washington *Post*, to which Cash applied. At the same time he had applied for a Guggenheim Fellowship with the intention of going to Mexico City and writing a novel. Mencken, who had supported Cash's two previous Guggenheim applications, was strangely skeptical about this one. "I am . . . in doubt about the novel he has in mind," he had written the Guggenheim committee. "Moreover, I see no reason why he should go to Mexico to get it. It would be much more rational to stay in North Carolina." But Cash, on the basis of his newly published book and outstanding editorial work for the Charlotte *News*, had been awarded the fellowship and made plans to depart for Mexico. He left Charlotte on May 30, gave the commencement address, "The South in a Changing World," at the University of Texas on June 2, and arrived in Mexico City three days later. The story of the next month Joseph Morrison has told well: Cash could not adjust to life in Mexico, found writing difficult, came to believe that he was being pursued by Nazi agents, and on July 1 hanged himself in a hotel room.[25]

The reason for Cash's suicide has never been determined. Some writers have assumed that his death, coming so shortly after a book basically critical of his homeland, could only be attributed to his fear of rejection and abuse from his fellow Southerners. Morrison believes, however, that illness—an "acute brain syndrome . . . almost certainly toxic in origin"[26]—led to the suicide. He argues that Cash seemed to be optimistic and confident when he left North Carolina, and nearly all the reviews of his book he had seen had been favorable. Besides, as Morrison points out, Cash's paranoid obsession in Mexico City was that Nazi agents, not Southerners, were out to get him.

But still one wonders. Although the Southern reviews of *The Mind of the South* were indeed favorable, Cash had feared they would not be, and his was a fear in the making for more than a decade. Morrison himself acknowledges that he had been "dreading" reviews of the book, and if anyone knew the force of the Southern savage ideal it was the author of that term. Although Cash in Mexico City seems to have been free of the threat of Southern reaction, his fear of Nazis was not without a modicum of justification: the previous few years he had written savage editorials against Hitler and Germany, essays that had won him a nomination for a Pulitzer Prize. Once he arrived in Mexico City he wrote an article, which he never published, reporting that Mexican towns "swarmed with Nazi and Communist agents."[27] And Cash's fear of Nazi Germany was not an isolated phenomenon. Not only Clarence Cason but Cash himself has seen European Fascists—with their belief in racial supremacy, their reliance on demagogy and violence, their suppression of free thought—as spiritual cousins to Southern racists. Cash's delusions, then, may indeed have stemmed partly from organic factors, but the form those delusions took was interesting. These were Nazis in Mexico City, not Kluxers in the American South, but one wonders if Cash had decided to spend

25. W. J. Cash, review of *Lanterns on the Levee*, Charlotte *News*, May 10, 1941, in Morrison, *W. J. Cash*, 290; W. J. Cash to H. L. Mencken, August 6, 1940, and H. L. Mencken to Henry Allen Moe [of the Guggenheim Foundation], November 27, 1940 (copy), both in Mencken Papers; Morrison, *W. J. Cash*, 107–135.

26. See in particular Grantham, "Mr. Cash Writes a Book," and King, *A Southern Renaissance*, 146–72; Morrison, *W. J. Cash*, 147.

27. W. J. Cash, "Report from Mexico," reprinted in Morrison, *W. J. Cash*, 305–309.

his Guggenheim year in Alabama or Mississippi—or North Carolina—if the delusions would have assumed a more Southern form.

Perhaps not. Certainly Cash did experience a severe culture shock in Mexico—a strange language, climate, and diet, to none of which he adapted, and all of which made him feel vulnerable in a way he would not have been in his native South. But he would still have had to deal with his book and the consequences of having finally finished it. One cannot discount the fact that it was a book which troubled him profoundly, which he both longed and dreaded to publish, one in which readers then and since have seen a certain bitterness. The week the book came out Will Percy's friend, David Cohn, wrote that it was a beautiful but "strangely embittered book" and described its author as both a "great despiser" and "great adorer" of the South. A quarter-century later Edwin M. Yoder, Jr., saw the same "muffled bitterness" in *The Mind of the South*. It was a book which, in spite of its dazzling style and its self-proclaimed affection for the South, was at bottom a severe indictment of Southern life: the South, it announced, had no cultural and intellectual tradition, it had a sham religion and a sham aristocracy, it was a closed society, an intolerant and violent society, and most of all a fraudulent one which possessed an unlimited capacity for self-deception. Cash refused, even at the end of his book, to be upbeat, as fellow Southern journalists Daniels, Dabney, and even Cason had been. He could only "hope, as [the South's] loyal son, that its virtues [would] tower over and conquer its faults"; but of the future he would "venture no definite prophecies" (p. 440). And although he had cultivated throughout *The Mind of the South* an apparent detachment from his subject—presuming to treat it intellectually rather than personally, writing rather loftily of "guilt complexes" but expressing little contrition himself—he did in fact feel a measure of guilt in exposing and attacking the South as he had. Even Morrison acknowledges that guilt, and attributes Cash's "writing block" of the mid- and late 1930s in part to his distaste for publicly exposing his own country. Cash himself wrote Alfred Knopf about his block, "I have never been able to approach the task of continuing [*The Mind of the South*] without extreme depression and dislike."[28]

But it was not guilt alone, or fear of abuse from other Southerners,

28. Cohn, "Tissues of Southern Culture," 7; Edwin M. Yoder, Jr., "W. J. Cash After a Quarter Century," in Willie Morris (ed.), *The South Today: 100 Years After Appomattox* (New York, 1965), 90; Cash, quoted in Morrison, *W. J. Cash*, 80–81.

which disturbed Cash the late spring of 1941. Nor was it fear that he had shamed his family. Suicide, after all, meant far greater shame than did authorship of *The Mind of the South*; as another South Carolina Baptist wrote the following year, self-destruction was "a disgrace to a person's entire family connection. . . . The Baptist Church has always told us we would go straight to hell for self-murder." What might have served equally as a disruptive influence in Cash's life during the spring of 1941 was, quite simply, that he had finally *finished* the book on which he had been working for more than a decade and contemplating in some form for the better part of two. Richard King suggests that Cash, like a patient under psychoanalysis, had poured out his fears and anxieties in *The Mind of the South* in the hope of freeing himself from them. Joseph K. Davis concludes that since history to Cash, as to Joyce's Stephen Dedalus, was the nightmare from which he was trying to awake, writing the book itself was the *means* of awakening, of escape.[29] In Cash's case, however, the process of writing, of completing the book, might have operated in a quite different way. What should have been cathartic and therapeutic was instead draining and damaging: the book's completion created a vacuum, a void in the author's life. Cash was, as we have seen, truly a one-book man: it was the book he began to consider in his early twenties and did not publish until his early forties. In this same span William Faulkner wrote a dozen books about the South, and Erskine Caldwell a dozen and a half. But Wilbur Cash wrote only one and into that one poured every original and imaginative thought about his subject he had ever had. It was the book that would rescue him—and did rescue him—from obscurity. What has sometimes been said of Henry James was perhaps even more true of Cash: the writing seemed more important than the man. It was not, of course, but it was the culmination of virtually everything the man had pondered and over which he had agonized. It was the novel he had never written. It would be misleading to say that he had lived only to write it, that it was the only book he had in him and when it was out of his system, he died. But like Edmund Ruffin, when he had said what he had to say, he may have experienced a great emptiness in his life.

29. Ben Robertson, *Red Hills and Cotton: An Upcountry Memory* (New York, 1942), 45; King, *A Southern Renaissance*, 157; Joseph K. Davis, "The South as History and Metahistory: The Mind of W. J. Cash," in Lewis P. Simpson (ed.), *The Poetry of Community: Essays on the Southern Sensibility of History and Literature* (Atlanta, 1972), 17.

Cash's critics, of course, are right about *The Mind of the South*. The book is oversimplified, unrepresentative, in places simply incorrect. In one respect, indeed, its author did not so much write Southern history as he contributed to its making, became an example of its forces at work. He illustrated the operation of that particular Southern tradition which required the critical thinker to detach himself, to cast himself outside the Southern community of spirit, in order to explore and explain his homeland. He was another of those Southerners, like Ruffin and Helper, Dabney and Davidson, for whom telling about the South became not simply professional obligation but compulsion. His book was true in the same way *I'll Take My Stand* was true, and just as *I'll Take My Stand* cannot be approached as good economics and sociology, *The Mind of the South* cannot be approached as good history. It contains, rather, a personal truth, an imaginative truth, charged with the power and the integrity of the individual vision.

IF W. J. CASH had to leave the Southern spiritual community in his search for truth and understanding, William Alexander Percy remained within that community as he wrote. He was a part of the community in a way very few other Southern writers before or since have been, indeed embodied most of its best qualities, and if the price he paid for his membership was a certain lack of perspective, the rewards he reaped were abundant. His vision was both more limited and more encompassing than that of Cash. He too wrote a single work explaining the South, but the title of his book, *Lanterns on the Levee*, suggested something quite different from Cash's. It was a localized title, a self-contained one, lacking the grandeur and the presumption of *The Mind of the South*. But it was at the same time more universal, for the lanterns of which Percy writes were more than the lights on the banks of the Mississippi near Greenville. They were stays against the darkness of the modern age that Percy saw engulfing not only the American South but Western civilization in its entirety.

William Alexander Percy has long had a curious reputation among Southerners. No one has been held in higher personal regard, yet few commentators on the South have agreed wholly with his ideas. The admiration expressed for him, as that for Cash, is nearly always qualified. Southern liberals in particular have been fascinated with Percy, the classic conservative; it is they, not the conservatives, who have been unable to resist discussing *Lanterns on the Levee*. Their verdict, almost unanimous, has been that this Mississippi planter was a misguided but well-intentioned, even noble man. Virginius Dabney called him "high-minded," humane, understanding, and tolerant, and believed he possessed a "genuine affection for the Negroes on his plantation"; but he was also "a paternalist of the paternalists" and was dead wrong in his defense of sharecropping. Ralph McGill called him a "gentle, much-loved man" but expressed total disagreement with his racial views. Jonathan Daniels, who visited Percy in Greenville in the late 1930s, admired his courage and his code of noblesse oblige, but added, "I had the feeling that Percy loved Negroes as another gentleman might love dogs." James McBride Dabbs of South Carolina was equally ambivalent. Percy, he wrote, felt pity for his fellow man; however, he failed "to feel himself involved beyond this mood of pity." He did not realize he had helped to make the limited world the black sharecropper inhabited. But Hodding Carter, whom Percy had brought to Greenville to edit the *Delta Democrat-Times*, was gentler. He agreed that Percy was a paternalist, but a paternalist of the best sort. A "gentleman unafraid," Carter called him, who fought the Klan, served as counselor for his town and region, and treated his sharecroppers fairly and generously. Ellis Arnall of Georgia agreed: "Every Negro cropper in Mississippi," he wrote in 1946, "wanted to work on his plantation; half the scamps in his county, black and white, lived at one time or another out of his smokehouse."[30]

William Alexander Percy was "a surviving authentic Southern aristocrat," Cash wrote—the last aristocrat to many of these Southern liberals. Percy himself sometimes made light of his ancestry, but he was highly aware of it all the same. He was the son of a first family of the Delta, descended on his father's side, it was rumored, from the earls of Northumberland and on his French grandmother's side from the Générelly de Rinaldis. More immediately, his grandfather, Colonel William Alexander Percy, had been a leader in the reestablishment of white rule in the Delta after the Civil War. His father, LeRoy Percy,

30. Virginius Dabney, "Paternalism in Race Relations Is Outmoded," *Southern Frontier*, III (July, 1942), 4; Dabney, *Below the Potomac*, 63; Ralph McGill, *The South and the Southerner* (Boston, 1963), 165; Daniels, *A Southerner Discovers the South*, 173; James McBride Dabbs, *Who Speaks for the South?* (New York, 1964), 122; Hodding Carter, *Where Main Street Meets the River* (New York, 1953), 67–78; Ellis Arnall, *The Shore Dimly Seen* (Philadelphia, 1946), 86.

was a planter who became a U.S. senator in 1910—only to be unseated in 1911 by Mississippi demagogue James K. Vardaman. Percy himself was educated in his home and in private schools, then attended Sewanee and, after a trip to Europe, Harvard Law School. He came back to practice law with his father in Greenville, reluctantly since he preferred the high culture of Europe and the Northeast. The small, slender man, devotee of art and beauty, was at first something of an enigma in Greenville. Fastidious and somewhat aloof, he was, Hodding Carter wrote, "perplexing to his father and suspect to his fellow river folk." His friend David Cohn called him "the loneliest man I have ever known," this "saddest of men who felt so sharply the world's agonies and its exaltations," a man "half in love with easeful Death."[31] Yet Percy gave much of himself to others. He never married, but when he was forty-five he took into his home and adopted three young cousins—including fourteen-year-old Walker Percy—whose father had committed suicide. And despite his loneliness Percy had many friends, and with those friends was a good conversationalist, thoughtful and cheerful. Nor did he lack for intellectual companionship. Greenville was a town of writers, Carter and Cohn among them, and Percy's rambling two-story house was a gathering place for the local intelligentsia and for those many writers, journalists, and sociologists who ventured into the Delta. And he did not reserve his hospitality and good will for friends alone. If his personal nature was private, his role as a Percy was to serve as benefactor and advisor to an entire community. He directed the 1927 relief program in the Delta after the great Mississippi flood, he counseled and defended the indigent without pay, he provided for the education of others. He even joined Rotary. Noblesse oblige was no abstraction to Will Percy.

But Percy was a poet as well as a citizen, and if in his public duties he served his present time, in his verse he seemed to escape to the past. His was a lyrical poetry, influenced both by the Romantics and by Browning. In the poems he dealt with fathers and sons, ambition and resignation, physical and spiritual love, and he was inclined to-

31. Cash, review of *Lanterns on the Levee*, 291; Carter, *Where Main Street Meets the River*, 70; David Cohn, "Eighteenth Century Chevalier," *Virginia Quarterly Review*, XXXI (Autumn, 1955), 562, 563. My biographical information on Percy is taken largely from Carter; Cohn; Phinizy Spalding, "A Stoic Trend in William Alexander Percy's Thought," *Georgia Review*, XII (Fall, 1958), 241–51, and "Mississippi and the Poet: William Alexander Percy," *Journal of Mississippi History*, XXVII (February, 1965), 63–73; and J. R. Welsh, "William Alexander Percy and His Writings," *Notes on Mississippi Writers*, I (Winter, 1969), 82–99.

ward ancient or medieval settings. He had begun writing poetry in earnest in 1911, shortly after he had returned to Greenville from Harvard, and he published three volumes of verse in the period between 1915 and 1924. Willard Thorp once wrote that Percy's verse appealed "to those who stopped reading poetry in 1915." Another reviewer, twenty-three-year-old William Faulkner, discussed Percy's second volume, *In April Once and Other Poems* (1920), for the *Daily Mississippian* in November, 1920. Percy, he wrote, was like "a little boy closing his eyes against the dark of modernity which threatens the bright simplicity and the colorful romantic pageantry of the middle ages with which his eyes are full."[32]

It was through his poetry and his interest in other poets that Percy became acquainted with the Fugitives of Nashville. Donald Davidson, who had seen his poetry and liked it, began to write him in the early 1920s. Percy appreciated Davidson's attention. "You & John McClure," he wrote in December, 1929, "are two of the few critics in America I listen to." He also commended the views Davidson expressed in his Nashville *Tennessean* book column, and shared his opinions on Southern literature in particular. He echoed in a letter to Davidson in May, 1930, Davidson's own complaint about—in Percy's words—"the expectation that all artists in prose or verse should write about the poor and the illiterate and the ill-bred." On another occasion he applauded Davidson's criticism of Frances Newman's iconoclastic Southern novel *The Hard-Boiled Virgin* (1926)—"an affected smart aleck book," Percy wrote, "that I could not finish." Further, he confided in Davidson his fears that his poetry was misunderstood, that he himself was being cast as one who was interested only in faraway times and places: "I get so damn tired of people assuming that because I use medieval and Greek themes, I am interested only in archaeology or history or literature. As far as I can recall neither Shakespeare nor Milton nor Dante nor any of the great Greeks used contemporary themes to any considerable extent, and yet their emotion and thought did not lag behind the emotion and thought of their own time."[33]

32. Aside from the three separate volumes of poetry (see n. 1, this chapter), Percy's *Selected Poems* was published in 1930 by the Yale University Press and his *Collected Poems* in 1943 by Knopf. Willard Thorp, quoted in Welsh, "William Alexander Percy," 83; William Faulkner, review of *In April Once, Daily Mississippian*, November 10, 1920, quoted in Carvel Collins (ed.), *William Faulkner: Early Prose and Poetry* (London, 1962), 72, and in Welsh, "William Alexander Percy," 83–84.

33. William Alexander Percy to Donald Davidson, [December, 1929], May 31, 1930, and May 18, 1928.

One of the issues of his time that interested Percy was the Agrarianism which Davidson had come to espouse in the late 1920s. He learned of *I'll Take My Stand* six months before its publication when Davidson wrote describing it. "I will be awfully glad," Percy responded, "to see your new book on the South." When Davidson sent him a copy autographed by six of the Agrarians, he responded with his assessment: "It is informing and valuable: valuable in calling the attention of the South to its own inheritance and for the clear analysis of what that inheritance is." That Southerners could "continue in the agrarian tradition" Percy "gravely" doubted, but they could "at least lose their apologetic attitude and recognize their past as precious." Percy could agree with the Agrarians in spirit, but he made no attempt to join their movement in any active way. Unlike Davidson, he was no polemicist. Rather than militantly taking his stand, he preferred to muse on the past. His relationship to the Nashville group, rather, resembled Cash's to Odum and the Regionalists: each man drew from the group, was stimulated by it. Through his correspondence Percy shared ideas with Davidson as Cash, in 1929, had with Odum. But neither man was temperamentally suited to lead in the debate of the 1930s. Each in his own way stood aloof. Neither was Percy doctrinaire in the manner of some of the Agrarians. He could appreciate ideas emanating from the liberal school of Southern thought as well as from the conservative. "Did you see the Cadets of Newmarket [*sic*] in December Harper's?" he asked Davidson of Gerald Johnson's essay in 1929. "Very fine, it left a lump in my throat."[34] And when it was time to advise Walker Percy on the choice of a university, he recommended Chapel Hill.

But it was Nashville, not Chapel Hill, whose spirit Percy came closer to sharing in *Lanterns on the Levee*. His unqualified defense of the planter class, his defense of sharecropping, his traditional attitude toward the Negro would find little support among liberal Southerners, no matter how highly they regarded the man himself. Percy had long considered a book on Southern life from the planter's point of view and had begun to write such a book sometime in the 1930s, then had abandoned it for a time before David Cohn had urged him to complete it. He felt compelled—in the spirit of community service, *obligated*—to write such a book. "I know nothing about the psychology of the negro nor of the poor white," he had written Donald Da-

34. Percy to Davidson, [December, 1930?], [December, 1929].

vidson as early as 1930. "But I do know something of the feelings and problems of the descedants [*sic*] of that class which was once the slave owner class in the South. Northern critics seem to forgive us anything except following our own best traditions." *Lanterns on the Levee* stemmed from a desire both to defend those traditions and to reminisce. In poor health, filled with melancholy and an awareness of death, he wrote "while the world I know is crashing to bits" (p. xx). He was a reluctant truth-sayer. "It is not pleasant to make these bald and bitter statements," he wrote in his chapter on race relations. "I make them because they are true" (p. 309).[35] The underlying assumption of *Lanterns on the Levee* is that the aristocracy of which the author was a part was doomed, was already nearly extinct, and the poor whites were taking over. Thus he had to set down his memories and creed while he could. "My generation, inured to doom, wears extinction with a certain wry bravado, but it is just as well the older ones we loved are gone" (p. 63). They had tragedy, but "the last act is vulgarity" (p. 63). A "tarnish" had "fallen over the bright world; dishonor and corruption triumph; my own strong people are turned lotus-eaters; defeat is here again, the last, the most abhorrent" (p. 343). His book, then, was "a pilgrim's script . . . valueless except as that man loved the country he passed through and its folk, and except as he willed to tell the truth. How other, alas, than telling it!" (p. xx).

Thus Percy sets out to tell his truth, to tell about his particular South, first its land and then its people. It was not a South that W. J. Cash would easily recognize. "The basic fiber, the cloth of the Delta population," Percy insisted, "is built of three dissimilar threads and only three"—the old slave-owning class, the "poor whites," and the Negroes (p. 19). The yeoman, that sturdy "man at the center" of Cash's South, had no place in Percy's. Having set forth the general, Percy then turns to the particular: the Percys of Mississippi. He remembers his grandmother on his father's side and his French mother's parents, Mère and Père, originally from New Orleans. He recalls his great-great-grandfather on the Percy side, a dashing rogue who received a Spanish grant. From the first, William Alexander Percy was assured, he was "as good as" anybody and better than most.

---

35. Percy to Davidson, May 31, 1930. Despite Percy's insistence that it was not always "pleasant" to tell the truth, at times he took a certain satisfaction in it. "There's a low malicious pleasure in telling the truth," he wrote in his chapter on sharecropping, "where you know it won't be believed" (p. 282).

He goes on to describe his father and his father's circle of friends, the Negro playmates of his early years, his early education in a Catholic school, his immersion in religion, his four years at Sewanee, the one in Europe, and three more at Harvard Law School. Thus ends the primary phase of the apprenticeship of William Alexander Percy. The remainder of the book, except for the chapter dealing with his experience in World War I, concerns Percy's life in and around Greenville: his father's campaign against James K. Vardaman in 1911, his battle against the Klan in 1922, his role in the relief effort after the flood of 1927, the creed he shares with his adopted sons, the administration of his 3,300-acre cotton plantation, and dealings with his Negro sharecroppers.

The book follows an approximate chronological order, but it is structurally unified by far more than chronology. It is a work of art, carefully conceived and executed. As James C. Rocks has written, the method of Percy's autobiography is "the art of opposition and tension"—the public man and the private are in opposition, the past and the present, order and change, good and evil, the ideal and the real.[36] Places, objects, and events mean more than they seem to: the garden which Percy cultivates is itself an ordered island, a stay against fragmentation. The "lanterns" of the title, as we have seen, are not only lights along the river but also warnings of danger of another sort: the flood of democracy was approaching, the world was getting out of its banks.

Lanterns on the Levee took its form in part from the *Meditations* of Marcus Aurelius, beginning, as did the *Meditations*, with a description of the author's inheritance from his forebears, and then going on to state his creed. But even more than its form, as several scholars have noted, the philosophy of Percy's book was influenced by Marcus Aurelius and the Stoicism he espoused. Because Stoicism thrives on adversity and virtually assumes an unkind world without, in some ways it was well suited to the South of Will Percy's childhood, as it had been for an even earlier South. Robert E. Lee had heeded the teachings of the Emperor, as his father had before him (though each had tempered Stoicism with Christianity), and many of the gentlemen of Thomas Nelson Page bore witness to its influence. "How fine

36. James C. Rocks, "The Art of *Lanterns on the Levee,*" *Southern Review*, New Ser., XII (Autumn, 1976), 814–23.

and noble that old man was," wrote Page of Gordon Keith's father, "sitting unmoved amid the wreck not only of his life and fortunes, but of his world" (p. 34). Will Percy, after a period of fervent Catholicism, had settled on this Stoicism of an older South. In particular, he wrote in *Lanterns on the Levee*, the election of 1911 in which his father had been defeated by Vardaman had taught him that the good usually did not triumph. He believed he lived, as Marcus Aurelius had, at the end of a proud era, at a time when traditional values were being eroded. But Percy's Stoicism, like that of Aurelius, was more than graceful acceptance of defeat. It affirmed the ability of men to effect at least limited change, not through sweeping reform, which was almost certainly doomed to failure, but through individual action in a restricted arena. Thus the importance of the community to Percy: it was the limited arena in which he could work. And thus the importance of individual integrity and courage, the qualities that inform *Lanterns on the Levee*. Although the world had decayed, although "the bottom rail" was "on top," there was still "left to each of us, no matter how far defeat pierces, the unassailable wintry kingdom of Marcus Aurelius, which some more gently call the Kingdom of Heaven. However it be called, it is not outside, but within, and when all is lost, it stands fast" (p. 313). The Emperor's "self-communings . . . convince a man he never need be less than tight-lipped, courteous, and proud, though all is pain" (p. 316). We should meditate "on Jesus and the Emperor" (p. 320).[37]

Although the Stoicism of Marcus Aurelius is the moving force behind *Lanterns on the Levee*, the book in fact resembles more closely a notable work of Percy's own century. If W. J. Cash read and was influenced by *The Education of Henry Adams* and shed tears as he stood before Chartres, and if, much earlier, Walter Hines Page made a weak attempt at writing such a spiritual autobiography, it was Percy who most nearly wrote the Southern *Education*. In Percy's case, it was probably not so much a matter of influence—although he had read and recommended the *Education*, he would have been unlikely to acknowledge any significant debt to a man who had drawn a terrible indictment of the South and the Southerner—as it was a matter of parallel lives: the authors of *The Education of Henry Adams* and *Lanterns on the Levee*, although removed in time and place, found themselves

37. For the fullest treatment of Percy and Stoicism, see Spalding, "A Stoic Trend in William Alexander Percy's Thought."

personally and historically in remarkably similar circumstances. It is instructive to consider Percy's classic expression of a particular Southern mind in relation to that classic of a particular New England mind, Adams' *Education*.

Like Henry Adams, Percy was the son of a strong father and a proud family—one rich in tradition but in decline as he wrote. And in his book, like Henry Adams, he paid great attention to his early influences, particularly that of his grandparents, and to his "education." He grew up respecting, above all, his father's circle of political friends and formed his notion of the good society from their views and actions. Like Adams, he attended Harvard, studied law, spent a formative period in Europe in his early twenties, returned to teach at his undergraduate institution, and considered himself a poor teacher— although his students thought him a great success. As a young man, like Adams, he saw his world shattered by the decline in the political fortunes of his father's circle, considered himself a victim of the excesses of democracy, and resented "the rise of the masses . . . the insolence of organized labor and the insolence of capital, examples both of the insolence of the parvenu" (p. 153). Vardaman was to Percy as Grant was to Henry Adams: after 1914, he wrote, "I was to be a bit of an Ishmael the rest of my days" (p. 158). For solace, like Adams, Percy turned to contemplation of the Middle Ages, to a circle of like-minded companions, and to travel.

But the greatest similarity in Adams and Percy lay not in their lives but in the works they produced—for in his autobiography Percy, like Adams, announced himself a failure, a son unworthy of his family and particularly his father, a child of an earlier century out of place in the twentieth. Like Adams (who was also attracted to Stoicism), he sat down in the latter part of his life, viewed the vulgarity and corruption of his age with disgust, but could do nothing but observe, reflect, hold to a high personal integrity—and write. The vitality of his ancestors was gone: a "sissy" Percy called himself, not the man of force and influence his father had been.

And the author of *Lanterns on the Levee* resembled the author of the *Education* in one other way: his confession of failure was in part a posture, a literary device, and his autobiographical self a persona. The *Education of Henry Adams* and *Lanterns on the Levee* shared most of all a tone, sometimes ironic, sometimes self-deprecating, that was appropriate for one who presumed to be a failure and had the awareness to recognize his condition. The two works shared a language, an imagery of drama and games. Adams had found himself a product of the eighteenth century required "to play the game of the twentieth," a game which "he never got to the point of playing . . . at all; he lost himself in the study of it, watching the errors of the players."[38] Percy preferred "to watch the spread and pattern of the game that is past rather than engage feebly in the present play." To reflect on the "game that is past" was appropriate for one who had "cut no very splendid figure in the show" (p. xix). In any event, for himself, Percy wrote, "the show is nearly over" (p. 127). The language of play and drama, in both cases, contributes to the notion of the autobiographical subject as passive observer, not active participant in life. Each watches and evaluates the "game" and reflects on his own shame at not having played in it. Percy equals Adams in his confession of inadequacies. "My incompetency is almost all-inclusive," he announces (p. 285). Like Adams, he searches for a suitable calling but insists he has found none. Adams had declared that he had in his twenties "made no step towards a profession . . . was as ignorant as a schoolboy of society . . . was unfit for any career in Europe, and unfitted for any career in America" (p. 88). Percy, describing the same stage of his own life, made a similar confession:

> For months (maybe for years, maybe until now) I hunted about for a good ambition. Money? No, positively—not because my financial future was assured or my financial present anything more than adequate to supply my simple needs, but it wasn't interesting and it wasn't worthy. . . . Fame as a lawyer? I had been a B man at the law school, which is eminently respectable but not brilliant. . . . Power? I knew nothing about it and it certainly wasn't my métier. Civic usefulness? Perhaps; that was getting warmer, but I had no desire to hold office and I knew no way of dedicating one's unendowed life to usefulness. (p. 127)

Percy catalogued his inadequacies throughout the book. He "was terrified at the thought of arguing a case, particularly before a jury," but somehow "steeled" himself "to do it and with some passion, though never brilliantly and never to this day without a spasm of nerves before and after" (p. 128). As Adams, who maintained in the *Education* that he had "failed" at "social experience" (p. 195), Percy "failed" socially: "Mother never understood or forgave in me a certain lack of enthusiasm for things social" (p. 130). Like Adams, he was

38. Henry Adams, *The Education of Henry Adams* (1918; rpr. New York, 1931), 4.

baffled by the mechanical age: he could not "drive a car or fix a puncture or sharpen a pencil" (p. 285). Like Adams, he lacked resolve: "I didn't exactly plunge into life, rather I tipped in, trepidly" (pp. 127–28). In "sheer lonesomeness and confusion of soul," he "often took to the levee" (p. 130). And at the end of his life he looked back: "One by one I count the failures—at law undistinguished, at teaching unprepared, at soldiering average, at citizenship unimportant, at love second-best, at poetry forgotten before remembered—and I acknowledge the deficit" (p. 348).

Much of this, again, was posturing. In fact William Alexander Percy, as Henry Adams, had been very successful in life. Just as Adams had succeeded as journalist, teacher, and historian, Percy had succeeded, if less conspicuously so, as planter, teacher, poet, and citizen—and the final irony was that each, in the very book in which he declared himself a failure, achieved a peculiar kind of literary success as well as a modest fame, a reputation which would ultimately exceed that of his father. Out of the confession of inadequacy came a measure of literary immortality. Indeed, what seems clear enough in *Lanterns on the Levee* is that Percy, like Adams, was in part making fun of the conventional idea of success. At times the author breaks through the persona and declares that prominence as lawyer and poet was not the end of life: "What have defeats and failures to do with the good life? . . . Of the good life I have learned what it is not and I have loved a few who lived it end to end. I have seen the goodness of men and the beauty of things" (p. 348).

But if the confession of failure was partly posturing, it was not entirely that. Percy may have succeeded in the eyes of his contemporaries, and he may seem a success to posterity, but again the standard by which he judged himself was that of his father and by that standard, at least as he interpreted it, he was indeed a failure. He would have subscribed wholeheartedly to Adams' assessment: "[My] father's character was therefore the larger part of [my] education" (p. 26), and "if [I] were to be useful at all, it must be as a son" (p. 208). LeRoy Percy emerges in *Lanterns on the Levee* as a man of courage and action, a brilliant dashing figure on the Elizabethan model. He read *Ivanhoe* once a year and epitomized noblesse oblige. The frail son idolized the father, and the son believed the father must be ashamed of him. Like Henry Adams, who "never played cards, and . . . loathed whiskey" (p. 298), Will Percy "was blessed with no endearing vices: drunkenness made me sick, gambling bored me, rutting per se, unadorned, I considered overrated and degrading. In charitable mood one might call me an idealist, but, more normally, a sissy. It must have been difficult for Father too. Enjoying good liquor, loving to gamble, his hardy vices merely under control, he sympathized quizzically and said nothing. But his heart must often have called piteously for the little brother I had lost, all boy, all sturdy, obstreperous charm" (pp. 125–26).

Richard King suggests that Percy was "in some fundamental way unmanned" by his father and concealed beneath his praise of LeRoy Percy a deep bitterness. It is significant, as King remarks, that Percy subtitled his book *Recollections of a Planter's Son*.[39] Percy himself was a planter, not merely a son. Indeed, it does appear that desire for his father's approval motivated him to take certain paths that he might otherwise not have taken. Henry Adams remained abroad in the early 1860s and regretted not participating in the war of his time. So at first, in 1917, did William Alexander Percy, but unlike Adams he then took action. He came home, enlisted, trained in Texas, became an officer, went to France and the front. There he found, he believed, the most intense experience of his life. Although he hated it, the possibility of death charged every moment with meaning. He had found a life in commitment that Henry Adams never found, one he sustained when he returned to America, fought the Ku Klux Klan, and headed the 1927 flood relief effort. Indeed, that commitment extended even to *Lanterns on the Levee*, a book which, despite its wry and ironic self-deprecation and its confession of failure, is a work of affirmation in a way *The Education of Henry Adams* is not. It is not, finally, so analytical, so cerebral, not even really so much a search for understanding as Adams' book was. The ideal of his father—often, as in the battle with the Klan, actually fighting by his side—turned Percy himself, if only for brief moments, into the forceful, courageous figure he said he could not be.

It was at these moments that he believed himself worthy of the tradition of the older South, for the idealization of his father was in many respects an idealization of what that South had been. LeRoy Percy was indeed the Southern aristocrat—the perfect Southern gentleman of Daniel Hundley (minus a certain prudishness), the cava-

39. King, *A Southern Renaissance*, 94, 97.

lier glorified by Thomas Nelson Page. It was this ideal gentleman, and the old order over which he presided, that Percy was celebrating in *Lanterns on the Levee*, and it was the death of this order that he announces and mourns at the end of his book. In the final chapter, "Home," the various tones of the book—self-deprecating, witty, ironic, even outraged—give way to acceptance, assurance, even a quiet joy. Percy returns to the Greenville cemetery and is drawn toward his family's plot. He sees the graves of his grandparents, his father and mother, "the small brother who should be representing and perpetuating the name" (p. 345). All men were sons of death, and Percy himself was moving in its direction, envisioning himself "home" with his family. This was the man Jonathan Daniels had described in the late 1930s—"I had a feeling that [his] weariness was deeper than the physical"[40]—and Percy, ill and drained, finds in death the same attraction the Romantics had found. He sees, finally, "among the graves in the twilight . . . one thing only," a long wall of a rampart and on the tower of the rampart "the glorious high gods, Death and the rest." He approaches the tower and the High God asks, "Who are you?" "The pilgrim I know," the author concludes, "should be able to straighten his shoulders, to stand his tallest, and to answer defiantly: 'I am your son'" (p. 348).

The author of *Lanterns on the Levee* cannot at the end see—does not want to see—beyond the grave: the death not only of an individual but of a way of life. Will Percy walked among the graves of his forebears and was preoccupied with death—at about the same time Wilbur Cash, visiting the Riverside Cemetery in Asheville, wept at the grave of Thomas Wolfe and himself reflected painfully on mortality.[41] But Cash was able in the moment he completed his book on the South to flee from the vision of death and to consider the future, if uncertainly. *The Mind of the South* is an open-ended book in a way *Lanterns on the Levee* is not, not prophetic so much as recognizing the need for prophecy. But Will Percy at the end of his book is beyond acknowledging even the need. His world, like that of Henry Adams, had moved from unity to multiplicity. It was a world—in Adams' words—which "cared little for decency" (p. 280), one—in Percy's words—

40. Daniels, *A Southerner Discovers the South*, 175.
41. See W. J. Cash, "His Sister Knew Thomas Wolfe Well," Charlotte *News*, July 30, 1939, in Morrison, *W. J. Cash*, 249–56.

turned upside down with "the bottom rail . . . on top" (p. 312). The old order was gone, and with its departure the author had witnessed "a disintegration of that moral cohesion of the South which had given it its strength and its sons their singleness of purpose and simplicity" (p. 74), and he himself was weary.

William Alexander Percy died ten months after his book appeared— in January, 1942, of a cerebral hemorrhage. Like Cash, he did not live to see his work become a classic, but he did live long enough to suspect it might. Even most of the Southern liberals responded kindly to *Lanterns on the Levee*, partly because, one suspects, despite their protests of paternalism they too had long been paternalistic toward the Negro, had embodied noblesse oblige. One of few harsh outcries came from Lillian Smith, who charged in her journal, the *North Georgia Review*, that *Lanterns on the Levee* was a "tasteless though muted expression of white arrogance," an "anachronism with a highly rubbed patina," a book—because written by an intelligent man—"more disturbing . . . than a Georgia demagogue's cheap tricks." W. J. Cash, a friend of Smith's and contributor to her journal, was kinder, though still taking issue with Percy's conclusions. In a review for the Charlotte *News*, which Percy probably never saw, Cash called him "that exceedingly rare thing, a surviving authentic Southern aristocrat," "an excellent and admirable man." But Percy had his blind spot, and that spot was not so much the Negro as the poor white. The author of *Lanterns on the Levee*, Cash contended, did not understand why the Mississippi peasants rejected rule by aristocracy and embraced Vardaman and Bilbo. It was because the aristocrats, the Percys, had not helped them enough but rather had been self-serving.[42] The leaders had not led that well.

Cash also chided Percy for his class division of Southerners, as well he might have. Percy, as we have seen, had divided the Delta population—and "the whole South"—into "three dissimilar threads and only three": the old slaveholders, the "poor whites," and the Negroes (p. 19). "*The whole South*," he had written, and "*only three*" classes [italics mine]: thus he made the same mistake that Cash had made in *The*

42. Lillian Smith, review of *Lanterns on the Levee*, *North Georgia Review*, Winter, 1941, reprinted in White and Sugg (eds.), *From the Mountain*, 15–16; Cash, review of *Lanterns on the Levee*, 291, 294.

Mind of the South, mistaking his part of the South for its entirety. In doing so, he supported the myth that Cash had written an entire book to disprove. The yeoman, Cash's man at the center, he had omitted, and although the yeoman was indeed less noticeable in Percy's Delta than in the rest of the South, even there he was present—as Percy himself comes close to acknowledging much later in the book. Throughout *Lanterns on the Levee*, however, he makes a mistake that his fellow Mississippian Faulkner—or indeed Donald Davidson— would never have made, confusing the plain and "poor" white. The degraded and malnourished poor white, Percy insisted, was "responsible for the only American ballads, for camp meetings, for a whole new and excellent school of Southern literature" (p. 20). It was not the poor white, in either the historical or the sociological sense, that Percy meant at all.

There were other points at which Cash could have taken issue with Percy, could have proved him "wrong," but there was just as much in *Lanterns on the Levee* that could serve to challenge Cash. Percy not only affirmed the existence of a Deep South aristocracy that Cash virtually denied, but in the very writing of *Lanterns on the Levee* presented himself as a good example of it. He himself *was* that cultivated gentleman educated in the classics who, according to Cash, rarely existed outside the Tidewater. His book also, in its description of the fall of the Percys and the rise of the Vardamans and Bilbos, with the accompanying shifts and changes in the affairs of the Delta and in Southern politics generally, challenged Cash's claim of continuity. When the bottom rail was on top, the same people were not in charge anymore.

As he read *Lanterns on the Levee* in the spring of 1941 Cash must have realized these discrepancies. In his review he did admit the claim of at least one Deep Southerner to aristocracy—Percy himself. And in a speech he made only a month before his death, the commencement address at the University of Texas, he himself dwelt on the central theme of *Lanterns on the Levee*, the importance of "tradition," and particularly "our Southern tradition." Cash's concern for Western tradition stemmed from his reading of events in Europe: the barbarians were threatening, "tradition [was] everywhere under attack."[43] Indeed, he had expressed a similar concern in the final pages of *The*

43. W. J. Cash, "The South in a Changing World," reprinted in Morrison, *W. J. Cash*, 297.

Mind of the South. For all his emphasis on continuity, at the end he saw only change and uncertainty: "It would be a madman who would venture [prophecies] in face of the forces sweeping over the world in the fateful year of 1940" (p. 440). In the remainder of his Texas speech Cash had not departed drastically from the themes of *The Mind of the South*—he still stressed the plebeian origins of Southern aristocracy—but the wonder seems to be that Cash, the iconoclast and Menckenite, would devote his last public remarks to a consideration of tradition. It was a sentiment more appropriate for William Alexander Percy.

Percy himself had little more to say after he completed *Lanterns on the Levee.* He did not need to. That one book had established him as perhaps the most eloquent spokesman in the Southern school of remembrance. If he had lived longer and had seen Southern society change, he might have broadened his perspective; or, as Walker Percy wrote in 1973, he might have found "himself closer to Cash in sorting out his heroes and villains."[44] But he could not have written with greater conviction and beauty than he did in 1940. Like Fitzhugh, Dabney, and Davidson, he saw the older South's cause as the cause of order and stability, of Western civilization itself, and like them he was a Cassandra, foreseeing only doom for an age which departed from its inheritance. Like them, he possessed a rage against abstraction, reform, radical change, and the planned society. Even sharecropping, his discussion of which drew more criticism than any other part of his book, he defended in precisely the same way as Fitzhugh had defended slavery. It was preferable to the "slave routine" of industrial workers. The Negro cropper received a house, free medical care, education, and, on the Percy plantation, free legal services: "I wonder what other unskilled labor for so little receives so much. Plantations do not close down during the year and there's no firing, because partners can't fire one another. Our plantation system seems to me to offer as humane, just, self-respecting, and cheerful a method of earning a living as human beings are likely to devise" (p. 280). When Percy considered his sharecroppers, he felt pity for unskilled laborers and clerks in modern society, "for their poor and fixed wage . . . their joyless habits of work, and their insecurity" (p. 280). If anyone suffered

44. Walker Percy, introduction to *Lanterns on the Levee,* xvii.

in the plantation system, it was the planter class, which took the risks, lost money, and carried "on its shoulders a weaker race and from the burden [lost] its own strength!" (p. 284).

Fitzhugh had said all this, yet Percy said it in a different voice. For Fitzhugh had been defending a plantation society he considered strong and vibrant, likely to prosper for years. Percy was at the other end of a historical era, looking back on the plantation system that now had nearly disappeared. Thus he differed in tone not only from Fitzhugh but the other earlier apologists as well. He lacked the defiance of Dabney and Davidson, the intensity and vigor. Their views had been polemical and militant, his were elegiac. Nor was he, in the strictest sense, even an agrarian. "I have no love of the land," he wrote in *Lanterns on the Levee* (p. 278), and although much else he wrote in that book suggests otherwise, indeed he did not have the close contact with the soil that Davidson and most of the other Agrarians valued. The plantation system and his sharecroppers came between him and his three thousand acres. They were closer to the fertile cotton land than he was. He cultivated only his garden.

But he cultivated that with the care of one who realized it was virtually the only thing over which he still had control. All else was chaos: the poor whites had seized command, the Negroes on his plantation did not exhibit the dignity and respect they had once exhibited, the world was beyond his understanding. Will Percy, as he tended his garden in 1940, was already an anachronism, and he knew it. "As a class I suppose the Southern aristocrat is extinct," he wrote in *Lanterns on the Levee* (p. 62), although he believed that what that class treasured lived on. Four decades later one wonders to what degree even that is true. As Walker Percy has written, paternalism and noblesse oblige at their best were finer concepts than we are now willing to admit: they gave humanity to an older South. But the upper classes have now abdicated their responsibility, and with that abdication have cast off noblesse oblige and the tradition of manners that often accompanied it. The gentleman planter in the Deep South who had been the Negro's champion was, a generation after Will Percy's death, rare indeed. Will Percy's class, as Walker Percy suggests, was not really fighting the battle anymore. Its heirs differed little in attitude from the upstarts; in some cases they had joined the Snopeses. Stoicism, Walker Percy has written, finally was not enough: "For the Stoic there is no real hope. His finest hour is to sit tight-lipped and ironic while the world comes crashing down around him."[45] But the modern Southerner, or rather the Southerner in a modern world, needed more than that, something more rewarding, more vital.

If William Alexander Percy was nearly an anachronism in 1940, he is even more so today. The big, rambling house in Greenville at the corner of State and Percy is now gone, and one finds only the trees which had shaded the house and a walk leading up to where a front door had been. Greenville's memory of Percy has faded, and in Southern history he is classified and labeled, his case closed: paternalistic planter, kind, outdated. He was not truly much of a Southern analyst anyway. Wilbur Cash, seven hundred miles away in the Carolina Piedmont, understood Thomas Sutpen of Yoknapatawpha better than did Will Percy one hundred miles away in the Delta. But Will Percy nonetheless has his legacy—in no small part, in the writing of Walker Percy, the sanest and most acute observer of the contemporary South, a writer who, while rejecting the Stoicism of his adoptive father, has retained Will Percy's commitment to values, has drawn from him an influence more beneficial than that William Alexander Percy drew from his father. Will Percy was a poet, as the most notable contributors to *I'll Take My Stand* were poets, and his vision of the good society must be viewed as theirs, poetically. His commitment to the code of the gentleman was genuine if antiquated, his regard for the Negro sincere if paternalistic, and if he were writing today, as Walker Percy says, he might even think better of the plain whites, whose sons have assumed leadership in the South and in some cases have not done so badly.

IN 1942, the year after *The Mind of the South* and *Lanterns on the Levee*, Alfred A. Knopf published still another remarkable book of Southern self-explanation, a book written about W. J. Cash's people but more nearly in the voice of William Alexander Percy. Ben Robertson in *Red Hills and Cotton* was reminiscent and poetic like Percy, not cerebral and analytical like Cash. His title, like that of Percy, was modest and

45. *Ibid.*, xiii, xvii; Walker Percy, "Stoicism in the South," *Commonweal*, July 6, 1956, p. 344. See also Walker Percy, "Mississippi: The Fallen Paradise," *Harper's*, CCXXX (April, 1965), 166–72.

localized, not sweeping and presumptuous as *The Mind of the South*; and his subtitle *An Upcountry Memory* resembled Percy's *Recollections*. For Robertson wrote only of his own people in the valleys of the Keowee and Twelve Mile rivers in upcountry South Carolina, and he presumed to speak of and for no other. The people he described were hardly aristocrats, but he prized and defended their way of life as strongly as Percy had defended the life of the Delta planter. His book was less interpretation than creed, an affirmation of faith in his family and his people. The creed went something like this: We believe in God, family, upcountry Carolina, the South and America, in cotton, the Baptist church, and the Democratic party. We believe the hills of northwestern South Carolina, which we have inhabited for two centuries, to be the finest place on earth. We believe small farms are best, but sometimes have large ones. We believe in self-reliance, self-improvement, total abstinence, total immersion, righteousness, and justice. We are rooted in place and have a sense of who we are and where we came from.

It is in this manner—using "we," not "I"—that Robertson speaks throughout his book. He was a native of that South Carolina upcountry he describes, born seventy-five miles away from Wilbur Cash and three years after him. Like Cash and Percy, he died less than a year after his book on the South was published by Knopf—at age thirty-nine, in a plane crash near Lisbon in February, 1943. Like Cash, he was a journalist, but of a far more exotic breed. He had attended Clemson College and the University of Missouri, then, while Cash was working in Boiling Springs, Shelby, and Charlotte, he had struck out for Hawaii, and later for India, Borneo, Java, and Australia. In 1940 he had gone to Europe as a war correspondent for the New York newspaper *PM*, and upon his return to the United States had collected his observations in a well-received book, *I Saw England* (1941). But Robertson, that most cosmopolitan of men, was at once the most provincial. In 1938 he had written—and printed at his own expense when he found no publisher—*Traveler's Rest*, a story based on the Robertson clan of Piedmont South Carolina. In 1942, while he was in Moscow covering the Russian front, Knopf published his second book on the South, *Red Hills and Cotton*.

It was a book written in a leisurely, conversational style, telling of the Robertsons, their beliefs and attitudes, and farm life in upcountry

South Carolina as it had existed for two centuries. That book too was well received[46]—and its author received a final measure of recognition when, as a war correspondent, he perished in the much-publicized crash of the *Yankee Clipper* several months later—but since 1943 both book and author have been largely ignored. One does not find Robertson in biographical and bibliographical guides to Southern literature. Neither literary scholars nor historians claim him. As Southern writer he is forgotten.

Red Hills and Cotton deserves better. One of the most beautifully written of those books of Southern self-exploration, it also shares many concerns with *Lanterns on the Levee* and *The Mind of the South*. Like Percy, Robertson writes with unashamed admiration for tradition and dwells on the past, on what he learned from the old people—his strong, gentle grandmother and public-spirited grandfather. Grandfather Bowen defended the South's agrarian heritage and was suspicious of the "factory system" of the North. Like Percy, Robertson defends the traditional Southern attitude toward the Negro and embodies the spirit of noblesse oblige, and also like Percy, he recommends "Southern Stoicism," although he means something different by the term: not Marcus Aurelius but John Calvin inspired the conduct Robertson calls stoical—a strong, rigid moral code, a preference for an austere life. But the author of *Red Hills and Cotton* would object to Percy's condescension to the plain white. Robertson's attitude toward the planters of the Delta would likely be the same as his attitude toward the planters of the Carolina low country: he disliked and distrusted them. His people, again, were Cash's people—plain white and Baptist. As a child he too worshipped the Confederate cause, and as a writer he dwelt on the same streaks of Puritanism and hedonism running parallel in the Southern temper. With the unbroken agrarian experience of the Robertsons, farming on the same land for two centuries, he could not help but affirm continuity in the Southern history he knew. But his approach to the upcountry people departed radically from that of Cash. His was a voice committed rather than detached.

46. See Stark Young, "More Souths," *New Republic*, October 5, 1942, p. 421; J. K. Paulding, "Biography," *Commonweal*, October 2, 1942, p. 369; "The Hill Gentry," *Time*, September 28, 1942, p. 92. The same year Knopf brought out *Red Hills and Cotton*, Harper & Brothers published *I Came Out of the Eighteenth Century*, another retrospective glance by a South Carolinian, Andrew Rice. Rice had grown up largely in a series of towns and cities, and his book is not the celebration of agrarian virtues that Robertson's book is. The son of a Methodist minister, Rice is most perceptive when discussing religion, particularly Southern Puritanism.

Cash assessed the Southern devotion to family and clan; Robertson presents himself as an example of that devotion. Cash saw spectacle and drama, contradiction and irony in Southern life. Robertson sees normalcy and harmony. He evokes poetically what Cash brilliantly dissects. Yet at the same time he is committed, even at times intensely personal, Robertson reveals very little of himself, where he had gone, what he has done. He writes not an autobiography of an individual but of a place, a community, a family. In the sense of a self endowed with personality, the self is refined out of the narrative. We know virtually nothing about Robertson save that he is one of the people of the valley, that he had gone to college, and apparently was in England in 1940. For all we know from the book, he is a farmer, not a journalist.

And in the final analysis, Robertson did not write precisely of Cash's people. For he wrote a Jeffersonian idyll: the people he celebrated had not yet left the land and gone to Greenville and Spartanburg and the other textile towns. They were still farmers, good country people before the fall—still whole, their lives still unified, organic. At the time Robertson wrote, the life he described was already passing. He had seen and reported the depression of the 1930s, and although he sometimes believed the collapse of industrial capitalism vindicated the Southern agrarian philosophy, he also knew that the older agrarian order could never return. He wrote, as well, with a knowledge that the war in Europe could change everything. In this respect he was not unlike the authors of *The Mind of the South* and *Lanterns on the Levee*. His book, like theirs, though conceived as a Southern expression, was completed with one eye on Europe. "Germany destroyed my world," Will Percy wrote in *Lanterns on the Levee* (p. 156), and although he was referring specifically to the First World War, the statement stood also for his attitude toward the Second. W. J. Cash, feverishly writing editorials on Hitler's Germany in the late 1930s, could not separate events abroad from events in the American South. Ben Robertson was in Europe, observing the war firsthand as he finished his book. The specter of Nazi Germany touched all three men and it was no accident that their classics of Southern self-expression appeared within a period of eighteen months in 1941 and 1942. It was no accident, because the threat to the old order, to Western civilization—of which, Cash said in his last public address, the American South was a prominent part—lent an air of emergency, however far away (to Cash and Percy, at least) the war might have been. It also brought a mood of retrospection. The situation for Cash, Percy, and Robertson in 1940 resembled, in one respect, that of the Southern writer just after the First World War—seeing his world rapidly changing and feeling the need to capture it while he could, before it disappeared entirely. With Hitler's armies sweeping across Europe, there was no assurance that the world as they had known it would not disappear. It was time to take stock, to reflect on a South that was already changing radically, to get it on record before it was too late.

PART III

No More Quentin Compsons?
   or
Dixie in the Sun

Look! We Have Come Through!
  D. H. Lawrence, 1917

The worlds of Wilbur Cash and William Alexander Percy survived the war if they themselves did not. The radical change they prophesied did not come immediately, but it came soon enough that, had they lived another generation, they would have found a South as foreign in many respects as their worlds had been from Appomattox. Increasing federal support for Negro demands in the immediate postwar years, the 1954 Supreme Court decision outlawing segregation in the public schools, the civil rights revolution of the 1960s: all brought the racial change the South had long resisted. Dixie was destined to change not only its racial habits but its way of making a living as well. The South emerged from World War II, as George B. Tindall has written, "with fewer sharecroppers but more pipefitters and welders, with less plowing and hoeing but more mowing and sowing, with less rural isolation and more urban sophistication." As the South of the Agrarians' imagination slipped further into the past, new industries came—not the least of which, as Edwin M. Yoder, Jr., has written, was producing books about the South.[1]

If pondering and examining the mind and the soul of Dixie had seemed a Southern affliction before 1945, it assumed epidemic proportions in the three decades thereafter. The attention riveted in the 1950s and 1960s upon Little Rock, Oxford, Birmingham, Selma, and other civil rights battlegrounds brought again to the region the reputation it had earned in the 1920s—the savage or benighted South. Reporters again flocked south in search of a story, and reformers came with a missionary zeal they had not exhibited since the days of Dayton and Gastonia and Scottsboro. Again Dixie occupied center stage, both sinned against and sinning in outrageous fashion. If the Northern interest in the South accelerated, the Southerner's desire to explain

1. George B. Tindall, *The Emergence of the New South, 1913–1945* (Baton Rouge, 1967), 731, ix [quoting Yoder].

himself—both to outsiders and to himself—grew correspondingly. Every journalist, politician, and scholar in the late Confederacy, it seemed, was probing his homeland, writing a book about it, assigning it a new label. *The Emerging South, The Changing South*, "The Disappearing . . . South," "The Vanishing South," *The Enduring South*, "The Distinctive South," "The American South," "The World South," "The Provincial South," *The Democratic South*, "The Embarrassing New South," "The South as a Counterculture," *The Romantic South, The Uncertain South, The Militant South*, "The Benighted South," "The Poetic South," "The Backward South," "The Progressive South," *The Lazy South*, "The Turbulent South," "The Squalid South," "The Solid South," "The Divided South," "The Devilish South," "The Visceral South," "The Massive, Concrete South"—such is only a partial list of titles of books, chapters, and essays written since 1945 on that land below the Potomac and Ohio.[2]

Few Southerners seemed to agree about what the South, most of all, was, or even what it had been. In 1958 Harry Ashmore, Pulitzer Prize–winning editor of the *Arkansas Gazette*, detected a disappearing South and issued an "Epitaph for Dixie." The year before John Westbrook, writing in the *Southwest Review*, had come to a similar conclu-

2. Thomas D. Clark, *The Emerging South* (New York, 1961); Raymond W. Mack (ed.), *The Changing South* (Chicago, 1970); Selz C. Mayo, "Social Change, Social Movements, and the Disappearing Sectional South," *Social Forces*, XLIII (October, 1964), 1–10; John Shelton Reed, "The Vanishing South," *The Enduring South*; Carl N. Degler, "The Distinctive South," *Place Over Time*; Louis D. Rubin, Jr., "The American South: The Continuity of Self-Definition," in Rubin (ed.), *The American South: Portrait of a Culture* (Baton Rouge, 1980); Marshall William Fishwick, "The World South" and "The Changing South," *Sleeping Beauty and Her Suitors: The South in the Sixties* (Macon, 1961); Lester J. Cappon, "The Provincial South," in George B. Tindall (ed.), *The Pursuit of Southern History: Presidential Addresses of the Southern Historical Association, 1935–1963* (Baton Rouge, 1964); Dewey W. Grantham, Jr., *The Democratic South* (Athens, Ga., 1963); Jack Temple Kirby, "The Embarrassing New South," *Media-Made Dixie: The South in the American Imagination* (Baton Rouge, 1978); Sheldon Hackney, "The South as a Counterculture," *American Scholar*, XLII (Spring, 1973), 283–93; Harnett T. Kane (ed.), *The Romantic South* (New York, 1961); Charles O. Lerche, Jr., *The Uncertain South: Its Changing Patterns of Politics in Foreign Policy* (Chicago, 1964); John Hope Franklin, *The Militant South* (Cambridge, Mass., 1956); George B. Tindall, "The Benighted South," *The Ethnic Southerners*; James McBride Dabbs, "The Poetic South," *Who Speaks for the South?*; John Samuel Ezell, "The Backward South" and "The Progressive South," *The South Since 1865* (New York, 1963); David Bertelson, *The Lazy South* (New York, 1967); George B. Tindall, "World War II: The Turbulent South," *The Emergence of the New South*; Stetson Kennedy, "The Squalid South," *Southern Exposure* (Garden City, N.Y., 1946); Samuel S. Hill, Jr., "The Solid South," in Hill and others, *Religion and the Solid South* (Nashville, 1972); Carl N. Degler, "The Divided South," *Reporter*, March 11, 1965, pp. 46–49; Jack Temple Kirby, "The Devilish South" and "The Visceral South," *Media-Made Dixie*; James McBride Dabbs, "The Massive, Concrete South," *The Southern Heritage* (New York, 1958).

sion: "The happy truth is that the South has lost its 'regional integrity.'" Yet that same year fourteen Southerners by birth or adoption, in the most impressive joint statement of its kind since *I'll Take My Stand*, issued a book entitled *The Lasting South*, and six years later historian Francis Butler Simkins, not to be outdone, entitled his book *The Everlasting South*. Even the social scientists, armed with tables and charts, could not agree. The president of the Southern Sociological Society proclaimed in his 1964 presidential address—and later in *Social Forces*—a "Disappearing Sectional South," and two years later another sociologist writing in the *Journal of Social Issues* agreed that the South was on its way to becoming "almost indistinguishable from any other region in the country." Five years after that, in the *American Sociological Review*, two other social scientists concurred that the South was "becoming increasingly indistinguishable from the rest of American society." But the next year John Shelton Reed, a sociologist in the tradition of Odum at the University of North Carolina, consulted *his* tables and charts and came to a completely different conclusion: the South endured. Southerners were different from non-Southerners even after they moved to city and suburb.[3]

The debate continued with no conclusive results—a debate not so much about what the South should be (as the debate of the 1930s between the Agrarians and Odum's Regionalists had been) but rather about what the South in fact was and had been. Mythology became a new frontier of Southern history, as George Tindall wrote; scholars debated not only what Dixie was in itself but what it represented in the nation. C. Vann Woodward focused on the burden of the Southern past, the special perspective that the Southerner's legacy of defeat and failure, unique within the American experience, had given him. Howard Zinn wrote of a "Southern mystique" and pronounced the South a "distorted mirror image" of the rest of the nation. Leslie Dunbar suggested that Dixie was "the place where American error and excess go to retire." Charles Grier Sellers, Jr., Grady McWhiney,

3. Harry Ashmore, *An Epitaph for Dixie* (New York, 1958); John Westbrook, "Twilight of Southern Regionalism," *Southwest Review*, XLII (Summer, 1957), 234; Louis D. Rubin, Jr., and James J. Kilpatrick (eds.), *The Lasting South: Fourteen Southerners Look at Their Home* (Chicago, 1957); Francis Butler Simkins, *The Everlasting South* (Baton Rouge, 1963); Mayo, "Social Change, Social Movements, and the Disappearing Sectional South"; Leonard Reissman, "Social Development and the American South," *Journal of Social Issues*, XXII (January, 1966), 115; McKinney and Bourque, "The Changing South," 399–412; Reed, *The Enduring South*. See also, for an excellent discussion of continuing Southern distinctiveness, Degler, *Place Over Time*.

George E. Mowry, and other historians stressed that the South was at least as American as it was Southern. And David M. Potter spoke perhaps for all of them when he wrote of "the enigma of the South."[4]

But in this explosion of literature on the condition and transcendent meaning of Dixie, some things remained the same. The Southern schools of shame and remembrance—still corresponding roughly to self-critic and defender, or liberal and conservative—endured, although, as we shall see, they assumed somewhat different forms and, between 1945 and 1970, the school of shame and guilt carried the day. If native Southern critics before 1945 had often trembled to pour out their true feelings about their homeland, and had in some cases poured out those feelings at risk to health and well-being, their descendants after 1945 could hardly be restrained. Liberal Southern congressmen, only peripheral members of the school of shame and guilt but often considered downright radical by their constituents, wrote books, often after forced retirements, describing their own profiles in Southern courage. Brooks Hays of Arkansas, Frank E. Smith of Mississippi, Charles Longstreet Weltner of Georgia, and Albert Gore of Tennessee were only four of those who proclaimed their love for the South while decrying its racial attitudes and waste of resources.[5] A reader in New York would have thought all Southern congressmen were liberal and wrote books.

But if the politicians were prolific they were also too pragmatic to be the true heirs of the Southern tradition of self-criticism. That legacy fell largely to liberal Southern journalists, those who felt comfortable with the rhetoric of sin and guilt and were in many respects the suc-

4. George B. Tindall, "Mythology: A New Frontier in Southern History," in Frank E. Vandiver (ed.), *The Idea of the South: Pursuit of a Central Theme* (Chicago, 1964); Woodward, "The Irony of Southern History"; Zinn, *The Southern Mystique*; Leslie Dunbar, "The Annealing of the South," *Virginia Quarterly Review*, XXXVII (Autumn, 1961), 495; Charles Grier Sellers, Jr., Grady McWhiney, John Hope Franklin, Thomas P. Govan, David Donald, George B. Tindall, L. D. Reddick, Dewey W. Grantham, Jr., and C. Hugh Holman, in Sellers (ed.), *The Southerner as American* (Chapel Hill, 1960); George E. Mowry, *Another Look at the Twentieth-Century South* (Baton Rouge, 1973); Potter, "The Enigma of the South," 142–51.

5. Brooks Hays, *A Southern Moderate Speaks* (Chapel Hill, 1959); Frank E. Smith, *Look Away from Dixie* (Baton Rouge, 1965) and *Congressman from Mississippi* (New York, 1964); Charles Longstreet Weltner, *Southerner* (Philadelphia, 1966); Albert Gore, *Let the Glory Out: My South and Its Politics* (New York, 1972). See also Arnall, *The Shore Dimly Seen*; Henry Savage, *Seeds of Time: The Background of Southern Thinking* (New York, 1959); and William T. Polk, *Southern Accent: From Uncle Remus to Oak Ridge* (New York, 1953). For a later book in the same vein, see Robert Canzoneri, *"I Do So Politely": A Voice from the South* (Boston, 1965).

cessors to Cash. The year after the war Stetson Kennedy, a thirty-year-old Florida newspaperman with roots in Georgia, produced *Southern Exposure*, a book that placed him squarely in the tradition of Helper and William H. Skaggs. Although "attached" to his "birthplace and home," he felt compelled to attack the Southern "slavocracy" and to pronounce the South "the nation's pathological problem No. I." Dixie was "insane" and its insanity "infected the entire nation." Most other Southern journalists, even those who objected to the South's economic and racial conduct, were not willing to go so far. Hodding Carter's *Southern Legacy* (1950), Ashmore's *Epitaph for Dixie* (1958), Ralph McGill's *South and the Southerner* (1963), Willie Morris' *North Toward Home* (1967), Larry King's *Confessions of a White Racist* (1971), and Pat Watters' *South and the Nation* (1969) and *Down to Now* (1971) all belonged in varying degrees to the Southern school of shame and guilt, although in each case the author's shame was tempered by a proper measure of Southern pride. Carter, editor of the *Delta Democrat-Times* of Will Percy's Greenville, was a "mild liberal," as C. Vann Woodward has written, although the mildness of his liberalism was sometimes mistaken in Mississippi for sheer lunacy.[6] In *Southern Legacy*, written in the late 1940s, he was cautious. He complained of "uninformed" outside critics of the South and declared that "any abrupt Federal effort to end segregation" would not only fail but would "dangerously impair the present progressive adjustments between the races" (pp. 89–90). Yet he expressed a strong distaste for Southern demagogues, spoke critically of Southern Agrarianism, and in a chapter entitled "The Deeper Wound" declared that racial prejudice and discrimination had "infected the white South with a moral sickness." The "soul" of the white South had suffered a wound deeper even than that inflicted upon the Negro (p. 175). Ashmore did not regard his Southern legacy so highly as did Carter. His "epitaph" for Dixie was issued largely without regret. Although he prized the grace and leisure of an earlier South, Dixie's racial sins nearly canceled its virtues in his mind. The history of the South was "tragedy," a tragedy lying "not in the battles we lost, but in the battles we never fought"

6. Kennedy, *Southern Exposure*, 78; Hodding Carter, *Southern Legacy* (Baton Rouge, 1950); Ashmore, *An Epitaph for Dixie*; McGill, *The South and the Southerner*; Willie Morris, *North Toward Home* (New York, 1967); Larry King, *Confessions of a White Racist* (New York, 1971); Pat Watters, *The South and the Nation* (1969; rpr. New York, 1971) and *Down to Now: Reflections on the Southern Civil Rights Movement* (New York, 1971); C. Vann Woodward, review of *Southern Legacy*, *Journal of Southern History*, XVI (August, 1950), 381.

(p. 179). Southern leaders had rarely led. Ashmore, like George W. Cable seventy-five years before, lamented a Silent South.

Ralph McGill of Atlanta shared the liberalism of Carter and Ashmore but not precisely their perspective. They lived and wrote in that part of Dixie that nineteenth-century Virginians had called the Far South; McGill was more in the tradition of Near South Piedmont liberalism. Ralph McGill is a somewhat paradoxical figure in twentieth-century Southern liberalism. Editor of the Atlanta *Constitution* from 1942 to 1969, he gained a great reputation as a courageous spokesman on racial matters. Yet some Southerners believed, as one of his acquaintances wrote after his death, that his "reputation was built on something that never was," and those detractors gave as evidence statements such as one he made a few weeks before the 1954 Supreme Court decision: "I personally hope the Supreme Court will not disturb segregation in the common schools." Yet his autobiography, *The South and the Southerner*, possesses the moral tone—the emphasis on Southern racial sins and a call for right action—that has characterized most Southern social criticism since Cable. It was called by more than one reviewer the finest work on the South since *The Mind of the South*, and superficially at least it had something in common with Cash's book. Cash's publisher, Alfred A. Knopf, had first interested McGill in writing such a book, and, like Cash, McGill was "beset by doubts and fears" while he was working on it. McGill's editor had first proposed the title "The Education of Ralph McGill," but the book was hardly that.[7] McGill did not really *absorb* his environment as such a title would suggest; rather he remained largely what he had been from the first, as his "stern Welsh-Scottish Calvinism" would have ordained it. He had gone from his native east Tennessee hills to Vanderbilt (where he disproved Donald Davidson's claim that one's college influences one's ideology) and then on to Atlanta; but he remained the east Tennessean with divided Southern sentiments who "early acquired a poor opinion of slaveholding people" (p. 54) and whose "Calvinist conscience was stirred by some of the race prejudice I saw" (p. 58). McGill spoke often of "conscience," "shame," and "guilt." "Guilt and accusation" made up "the mosaic of Southern conscience,"

7. George McMillan, "Portrait of a Southern Liberal," *New York Review of Books*, April 18, 1974, p. 33; Ralph McGill to Alfred A. Knopf, July 24, 1963 (copy), McGill to Edward Weeks, July 8, 1959 (copy), and Peter Davison to McGill, May 27, 1959, all in Ralph McGill Papers, Emory University Library, Atlanta.

he wrote in *The South and the Southerner* (p. 218), and the South had "consistently and almost embarrassingly revealed its troubled conscience" (p. 217).

If McGill represented the Southern tradition of racial shame and guilt in its early 1960s phase, a lesser-known Atlanta journalist, Pat Watters, represented the same tradition at a still later stage. McGill had written his book just before the great civil rights activity of the mid-1960s; Watters wrote just after it and the passing of a few years made a vast amount of difference. The author of *The South and the Nation*, as Sheldon Hackney wrote, was a moralist, and "outrage and compassion" were his reactions to the South.[8] But a book which better illustrates Watters' moralism, although it attracted far less attention, was *Down to Now: Reflections on the Southern Civil Rights Movement*, which might well have borne the title "Up From Segregation." Here Watters, a reporter who had covered the movement, wrote as one "whose life was essentially changed by it" (p. x). His tone was emotional, unashamedly sentimental; he was one of the repentant and converted, and he spoke the language of sin and guilt. His "deep, personal awakening" had been "in the real sense a religious experience" (p. 3). "And how," he exclaimed of his Southern childhood, "*how* were we able to achieve such insensitivity, such cruelty, with never a pang of conscience?" (p. 30). There had been "evil brooding over us" (p. 31), but Southern whites "shut out from consciousness the bad and the evil" (p. 30). Segregation was "surely insane, surely the worst sin" (p. 38). The "southern movement" had set out to "heal the insanity in southern society, to end the sin of it, to allow expiation of it" (p. 38). He recalled in particular a night in Atlanta when he had gone to see Negro students greet Martin Luther King, who had just returned from jail. Watters heard the students sing "We Shall Overcome," was struck with the knowledge of "all my life of acquiescence in the evil," and "cried unabashedly, cried for joy—and hope" (p. 54).

For all its seeming sentimentality, *Down to Now* is a moving story. The conversion of a sinner usually is. It is a book Ralph McGill, for all his discussion of guilt and conscience, could never have written. Watters' voice is that of a white Southerner who has finally crossed barriers of separation and—as he writes—has learned how to live. Mc-

8. Sheldon Hackney, review of *The South and the Nation*, *Journal of Southern History*, XXXVI (August, 1970), 470–71.

Gill's too was a committed voice, but one always in control, never betraying too much—in the final analysis, perhaps, the semi-official voice of the City Too Busy to Hate, as Atlanta proclaimed itself in the 1960s. The concern of McGill, to his credit, went deeper than that of the slogan-makers: he was not only too busy but too compassionate for hatred. And he wrote his book before 1964, before the spiritual power of the civil rights movement had fully stirred the consciences of sensitive white Southerners. But even if McGill had written in 1969, one suspects, he was too much the reporter to bare his emotions. As one of his contemporaries wrote, he was perhaps "protected from complete involvement" with the South because of his newspaperman's temperament and east Tennessee heritage.[9] Were not sin and guilt, in *The South and the Southerner*, at least in part abstractions, intellectual constructs?

And were they not, to some extent, abstractions as well for Willie Morris and Larry King, two latter-day Southerners who belong by design and by rhetoric to the Southern school of shame and guilt? Unlike Carter, Ashmore, McGill, and Watters, the younger Southerners Morris and King had gone north by the time they wrote their books of self-revelation in the late 1960s. Theirs was, in this respect, the older tradition: Cable and Walter Hines Page had also left Dixie for the Northeast when they wrote. But Morris and King also contributed significantly to the literature of Southern self-exploration. In *Confessions of a White Racist*, King, who had grown up in a Texas as much Western as Southern, issued a forthright admission of racial guilt—for himself, other Southerners, other Americans, and humanity in general. He traced his own attitude from the racial insensitivity of his youth through a timid racial liberalism of the 1950s and early 1960s to a sympathetic understanding in the late 1960s of the black rage for revenge. Throughout he was earnest, terribly earnest. Larry King's was a personal statement, he insisted in the beginning, one he had to make even if it hurt his family.

Willie Morris in *North Toward Home* was less guilt-ridden, but he too wrote in the tradition of those Southerners who have felt compelled to come to terms with the South and themselves as Southerners. His book, indeed, is perhaps illustrative of what happened to the South-

9. James McBride Dabbs, "McGill and the South," Atlanta *Constitution*, March 24, 1963.

ern tradition of self-exploration as it moved into the post–civil rights era. A white Mississippian from the fringes of the Delta, Morris described in *North Toward Home* his journey from the Deep South to the University of Texas, where he had become editor of the campus newspaper, then to Oxford as a Rhodes scholar, and finally to the Northeast, where he found himself pondering the South. He seems at first glance a latter-day Quentin Compson, the Mississippian possessed of a love-hate relationship with his homeland who sits in the iron-cold North and pours out his feelings about Dixie. But in fact, rather than the tortured Quentin, Morris resembles more the real-life Thomas Wolfe, another small-city Southerner of modest origin and high ambition who was first awakened to the power of ideas at a liberal Southern state university, became editor of his campus newspaper, lived for a while in Europe, than settled in New York, where he sought his literary fortune and found himself able to utilize his Southernness to literary advantage: he could work out his feelings about the South on paper in a way Faulkner's Quentin never could. Morris, like Wolfe, found New York cold and impersonal; like Wolfe, he called it "the Cave." But like Wolfe as well, he was a man of ideas who felt at home in a place that valued ideas, and his relationship to his homeland was also similar. It was the definition of *home* that principally concerned him, as it concerned the author of *Look Homeward, Angel*. Even the title of Morris' book is a variation on that of Wolfe's later novel, *You Can't Go Home Again*.

But if Morris was the sensitive Southern artist gone north, he was also the Southern Horatio Alger, or Horatio Alger as man of letters, the embodiment of the Southern success story. In this role he was less Thomas Wolfe than Walter Hines Page, that earlier Southern journalist of solid stock and good sense who became a successful editor in New York, took sentimental, even painful journeys back to Dixie, wrote one autobiographical work exploring his relationship to the South and decided, after all, that he must return north to live. Morris would always have Mississippi in his blood, he insisted in *North Toward Home*. Nowhere else was his entire being so fully engaged. He had grown up in Yazoo City an apprentice good old boy, a plain white who disproved Will Percy's contention that the Delta contained, among Caucasians, only aristocrats and poor whites. But his father had told him to get out of Mississippi, and just after he completed high school he did. He returned often, but after the years in Austin and England he found himself "sickened" by the racial attitudes, the lack of free inquiry, the narrowness of vision of most Mississippians, and realized he was alienated from his people. He ended his book about the South by describing one such visit and the emotions he experienced flying out of Jackson to New York, "north toward home": "Why was it, in such moments just before I leave the South, did I always feel some easing of a great burden?" (p. 437).

It was an attempt to come to terms with Mississippi, an expression of ambivalence over his relationship with his homeland; but it was hardly Quentin's "I dont hate it. . . . I dont. I dont." It was a rational response, an analytical one, not the uncontrolled, anguished outpouring of love and hate of that earlier imaginary Mississippian, or indeed of several actual Southerners we have discussed. Willie Morris, to be sure, like McGill and Watters, Ashmore and Carter and King, undertook his writing with a purpose that went beyond professional interest and intellectual curiosity; he too savored and protested his Southernness at one and the same time. Yet in Morris, as in all these other writers save Watters in Down to Now and, perhaps, King in his Confessions, something was missing: the tone was not quite so urgent. The literature of self-exploration, even of confession and shame and guilt, had become, as I have said earlier, somewhat stylized, had become in part a habit, an aesthetic ritual. The talented, sensitive Southerner who left his home, or even remained, wrote his obligatory self-study, his love-hate drama, in part because his predecessors had. It was, to some degree, expected of him. But his South had changed in a way that would strip a certain measure of urgency and anguish from his writing. Cash's savage ideal, though certainly not dead, was dying by 1960. Cable fled the South, and Cason and Cash committed suicide. McGill remained in Atlanta and was lionized. And when Willie Morris returned to Mississippi in 1980 it was not to be lynched; it was to be writer in residence in Oxford. What was different was that the paralyzing fear of telling the truth about the South had diminished. It was a condition partly of these writers' making—Carter and Ashmore and McGill had helped to create a climate in which honest self-appraisal was possible—and it was a condition at which they surely rejoiced. But it also leads to a question: When they wrote their confessionals and self-revelations did they really *mean* it anymore, or mean it in the way Cable and Cash and Cason assuredly had?

Lillian Smith

One among the postwar writers did mean it, and she spoke with a remarkably different voice. Lillian Smith of north Florida and Georgia was in many respects the last holdout, the last angry, absolute, and unselfconscious member of the Southern school of shame and guilt. "A modern, feminine counterpart of the ancient Hebrew prophets Amos, Hosea, Isaiah and Micah," McGill called her; the William Lloyd Garrison of the South, Virginius Dabney believed. Herself in some respects the "tortured southern liberal" she described in her writing, she represented a return to those all-or-nothing Southerners of an earlier generation. She kept her sanity, but otherwise she spoke with the fury of Helper or Ruffin or Robert Lewis Dabney. She might be seen, indeed, as a sort of twentieth-century mirror image of Edmund Ruffin—a crusader and cheerleader, one of the truly committed. Just as Ruffin in the 1850s and early 1860s had traveled to Charleston and Montgomery and Atlanta preaching the cause of secession, so Smith in the 1950s and early 1960s traveled to Atlanta and Montgomery and Washington preaching the cause of civil rights. Like Ruffin she sometimes felt abused and like Ruffin, as well, she suffered. Twice her house burned—once the fire was set by arsonists—and many of her papers and manuscripts were destroyed. In 1953 she learned she had cancer, and thus began a battle which lasted the remaining thirteen years of her life. But more important, like Ruffin, she often felt unappreciated. "I have been curiously smothered during the past nine years," she wrote in the early 1960s. "When southern writers are discussed, I am never mentioned; when women writers are mentioned, I am not among them. . . . Whom, among the mighty, have I so greatly offended!"[10]

10. Ralph McGill, "A Matter of Change," *New York Times Book Review*, February 13, 1955, p. 7; Virginius Dabney, in Morton Philip Sosna, "In Search of the Silent South: White Southern Racial Liberalism, 1920–1950" (Ph.D. dissertation, University of Wisconsin, 1973), 309; Lillian Smith, *The Winner Names the Age*, ed. Michelle Cliff (New York, 1978), 217–18, in subsequent citations, *WNA*. For biographical information about Smith, I rely principally on Smith's own autobiographical works and Margaret Long, "The Sense of Her Presence: A Memorial for Lillian Smith," *New South*, XXI (Fall, 1966), 71–77; Margaret Sullivan, "Lillian Smith: The Public Image and the Personal Vision," *Mad River Review*, II (Summer-Fall, 1967), 3–21; Rose Gladney, "The Legacy of Lillian

Her fellow Southern liberals, in part, she must have realized, for the way she treated them was anything but respectful. Her harsh treatment of the Southern reactionaries was to be expected: she saw them as cruel and sick. But those advocates of racial progress with whom she seemed to be aligned she similarly alienated at times. In 1944 she accused Virginius Dabney, John Temple Graves, and other liberals of forsaking the Negro's cause during wartime, of being "racial thumb-suckers" who regressed to childhood prejudices during times of stress. The same year she attacked the racially progressive Southern Regional Council for its failure to take a stand against segregation. She was indeed, as McGill said, akin to the prophets of old, and like them she would not compromise. Racial prejudice and discrimination were to her as the "perfidious Yankees" had been to Ruffin or the slavocracy to Hinton Helper—or the whale to Ahab. It had to be destroyed at any cost. If segregation to Howard Odum was a cause and an example of the Southern waste of human resources, and if to Cash it was a curious manifestation of the Southern mind, to Lillian Smith, "segregation [was] evil." "Try to forget that you are white," she urged her fellow Southerners. The rhetoric of good and evil, sin and guilt, came easily for her. All her major books—the novel *Strange Fruit* (1944) and the autobiographical treatises *Killers of the Dream* (1949) and *The Journey* (1954)—were highly charged works, in the deepest sense *religious* works, and so were the essays she wrote for the *New Republic, Saturday Review*, and other magazines. She wrote of the South's "dark tangled forest full of sins and boredom and fears" and of the Southern conscience "stretched so tightly on its frame of sin and punishment and God's anger." "Guilt" was "the biggest crop raised in Dixie, harvested each summer" during the August revivals, "just before cotton is picked," and she herself was hardly immune to its power. She wrote *Killers of the Dream*, she later explained, "in a way [as] an act of penance. . . . It was also for me . . . a step toward redemption." Such language, at least on such a personal level, was foreign to Odum and Virginius Dabney, McGill and Ashmore and Hodding Carter, as to Walter Hines Page before them. It would have violated the integrity of their basically pragmatic vision. But Smith was possessed of a different vision: she longed to create a "Christian

---

Smith," manuscript of speech given to the Southern Regional Council, Atlanta, May, 1980; and Louise Blackwell and Frances Clay, *Lillian Smith* (New York, 1971).

democratic culture" in the American South.[11] With her, it might be said, for the first time since the postbellum Calvinists Cable and Robert Lewis Dabney, God truly reentered the Southern picture.

Like Odum and the other Southern liberals, Smith recognized and dealt with a problem South. But if Odum ministered to Dixie's physical needs, and Cash to its mind, Smith plumbed its very soul. Segregation she found "a way of life so wounding, so hideous in its effect upon the spirit of both black and white" that it was without any redeeming feature. But the rhetoric of Southern religion sometimes was merged with the language of modern psychology. There was much, she wrote, "that reminds one of mental illness in [the Southern] catalog of sins." Southerners had "split [their] lives in a way shockingly akin to those sick people whom we call schizophrenics"; they suffered "delusions of persecution." Indeed, "perhaps the psychology of no group of people shows heavier traces of guilt and fear and hate than that of our South." Writing her controversial novel *Strange Fruit* was "therapy," Smith insisted, which "removed a long amnesia about my hometown." "I wrote down things I did not know were true until I saw them staring back at me on the page." Like Edmund Ruffin, she felt compelled to speak. "I had to write this book," she said of *Killers of the Dream*. "It was like a ghost flitting in and out of my mind until I did."[12]

Lillian Smith was fascinated by the process of self-exploration and truth-seeking. "Call Me Ishmael" she entitled one of her late essays, and like that earlier Ishmael she was a wanderer. Although she demonstrated great warmth and affection for the children of the South, she was at the same time detached from most of her other fellow Southerners. Indeed, the power of her truth-telling stemmed in part from her detachment. Unlike Odum and Dabney, Carter and Ashmore and McGill, all very conscious of their roles not only as South-

11. Lillian Smith, "Humans in Bondage," February 15, 1944, *WNA*, 37, 48, 46; acceptance speech for the Charles S. Johnson Award, *WNA*, 101; Lillian Smith, *Killers of the Dream* (1949; rpr. Garden City, N.Y., 1963), 100, 84, 87; Lillian Smith, "Autobiography as a Dialogue Between King and Corpse," *WNA*, 197. See also Lillian Smith, "Are We Not All Confused?," in White and Sugg (eds.), *From the Mountain*, 103–109.

12. Lillian Smith, "Putting Away Childish Things," *South Today*, Spring-Summer, 1944, in White and Sugg (eds.), *From the Mountain*, 133; Smith, *Killers of the Dream*, 184; Smith, "Humans in Bondage," 38; Smith, quoted in Blackwell and Clay, *Lillian Smith*, 34; Lillian Smith to Maxwell Geismar, January 1, 1961, in *WNA*, 214, 216; Smith, quoted in John K. Hutchens, "Lillian Smith," *New York Herald Tribune Book Review*, October 30, 1949, p. 2.

ern writers but as Southern *spokesmen*—and Southern leaders who could not leave their followers too far behind—she was bound by no institutional ties, restricted by no role as official spokesman. She possessed a freedom they did not because of her position outside the liberal mainstream—and also, she felt, because of her sex. The Southern woman, she believed, had a special position and a special calling if she would only recognize it. Removed from Southern political and economic life by history and tradition, she was free to concentrate on the religious and the moral. But Southern woman all too often had neglected her calling; rather she had belonged to the school of thought associated with the United Daughters of the Confederacy, reinforcing rather than questioning Southern tradition. It was largely for the benefit of Southern woman, after all, that Southerners insisted segregation had to be maintained, and it was for her protection that even lynching was justified. Woman, as Cash had written in *The Mind of the South*, was the "South's Palladium . . . the shield-bearing Athena gleaming whitely in the clouds . . . the lily-pure maid of Astolat and the hunting goddess of the Bœotian hill. . . . Merely to mention her was to send strong men into tears—or shouts" (p. 89). It was no wonder that gyneolatry arose, that women such as Mildred Lewis Rutherford and Dolly Blount Lamar of Georgia wrote books unswerving in their devotion to the late Confederacy, or that another Georgian, Margaret Mitchell, wrote *Gone With the Wind*—a "curious puffball" of a book, according to Lillian Smith.[13] Yet if there existed a UDC school of Southern thought, there existed as well a tradition of dissent among Southern women extending back to the Grimké sisters of Charleston and manifesting itself in the early twentieth century in antilynching crusades. It was in that tradition that Lillian Smith belonged, a tradition with its origins largely in religion. Lynching— or, in Smith's mind, segregation—was morally wrong; thus it must be fought.

But before Lillian Smith, very few Southern women had written books announcing it was wrong. Women of the 1920s, Julia Collier Harris of Columbus, Georgia, and Nell Battle Lewis of Raleigh, had

---

13. Lillian Smith, "Call Me Ishmael," *WNA*, 199–200; Dolly Blount Lamar, *When All Is Said and Done* (Athens, Ga., 1952); Mildred Lewis Rutherford, *The South in History and Literature* (Atlanta, 1907) and *Truths of History* ([Athens, Ga.], 1920); Lillian Smith, "One More Sign for the Good Old South," *Pseudopodia*, Fall, 1936, in White and Sugg (eds.), *From the Mountain*, 30.

combated the UDC position in newspaper articles, and Frances Newman of Atlanta had satirized it in her iconoclastic novel, *The Hard-
Boiled Virgin* (1926). Another Georgian of Smith's own generation,
Katharine DuPre Lumpkin, wrote *The Making of a Southerner* (1947), a
perceptive account of how she became aware of "glaring incongrui-
ties" in Southern life, came to question her "old heritage," "wrestle"
with her "Southernness," and reject the notion of white supremacy.
But none of these writers possessed the moral indignation of Lillian
Smith, and certainly none sustained it for so long. And none was
so totally aware of her unique responsibility as *woman*, particularly
Southern woman, as Lillian Smith was. Men, she wrote, were creatures of abstraction and design; women perceived reality concretely.
Men possessed a "mass-lust for power" and warfare; women, giving and nurturing life, cherished it more. For this reason Southern
women had "never been as loyal to the ideology of race and segregation as have southern men." Woman had "smelled the death in the
word *segregation*"—because she herself had been segregated. Because
of his "unending secret enmity against woman," man had placed her
on a "pedestal—segregating her . . . putting her always and forever
in her 'place.'" Women in the South had been an "oppressed group"
whose minds "man put . . . in prison"; worse, "we have grown to
love our chains."[14] Racism and sexism, then, were intertwined in the
mind of Lillian Smith. Neither Negro nor woman was truly separate
but equal: each faced barriers white man had erected. Both, Smith
reasoned, were victims of the aggression and the passion for abstraction of the dominant male, particularly the Southern variety.

The route by which Lillian Smith arrived at such conclusions was long
and circuitous. Save for a maternal grandfather from New York, there
was nothing suspect about her Southern origins. She was born in the
north Florida town of Jasper in 1897 to a prosperous businessman and
his well-bred wife. The Smiths were perhaps the leading family in
town. The seventh of nine children, Lillian grew up in a sixteen-room
house surrounded by live oaks in a town that was predominantly
Negro. Although she later spoke of the "haunted" nature of South-

14. Frances Newman, *The Hard-Boiled Virgin* (New York, 1926); Katharine DuPre
Lumpkin, *The Making of a Southerner* (New York, 1947), 239, 182, 198; Lillian Smith,
"Man Born of Woman," in White and Sugg (eds.), *From the Mountain*, 240, 247; Smith,
"Autobiography as a Dialogue Between King and Corpse," 191.

ern childhood, her own seemed on the surface pleasant enough, as she herself acknowledged in her autobiographical *Memory of a Large Christmas* (1962). She left Jasper, however, at age seventeen when her father's financial fortunes suffered and the Smiths moved to their summer home in north Georgia. After attending Piedmont College in Georgia for one year and studying piano for four at the Peabody Conservatory in Baltimore, she left for China, where she taught music for three years in a mission school. The stay in China had upon her the same effect that similar periods of residence outside the American South had upon other Southern writers of her generation: with geographical distance came emotional detachment and a new perspective she could not have found at home. The new insight was particularly keen in Smith's case. In the manner in which white Westerners dominated the Chinese she saw reflections of what she had left behind in the American South.

She returned to America in 1925 and took over the summer camp for girls that her father had begun. Here, at the Laurel Falls Camp on Old Screamer Mountain outside Clayton, Georgia, she would spend much of the rest of her life. In the summers from 1925 until the camp closed in 1949 she would supervise the moral and emotional growth of Southern girls from well-to-do families. Laurel Falls, as Rose Gladney has written, was "a lab school for human growth and understanding." The rest of the year Smith found time to read, especially Freud, and to write—a first novel, growing out of her China experience, which was first rejected by publishers for being too controversial and later was destroyed by fire. The novel, entitled "Walls," suggests much about Smith's thinking as she viewed the South from Old Screamer Mountain. Walls, barriers of any sort—but particularly racial segregation—were the enemies, she concluded, and it was partly to tear down such walls, as well as to create an outlet for other Southern writers, that Smith and her friend Paula Snelling began in 1936 a little magazine named, first, *Pseudopodia*, then the *North Georgia Review*, and finally *South Today*. In their quarterly, the editors announced in their first issue, they intended to nurture the pseudopod, "a temporary and tender projection of the nucleus of the inner-self." [15] In the

15. Gladney, "The Legacy of Lillian Smith," 8; White and Sugg, introduction to *From the Mountain*, xii. For an excellent selection of editorials and essays from *Pseudopodia*, the *North Georgia Review*, and *South Today*, see *From the Mountain*.

nine years that followed they published essays by W. J. Cash and W. E. B. Du Bois, fiction and poetry by dozens of young Southerners, and editorials in which they pleaded for an end to white supremacy and racial segregation. Theirs was not only a bold Southern voice for the 1930s, it was unique. Rare indeed was the Southern liberal who had decided against segregation by 1935. Rarer still was one who would announce such a decision.

But Smith was not nearly so interested in the politics of segregation as she was in its psychology. Her recurring theme in *South Today*, as in her other work, was the shame and guilt of white Southerners. It seemed at first that she and Paula Snelling were carrying on the tradition of the iconoclastic Southern little magazines of the 1920s, the *Reviewer* of Richmond and the *Double Dealer* of New Orleans. "We are not interested in perpetuating that sterile fetichism [*sic*] of the Old South," they announced in their first issue, and in later issues Smith spoke of the South as "this old intelligence-drained region," hailed the "intellectual vigor of the southern sociologists," and announced, as the *Reviewer* editors had in the 1920s, that she preferred "the cruelest analysis" of the South "to self-pity." But Smith's editorials lacked the exuberance, the sheer delight, of *Reviewer* and *Double Dealer* editorials. Her voice was not, as theirs had been, Mencken with a Southern accent, but rather the voice of the Southern moralist. Time and again she wrote of the "profound guilt for our treatment of the Negro" and "the rationalizations by which the white man eases his guilt." She spoke of "racial fear and hate" among white Southerners, a Southern way of life "hideous in its effect" upon Negroes and whites. The Southern guilt was of two varieties: the guilt the Southerner felt openly but should not have felt—for petty offenses which the Southern church made major—and the deeper racial guilt which he felt within but tried to deny. Smith wanted to rid the Southerner of the former, to bring the latter to the surface. Her own shame and guilt she confessed as openly as the early Puritans had proclaimed their sinfulness. "We in the South who feel so much shame are not without sin," she announced in an editorial entitled "Act of Penance." "We can now perform the ancient rites of handwashing—this editorial is no more than that—but we shall not be free of guilt until we rid our region of inertia and ignorance and poverty . . . until we rid ourselves of the haunting sense of inferiority which manifests itself

through the compensatory mechanisms of Nordic bluster and para-
noiac destructiveness."[16]

Smith freely acknowledged her reformer's zeal. "We sound like
missionaries with a powerful solemn purpose," she wrote a Rosen-
wald Fund official in 1939. That zeal extended as well to the novel she
wrote at the same time she was writing hortatory editorials, a book
which dramatized many of the themes with which she was concerned. The picture she painted in *Strange Fruit* (1944)[17] was of a South
benighted and savage, cruel and ignorant. The contemporary South
and its people were the "strange fruit" of a dehumanizing system
of racial prejudice and segregation. The story, which takes place in
a Deep South lumber town similar to Smith's Jasper, treated the
most taboo of Southern subjects, miscegenation. Nonnie Anderson, a
college-educated Negro in her early twenties, becomes pregnant with
the child of Tracy Deen, son of the town's white doctor. The restrictions of caste—which permit Tracy to have sexual relations with Nonnie but not to love and acknowledge her—lead to the story's predict-
able end. Tracy deserts Nonnie and is killed by her vengeful brother,
the wrong Negro is lynched, then the town of Maxwell returns to
normal.

It was a story sensational enough to sell three million copies and to
give Lillian Smith fame, notoriety, and financial security. If it was in
any particular Southern literary tradition, it seemed at first to be that
of T. S. Stribling and the forgotten Southern realists of the 1920s. Like
Stribling, Smith describes a culturally barren Southern town, and she
populates her town with stock Stribling characters—the evangelist,
the town radical, the confused young man. But Smith's novel, unlike
Stribling's work, is not satire. It is a tragedy of separation, of barriers
people create through abstraction and inhumanity; like her earlier unpublished novel, it could well have been entitled "Walls." The novel
drew at least superficially on Lillian Smith's own early life. The Harris
family, the "decent" white family, was based on her own. In *Strange
Fruit*, as in the draft of an earlier novel "Tom Harris and Family," Mr.

16. Lillian Smith and Paula Snelling, quoted in White and Sugg (eds.), *From the
Mountain*, xii; Lillian Smith, "Act of Penance," Spring, 1938, p. 67; Lillian Smith, "Dope
with Lime," Fall-Winter, 1938–1939, p. 11; Lillian Smith, "Wisdom Crieth in the Streets,"
Fall, 1937, p. 42; Smith, "Are We Not All Confused?," 106; Smith, "Putting Away Childish Things," 133; Smith, "Act of Penance," 67. All in *From the Mountain*.

17. Lillian Smith to George Reynolds, August 7, 1939, quoted in Sosna, "In Search of
the Silent South," 327; Lillian Smith, *Strange Fruit* (New York, 1944).

Harris is the most important man in town. He owns the town's saw-mill and turpentine works, as Calvin Smith had. He builds a mill town for his workers as Mr. Smith had, and he too has nine children. One of the children, Harriet, resembles Lillian Smith. She is ambitious—"too ambitious, too restless to stop at Maxwell" (p. 186)—"always protesting, even as a child, what other folks took for granted" (p. 44), and is sharply critical of her town. At the end of the novel she and her family discuss the future of the South and conclude there may be no way out. Dixie is too deep in darkness and ignorance ever to change. White Southerners, Harriet Harris concludes, are paranoid (p. 357).

Critical response to *Strange Fruit* was mixed. It was an important novel, most reviewers agreed, a bold and passionate one, but not an unqualified artistic success. Smith's commitment and courage, Malcolm Cowley wrote, outweighed her literary gifts. "It is possible," he speculated, "that her talents will lead her eventually into some other field than the novel."[18] This assessment Lillian Smith rejected, but it was prophetic. She published only one novel after *Strange Fruit*, and that novel was less important than her works of nonfiction. Her method as a writer was personal and confessional, not dramatic. Even artistically she was more successful in the works of self-revelation.

Her first major work in this vein, *Killers of the Dream*, appeared in 1949. Of all Smith's books, this is the boldest, the most starkly revealing—perhaps the harshest portrait of the South by a notable white Southerner since Hinton Helper's *Impending Crisis*. It depicted Southern life, one reviewer said, as "a schizophrenic invention without parallel, an insane dichotomy from the cradle to the grave." But Smith had undertaken her writing not to expose the South so much as to understand herself. "As was *St. Augustine's Confessions*," she later said, "I began the book not to give answers but to find the big questions that I could and must live with in freedom." Hers was a book, she explained, that could have been written only "in a tight, closed culture." "A German, reared as a child in the Nazi days," might have produced it.[19]

Smith later denied that *Killers of the Dream* had been a Freudian

18. Malcolm Cowley, "Southways," *New Republic*, March 6, 1944, p. 322.
19. Vincent Sheean, review of *Killers of the Dream* in *New York Herald Tribune Book Review*, quoted on back cover of 1963 Anchor edition; Smith, "Autobiography as a Dialogue Between King and Corpse," 197.

study, but it was indeed informed by her early reading in Freud, and a reviewer in *Psychoanalytic Quarterly* called it "a psychological study in the best sense," a book "of importance for psychoanalysts." [20] Her thesis was familiar: the South was a sick society, plagued by sin and guilt, tormented by racial segregation. A Southern childhood was a "haunted childhood": "This terrifying sense of impending disaster hung over most of us" (p. 77). To Southern children, racial tension "was a vague thing weaving in and out of their play, like a ghost haunting an old graveyard. . . . We knew guilt without understanding it" (pp. 15–16). Smith's own parents, she insisted, had been kind and tolerant, teaching their children Christian and democratic ideals. Yet they were blind, had seen no apparent evil in racial segregation. "We southerners had identified with the long sorrowful past on such deep levels of love and hate and guilt that we did not know how to break old bonds without pulling our lives down" (p. 16). "From the day I was born, I began to learn my lessons" (p. 18). The lessons she learned were rooted in fear and guilt, in lies and defense mechanisms. "For deep down in their hearts, southerners knew they were wrong. They knew it in slavery just as they later knew that sharecropping was wrong, and as they know today that segregation is wrong. It was not only the North's criticism that made them defensive, it was their own conscience" (p. 47). Even in the late nineteenth century when it seemed "as if the whole white South suffered a moral breakdown," the "South's conscience hurt." Always "there were doubts and scruples; always hate was tempered with a little love" (p. 54). Because of his fragmented sensibility, the Southerner was a broken creature, and his culture a fraudulent thing, denying not only the Negro's humanity but his own sexuality: "Not only Negroes but everything dark, dangerous, evil must be pushed to the rim of one's life" (p. 75). The Southern child loved his black mammy, but as he grew older she was replaced by his own mother—although he still crawled back to his mammy when he was miserable. And the black woman he wanted for sexual pleasure was his mammy in another form. Those "ghost relationships still haunt the southern mind" (p. 99).

Such was Smith's psychoanalysis of the white Southern mind, an analysis which for all its protest against rank and privilege betrayed a certain elitism on her part. Her portrait presupposed a Southern child

---

20. William G. Barrett, "Killers of the Dream," *Psychoanalytic Quarterly*, XX (January, 1951), 129–30.

who had *had* a mammy as Smith herself had, and also a refined, aristocratic mother who would make the mammy earthy and appealing by comparison. Such was not the case among most Southerners. But if Smith took no notice of the plain and poor Southern white in her psychological portrait, she accorded him a central role in her economic interpretation of Southern history. Like W. J. Cash, she saw Southern history as an interaction between "Mr. Rich White" and "Mr. Poor White" who struck a bargain to keep the black man in his place, all the while Mr. Rich White was economically exploiting Mr. Poor White. But the deeper trouble in the South transcended economics: no Southerner would tell the truth about himself. Politicians, ministers, writers, all spoke as propagandists for the official Southern culture.

Smith later called *Killers of the Dream* "the book that turned the South against me . . . blasted me out of existence. . . . Men like Hodding Carter and Ralph McGill and others on the [Atlanta] *Constitution* did a dirty job on me." In fact the reaction of the Southern liberals was not that hostile. McGill and Carter, both in their response to *Killers of the Dream* and in other remarks on Smith, were publicly respectful, although they viewed her as overly idealistic and sometimes tended to patronize her—which to Lillian Smith might have been the worst treatment of all. When her treatise *Now Is the Time* appeared in 1955, urging Southern leaders to end segregation immediately, Carter gave somewhat condescending praise to her "dramatic little primer on racism," and McGill called her a courageous moralist who was "a bit dogmatic, or firmly naive." To Smith's claim that it was up to Southern leaders to see that school integration proceeded smoothly, McGill replied with caution, "It isn't quite that simple"; and to her belief that Southern attitudes could change reasonably quickly with proper guidance, he said, "It's too bad Miss Smith isn't right about it." Howard Odum, who resented Smith's occasional attacks on the Southern Regional Council, also harbored doubts. Smith seemed more interested in "Freudian promotion," he wrote a colleague, than in securing Negro rights.[21]

But Smith had never pleased the ranking Southern liberals, and she

---

21. Lillian Smith, quoted in Jo Ann Robinson, "Lillian Smith," *Southern Exposure*, IV (Winter, 1977), 46; Hodding Carter, "Hope in the South," *Saturday Review*, April 2, 1955, p. 35; McGill, "A Matter of Change," 7; Howard W. Odum to Guy Johnson, June 20, 1944, quoted in Sosna, "In Search of the Silent South," 347.

continued in the 1950s to chart her own course. In 1953 she began the bout with cancer that would lead to her death in 1966. The ordeal did not cause her to retreat from her role as Southern gadfly; if anything, it motivated her to proceed with greater determination and fervor. It was not quite true, as it had been with sick, old Edmund Ruffin, that her cause became her life, but such could have been suspected. In speeches to students black and white, and in essays in journals North and South, she continued to pursue the demon, segregation. Racial segregation was "a symbol of the deep pervasive illness in our culture that has dehumanized us all." It meant "the cleavage Western mind has dug between subject and object; it means loss of communication with our own self; it means that estrangement from God which oppresses modern man; it subsumes all the fragmentations of modern times." Racial segregation was part of the white Southerner's "personal defense system against the world," white supremacy a "psychic defense," she told a predominantly Negro audience at Kentucky State College. Southerners had been "brain-washed . . . for nearly eighty years," she declared at the University of Arkansas. Racial guilt remained Smith's central theme of Southern history: "To stem our guilt, we began to defend the indefensible: we declared that God had made the white race superior to other races." But "it is not wise to let ourselves be overwhelmed with guilt. We can reduce our guilt by accepting our responsibilities."[22]

Southern moderates continued to draw Smith's wrath in the speeches of the 1950s and early 1960s. They were "suffering from temporary moral and psychic paralysis," she told an audience in Montgomery, in a speech delivered for her because of her illness, and she drew an indictment of moderation resembling nothing so much as Emerson's attack on consistency:

> Moderation is the slogan of our times. But moderation never made a man or a nation great. Moderation never mastered ordeal or met a crisis successfully. Moderation never discovered anything, never invented anything, never dreamed a new dream. . . . It would be difficult to imagine Jesus as a "moderate." Difficult to imagine Leonardo da Vinci as a moder-

22. Lillian Smith, "Words That Chain Us, Words That Set Us Free," *New South*, March, 1962, *WNA*, 157, 158; Lillian Smith, "Out of New Creative Tensions Will Come Peace," *Saturday Review*, December 24, 1960, *WNA*, 129; Lillian Smith, "Ten Years From Today," speech of June 5, 1951, *WNA*, 62; Lillian Smith, "No Easy Way Now," speech of October 23, 1957, *WNA*, 85; *Now Is the Time* (New York, 1955), 36.

ate. Imagine Gandhi as a moderate. Imagine Shakespeare or Einstein as a moderate.

Southern moderates who lacked courage supported a South nearly as silent as that of Cable's time: "We are acutely anxious, almost in panic," she wrote in 1957, "because silence has delivered us not only to the mob in the street but to the primitive, mob-like part of our own natures." "We have lost our freedom to question, to learn, to do what our conscience tells us is right, to criticize ourselves." Smith valued the civil rights movement—she preferred the term *human rights*—because it had *not* lost that freedom and courage. The movement of the late 1950s and early 1960s, in fact, could hardly have been different if Smith herself had planned it: as an admirer of Gandhi since her early days in Asia, she applauded the nonviolent resistance, the emphasis on love, of the movement. It was to her, in the deepest sense, religious. "By the reiteration of those powerful words *love, compassion, redemption, grace,* [it] is compelling us to search for truth, that of our region and of ourselves."[23]

Such was the message of Lillian Smith's last years. Finally, she was no longer alone in the South. She was hailed by civil rights workers as something of a priestess; she came to have apostles. But she continued to look within as well, to renew her journey in self-discovery. The year after she discovered she had cancer, she produced a book, *The Journey,*[24] which was as close to a spiritual autobiography as anything she ever wrote. The book was, in many respects, an attempt to come to terms with pain and suffering and human tragedy, and perhaps, in a deeper sense, with her own mortality. In it she wrote of people she had met on an actual journey down the Carolina and Georgia coast toward her old home and of people she remembered from earlier years—a crippled boy, a mute, a paraplegic, a Korean War widow. Again her themes were universal: brokenness, loneliness, adversity,

23. Lillian Smith, "The Right Way Is Not the Moderate Way," December, 1956, *WNA*, 68; Smith, "No Easy Way Now," 86; Lillian Smith, "The Students' Non-Violent Protest," speech of April, 1960, *WNA*, 95; Lillian Smith, "A Strange Kind of Love," *Saturday Review*, October 20, 1962, p. 20. Compare Smith's attack on moderation to Emerson's attack on consistency: "With consistency a great soul has simply nothing to do. He may as well concern himself with his shadow on the wall. Pythagoras was misunderstood, and Socrates, and Jesus, and Luther, and Copernicus, and Galileo, and Newton, and every pure and wise spirit that ever took flesh. To be great is to be misunderstood" ("Self-Reliance").

24. Lillian Smith, *The Journey* (1954; rpr. New York, 1965).

and endurance. Again, racial segregation operated as metaphor and as fact. It had "almost smothered the goodness in us" (p. 34). Again childhood was depicted as haunted. Birth and death, race and sex: each was mysterious and frightening, none was faced openly. Although Freud had removed part of the mystery and fear from childhood, the human loneliness remained. Smith longed to break down the barriers of loneliness, to "bring together the fragments" (p. 254).

The Journey was a Whitmanesque performance, with a persona who dared take the broken and dispossessed into herself, a compassionate ego expanding to embrace the suffering. Smith maintained a similar stance in certain other of her late works, although in still others she returned to her old combativeness. She struggled in the late 1950s and early 1960s to complete or revise books she had earlier conceived. In 1959 she published her second novel, *One Hour*, a deep and involved story which probes the conscience of a community in which a prominent scientist is unjustly accused of rape. The town is Southern but it could as well have been in Hawthorne's New England or Sherwood Anderson's Midwest: the sin and guilt which Lillian Smith had discovered in the South she had learned were universal. Shortly afterward she published a revised and updated version of *Killers of the Dream*, to which she added chapters indicting those such as the Southern Agrarians who she believed had worked to destroy the dream of Southern brotherhood and lauding those like Martin Luther King who might yet revive it. The severity of her attack on the Agrarians surpassed that of their traditional liberal critics. "No writers in literary history," she insisted, had "failed their region as completely as these did" (p. 199). They had failed to recognize that the dehumanization they feared would accompany industrialization had in fact already existed in the South of segregation and sharecropping. Instead of confronting . . . new realities" they "turned away" (p. 199). They "urged their students . . . to support the 'New Criticism' instead of a new life" (p. 200). "The tone was southern, but if one listened carefully one could hear echoes of post-World War One German thinking" (p. 200).

The words were damning, far more so than those of Odum, Cash, Gerald W. Johnson, or any other of the Agrarians' early detractors. But illness was about to silence Lillian Smith as her adversaries could not. Except for *Our Faces, Our Words*, a brief tribute to the civil rights movement published in 1964, the expanded *Killers of the Dream* would be her final book. A novel, "Julia," which she had written as early as the 1930s, she was reluctant to publish. A highly personal story about the role of a Southern lady, it still remains in a bank vault. Other projects she had conceived she was unable to complete—particularly the autobiography she wanted to write because, she believed, no other Southern woman had ever written a complete and honest one. Southern women had dared not "tell the truth about themselves for it might radically change male psychology." [25]

Lillian Smith's death in 1966 prevented her from writing the autobiography she believed would be her final and greatest testament of truth. But, in fact, her work all along had been a sustained act of very personal truth-telling unsurpassed by any other white Southerner of her generation. She was, like all radical truth-sayers, so devoted to her particular truth that she sometimes lost sight of all others. That single truth, as we have seen, was the destructive power of segregation by race and sex, and segregation she continued to pursue with a fury that did not diminish as she lay dying. The Southern tradition was completely discredited for her because it was a tradition of white supremacy. As she said in *Killers of the Dream*, the Southern way of life "began destroying its children long before they were born" (p. 133). It was a "troubled way of life that threatens to rise up and destroy all the people who live it" (p. 142). Ironically, Smith came to see the South in a manner not unlike that in which her greatest adversaries, the staunchest segregationists, saw it in the 1950s: the Southern way of life *was* segregation and it seemed to be little else. Such a belief caused Smith to miss much of what else the South was and had been. She could not appreciate the Agrarians: they seemed to her only racists, at best insensitive escapists, at worst American Fascists. She could not appreciate William Alexander Percy: his *Lanterns on the Levee*, praised by every other Southern liberal for its grace and beauty, appeared to her "tasteless" and arrogant. She could not fully appreciate Faulkner: he created only "moral sleepwalkers," "moronic pygmies." She could not even fully acknowledge the achievements of her fellow Southern liberals. She may, finally, in her eagerness to indict the Southern man for his lack of sensitivity, have overestimated the wisdom and sen-

25. Lillian Smith, *Our Faces, Our Words* (New York, 1964); Smith, "Autobiography as a Dialogue Between King and Corpse," 188.

sitivity of Southern woman. Not all Southern women in 1962, not even most, "smelled the death in the word *segregation*."[26]

But not even her supporters would contend that Lillian Smith was always capable of balance. The prophets rarely are. Nor was she always capable of diplomacy, as the "official" Southern liberals had to be. Like Helper and Ruffin and the earlier Dabney, she was in some measure isolated from her fellow Southerners, although not for the same reasons they were: her sex, her early experience in China, finally her thirteen-year battle with cancer gave her a unique perspective. Like those other Southerners who had expressed their truth too boldly, she felt the wrath of her countrymen, although, in some measure, she was protected from the full extent of their wrath because she was that most cherished of Southern icons, a Southern lady, and came from that most revered of Southern institutions, a good family. Lillian Smith, who protested the pampering of Southern women, must have appreciated the irony. But she must have realized, too, that her position as well-bred Southern lady modified Cash's savage ideal as it operated in her case. She was occasionally plagued by her enemies, but she was neither silenced nor chased out of Dixie.

Despite her advanced racial attitudes, Smith was in some ways, as she once said of Will Percy, an anachronism: in her manner of expression she belonged to an earlier age. And like her predecessors, critics and apologists, she expanded her vision and her mission as she grew older. Just as Fitzhugh and Dabney and Davidson came to see the South fighting a battle for civilization, so in a quite different way did Lillian Smith. Racial segregation, in the form of its "twin brother" colonialism, infected not only the American South but the world. Segregation was abstraction, fragmentation; thus the fight against segregation was a fight for humanity. But at the same time Smith's vision remained distinctly Southern, and to the end that vision was a critical one. Despite her occasional profession of love for her homeland, the fear and the shame are what one finally is left with. She tells a story in *The Journey* of a night she spent in a motel near the Georgia-Florida border, not far from her childhood home, and in that story one finds a metaphor for her relationship to the South. The motel owner was kind and considerate; he brought her lemonade, a sandwich, and a piece of his wife's marble cake, and he talked with her of home. His

26. Smith, review of *Lanterns on the Levee*, 16; Lillian Smith, "A Trembling Earth," *WNA*, 123; Smith, "Autobiography as a Dialogue Between King and Corpse," 191.

wife showed Smith their prize magnolia. But her host was also an outspoken segregationist and white supremacist, and as she left the next morning Lillian Smith could barely remember his magnolia or his kindness. She recalled only the racial prejudice, the fear of outsiders which obsessed him, "wanted only to get away from this haunted place" (p. 97).

Richard M. Weaver

One finds another recurrence of that pervasive Southern irony in the fact that the South's harshest white critic in the mid-twentieth century, Lillian Smith, remained in Dixie to the end of her days, and its most eloquent defender, Richard M. Weaver, left in his thirties and never returned. Traditionally, of course, it had been the other way. Helper, Cable, and Walter Hines Page had left the South; the apologists had remained. But Weaver, professor of English at the University of Chicago and the foremost latter-day proponent of Southern Agrarianism, saw nothing at all inconsistent in his Northern residence. "The sections fade out, and one looks for comrades wherever there are men of good will and understanding," he wrote in 1950 in an attempt to explain why so many of the original Agrarians had left the South. He did not mean it literally: no one held more to the idea of an American South as enduring geographical section than did Richard Weaver. But what he meant was that in a South increasingly controlled by progressives, Southern Agrarians and conservatives had to seek allies wherever they could find them. The South was many things to Weaver but among them it was a metaphor for a humane, civilized life. Southernness was, to some extent, a state of mind, identified with Christian humanism and conservatism and opposed to "universal materialism," "technification," and radicalism.[27] His view was not unlike that expressed by George Fitzhugh one hundred years before.

Richard Weaver of Weaverville, North Carolinia, was one Tar Heel whom Donald Davidson would have exempted from his indictment of Carolinians. He was born in 1910 in the Carolina mountains, ten miles from Thomas Wolfe's Asheville, but unlike Wolfe—who, Davidson said, would have been a different writer if he had gone to Vander-

27. Richard M. Weaver, "Agrarianism in Exile," *Sewanee Review*, LVIII (Autumn, 1950), 602. For an excellent discussion of Weaver's views, see M. E. Bradford, "The Agrarianism of Richard Weaver," *Modern Age*, XIV (Summer-Fall, 1970), 249–56.

bilt—Weaver did choose to go to Nashville, not east to Chapel Hill, and in his case the choice did make a difference. But the route by which he arrived at Vanderbilt was an indirect one, and that by which he arrived at Southern Agrarianism more circuitous still. His was a modern conservative's *Pilgrim's Progress*: coming from a traditional religious background in North Carolina, he wound up in Chicago as the strongest of conservatives, but he encountered numerous diversions and temptations along the way. He described his journey in a 1958 essay, "Up From Liberalism,"[28] and he spoke with a fervor only the converted can summon. Like the converted, too, he dwelt on his former days in sin—and on the manner in which he had come to see the light. At an early age he had moved with his family from Weaverville to Lexington, Kentucky, and as a student at the University of Kentucky in the early 1930s he had been taught by "social democrats," had become enamored of "science, liberalism, and equalitarianism" (p. 131), and had joined the American Socialist party. In 1932, however, he had gone to Vanderbilt for graduate work in English, had written an M.A. thesis, "The Revolt Against Humanism," under the direction of John Crowe Ransom, and had become acquainted with the Agrarians. Although at first he disagreed with their politics, he liked them personally and took their influence with him when he left Nashville in 1936. During a year teaching in Alabama and three years in Texas he became fully converted to the Agrarian cause. In 1940 he went to Louisiana State University to pursue a Ph.D. in English and spent three years immersed in Southern history and literature of the Civil War and the late nineteenth century. His dissertation, written under the direction of Cleanth Brooks, bore the title "The Confederate South, 1865–1910: A Study in the Survival of a Mind and Culture," and in the process of writing it the author defined his own relationship to the South. One pictures Richard Weaver of Weaverville during these years in Baton Rouge—not unlike Robert Penn Warren's Jack Burden of Burden's Landing, the graduate student who inhabited the same place at approximately the same time—pondering Southern history and, out of his study of it, coming to understand himself. In his contemplation of the past Weaver came to chart a course for his future: he became, and would remain, a committed Southerner.

Weaver left Louisiana in 1943 and went in 1944 to the University of

28. Richard M. Weaver, "Up From Liberalism," *Life Without Prejudice and Other Essays* (Chicago, 1965).

Chicago as a member of the English faculty, but the lessons he had learned in Nashville and Baton Rouge stuck with him as the democratic socialism of his youth had not. A bachelor given to solitude and frugality, he settled into a life of plain living and high thinking. Less Jack Burden than Henry Adams, he began a search for order in the modern world that would last until his death. Like Adams, he had long viewed his own progress through life as a form of education, although his regard for that education seemed to be higher than Adams'. "I wish, in this testament, to discuss education as one of the proven means of doing something about the condition of man," he had written in "Up From Liberalism" (p. 129), and later in that essay had described his "re-education" (p. 153) from liberalism to conservatism. Henry Adams, Weaver wrote in that same essay, had also "felt an impulse" to penetrate the clichés and generalizations of his day, and "his inquiry led him—this bloodless, self-questioning descendant of New England Puritans—to ponder the mystery of the Virgin" (p. 139). Like Adams, Weaver found his ideal society to some degree in medieval Europe, specifically in that period before the fifteenth century in which man had not yet abandoned "his belief in the existence of transcendentals" and had not begun his worship of science, rationalism, and materialism. But Weaver found an even better ideal, one realized more concretely than medieval Europe, in the traditional American South. He valued the South for some of the same reasons Adams had valued medieval Europe: it had put its faith in something other than science, rationalism, and materialism. Weaver possessed a conviction, Lewis Simpson has written, that the South "in its historical existence" represented "a permanent moral reality."[29]

Weaver was a "moral historian," as Simpson writes, and he found continuity between past and present in a way Henry Adams might have envied. But the search was not easy. Weaver's first book, *Ideas Have Consequences* (1948), dwelt almost exclusively on modern cultural fragmentation. The breakdown of distinction and hierarchy, the cult of egotism in modern art and literature, the reverence for "fact" as opposed to "truth," the reign of journalism, advertising, and public relations: these were among the problems of modern civilization, and their correctives lay in a "restoration of language," a regard for "small-

29. Richard M. Weaver, *Ideas Have Consequences* (Chicago, 1948), 3; Lewis P. Simpson, "The South and the Poetry of Community," in Simpson (ed.), *The Poetry of Community*, xviii.

scale private property," and "the chivalry and spirituality of the Middle Ages" (p. 187). *Ideas Have Consequences* seemed in no way a book about the South, but Weaver would have said that it was in every way a book about the South, a book about values he had come to esteem, and certain attitudes he had come to deplore, in the three years he had pondered the Southern past. What was he saying that Ransom, Tate, and Davidson had not said in *God Without Thunder*, *I'll Take My Stand*, *Who Owns America?*, and *The Attack on Leviathan*? Davidson recognized a likeness of mind and wrote commending Weaver as soon as the book appeared. The author replied that he had tried to tell the truth "in words as hard as cannon balls." [30]

Weaver's work in the area of rhetoric during the late 1940s and 1950s earned him a lofty reputation—*The Ethics of Rhetoric* (1953) remains one of his principal works—but he maintained at the same time a distinctly Southern point of view. Indeed, he felt, he was classical rhetor in part because he was first a Southerner. The two callings were related. His Southern legacy had taught him a reverence for the word, a respect for rhetoric which, in any case, was more "Southern" than dialectic. Living in Chicago may also have intensified his Southernness—a reaction to voluntary exile not unusual for Southerners. Even Dixie's liberals became sentimental when they lived too long above the Potomac and Ohio; how much greater the effect on a traditionalist such as Weaver? In 1948, shortly after the appearance of *Ideas Have Consequences*, he published an essay, "Lee the Philosopher," in which he proclaimed Robert E. Lee not only a great general but a subtle and profound thinker as well. Two years later he wrote "Agrarianism in Exile," an essay prompted, one suspects, not only by the residence of many of the former Vanderbilt writers in the North but also by that of their Chicago-based disciple. Weaver wrestled with the essay for many months and wondered in a letter to Davidson if publishing it "would burn my bridge to the South." [31] In his essay he explained the flight of the Agrarians in this manner: they were Faulknerian Sartorises—albeit ones with greater resources for coping with the present than Faulkner's originals had—but they had lived in a South in which the Snopeses had assumed many positions of leadership. The

30. Richard M. Weaver to Donald Davidson, February 28, 1948.
31. Richard M. Weaver, "Lee the Philosopher," *Georgia Review*, II (Fall, 1948), 297–303; Richard M. Weaver to Donald Davidson, March 8, 1949.

Agrarians were not being heeded in Dixie; "thus what has been represented as the flight of the Agrarians may appear on closer examination to be a strategic withdrawal to positions where the contest can be better carried on" (p. 602). Allies, as Weaver himself had discovered, could be found in the North as well as in the South.

Weaver wrote numerous other essays on Southern culture in the years that followed,[32] and discussed many of them in his letters to Davidson. The two men shared similar views on numerous subjects, particularly racial integration and the "levelling process," the "cultural and intellectual decadence" of the East, and the threat of journalism. "Half-educated journalists," Weaver wrote in 1963, "talk of 'seeds of Southern change' or write 'epitaphs for Dixie.'" Journalism was "a monstrous discourse of Protagoras which charms by hypnotizing." Davidson's bête noire, social science, was his as well. In "Agrarianism in Exile" he disparaged "stuffy treatises of social science which emerge from university presses" (p. 593), and there was no doubt that he was looking toward his native North Carolina as he wrote. In a subsequent essay, "The Rhetoric of Social Science," he was as critical as Davidson had even been, although he proceeded on different grounds. Weaver objected chiefly to the debasement of language which he perceived in social scientists: "They have not set themselves to learn the principles of sound rhetorical exposition." But, he contended, the confusion of language betrayed a greater confusion about the social scientist's role and purpose. He was "a dialectician without a dialectical basis."[33] His "facts" were not as indisputable as those of natural scientists: a "slum" is relative. Neither was he given to metaphor as the poet was—and in so contending Weaver suggested why Howard Odum and his lieutenants could not fully appreciate *I'll Take My Stand*, a book conceived by poets given in the deepest sense to truth by metaphor.

Increasingly, as Weaver pondered the South in the 1950s, he came to see it as unique in Western civilization. In the essay "Aspects of the

---

32. See in particular Richard M. Weaver's essays "The Tennessee Agrarians," *Shenandoah*, III (Summer, 1952), 3–10; "Contemporary Southern Literature," *Texas Quarterly*, II (Summer, 1959), 126–44; "The Regime of the South," *National Review*, March 14, 1959, pp. 587–89; and "The Southern Phoenix," *Georgia Review*, XVII (Spring, 1963), 6–17.

33. Weaver to Davidson, February 28, 1948, January 27, 1954; Weaver, "The Southern Phoenix," 16; Weaver, *Ideas Have Consequences*, 97; Richard M. Weaver, "The Rhetoric of Social Science," *The Ethics of Rhetoric* (Chicago, 1955), 186, 189.

Southern Philosophy," first published in the *Hopkins Review* in 1952, then in *Southern Renascence* (1953),[34] he set out to show just how and why it was unique. The characteristics he identified in the "Southern philosophy" were similar to those we have previously discussed—a distrust of analysis, statistical evidence, sociology, and abstraction— but Weaver went further than his predecessors. The Southerner, he contended, had a reverence for the word, and he respected nature too much to change it without good reason. He was theatrical, sometimes too extreme to seem real. Most of all, he had a discipline in tragedy and failure which gave him a perspective unique in the United States. For this reason among others, if America had dark times ahead, the South could provide counsel for the rest of the nation.

One is struck by the similarity of Weaver's conclusion to that of an- other Southerner whose essay appeared thirty-five pages after his in *Southern Renascence*. C. Vann Woodward in "The Irony of Southern History" viewed the South from a different vantage point, but he con- curred: the Southerner, schooled in suffering and failure, had some- thing to teach America. It was an idea that would be echoed fre- quently by Southerners during the next quarter-century, and one that Weaver himself had a chance to develop further when, four years later, he contributed an essay to Louis Rubin and James J. Kilpatrick's *Lasting South*.[35] The opportunity to join with other Southerners in is- suing a new manifesto from the South must, in itself, have proved a great satisfaction for a man who had missed the original one. In 1930, when *I'll Take My Stand* appeared, he had been a twenty-year-old lib- eral in Kentucky. Now a neo-Agrarian in his mid-forties—in a volume in the tradition of that earlier book—he could finally take his stand.

The Southerner, Weaver wrote in "The South and the American Union," was similar to "Classical man" and had "tended to live in the finite, balanced, and proportional world which Classical man con- ceived" (p. 54). He was not the idealist, the frenzied romantic; rather he was the "Apollinian," and he rejected the "Faustian concept" of the Northern mind which manifested itself in the idea of progress (p. 54). The South had suffered and had "in a way made a religion of its his- tory. . . . Being a Southerner is definitely a spiritual condition, like

34. Richard M. Weaver, "Aspects of the Southern Philosophy," *Hopkins Review*, V (1952), 5–21, and in Rubin and Jacobs (eds.), *Southern Renascence*, 14–30.
35. Richard M. Weaver, "The South and the American Union," in Rubin and Kilpat- rick (eds.), *The Lasting South*, 46–68.

being a Catholic or a Jew" (p. 64). But because the South remained "a great stronghold of humanism, perhaps the greatest left in the Western World" (p. 65), it was destined to play a great role in world affairs. "If the future of the world shapes up as a gigantic battle between communism and freedom" (p. 67), the South would lead: it had proved itself against scientific materialism, had "maintained a respect for personality," and had "proved its conviction that when principles are at stake, economics is nowhere" (p. 67). It had "earned the moral right" to lead "in the more general renascence of the Human way of life." "The stone which the builders have so persistently rejected," he wrote, "may become the headstone of the building" (pp. 67–68).

Weaver's emphasis in "The South and the American Union" was on the South's role as savior for a troubled world: his was a majestic vision. But, if only briefly, another, more familiar Southern tone also found its way into the essay—an embattled tone, that of a man who seemed convinced that his South could save the world but only if it could first save itself; or, rather, if it could be saved from enemies within the nation. Weaver wrote not long after the 1954 Supreme Court decision on school desegregation, a decision which he, like Davidson, feared would destroy the Southern way of life as he had known it. The 1954 decision, he believed, had accomplished more than outlawing segregated schools; it had "the look of a second installment of Reconstruction" (p. 66). That decision and the turmoil it created seemed, in this essay and others, to involve Weaver even more directly in the South of his own day, and in a way that was not always beneficial. It was not that he ceased being philosopher and became polemicist—he would always be philosopher and he had always been, in some measure, polemicist—but rather that his voice assumed, if only to the slightest degree, the sharpness that characterized numerous other Southern voices during the late 1950s and inspired defenses of the Southern tradition that were in fact only defenses of segregation. *The Lasting South* was not one of them. As Rubin wrote in his essay on the threat to the "Southern way of life," "I am not now talking about segregation, or integration, or creeping socialism, or anything so topical as that" (p. 2). But some Southern traditionalists—just as Southern iconoclasts such as Lillian Smith— could think of the South solely or largely in terms of segregation. Francis Butler Simkins, Southern historian and native South Carolinian, collected several essays in *The Everlasting South* which proclaimed the fundamentals of social hierarchy and privilege—and wrote elsewhere that that South was dead if segregation were dead. Another South Carolinian, William D. Workman, Jr., wrote an even more fervent book, *The Case for the South* (1960), and confessed: "Much of it has been written on the edge of anger, for there are emotional factors involved which evoke response from the pressure-sensitive Southerner, and which frequently provoke his resentment against those who cannot, or will not, accept the sincerity of his views or the weight of his arguments." [36] Workman was not alone in the South of 1960.

Weaver was too much the controlled rhetor to yield to anger in writing. His rage was only for order. But, after 1954, a certain combative quality did at times inform his voice—in one instance, in a 1959 essay, "The Regime of the South," in which he vigorously defended segregation and struck out at liberals who "hate the very idea of regime" (p. 589) or "way of life" (p. 587). Weaver had been in Chicago for fifteen years when he wrote this, and he sometimes misread events when he looked south. Had he, as Henry James was wont to say, been in foreign parts too long? Was the segregated Southern society he saw truly the ideal, organic society he envisioned, or was it something altogether different, something meaner and more petty? And did he not realize that racial segregation itself was one of the abstractions he should have feared? He maintained contacts in the South certainly—with Davidson and other like-minded Southerners—and he annually returned for visits, but he found it hard to comprehend Southerners who held other points of view, particularly those who had changed their minds about segregation. "Can you tell me what has happened to Red Warren?" he wrote Davidson in 1961. "I was dismayed by his *Legacy of the Civil War*. Some things in there seemed to me incredible for a man of his background." [37]

Whatever the case, it seemed that Weaver in the late 1950s and early 1960s was defending the South and his idea of Southernness with even greater fervor than before. But from the beginning of his Chicago exile, the impulse to defend and to justify had existed. Persecu-

36. William D. Workman, Jr., *The Case for the South* (New York, 1960), ix. David M. Potter, in his review of *The Everlasting South*, described Simkins as "almost the only practicing historian of the South who defends the major and historic Southern institution of segregation" ("On Understanding the South," *Journal of Southern History*, XXX [November, 1964], 458).

37. Richard M. Weaver to Donald Davidson, October 5, 1961.

tion, as Ransom once wrote, merely intensified one's tradition.[38] It was as if in leaving the South—particularly after he had just discovered it through his three-year immersion in Southern history—that Weaver felt he would lose his Southernness if he did not constantly affirm it. Even essays such as "Aspects of the Southern Philosophy" and "The South and the American Union," which insisted upon the enduring distinctiveness of the South, might be said to have grown in part from an unacknowledged fear that the South might be gradually losing that distinctiveness. Throughout Southern history, there had existed no great need to define the Southern order until that order was threatened—a phenomenon which might account for all the attempts to define and explain it both in the 1850s and in the 1950s, two decades when its existence had seemed seriously endangered. But in the very attempt to define Southern identity, that which had been to some extent unconscious became self-conscious. Weaver, if anyone, must have recognized that the South would change drastically in his long absence, that when at last he returned to it, as he planned to after his retirement, it would be no longer the same.

He did not live to return. He died in 1963, at age fifty-three, in his rented room in a Chicago hotel—a few months before he would have gone to Vanderbilt to assume, at least for a year, Donald Davidson's chair in the English department. Dying alone in a hotel on Chicago's South Side seems a bleak death for any man, one more befitting an inhabitant of Eliot's Waste Land than a loyal son of the rural South. It seems an especially bleak and inappropriate death for a Southern Agrarian. The "Hated Helper," one recalls, had died alone in a drab Washington rooming house. But in just such an environment Weaver had written many of his books and essays on the condition and promise of the South, and at his death had published only a portion of what he had actually written.

Much of that writing did appear after his death, due mainly to the efforts of M. E. Bradford and George Core, who brought together and published large portions of it. At the time of his death, as Bradford has written, Weaver "was finally ready to make his case for the South." Many of the essays he left behind which were not specifically on the South—although, Weaver would have said, informed by

38. John Crowe Ransom, "The South Defends Its Heritage," *Harper's*, CLIX (June, 1929), 113.

Southern values—were published posthumously in two of his finest volumes, *Visions of Order: The Cultural Crisis of Our Time* (1964) and *Life Without Prejudice and Other Essays* (1965). Other projects—a series on Southern letters and, Bradford writes, "an American Plutarch, contrasting exemplary Southern and Northern types"—he had partially completed. He had written an essay on William Byrd and Cotton Mather, another on Daniel Webster and Robert Hayne, a third on Thoreau and John Randolph of Roanoke. But the work that would particularly "make his case" for the South was Weaver's doctoral dissertation on the nineteenth-century Southern apologists, written twenty years before but never published. It had been rejected for publication in the 1940s, and Weaver apparently had not tried to publish it again, perhaps, as Core suggests, because he was never quite satisfied with it.[39] But before his death he had taken the manuscript out, had written a new introduction, and was prepared to publish it when he died.

In the expanded version of the dissertation, published under the title *The Southern Tradition at Bay*, the author himself did what he charged the earlier Southern apologists had failed to do: he presented a strong and eloquent argument on behalf of the South. The volume, when it appeared in 1968, seemed something of a latter-day Agrarian symposium in itself, with three generations of Southern traditionalists contributing. Weaver had written the body of the book in addition to the introduction and epilogue; Donald Davidson, less than a year before his own death, wrote the foreword to the book; and Core and Bradford, who edited the work, also wrote an insightful preface. Weaver's contribution was of two kinds. The body of the book, written in his early thirties, was conventional historical scholarship for the most part, with just enough personal commentary entered to persuade the reader that the earlier South was the guardian of Western civilization. In chapters on the Southern cultural heritage, Southern apologists, Confederate soldiers, Confederate diaries, postwar fiction, and critics of the Southern tradition, Weaver provided the best account of the nineteenth-century Southern apologia published to that time. His discussions of Alfred Taylor Bledsoe, Edward A. Pol-

39. Bradford, "The Agrarianism of Richard Weaver," 252. See Weaver, *The Southern Tradition at Bay*; Richard M. Weaver, "Two Orators," ed. George Core and M. E. Bradford, *Modern Age*, XIV (Summer-Fall, 1970), 226–42; and George Core, "One View of the Castle: Richard Weaver and the Incarnate World of the South," in Simpson (ed.), *The Poetry of Community*, 1.

lard, Alexander Stephens, John Esten Cooke, Thomas Nelson Page, Thomas Dixon, and other defenders of the South were generally well reasoned and fair, and so for the most part were his assessments of Walter Hines Page and "the first liberals."

But it was in his introduction and epilogue that Weaver the moral historian emerged. As he had in the essays of the 1950s, he identified those aspects of the Southern philosophy he believed had been present from the South's early days: a recognition of rank and distinction, a suspicion of science, indeed "of all theory, perhaps of intellect" (p. 42), and an especial piety. "The North had Tom Paine . . . the South had Burke and his doctrine of human fallibility and of the organic nature of society" (p. 39). The apologists of the nineteenth century had been right, but they had failed the South because they were not as profound or as convincing as they might have been. The nineteenth-century South had failed "to study its position until it arrived at metaphysical foundations" (p. 389). The apologists had used the Bible and Aristotle, but they could have used them far more effectively. Most damning of all, the South after the war had surrendered the initiative: it had given up too easily.

In one respect the nineteenth-century apologists had not failed as dismally as Weaver suggested—for through their writings they had convinced one twentieth-century Southerner, Weaver himself, that the Southern tradition was well worth pondering and affirming. It was with a personal affirmation that Weaver concluded *The Southern Tradition at Bay*. Western civilization was in deep peril: "The state becomes a monolith, rigid with fear that it has lost control of its destiny. We all stand today at Appomattox, and we are surrendering to a world which this hypostatized science has made in our despite" (pp. 393–94). As "*the last non-materialist civilization in the Western World*," the South could "save the human spirit by re-creating a nonmaterialist society." "Only this can rescue us from a future of nihilism" (p. 391).

Thus Weaver wound up proclaiming what Fitzhugh and Dabney, Thomas Nelson Page and Davidson had declared before him: the American South, guardian of Christian civilization against science and rationalism, was in a most literal sense the hope of the world. And he could have said with Fitzhugh in *Cannibals All!*: "By a kind of alliance . . . with the South, Northern Conservatism may now arrest and turn back the tide of Radicalism" (pp. 356–57). He was in the tradition of those earlier apologists, yet he had opportunities—and faced obstacles—they had not. Since he did most of his writing outside the South—even the most fervent parts of *The Southern Tradition at Bay* were written in Chicago, not Baton Rouge—he had a basis for comparison that the earlier apologists had lacked. But he also wrote at a time less receptive to the Southern apologist than were the times of his predecessors. In a Southern generation whose dominant voices were liberal—Dabney and Daniels, McGill and Hodding Carter—he professed to have come "up from liberalism" and his was a minority voice. Nor did he ever enjoy the companionship of kindred spirits— at least not Southern ones—as the earlier Agrarians had at Vanderbilt in the 1920s and 1930s.

Every established order writes its apologia only after it has been fatally stricken, Weaver wrote in *The Southern Tradition at Bay*, and perhaps that is why, in the early 1960s, he felt an acute need to publish his own. The South as he had known it was in grave danger: the reforming impulse of latter-day "abolitionists" in the 1950s and early 1960s had ensured that. This Weaver deeply believed. But, again, one wonders just how well he *knew* his contemporary South. Were the liberals the Snopeses, as he had earlier suggested, and the conservatives the Sartorises? Or was it, in some instances, the other way around? One wonders if Weaver, geographically removed in Chicago, in some respects knew the South of the nineteenth century better than the South of his own day—or if he knew it as metaphor better than he knew it in fact. Perhaps not. Certainly he did recognize some of the defects of the contemporary South far more than his critics would allow. He recognized, too, some of the implications of his own thought. "It is undeniable," he wrote near the end of his life, "that there are numerous resemblances between the Southern agrarian mind and the mind of modern fascism" (p. 395).[40] And if he sometimes betrayed an incomplete understanding of the contemporary South, he also possessed a vision of the South and its larger meaning unsurpassed in his generation. In the process of writing his book

40. Weaver discussed fascism and the Southern mind in a much earlier essay, "The South and the Revolution of Nihilism," *South Atlantic Quarterly*, III (April, 1944), 194–98. Here he contends that the South—which, in many respects, seemed sympathetic to fascism—was in fact deeply opposed to it because twentieth-century European fascism was only a stage in "radical democracy." The Southern ideal, Weaver maintained, was pre–French Revolution; fascism was post–French Revolution. Thus, "the South perceived intuitively that the new radicalism of Europe represented a final assault upon society as that term has been understood in Western civilization" (p. 196).

about the Southern apologists, he joined their number, indeed became one of the greatest of them. Perhaps the last truly committed member of the school of remembrance—the times after him would allow for no more—he continued in its tradition of seeing the South as America's salvation. The nineteenth-century South "needed a Burke or a Hegel" (p. 389), he wrote in *The Southern Tradition at Bay*. Or, one might add, it needed Weaver.

James McBride Dabbs

The Southern traditions of remembrance and shame, at least as they have operated throughout this study, might be said to have come to an end with Richard M. Weaver and Lillian Smith. There were historical and sociological reasons for the breakdown of the old dialectic, as we shall see, reasons associated with the Southern civil rights movement of the 1960s and the South's new relationship to the rest of the nation. But before I discuss that breakdown, I should like to look at one other Southerner of the generation of Smith and Weaver who, in his own way, incorporated elements of both traditions. To belong both to the school of remembrance and that of shame was rare, if not unprecedented, in Southern self-explanation. The Southern apologists in making their case for the South as redemptive community had rarely focused on its shame and guilt; the Southern critics, in examining a problem South, had rarely seen it as the nation's salvation. The nature of the dialectic ensured that. But something in the nature of the Southern civil rights struggle of the 1950s and 1960s—something identified more with the realm of the religious or spiritual than with the political—made such a fusion possible. One could see the South as sinful, savage, and superstitious—a problem South at its worst—*and* see it, despite itself, as a redemptive community. Or at least one could if he had the particular vision of James McBride Dabbs. If Lillian Smith and Richard Weaver were the last two representatives of the traditional Southern dialectic, Dabbs was the new synthesis.

James McBride Dabbs of Rip Raps plantation in South Carolina was, in various stages of his life, college teacher, farmer, leader in the Presbyterian church, and, from 1957 to 1963, president of the Southern Regional Council. Born near Mayesville, South Carolina, in 1896—he came in with *Plessy* v. *Ferguson*, he wrote—he became in the 1950s and 1960s nearly as vocal as Lillian Smith in his support of the civil rights movement, and even more insistent that the movement was indigenously Southern. "The great creative moment of Southern culture, perhaps within our lifetime," he wrote in 1961, was that moment on February 1, 1960, when Negro students sat in at a lunch counter in Greensboro, North Carolina, and began the movement. Like Smith—although, as we shall see, not precisely in the same way—Dabbs was preoccupied with racial shame and guilt, the sins of his fathers and those of his own early life. Though perhaps not "haunted by God," as he pronounced the larger South, he nonetheless drew his strength from a deep religious faith. Less Quentin Compson than Isaac Mc-Caslin, the history-burdened Southerner of Faulkner's "The Bear," Dabbs sat in the study of his family's antebellum home, pondered the role of God in Southern affairs, and concluded finally that God so loved the South and intended for it such a great destiny that God had caused it to suffer and to be instructed through its suffering. That God loved the South, that it was divinely ordained, was not an original sentiment for the Southern *apologist*: that in effect had been his thesis from the beginning. It had even been suggested on occasion by the native Southern critic. "For is it not written that whom He loves He chastens?" Cash had written in *The Mind of the South* of the mood of the fallen Confederacy. "Did he not suffer the first Chosen People to languish in captivity?" (p. 135). But Cash hardly meant it as a personal statement: he was reporting, not affirming. Dabbs did mean it, and if one searches for his predecessors in the tradition of Southern self-criticism one finds them not in Walter Hines Page and Odum and Cash, the secular critics, but rather in such nineteenth-century Southerners as George W. Cable and Atticus Haygood whose social criticism had its origin in deeply held religious beliefs. It was they he resembled even more than he resembled his God-centered contemporary Lillian Smith. He was not one of the "tortured Southern liberals" to whom she referred and in whose number she might be included. (He was burdened but not tortured.) Smith's portrait of a Southern childhood in *Killers of the Dream* was one of barely relieved darkness; Dabbs's portrait in his books contains more joy than terror and gloom. Nor did he see segregation as the entire truth about the South, as Smith sometimes did; rather, to him, segregation was not organically Southern at all but instead an aberration in the basically wholesome Southern tradition. James McBride Dabbs, then, *was* something of a phenomenon—a Southerner both preoccupied with Southern guilt *and* certain of Southern salvation, a man who affirmed more than once that the Negro was brought to the American South to test and to teach the white Southerner, to show him his own limitations and to strengthen and prepare him through suffering to provide spiritual leadership for a troubled world.

It was a belief out of the world of nineteenth-century Southern Calvinism, the world of Cable and Haygood—or Faulkner's Isaac McCaslin, who in "The Bear" sits in the commissary of *his* family's plantation and tries to come to terms with the Southern past and his family's role in it. God had "permitted" Southerners to own both slaves and land, Ike McCaslin had insisted, "land already accursed" but also blessed—"this land which He still intended to save because He had done so much for it." God had also predetermined the Civil War and its outcome. White Southerners could "learn nothing save through suffering," black Southerners would "endure," would "outlast us. . . . They are better than we are. Stronger than we are." And, much later, it was Dabbs speaking, but except for the reference to segregation it could as well have been Faulkner's Isaac: "[God] was in the picture, in the patience and trusting faith of the Negro, and in the acceptance of life as imperfect and sinful on the part of the white. He remained in the picture through the South's defeat, willing that defeat and the great lessons it spread before us. He was with the Negro when he was shoved aside through segregation, into a sort of Babylonian Captivity, where, partly because he was out of the mainstream, he could both retain the best of the past and prepare through long, hard years for the future." [41]

This was the message of all Dabbs's major work. The South was "a pilot plant, set up [by God] under fortunate circumstances, where the white and colored races can learn how to settle the frontier that now divides them. . . . Those who are Calvinists might well believe that the South, like Queen Esther, has come to the kingdom for such a time as this." [42] Dabbs himself was the descendant of such Calvinists, and himself possessed the certainty, the integrity of vision, of the Calvinist at his most committed. Even, in one respect, Dabbs's own life

41. William Faulkner, "The Bear," from *Go Down, Moses* (1942), in Malcolm Cowley (ed.), *The Portable Faulkner* (rev. ed.; New York, 1967), 256, 279, 280, 287; Dabbs, *Who Speaks for the South?*, 379.
42. Dabbs, *The Southern Heritage*, 215–16.

seems part of the drama of Southern history which he read as pre-determined or at least foreknown by God: he died the day, May 30, 1970, he wrote the last lines of his final book.

James McBride Dabbs, however, was something besides idealist and prophet. He was also a Southerner who lived within and understood the requirements of his own time and place, who prided himself on his realism. Despite his own private burden of Southern history, he did not (like Faulkner's Isaac) relinquish the family plantation, nei-ther did he escape his calling among men. That calling was, in large measure, to speak to them, and so he wrote three books which sought to explain the South and himself as Southerner, *The Southern Heritage* (1958), *Who Speaks for the South?* (1964), and *Haunted by God* (1972). The first of the three brought praise from Jonathan Daniels, Gerald W. Johnson, Ralph McGill, C. Vann Woodward, and other Southerners, and prompted Leslie Dunbar to call it "the likeliest can-didate of recent years to stand beside the classic interpretations of Cash and Lillian Smith."[43] The two latter books drew equally lavish praise from various quarters. But the book which reveals the essential Dabbs, which suggests the forces that drove him to write his better-known books about the South, was a little-known spiritual auto-biography, *The Road Home*, written long before any of the others al-though not published until 1960. It is a terribly earnest book, pious and somewhat didactic, certainly not the sort of autobiography easily appreciated by one accustomed to the irony and self-deprecation of Henry Adams or Will Percy. It is, however, the progress of a Southern pilgrim much different from Richard Weaver, a book poetic and mov-ing, particularly in the early chapters on Dabbs's youth near Mayes-ville on the upper edge of the South Carolina coastal plain.

The Road Home is more about the growth of a mind and spirit, the development of a consciousness, than anything else. Dabbs's memory of childhood was one of wonder and fascination. It was also one of isolation: the outside world seemed far away. Like Odum and Lillian Smith, James McBride Dabbs came from a family privileged on his

43. Jonathan Daniels, "A Lancelot for Little Rock," *Saturday Review*, September 6, 1958, p. 40; Gerald W. Johnson, "Dixie, My Dixie," *New Republic*, September 22, 1958, p. 20; Ralph McGill, "Times Unforgotten—And a Burden Passed Along," *New York Times Book Review*, August 31, 1958, p. 3; C. Vann Woodward, "Double Maverick," *Nation*, November 15, 1958, p. 365; Dunbar, "The Changing Mind of the South," 19, n. 15.

mother's side, unpretentious on his father's. The McBrides were conservative planters, "the inheritors of the culture of the old South."[44] The Dabbs clan Cash would have called "yeoman." Eugene Whitefield Dabbs had come to South Carolina as an overseer, married Maude McBride, and acquired thousands of acres of land. James McBride Dabbs grew up in his father's farmhouse, but the columned McBride home was only a mile away.

The young Dabbs who emerges in *The Road Home* was, most of all, a seeker after religious faith, and religion to the young man meant woman and nature. He idealized woman, first his mother (who died when he was twelve), then a cousin, and later girls and women his own age. Nature, which was to say farm life, taught religion through dependency, and Dabbs was early moved by the rhythms of nature, the farmer's "fields of faith." The stern Presbyterian faith of his fathers he believed at first a negative force. The poetry of Homer and Wordsworth meant more than his Calvinist inheritance, and exalted woman—finally incarnate in Jessie Armstrong, whom he married in 1918—more than an Old Testament God. Dabbs was first a student at the University of South Carolina and Clark University, then a soldier in France, a graduate student at Columbia University, and chairman of the English department at Coker College in Hartsville, South Carolina. Life, as he described it in *The Road Home*, had progressed much as he had expected, until the late 1920s when his wife, whose health had long been poor, became an invalid. In 1933 she died. Her death was the central event of Dabbs's life: he was struck with the loneliness and tragedy of the human condition, with the need in a seemingly naturalistic world for love and community. Also, although he did not realize it at the time, the seeds of his concern for the Negro were sown. In the late 1930s he married again, left full-time teaching, and moved back to the old McBride home to farm, to think, and to write. But he was not to think and write about race and the South until the 1940s, and then only because he decided that segregation was an unnecessary burden for people already laden with too many burdens in life.

Dabbs's deep need to write about the South and the Southerner, thus, developed out of his personal situation, out of the need for one-

44. James McBride Dabbs, *The Road Home* (Philadelphia, 1960).

ness which possessed him after his wife's death. First he retreated from the world of duty and obligation into himself and into nature to construct a new life; later he emerged as a compassionate critic of his society. It is no coincidence that one of the greatest influences during his middle years was Henry David Thoreau, another man whose social commitment followed and grew out of a retirement into self and nature (but who insisted, as Dabbs later did, that he was no reformer). In *The Road Home* Dabbs discussed Homer and Wordsworth as his primary inspirations, but it was Thoreau whom he quoted and whose thinking he often mirrored. In fact, he had echoed and quoted Thoreau from the time of his earliest articles in the 1920s. In 1933, the year of his wife's death, he had announced in a *Scribner's* essay that he was fleeing from the "highly organized world" and "going home" to nature and "self-dependence." In another essay the following year he announced, "This is my religion. The universe throbbing with life gives of this life, carelessly indeed but lavishly, to those who know and are fortunate." In subsequent essays he returned to Thoreau and in 1947 wrote, for the *Yale Review*, "Thoreau: The Adventurer as Economist" in which he praised the philosophy of *Walden*.[45] In *The Road Home* the influence is equally pronounced. Like Thoreau, Dabbs prefers to stay at home and let the mind travel, to observe nature closely in its various seasons, to live "economically," and to drive life into a corner. His celebration of the "Homeric Morning" seems inspired by *Walden* and even his rationale for opposing racial segregation is Thoreauvian. Segregation violated the transcendental concept of oneness: "I had finally to oppose all division and separation, both within myself and within that outer picture of myself, the world" (p. 228). Besides, segregation was not practical or, in Thoreau's word, "economical."

The making of the Southerner James McBride Dabbs was essentially accomplished by the mid-1940s, although he had just begun to think about the South itself. "I only sensed with a vague uneasiness," he later said, "the fact that we [Southerners] were haunted; haunted by institutions and attitudes that, however vital in their inception, had now become pale and unreal" (pp. 218–19). "Life had pretty well

45. James McBride Dabbs, "I'm Going Home," *Scribner's Magazine*, XCIII (March, 1933), 173–76; James McBride Dabbs, "The Religion of a Countryman," *Forum*, XCI (May, 1934), 309; James McBride Dabbs, "Thoreau: The Adventurer as Economist," *Yale Review*, XXXVI (June, 1947), 667–72.

stripped me of most of what I valued, and I saw that I didn't have much left but my basic humanity. . . . I was tired already. Segregation seemed to me not so much an evil thing as a useless, foolish thing." [46]

Thus Dabbs began in the 1940s and 1950s to write on Southern race relations for the *Christian Century* and other national journals, to write pamphlets and public letters addressed to other Southerners,[47] and in 1958, in *The Southern Heritage*, to take his stand firmly against segregation. It was a stand he had considered almost two decades earlier in the essay "Is a Christian Community Possible in the South?" but from which he had retreated. Then he had acknowledged that segregation made true community impossible in the South, and further, "I do not see that we shall make any radical changes in this community—and this is the south—in generations, perhaps in centuries. . . . We have got ourselves into a situation where, as I see it, it is impossible without revolutionary change to establish a Christian community. I am no revolutionist. If a Christian community is what . . . it appears to be, then I am not in favor of a Christian community here and now." [48] But Dabbs did not include the future, and by 1958 in *The Southern Heritage* it was clear that he had changed his mind.

That heritage, as Dabbs explained it in his first published book, did not consist solely of racial guilt and shame, but shame and guilt overwhelmingly concerned Dabbs himself at this point. In the white Southerner's treatment of the Negro, "we were terribly wrong much of the time, and much of the time we knew it at the time, not merely in retrospect" (p. 94). The great sins of the Old South, he wrote, were its overweening pride and a greed which drove it to use Negroes for personal gain. And the Negro was always "before our eyes, the symbol of our sin. . . . There's little health left in us." But there was a chance for redemption because "we know we need a physician. . . . Our conscience continually stirs. . . . Through the processes of his-

---

46. Dabbs, quoted in John Egerton, *A Mind to Stay Here* (New York, 1970), 37–38.

47. See, for example, James McBride Dabbs, *Where Justice and Expediency Meet* (pamphlet published by the South Carolina Division of the Southern Regional Council, 1947); and a letter to the Columbia *State*, April 21, 1944, in which Dabbs protests a special session of the South Carolina legislature called, in Dabbs's words, to "insure white supremacy." These and some two hundred other short works are included in Thomas L. Johnson, "James McBride Dabbs: Uncollected Short Prose" (Ph.D. dissertation, University of South Carolina, 1980).

48. James McBride Dabbs, "Is a Christian Community Possible in the South?," *Christian Century*, July 10, 1940, p. 876.

tory and the grace of God we have been made one people," and "if we would be our deepest selves, there is no telling what great age might develop in the South" (pp. 267–68).

It was this belief in the future and in the hand of God that, despite Dabbs's preoccupation with sin and guilt, made *The Southern Heritage* in fact a positive statement—a book that, if anything, was too optimistic. It was also a book that, despite its criticism of the Southern past, was less likely to antagonize traditional Southerners than many a less "liberal" work—partly because, slavery and segregation excepted, Dabbs actually found much to admire in the Southern past; and even more because he professed himself a "confused" Southerner, searching for answers rather than giving them. He wrote, then, to discover himself "and especially to get a clearer view of the road ahead" (p. 3). He reviewed his own past, recalling especially the "actions, scenes, and people" that "suggest some clue to my present situation: A Southerner slowed down by racial fog but determined to find a way out" (p. 3). "I have no desire," he declared, "to reform the South. . . . What I should like to do is to learn what the South is striving to be" (p. 16). Dabbs's strategy in this book was clear: he would not, like Lillian Smith, say no to segregation in thunder. His voice would be more muted. He recognized his penchant for preaching and wanted as fully as possible to avoid it, so he made himself one *of* those Southerners with fears and doubts about ending segregation and the particular Southern way of life that rested on it. In fact, despite Dabbs's rhetoric of doubt and confusion, he had pretty certainly made up his mind that a South without segregation was the South he preferred.

"I feel the throb of this land in my blood" (p. 3), Dabbs insisted in the beginning of *The Southern Heritage*, and he confessed his own early mistreatment of Negroes—his assumption of white superiority, his verbal abuse of a small Negro girl who on one occasion would not move from his path, his total insensitivity to the Negro's plight when he was in college and in the army. He praised, as fully as any professional Southerner might, the "Southern way of life"—hospitality, leisure, manners, love of the land, a sense of place and family and tradition. All this, though sincerely expressed, was a part of his strategy, for next he insisted that segregation was *not* a part of that way of life, that it was "in sharp contrast to the rest of Southern life . . . a constrictive force in a genial society" (p. 36). For a moment, sensing he was too far in advance of his Southern readers, he retreated to declare that segregation, after all, might "be necessary"—but having so conceded, he then went on to show why it was *not* necessary. In doing so, he confronted point by point the arguments of the segregationists. If racial segregation was "instinctive," why bolster it by law? If Negroes were "inferior" to whites, could not environment rather than biology account for the "inferiority"? Dabbs denied that integration would corrupt white morals or lead to intermarriage (except perhaps in the distant future, which he would let take care of itself). Dabbs, that is, saw nothing good in segregation. Slavery may have created some Southern virtues—manners and leisure among them—but segregation had eroded these virtues and added no new ones. And it was impossible for Dabbs to discuss the South and race without finally coming around to the role of Providence in Southern affairs. The South was destined, he suggested, to show the way to the rest of the world, to be a "pilot project." This was a claim often heard from the apologists, from George Fitzhugh forward, but rarely from a member of the school of shame. But to Dabbs, the Southerner would lead because of his "basic goodness" and because "we are also better fitted than most men to do the social pioneering the day demands" (p. 220). And not only the Southern white: "Though one may not say where the spirit of God will move, it is possible we shall find [men of large, generous, and magnanimous natures] more frequently among Negroes than among whites" (p. 257).

Dabbs was poetic, impassioned, and at times prophetic in *The Southern Heritage*, and although his view of Southern history might be disputed, his only failing in viewing the contemporary South was in underestimating the rage of the Negro whom he championed. "Has there ever been any cry from the Negroes of 'black supremacy'?" he asked, and he answered no, except "maybe, during the darkest days of Reconstruction, a few faint cries, but that situation is gone forever. . . . I have known them for sixty years: from playmates, through hoe-hands and plow-hands, to university presidents. I think I could count on the fingers of my two hands the words of bitterness I have heard from them" (p. 99). The Southern liberal, a later critic might say, seeing the Negro for something other than he is—but Dabbs was hardly the only Southerner, liberal or otherwise, in the year 1958 to underestimate the capacity for rage in the black American.

If *The Southern Heritage* was a powerful plea for racial understanding and justice, Dabbs's next book *Who Speaks for the South?*, was even more forceful—and even bolder in proclaiming the role of God in Southern history. Although the book received less attention than Dabbs's first work, Carl Degler wrote that it surpassed all other attempts to explain the South "except its prototype, W. J. Cash's *The Mind of the South.* . . . In some ways [Dabbs's] book is even superior to Cash's; it is more temperate, more lucid, and less diffuse."[49] It had also a most misleading title, because the reader soon discovers that it is Dabbs himself who hopes to speak for the South, and he does not alway speak as clearly and as originally, or as temperately, as Degler suggests. In this book Dabbs assumed the role of historian and attempted, in the first two-thirds of the work, to trace the formation of the Southern mind and character. His picture, simplified, is this: From colonial days the Southerner was a rather simple creature, was more willing to accept his world as it was than was the Yankee; he saw slavery as a way to build the good life, and slavery also taught the Southerner to prize place more than space (or movement). The coming of the Scotch-Irish—the "Southern Puritans"—changed the South somewhat. The Scotch-Irish were more aggressive, more energetic, and more introspective, though not as introspective as the New England Puritans: Southern Calvinism tended to be "emotional" rather than intellectual. But so powerful was the attraction of the earlier "English" South that even the Scotch-Irish were tamed to some extent; they too came to appreciate slavery and place. Slavery thus prospered, and as it grew it restricted the original spacious Southern vision and warped and narrowed the Southern mind, indeed rendered the Southerner almost incapable of thought. The Scotch-Irish brought with them also a penchant for guilt, which at first seemed to have been a healthy addition to a South which had lacked a capacity for guilt and had experienced on occasion only "shame" over slavery (shame being a more social and public and less deeply held commodity than guilt—and even at that, shame more over occasional mistreatment of slaves than over slavery itself). But the Scotch-Irish contribution of guilt eventually became a Southern liability: the guilt came to be repressed and resulted only in harsher treatment of slaves and, in general, a sicker society.

Thus, James McBride Dabbs on antebellum Southern history, and

49. Degler, "The Divided South," 47.

he is no more and no less to be believed than, say, W. J. Cash. For one thing Dabbs, like Lillian Smith in her discussions of the Southern racial past, was concerned almost exclusively with the slaveholding planter and very little with the plain and poor white. For another, some Southerners before the coming of the Scotch-Irish did express guilt over slavery. But Dabbs's conclusion was clear enough: the Old South as a society was a failure in almost every important respect. It lacked a sense of community, it lacked anything other than a shallow spirit and a shallow philosophy, it had worked out no *raison d'être* (Dabbs ignores those Southerners such as Fitzhugh who did state a *raison d'être*). Most of all it lacked—as Allen Tate had remarked before—a proper religion. The highly individualistic religion of the South with its emphasis on personal salvation and damnation failed to serve a proper social function; thus the politicians took over. No matter how much the South hoped to model itself on medieval life, Dabbs contended, it failed because the wholeness and chivalry of feudal life were centered in religious life, the Church; in the South they were not. He conceded that the Old South had manners, leisure, charm, and a confidence and noblesse oblige among its aristocrats; and, unlike Cash, he conceded that the South did have an "aristocracy" in the sense of public figures who illustrated the possibilities of splendor and charm. But these virtues were decidedly inferior ones to Dabbs, himself after all the lineal and spiritual descendant of those Scotch-Irish Calvinists who valued a moral sense more than an aesthetic one.

If Dabbs was essentially the secular historian and analyst in the first two-thirds of *Who Speaks for the South?*, he became again the proponent of God's Providence in the latter parts of the book. After treating rather briefly the South between 1865 and 1914, and concluding that Southern demagogy was the result of a culture of manners and gestures and rhetoric gone sour, he assumed the role in which he felt most comfortable: a twentieth-century Isaac McCaslin holding forth from his old plantation on—in Dabbs's words—"the racial sins the white South has committed and, consequently . . . the justice of its being defeated and thwarted" (pp. 343–44). Out of this "judgment of God," he suggested, came the grace of God: "The Negro in America was defeated and thwarted, unjustly. The white Southerner was defeated and thwarted, in the broad sense, justly. . . . We should thank God for this, thank Him even for the defeats and the hardships"

(p. 344). Suffering had prepared the South for moral leadership, had equipped it to be God's "pilot project learning . . . to do within a limited area what now has to be done in the world if civilization is to survive" (p. 371). But before the white Southerner was ready to assume this responsibility, he had to confess his guilt: "The greatest, the essential injury was simply our assumption that we were different from and better than Negroes," and we may "heal this injury" by "admitting, in thought and action, that we are not better" (p. 378). We must "admit that we ourselves have failed; that we should not have permitted the racial injustice to go on; that we have been selfish, overprudent, cowardly" (p. 377).

To conclude his argument in *Who Speaks for the South?*, Dabbs proposed still another irony of Southern history: the despised, the Negro, becomes redeemer for the despiser, the Southern white. The idea was not entirely new. C. Vann Woodward, David Potter, and other historians had suggested that the Negro might be the quintessential Southerner, and still others had remarked that the Southern traditions of manners and dignity characterized the civil rights movement. But Dabbs went further:

> Here is the man the South was trying unconsciously to produce. The paradox is that his forefathers were brought here simply as means for the creation of Southern ends, and he has become, through a strange inversion of roles, the best exponent of the ends the South was seeking. If he should become generally accepted in this role, the possibilities of achievement for the South are almost unlimited. This acceptance can take place only at the religious level.
>
> Here, then, if anywhere, is the working of God's grace. . . . A despised minority, excluded from the common life, returns at last more in love than in hatred to reveal to the majority, not only that possibility of community that has always haunted the mind of the South, but also and far more importantly a vision of the universal meaning of failure and defeat, revealing how men become human through the positive acceptance and affirmation of defeat. The man who was once servant reveals through his suffering to the man who was once master the meaning of suffering, and in this common realization paternalism breaks down and a democracy richer than we have yet known may arise. (pp. 380–81)

Again, Dabbs was in the tradition of the nineteenth-century Southerners. He might well have said with Daniel Hundley one hundred years before—although he would have meant something entirely different—"We honestly believe, therefore, that God had a design in permitting the old slave trade—a design to bless and benefit the human race."[50]

The course of racial events in the South in the mid- and late 1960s seemed to confirm much of what James McBride Dabbs had been saying for a decade: that segregation was not the Southern "way of life"; that a "basic goodness" could be found in the white Southerner (and, although Dabbs had not so claimed, a habit of finally conceding to federal force); that the Southern Negro might demonstrate Southernness at its best; and that the South could in some instances provide an example in race relations for the rest of America. As Dabbs sat in his study at Rip Raps in the late 1960s he might have taken some satisfaction in a Southern racial progress which he, as president of the Southern Regional Council, had helped to bring about—and he might even, as numerous other Southerners, have indulged in self-congratulation at having nearly come through. Instead, he continued to ponder Southern racial sin and guilt, and the result was a book, *Haunted by God* (1972), in which he returned to a subject he had earlier explored—the failure of Southern Protestantism.[51] The only one of Dabbs's major works to be poorly received—reviewers found it confusing and unoriginal—*Haunted by God* was also his harshest portrait of the South. Just as his second book was more critical than the first, this third was more critical than the second. This would be his last; he wrote it in his early seventies and drew "more or less on everything" he knew for it, tried to put his "philosophy of life" into it.[52] There was no holding back. As Edgar T. Thompson wrote in his foreword to the book, "In the manner of the prophets of the Old Testament," Dabbs was "calling upon the people of this region to face up to their racial as well as their individual sins, and to repent" (p. 7). And in the manner of the prophets, that manner of Southern history which Richard Weaver called dramatic, Dabbs departed dramatically: he died, as I have said, the day he completed the first draft of the work.

It would have been a better book, though not a more honest one, if he had lived. A revision might have remedied some of the confusion,

50. Hundley, *Social Relations in Our Southern States*, 280.
51. James McBride Dabbs, *Haunted by God* (Richmond, 1972). Not long before he wrote *Haunted by God* Dabbs wrote *Civil Rights in Recent Southern Fiction* (Atlanta, 1969), a generally unsuccessful attempt to combine literary and social criticism.
52. Edith M. Dabbs, preface to *Haunted by God*, 5.

repetition, and fragmentation. Other flaws—a tendency to belabor the obvious, to generalize, and to exaggerate the South's uniqueness—might have survived a revision. And the book could not have been made more earnest, and not much more critical. Again, Dabbs traced the roots of Southern culture and concluded that of the three basic Southern institutions—the family, the plantation, and chattel slavery—the latter two were disgraceful. "To expect anything positive from the South with this background," he wrote, "seems to be to expect the impossible" (p. 40). The Southern land—he again echoed Ike McCaslin—was both blessing and curse: "God's gift to the South" became "the Southerner's chief temptation," and pride of ownership—of land and human beings—doomed the South. As for slavery, Dabbs exclaimed in anguish, "We are still inclined to cry out, *why?*" (p. 40).

But Dabbs's concern with history in *Haunted by God* was largely pragmatic; he wanted to know what men had done so that he might live better. The concern with history was also religious: history was the expression of the will of God. Much of what Dabbs said here he had said before, but his treatment of judgment and grace was new. The South had had plenty of both, he wrote, and the one was the absence of the other: "The basic fault of the South has been that it has misused God's gift [a "rich and sunny land"], thereby turning his grace into judgment. But the gift was not entirely misused, and so some of the original grace continued" (p. 154). A second major fault of the older South, he emphasized, was its institutional religion, a religion inadequate in almost every way to public needs. To those failings of the nineteenth-century Southern church already enumerated in his previous work Dabbs added others: it was "moralistic and private"; it pretended order and decorum in a world which possessed little of either; and it was not sufficiently strong to enable Southerners to feel that they were "a consecrated, chosen people" as the New England Puritans had. Thus when Southerners lost the Civil War "there were no real grounds upon which to rest a prophetic explanation of their fate. If they could have been convicted of breaking their covenant with God, they might have repented and been blessed by his forgiveness" (p. 206). Instead, the South attributed its defeat to fate.

The postbellum church, Dabbs believed, had served little better. It had conformed to society rather than transforming it, had sanctioned and supported the Southern worship of the past, had accepted racial injustice—had left the community little better than it found it. The church Dabbs blamed for numerous Southern failings, and he concluded his book with his most severe thrust of all: "The church continued and continues to spend too much time repenting of its sins . . . too little time celebrating the presence of the Holy Spirit in the world. . . . The church of my boyhood . . . did not give me what I needed. I needed God. . . . But the Protestant Church was not made for the celebration of life; it was made for repentance" (p. 250). As for himself, Dabbs had rather praise God—"polish . . . the pinnacles of heaven"—and he would wish the Southern church to "become a city set upon a hill, a light unto all the people" (p. 251).

It is fitting, one is tempted to say, that Dabbs ended his book—the last page he ever wrote for publication—not with the words of a Southern divine but the words of the New England Puritan John Winthrop. For what, his critics contended, were Southern dissenters like Dabbs anyway if not spiritual New Englanders—analysts, critics, reformers, latter-day abolitionists, outside the Southern grain. And if those same critics were inclined to take an overly dramatic view of Southern history—and considered that Dabbs, the severe critic of the Southern church, was also a leading Southern churchman and ruling Presbyterian elder—they might also conclude that Dabbs died of a heart attack the day he wrote these lines against the church for the same reason Wilbur Cash and Clarence Cason committed suicide shortly after they completed their books on the South: he too felt shame and guilt.

But if such were true for Cason, even partly for Cash, it was not for Dabbs. He had taken the criticism for two decades, and he was very sure of his ground. And despite his reliance on New England divines, and his views on segregation (and not even these, if we follow his own reasoning), Dabbs was as fully a traditional Southerner as one could wish, was in fact that most traditional of Southerners, an agrarian. It was no accident that the author of *Haunted by God* wrote an essay, "The Land," for *The Lasting South* in 1957, or that his position in that volume, between segregationists Richard Weaver and Francis Butler Simkins, did not make him noticeably uncomfortable. If he had been writing a quarter-century earlier, he could as easily have appeared with Ransom, Davidson, Tate, and Warren in *I'll Take My Stand*. For Dabbs had a better claim to agrarianism than most of the

Agrarians: he was a working farmer for much of his life and had tested his love of the land. Like Tate, he maintained that one's religion, one's entire outlook, stemmed from the way one made one's living, and farming he believed the best of ways. The farmer was in close contact with nature and with God. He assumed mystery in the universe, he learned the lesson of dependency. The farmer had a whole life, Dabbs insisted in his *Lasting South* essay: "His work is inwoven with his life, his life inwoven with the family . . . he belongs to the natural world, in coöperation with which he-and-the-family gain their livelihood. His life is all of a piece; he is integrated; he has integrity." Dabbs shared equally the Agrarian fear that unrestrained industrialism would destroy the Southern way of life: "We shall then be cut loose from ourselves; we shall lose the old integrity of the individual standing with his family amid the elements. We shall lose the sense of belonging. We shall lose the heart out of our religion." [53] He reiterated his fear the following year in *The Southern Heritage*: "That there might be an industrial way of life uncongenial to ours isn't deeply considered" (p. 186). As yet "the South isn't deeply concerned to find the spiritual security sought by modern man, because she hasn't really lost it. But she will lose it if she merely grabs the offered factories and plants them in the fields" (p. 197).

Dabbs shared not only the Agrarian fear of industrialism but also that deeply held fear of abstraction expressed by the Southern apologists. The two were related in his mind. "Industrialism," he wrote in *The Southern Heritage*, "is a high abstraction that, unless modified, will make abstractions of us all" (p. 170). If to embrace the concrete and to rage against abstraction is to prove one's Southernness, Dabbs was that most Southern of men, for in each of his books he struck out at anything that violated the massiveness of experience. Much of what he wrote about the Southern fear of abstraction had been said before. But he was more perceptive, perhaps more honest, in his appraisal of the *reasons* for the nineteenth-century Southerner's fear of abstraction than his predecessors had been. Aside from causes stemming from a rural tradition, the South was "afraid of abstractions . . . because it had built its life upon an abstraction it couldn't justify"—

53. James McBride Dabbs, "The Land," in Rubin and Kilpatrick (eds.), *The Lasting South*, 82, 83.

slavery. The South had "also feared abstractions, certainly theories about the nature of society, because it was too well pleased with the society it had created. Knowing the doubtful base upon which it had been built, it feared that investigation might result in disaster" (p. 171). After slavery was abolished, racism and segregation became the great Southern abstractions; they violated as nothing else could the totality of human experience. "No wonder we are afraid of abstractions," wrote Dabbs in 1958. "We are dying of one" (p. 266).

Dabbs, then, was not only one of the most committed and compassionate interpreters of the South but also one of the most astute—a quality even his supporters did not always recognize in him. They called him courageous and dedicated, but they sometimes failed to point out just how well he *understood* the South. Perhaps they were a little embarrassed by his divine view of Southern history: how, one might ask, could a modern man, a liberal and an intellectual, affirm in all seriousness that God was directing and overseeing Southern affairs? The piety and earnestness with which he wrote are also out of fashion. Modern man equates brilliance with irony, and there is little irony in the writing of James McBride Dabbs. (There is awareness of irony in Southern history, but that is quite another thing.) One can hardly contend that Dabbs mastered the Southern mind in all its intricacies; like Cash, even more than Cash, he was limited by his perspective—he wrote largely about the South he himself knew—and he had his own special faults of being, on the one hand, too optimistic and, on the other, preoccupied with race. Nor was he sufficiently detached from his homeland to always see it accurately; he did not have that "protection" from involvement he saw in Ralph McGill. He was, to be sure, mightily displeased with Southern institutions, but he was also the only major native Southern critic—the only prominent member of the school of shame—who saw more good than ill in the Southern tradition; and if he more often stressed the ill than the good it was because he was at heart a preacher who knew what his Southern parishioners needed to hear. His notable twentieth-century predecessors, Cash and Smith, were tormented and consumed by the South in a way Dabbs never was. His nineteenth-century antecedents—Cable and the young Walter Hines Page, not to mention Hinton Helper—had to leave the South to tell about it freely. Dabbs both remained and prevailed. He was notable in his tradition in this respect, and he is also notable because, like Lillian Smith and Richard Weaver, he may have been the last of his line.

THEY WERE the last perhaps because the South for which and to which they spoke in some measure went out with them—to be succeeded by a South more concerned with power and public relations than the burden or glory of its past, a South not about to fight any more battles or take any more stands, not noticeably haunted by God, and not likely to take sin and guilt *or* redemption so seriously as Smith and Weaver and Dabbs did. What had been the South—poor, violent, pessimistic, tragic, and mysterious—was christened in the 1970s, within a decade of their deaths, the Sun Belt—successful, optimistic, prosperous, and bland. The Sun Belt, of course, was not precisely the South. Rather the Sun Belt civilization was one that in some respects had been lifted out of the Northeast and placed in that geographical area designated the South—with an extension all the way across the "southern rim" to the Pacific. It was a land of aerospace, oil, agribusiness, real estate, military installations, and leisure, according to its prophets and press agents;[54] its inhabitants, like its values, tended to be transplanted Northern as much as Southern; and its goals had little in common with those of Jefferson or Edmund Ruffin or Will Percy. The Sun Belt was slick and polished, air-conditioned and comfortable, corporate and wealthy. Donald Davidson would not have recognized it.

But if the Sun Belt was not precisely the South, it played some role in the way America viewed the South and in the way the South came to see itself. Success on its soil, whatever the reason, brought confidence. When the Sun Belt was wrapped around Dixie, the schools of shame and guilt and perhaps even remembrance—at least as they had existed—were gone forever. Southern sons and daughters now wrote books entitled *The Good Old Boys* and *Southern Ladies and Gentlemen*—entertaining books, delightful books, but books focusing on the picturesque, on the South as cultural museum of charms and oddities. An occasional serious volume in the old vein would appear— most notably, *Why the South Will Survive* (1981), a collection of essays in the tradition of *I'll Take My Stand* and *The Lasting South* which pro-

54. See Kirkpatrick Sale, *Power Shift: The Rise of the Southern Rim and Its Challenge to the Eastern Establishment* (New York, 1975).

claimed an enduring Southern distinctiveness while acknowledging change—but even books of that sort were written from a new spirit of Southern confidence, and authorship no longer appeared a life and death matter.[55] As for the rest of Dixie, its compelling sin by the year 1980 had become not racism but excessive public relations, and that sin hardly aroused the same sort of impassioned feelings that Jim Crow laws and lynching parties had. The rise of the Sun Belt was replete with many contradictions and ironies, only one of which was that the South, which had always regarded leisure more highly than business, came to make a business out of leisure. With the new image, in any case, came a new version of the superior South, not so much the South as redemptive spiritual community, as it had been to Fitzhugh and Dabney and Davidson and Weaver, but a South whose superiority rested on *material* advantage—new, shining cities, amusement complexes, and real estate booms. If Weaver had lived to see it, he would have questioned, rightly so, whether the new superior South, confident and optimistic, possessed the discipline and integrity of the old.

In one regard, however, the new Southern confidence was not mere happenstance, not based entirely on something so external as the coming to Dixie of Yankee dollars, air conditioning, and major league sports. Rather it was, in part, justified, deserved by virtue of having come through the racial ordeal of the 1960s, having exited better than it entered. For the first time in a century and a half the South could face the nation without the taint of racism, no more than the rest of America anyway. Its 1960s mood of self-scrutiny gave way in many quarters to celebration—to the sort of boasting and exaggeration not out of keeping with its old tradition of Southwest humor. It was the self-congratulatory South. One might have concluded, thus, that the old Southern apologists had been right after all, if for the wrong reasons: the South indeed had a cause, a special mission. It was not the cause of Dabney and Davidson and Thomas Nelson Page—white supremacy—but rather its antithesis: as one Southerner expressed it, "the world['s] finest grand example of two races of men living together." The South, Robert Penn Warren had written early in the civil rights movement, might achieve "moral identity" and con-

55. Paul Hemphill, *The Good Old Boys* (Garden City, N.Y., 1975); Florence King, *Southern Ladies and Gentlemen* (New York, 1975); *Why the South Will Survive: Fifteen Southerners Look at Their Region a Half Century After I'll Take My Stand* (Athens, Ga., 1981).

tribute leadership to the nation because it had been forced "to deal concretely with a moral problem." "Out of its travail and sadness and requited passion," Leslie Dunbar had written shortly afterward, the South would bring forth human brotherhood. Its "heroic age" was beginning. Lewis M. Killian in his book *White Southerners* (1970) agreed that Southerners might "show the nation the way to racial harmony" and Samuel S. Hill in 1972 ended his book on Southern religion by proclaiming that the South was "now in a position to reclaim and give guidance to the entire nation." It was, Joseph Cumming wrote in *Esquire*, a "Good South" and it grew from the feeling that Dixie had "all the natural resources—especially in human resource and especially including all the qualities out of the black experience which have never been allowed their proper input—to lead the way . . . [into] a time of the world that will be more simple, quiet and joyous than the present confusion in the way a jet plane is more simple than an old-fashioned propeller-driven one." [56]

The role of moral superiority appears a strange one for Dixie. It was New England, as Warren has written, that had moral virtue on its side for more than a century. The South had only "the Great Alibi." [57] But it is a role with which the South has become familiar and in which it feels increasingly comfortable. Having dispensed, finally, with the Great Alibi, it has claimed its own Treasury of Virtue.

56. Dunbar, "The Annealing of the South," 507; Robert Penn Warren, *Segregation* (New York, 1956), 115; Dunbar, "The Annealing of the South," 507; Lewis M. Killian, *White Southerners* (New York, 1970), 135; Hill, *Religion and the Solid South*, 208; Joseph Cumming, "Been down home so long it looks like up to me," *Esquire*, LXXVI (August, 1971), 110.

57. Robert Penn Warren, *The Legacy of the Civil War* (New York, 1961), 54.

Bibliography

Manuscript Collections

Alderman, Edwin A. Papers. University of Virginia Library, Charlottesville.
Davidson, Donald. Papers. Special Collections, Vanderbilt University Library, Nashville.
Green, Paul. Papers. In possession of Mrs. Paul Green, Chapel Hill.
Harris, Julian, and Julia Collier. Papers. Emory University Library, Atlanta.
Hedrick, Benjamin. Papers. Duke University Library, Durham.
Hundley, Daniel R. Diary. In possession of Mrs. J. Dexter Nilsson, Rockville, Maryland. Copy in the University of Alabama Library, Tuscaloosa.
McGill, Ralph. Papers. Emory University Library, Atlanta.
Mencken, H. L. Microfilm Collection. Princeton University Library, Princeton.
————. Papers. New York Public Library, New York.
Odum, Howard W. Papers. Southern Historical Collection, University of North Carolina, Chapel Hill.
Page, Thomas Nelson. Papers. Duke University Library, Durham.
————. Papers. University of Virginia Library, Charlottesville.
Ruffin, Edmund. Papers. Southern Historical Collection, University of North Carolina, Chapel Hill.
Tate, Allen. Papers. Princeton University Library, Princeton.

Other Unpublished Sources

Brazil, Wayne D. "Howard W. Odum: The Building Years, 1884–1930." Ph.D. dissertation, Harvard University, 1975.
Cardoso, Joaquin Jose. "Hinton Rowan Helper: A Nineteenth Century Pilgrimage." Ph.D. dissertation, University of Wisconsin, 1967.
Gladney, Rose. "The Legacy of Lillian Smith." Manuscript of speech given to the Southern Regional Council, May, 1980. In the possession of Rose Gladney.
Holman, Harriet. "The Literary Career of Thomas Nelson Page, 1884–1910." Ph.D. dissertation, Duke University, 1947.
Johnson, Thomas L. "James McBride Dabbs: Uncollected Short Prose." Ph.D. dissertation, University of South Carolina, 1980.
King, Kimball. "George Washington Cable and Thomas Nelson Page: Two Literary Approaches to the New South." Ph.D. dissertation, University of Wisconsin, 1964.
Overy, David Henry. "Robert Lewis Dabney: Apostle of the Old South." Ph.D. dissertation, University of Wisconsin, 1967.

Page, Thomas Nelson. "The Old South." Speech delivered at Washington and Lee University, 1887. Manuscript in University of Virginia Library, Charlottesville.

Park, Leah Marie. "Edwin Mims and the Advancing South, 1894–1926: Study of a Southern Liberal." M.A. thesis, Vanderbilt University, 1964.

Sosna, Morton Philip. "In Search of the Silent South: White Southern Racial Liberalism, 1920–1950." Ph.D. dissertation, University of Wisconsin, 1973.

Books, Articles, and Pamphlets

Abbott, Martin. "The First Shot at Fort Sumter." *Civil War History*, III (March, 1957), 41–45.

Adams, Henry. *The Education of Henry Adams*. 1918; reprint. New York: Modern Library, 1931.

Agee, James, and Walker Evans. *Let Us Now Praise Famous Men*. Boston: Houghton Mifflin, 1941.

Aitken, Hugh G. J., ed. *Did Slavery Pay? Readings in the Economics of Black Slavery in the United States*. Boston: Houghton Mifflin, 1971.

Alden, John. *The First South*. Baton Rouge: Louisiana State University Press, 1961.

Aristotle. *The Politics*. Translated by H. Rackham. New York: G. P. Putnam's Sons, 1932.

Arnall, Ellis. *The Shore Dimly Seen*. Philadelphia: Lippincott, 1946.

Arnold, Matthew. "Preface to *Poems*, 1853." In *The Portable Matthew Arnold*, edited by Lionel Trilling. New York: Viking, 1949.

Ashmore, Harry. *An Epitaph for Dixie*. New York: Norton, 1958.

Bailey, Hugh C. *Hinton Rowan Helper: Abolitionist-Racist*. Tuscaloosa: University of Alabama Press, 1965.

Bain, Robert, Joseph M. Flora, and Louis D. Rubin, Jr., eds. *Southern Writers: A Biographical Dictionary*. Baton Rouge: Louisiana State University Press, 1979.

Barr, Stringfellow. "Catching Up with America." New York *Herald Tribune*, October 26, 1930.

———. "Shall Slavery Come South." *Virginia Quarterly Review*, VI (October, 1930), 481–94.

Barrett, William G. "Killers of the Dream." *Psychoanalytic Quarterly*, XX (January, 1951), 129–30.

[Bassett, John Spencer]. "Stirring Up the Fires of Race Antipathy." *South Atlantic Quarterly*, II (October, 1903), 297–305.

Beatty, Richmond Croom. Review of *The Mind of the South*, by W. J. Cash. Nashville *Banner*, February 26, 1941.

Beatty, Richmond Croom, and George Marion O'Donnell. "The Tenant Farmer in the South." *American Review*, V (April, 1935), 75–96.

Berry, Wendell. *The Hidden Wound*. Boston : Houghton Mifflin, 1970.

Bertelson, David. *The Lazy South*. New York: Oxford University Press, 1967.

Beverley, Robert. *The History and Present State of Virginia*. 1705; reprint, edited by Louis B. Wright. Chapel Hill: University of North Carolina Press, 1947.

Billington, Monroe Lee, ed. *The South: A Central Theme?* New York: Holt, Rinehart & Winston, 1969.

Blackwell, Louise, and Frances Clay. *Lillian Smith*. New York: Twayne, 1971.

Blair, Lewis H. "The Southern Problem and Its Solution." In *Forgotten Voices: Dissenting Southerners in an Age of Conformity*, edited by Charles E. Wynes. Baton Rouge: Louisiana State University Press, 1967.

————. [*A Southern Prophecy*]: *The Prosperity of the South Dependent Upon the Elevation of the Negro*. 1889; reprint, edited with introduction by C. Vann Woodward. Boston: Little, Brown, 1964.

Blassingame, John W. *The Slave Community: Plantation Life in the Antebellum South*. New York: Oxford University Press, 1979.

Bledsoe, Alfred Taylor. "Chivalrous Southrons." *Southern Review*, VI (July, 1869), 96.

————. *An Essay on Liberty and Slavery*. Philadelphia: Lippincott, 1856.

————. *Is Davis a Traitor?, or Was Secession a Constitutional Right Previous to 1861?* Baltimore: Innes & Company, 1866.

Blotner, Joseph L. *Faulkner: A Biography*. 2 vols. New York: Random House, 1974.

Boney, F. N. "Look Away, Look Away." *Georgia Review*, XXIII (Fall, 1969), 368–74.

Bradford, M. E. "The Agrarianism of Richard Weaver." *Modern Age*, XIV (Summer-Fall, 1970), 249–56.

————. "A Durable Fire: Donald Davidson and the Profession of Letters." *Southern Review*, New Ser., III (Summer, 1967), 721–41.

Bridenbaugh, Carl. *Myths and Realities: Societies of the Colonial South*. Baton Rouge: Louisiana State University Press, 1952.

Brownell, Blaine A. *The Urban Ethos in the South, 1920–1930*. Baton Rouge: Louisiana State University Press, 1975.

Brugger, Robert J. "The Mind of the Old South: New Views." *Virginia Quarterly Review*, LVI (Spring, 1980), 277–95.

Bryan, Edward B. *The Rightful Remedy, Addressed to the Slaveholders of the South*. Charleston: Walker & James, 1850.

Buck, Paul. *The Road to Reunion*. Boston: Little, Brown, 1937.

Butcher, Philip. *George W. Cable: The Northampton Years*. New York: Columbia University Press, 1959.

Cable, George W. *Bonaventure*. New York: Scribner's, 1888.

————. *Bylow Hill*. New York: Scribner's, 1902.

————. *The Cavalier*. New York: Scribner's, 1901.

————. *The Creoles of Louisiana*. New York: Scribner's, 1884.

————. *Dr. Sevier*. Boston: Rockwell & Churchill, 1884.

————. *The Flower of the Chapdelaines*. New York: Scribner's, 1918.

————. "The Freedman's Case in Equity." *Century*, XXIX (February, 1885), 409–418.

——. *Gideon's Band*. New York: Scribner's, 1914.

——. *The Grandissimes*. 1880; reprint. New York: Hill & Wang, 1957.

——. *John March, Southerner*. New York: Scribner's, 1895.

——. *Kincaid's Battery*. New York: Scribner's, 1908.

——. *Lovers of Louisiana*. New York: Scribner's, 1918.

——. *Madame Delphine*. New York: Scribner's, 1881.

——. "My Politics." See Turner, *The Negro Question*.

——. "The Negro Question." See Turner, *The Negro Question*.

——. *Old Creole Days*. New York: Scribner's, 1879.

——. "The Silent South." *Century*, XXX (September, 1885), 674–91.

——. "Thomas Nelson Page: A Study in Reminiscence and Appreciation." *Book-News Monthly*, XXVIII (November, 1909), 139–41.

Callaway, Elvy E. *The Other Side of the South*. Chicago: Daniel Ryerson, 1934.

Canzoneri, Robert. *"I Do So Politely": A Voice from the South*. Boston: Houghton Mifflin, 1965.

Cappon, Lester J. "The Provincial South." In *The Pursuit of Southern History: Presidential Addresses of the Southern Historical Association, 1935–1963*, edited by George B. Tindall. Baton Rouge: Louisiana State University Press, 1964.

Carmer, Carl. *Stars Fell on Alabama*. New York: Farrar & Rinehart, 1934.

Carpenter, Jesse Thomas. *The South as a Conscious Minority 1789–1961*. New York: New York University Press, 1930.

Carter, Hodding. "Hope in the South." *Saturday Review*, April 2, 1955, p. 35.

——. *Southern Legacy*. Baton Rouge: Louisiana State University Press, 1950.

——. *Where Main Street Meets the River*. New York: Rinehart, 1953.

Carter, Hodding, III. *The South Strikes Back*. Garden City, N.Y.: Doubleday, 1959.

Cash, W. J. "Buck. Duke's University." *American Mercury*, XXX (September, 1933), 102–110.

——. "Close View of a Calvinist Lhasa." *American Mercury*, XXVIII (April, 1933), 443–51.

——. "Genesis of the Southern Cracker." *American Mercury*, XXXV (May, 1935), 105–108.

——. "Holy Men Muff a Chance." *American Mercury*, XXXI (January, 1934), 112–18.

——. "Jehovah of the Tar Heels." *American Mercury*, XVII (July, 1929), 310–18.

——. "Literature in the South." *Saturday Review*, December 28, 1940, pp. 3–4, 18–19.

——. "The Mind of the South." *American Mercury*, XVIII (October, 1929), 185–92.

——. *The Mind of the South*. 1941; reprint. New York: Vintage Books, 1960.

——. "Paladin of the Drys." *American Mercury*, XXIV (October, 1931), 139–47.

——. "The Reign of the Commonplace." *Pseudopodia* (Autumn, 1936). In *From the Mountain*, edited by Helen White and Redding S. Sugg, Jr. Memphis: Memphis State University Press, 1972.

———. "Southland Turns to Books With New Vigor." Charlotte *News*, February 9, 1936.

———. "The War in the South." *American Mercury*, XIX (February, 1930), 163–69.

Cason, Clarence. *90° in the Shade*. Chapel Hill: University of North Carolina Press, 1935.

Cass, Michael M. "Charles C. Jones, Jr., and the 'Lost Cause.'" *Georgia Historical Quarterly*, LV (Summer, 1971), 222–33.

Clark, Thomas D. *The Emerging South*. New York: Oxford University Press, 1961.

Clayton, Bruce. *The Savage Ideal: Intolerance and Intellectual Leadership in the South, 1890–1914*. Baltimore: Johns Hopkins University Press, 1972.

Cohn, David. "Eighteenth Century Chevalier." *Virginia Quarterly Review*, XXXI (Autumn, 1955), 561–75.

———. "Tissues of Southern Culture." *Saturday Review*, February 22, 1941, pp. 7, 16–17.

———. *Where I Was Born and Raised*. Boston: Houghton Mifflin, 1948.

Coles, Robert. *Children of Crisis*. Boston: Little, Brown, 1967.

———. *Farewell to the South*. Boston: Little, Brown, 1972.

Collins, Carvel, ed. *William Faulkner: Early Prose and Poetry*. London: J. Cape, 1962.

Cooke, John Esten. *The Heir of Gaymount*. New York: Van Evrie, Horton & Company, 1870.

———. *A Life of General Robert E. Lee*. New York: D. Appleton, 1871.

———. *Surry of Eagle's-Nest*. New York: Bunce and Huntington, 1866.

Cooper, John Milton. *Walter Hines Page: The Southerner as American, 1855–1918*. Chapel Hill: University of North Carolina Press, 1977.

Cooper, William J., Jr. "Daniel R. Hundley." Introduction to *Social Relations in Our Southern States*, by Daniel R. Hundley. Reprint. Baton Rouge: Louisiana State University Press, 1979.

Core, George. "One View of the Castle: Richard Weaver and the Incarnate World of the South." In *The Poetry of Community: Essays on the Southern Sensibility of History and Literature*, edited by Lewis P. Simpson. Atlanta: Georgia State University, 1972.

Couch, W. T. "The Agrarian Romance." *South Atlantic Quarterly*, XXXVII (October, 1937), 419–30.

———. "Reflections on the Southern Tradition." *South Atlantic Quarterly*, XXXV (July, 1936), 284–97.

———, ed. *Culture in the South*. Chapel Hill: University of North Carolina Press, 1934.

Coulter, E. Merton. "The New South: Benjamin H. Hill's Speech Before the Alumni of the University of Georgia, 1871." *Georgia Historical Quarterly*, LVII (Summer, 1973), 179–99.

Cowan, Louise. *The Fugitive Group*. Baton Rouge: Louisiana State University Press, 1959.

Cowley, Malcolm. "Southways." *New Republic*, March 6, 1944, pp. 320–22.

Craven, Avery O. *The Growth of Southern Nationalism, 1848–1861*. Baton Rouge: Louisiana State University Press, 1953.

———. *Edmund Ruffin, Southerner*. 1932; reprint. Baton Rouge: Louisiana State University Press, 1966.

———. *The Repressible Conflict, 1830–1861*. Baton Rouge: Louisiana State University Press, 1939.

Cumming, Joseph. "Been down home so long it looks like up to me." *Esquire*, LXXVI (August, 1971), 84–90, 110–14.

Dabbs, James McBride. *Civil Rights in Recent Southern Fiction*. Atlanta: Southern Regional Council, 1969.

———. *Haunted by God*. Richmond: John Knox Press, 1972.

———. "I'm Going Home." *Scribner's Magazine*, XCIII (March, 1933), 173–76.

———. "Is a Christian Community Possible in the South?" *Christian Century*, July 10, 1940, pp. 874–76.

———. "The Land." In *The Lasting South: Fourteen Southerners Look at Their Home*, edited by Louis D. Rubin, Jr., and James J. Kilpatrick. Chicago: Regnery, 1957.

———. "McGill and the South." Atlanta *Constitution*, March 24, 1963.

———. "The Religion of a Countryman." *Forum*, XCI (May, 1934), 305–309.

———. *The Road Home*. Philadelphia: Christian Education Press, 1960.

———. *The Southern Heritage*. New York: Knopf, 1958.

———. "Thoreau: The Adventurer as Economist." *Yale Review*, XXXVI (June, 1947), 667–72.

———. *Who Speaks for the South?* New York: Funk & Wagnalls, 1964.

Dabney, Robert Lewis. "The Crimes of Philanthropy." *The Land We Love*, II (December, 1866), 81–93.

———. *A Defence of Virginia and Through Her of the South*. New York: E. J. Hale & Son, 1867.

———. "The Duty of the Hour." *The Land We Love*, VI (December, 1868), 108–119.

———. "Industrial Combinations." *The Land We Love*, V (May, 1868), 25–34.

———. "Laus Iracundiæ." *New Eclectic*, V (July-December, 1869), 524–29.

———. *The Life and Campaigns of Lieut.-Gen. Thomas J. Jackson*. New York: Blelock, 1866.

———. *The New South: A Discourse Delivered at the Annual Commencement of Hampden-Sydney College*. Raleigh: Edwards, Broughton, 1883.

Dabney, Virginius. *Below the Potomac: A Book About the New South*. New York: Appleton-Century, 1942.

———. *Liberalism in the South*. Chapel Hill: University of North Carolina Press, 1932.

———. "Paternalism in Race Relations Is Outmoded." *Southern Frontier*, III (July, 1942), 4.

Daniels, Jonathan. "A Lancelot for Little Rock." *Saturday Review*, September 6, 1958, p. 40.

———. *A Southerner Discovers the South*. New York: Macmillan, 1938.

———. *Tar Heels: A Portrait of North Carolina*. New York: Dodd, Mead, 1941.

Davenport, Francis Garvin. *The Myth of Southern History*. Nashville: Vanderbilt University Press, 1970.

Davidson, Donald. "The Artist as Southerner." *Saturday Review*, May 15, 1926, pp. 781–83.

———. *The Attack on Leviathan: Regionalism and Nationalism in the United States*. Chapel Hill: University of North Carolina Press, 1938.

———. "The Class Approach to Southern Problems." *Southern Review*, V (Autumn, 1939), 261–72.

———. "Criticism Outside New York." *Bookman*, LXXIII (May, 1931), 247–56.

———. "Dilemma of the Southern Liberals." *American Mercury*, XXXI (February, 1934), 227–35.

———. "Erskine Caldwell's Picture Book." *Southern Review*, IV (Summer, 1938), 15–25.

———. "First Fruits of Dayton." *Forum*, LXXIX (June, 1928), 896–907.

———. "The Future of Poetry." *Fugitive*, IV (December, 1925), 126–28.

———. "Gulliver With Hay Fever." *American Review*, IX (Summer, 1937), 152–72.

———. "Howard Odum and the Sociological Proteus." *American Review*, VIII (February, 1937), 385–417.

———. " 'I'll Take My Stand': A History." *American Review*, V (Summer, 1935), 301–321.

———. "Lands That Were Golden: New York and the Hinterland." *American Review*, III (October, 1934), 545–61.

———. "Lands That Were Golden: The Two Old Wests." *American Review*, IV (November, 1934), 29–55.

———. *Lee in the Mountains and Other Poems*. Boston: Houghton Mifflin, 1938.

———. "A Meeting of Southern Writers." *Bookman*, LXXIV (January-February, 1932), 494–96.

———. "Mr. Cash and the Proto-Dorian South." *Southern Review*, VII (Summer, 1941), 1–20.

———. "The New South and the Conservative Tradition." *National Review*, September 10, 1960, pp. 141–46.

———. *The Outland Piper*. Boston: Houghton Mifflin, 1924.

———. "Preface to Decision." *Sewanee Review*, LIII (July-September, 1945), 394–412.

———. "The Sacred Harp in the Land of Eden." *Virginia Quarterly Review*, X (April, 1934), 203–217.

———. "Sectionalism in the United States." *Hound and Horn*, VI (July-September, 1933), 561–89.

———. "A Sociologist in Eden." *American Review*, VIII (December, 1936), 177–204.

———. "The Southern Poet and His Tradition." *Poetry*, XL (May, 1932), 94–103.

———. *Southern Writers in the Modern World*. Athens: University of Georgia Press, 1958.

————. "Still Rebels, Still Yankees." *American Review*, II (November, 1933), 58–72; II (December, 1933), 175–88.

————. *Still Rebels, Still Yankees*. Baton Rouge: Louisiana State University Press, 1957.

————. *The Tall Men*. Boston: Houghton Mifflin, 1927.

————. "That This Nation Might Endure: The Need for Political Regionalism." In *Who Owns America? A New Declaration of Independence*, edited by Herbert Agar and Allen Tate. Boston: Houghton Mifflin, 1936.

————. "The Trend of Literature." In *Culture in the South*, edited by W. T. Couch. Chapel Hill: University of North Carolina Press, 1934.

————. "Where Regionalism and Sectionalism Meet." *Social Forces*, XIII (October, 1934), 23–31.

Davidson, Eugene. "Richard M. Weaver—Conservative." *Modern Age*, VII (Summer, 1963), 226–30.

Davis, Jefferson. *The Rise and Fall of the Confederate Government*. 2 vols. New York: D. Appleton, 1881.

Davis, Joseph K. "The South as History and Metahistory: The Mind of W. J. Cash." In *The Poetry of Community: Essays on the Southern Sensibility of History and Literature*, edited by Lewis P. Simpson. Atlanta: Georgia State University, 1972.

Davis, Richard Beale. "Early Southern Literature." In *Southern Literary Study*, edited by Louis D. Rubin, Jr., and C. Hugh Holman. Chapel Hill: University of North Carolina Press, 1975.

————. *Intellectual Life in the Colonial South, 1585–1763*. Knoxville: University of Tennessee Press, 1978.

Dearmore, Tom. "The Enigma of W. J. Cash." In *Reporting the News*, edited by Louis M. Lyons. Cambridge: Harvard University Press, 1965.

"The Death of Edmund Ruffin." *Tyler's Quarterly Magazine*, V (January, 1924), 193–95.

De Bow, James D. B. *The Interest in Slavery of the Southern Non-Slaveholder*. Charleston: Evans & Cogswell, 1860.

Degler, Carl N. "The Divided South." *Reporter*, March 11, 1965, pp. 46–49.

————. *The Other South: Southern Dissenters in the Nineteenth Century*. New York: Harper & Row, 1974.

————. *Place Over Time: The Continuity of Southern Distinctiveness*. Baton Rouge: Louisiana State University Press, 1977.

Dew, Thomas. *Review of the Debate in the Virginia Legislature of 1831 and 1832*. Richmond: T. W. White, 1832.

Dixon, Thomas. *The Clansman*. New York: Doubleday, Page, 1905.

————. *The Leopard's Spots: A Romance of the White Man's Burden*. New York: Doubleday, Page, 1902.

————. *The Traitor*. New York: Doubleday, Page, 1907.

Dodd, William E. *The Cotton Kingdom: A Chronicle of the Old South*. New Haven: Yale University Press, 1919.

————. "The Social Philosophy of the Old South." *American Journal of Sociology*, XXIII (March, 1918), 735–46.

Dollard, John. *Caste and Class in a Southern Town*. 1937; reprint. Garden City, N.Y.: Doubleday, 1957.

Donald, David. *The Politics of Reconstruction, 1863–1867*. Baton Rouge: Louisiana State University Press, 1965.

———. "The Pro-Slavery Argument Reconsidered." *Journal of Southern History*, XXXVII (February, 1971), 3–18.

Downs, Robert B. *Books That Changed the South*. Chapel Hill: University of North Carolina Press, 1977.

Dunbar, Leslie. "The Annealing of the South." *Virginia Quarterly Review*, XXXVII (Autumn, 1961), 495–507.

———. "The Changing Mind of the South: The Exposed Nerve." *Journal of Politics*, XVII (February, 1964), 3–21.

Dykeman, Wilma, and James Stokely. *Neither Black Nor White*. New York: Rinehart, 1957.

Eaton, Clement. *Freedom of Thought in the Old South*. Durham: Duke University Press, 1940. Expanded and issued as *The Freedom of Thought Struggle in the Old South*. New York: Harper Torchbooks, 1964.

———. *The Growth of Southern Civilization, 1790–1860*. New York: Harper & Row, 1961.

———. *The Mind of the Old South*. Baton Rouge: Louisiana State University Press, 1964.

———. *The Waning of the Old South Civilization, 1860s–1880s*. Athens: University of Georgia Press, 1968.

Egerton, John. *The Americanization of Dixie*. New York: Harper's Magazine Press, 1974.

———. *A Mind to Stay Here*. New York: Macmillan, 1970.

Elliott, E. N., and others. *Cotton Is King, and Pro-Slavery Arguments*. Augusta: Pritchard, Abbott & Loomis, 1860.

Ezell, John Samuel. *The South Since 1865*. New York: Macmillan, 1963.

Fain, John Tyree, ed. *The Spyglass*. Nashville: Vanderbilt University Press, 1963.

Fain, John Tyree, and Thomas Daniel Young, eds. *The Literary Correspondence of Donald Davidson and Allen Tate*. Athens: University of Georgia Press, 1974.

Faulkner, William. *Absalom, Absalom!* 1936; reprint. New York: Vintage Books, 1972.

———. "The Bear." In *The Portable Faulkner*, edited by Malcolm Cowley. Rev. ed. New York: Viking, 1967.

Faust, Drew Gilpin. *The Sacred Circle: The Dilemma of the Intellectual in the Old South, 1840–1860*. Baltimore: Johns Hopkins University Press, 1977.

Fishwick, Marshall William. *Sleeping Beauty and Her Suitors: The South in the Sixties*. Macon: Southern Press, 1961.

Fitzhugh, George. *Cannibals All!* Richmond: A. Morris, 1857.

———. "Cuba." *De Bow's Review*, XXX (January, 1861), 30–42.

———. "Disunion Within the Union." *De Bow's Review*, XXVIII (January, 1860), 1–7.

———. "Frederick the Great by Thomas Carlyle." *De Bow's Review*, XXIX (August, 1860), 151–67.

———. "German Literature." *De Bow's Review*, XXIX (September, 1860), 280–90.

———. "Love of Danger and of War." *De Bow's Review*, XXVIII (March, 1860), 294–305.

———. "The Message, the Constitution, and the Times." *De Bow's Review*, XXX (February, 1861), 156–67.

———. "The Northern Neck of Virginia." *De Bow's Review*, XXVII (September, 1859), 279–95.

———. "Origin of Civilization." *De Bow's Review*, XXV (December, 1858), 653–64.

———. "The Politics and Economics of Aristotle and Mr. Calhoun." *De Bow's Review*, XXIII (August, 1857), 163–72.

———. *Sociology for the South*. Richmond: A. Morris, 1854.

———. "Southern Thought." *De Bow's Review*, XXIII (October, 1857), 337–49.

———. "Southern Thought Again." *De Bow's Review*, XXIII (November, 1857), 449–62.

———. "Superiority of Southern Races." *De Bow's Review*, XXXI (October-November, 1861), 369–81.

———. "Uniform Postage, Railroads, Telegraphs, Fashions, Etc." *De Bow's Review*, XXVI (June, 1859), 662–64.

———. "The Uses and Morality of War and Peace." *De Bow's Review*, New Ser., I (January, 1866), 75–77.

———. "Wealth and Poverty—Luxury and Economy." *De Bow's Review*, XXX (April, 1861), 399–407.

———. "Wealth of the North and the South." *De Bow's Review*, XXIII (December, 1857), 587–96.

Fogel, Robert William, and Stanley L. Engerman. *Time on the Cross: The Economics of American Negro Slavery*. Boston: Little, Brown, 1974.

"Foreword." *Fugitive*, I (Spring, 1922), 2.

Franklin, John Hope. *The Militant South*. Cambridge: Harvard University Press, 1956.

Fredrickson, George M. *The Black Image in the White Mind*. New York: Harper & Row, 1971.

Friedman, Lawrence J. *The White Savage: Racial Fantasies in the Postbellum South*. Englewood Cliffs, N.J.: Prentice-Hall, 1970.

Gaines, Francis Pendleton. *The Southern Plantation: A Study in the Development and the Accuracy of a Tradition*. New York: Columbia University Press, 1925.

Gaither, Gerald, and John Muldowny, eds. "Hinton Rowan Helper, Racist and Reformer." *North Carolina Historical Review*, XL (Autumn, 1972), 377–83.

Gaston, Paul M. *The New South Creed*. New York: Knopf, 1970.

———. "The South and the Quest for Equality." *New South*, XXVII (Spring, 1972), 2–13.

Gatewood, Willard B., Jr. "Embattled Scholar: Howard W. Odum and the Fundamentalists, 1925–1927." *Journal of Southern History*, XXXI (November, 1965), 375–92.

————. *Preachers, Pedagogues, and Politicians: The Evolution Controversy in North Carolina, 1920–1927*. Chapel Hill: University of North Carolina Press, 1966.

Gee, Wilson. "The Distinctiveness of Southern Culture." *South Atlantic Quarterly*, XXXVIII (April, 1939), 119–29.

Genovese, Eugene. *The Political Economy of Slavery*. New York: Pantheon, 1965.

————. *Roll, Jordan, Roll: The World the Slaves Made*. New York: Pantheon, 1974.

————. *The World the Slaveholders Made*. New York: Pantheon, 1969.

Gildersleeve, Basil. "The Creed of the Old South." *Atlantic Monthly*, LXIX (January, 1892), 75–87.

————. *The Creed of the Old South, 1865–1915*. Baltimore: Johns Hopkins University Press, 1915.

————. "A Southerner in the Peloponnesian War." *Atlantic Monthly*, LXXX (September, 1897), 330–42.

Gladney, Rose. "The Liberating Institution: Lillian Smith and the Laurel Falls Camp." In *Southeast American Studies Association Proceedings, 1979*, edited by Don Harkness. Tampa: American Studies Press, 1979.

[Goodloe, Daniel]. *Inquiry Into the Causes Which Have Retarded Accumulation of Wealth and Increase of Population in the Southern States*. Washington, D.C.: W. Blanchard, 1846.

[————]. *The South and the North*. Washington, D.C.: Buell & Blanchard, 1849.

————. *The Southern Platform: or, Manual of Southern Sentiment on the Subject of Slavery*. Boston: J. P. Jewett, 1858.

Gore, Albert. *Let the Glory Out: My South and Its Politics*. New York: Viking, 1972.

Grady, Benjamin Franklin. *The Case of the North Against the South*. Raleigh: Edwards & Broughton, 1899.

Grady, Henry W. "In Plain Black and White: A Reply to Mr. Cable." *Century*, XXIX (April, 1885), 909–917.

————. *The New South and Other Addresses*. New York: Merrill Company, 1904.

Grantham, Dewey W., Jr. *The Democratic South*. Athens: University of Georgia Press, 1963.

————. "Interpreters of the Modern South." *South Atlantic Quarterly*, LXIII (Autumn, 1964), 521–29.

————. "Mr. Cash Writes a Book." *Progressive*, XXV (December, 1961), 40–42.

Graves, John Temple. *The Fighting South*. New York: G. P. Putnam's Sons, 1943.

Gray, Richard. *The Literature of Memory: Modern Writers of the American South*. Baltimore: Johns Hopkins University Press, 1977.

Grayson, William J. *The Hireling and the Slave*. Charleston: McCarter & Company, 1856.

————. *Letters of Curtius*. Charleston: A. E. Miller, 1851.

Green, Paul. "A Plain Statement About Southern Literature." *Reviewer*, V (January, 1925), 71–76.

Gross, Theodore. *Thomas Nelson Page*. New York: Twayne, 1967.

Haas, Paul H., ed. "A Volunteer Nurse in the Civil War: The Diary of Harriet Douglas Whetton." *Wisconsin Magazine of History*, LXVIII (Spring, 1965), 205–221.

Hackney, Sheldon. "The South as a Counterculture." *American Scholar*, XLII (Spring, 1973), 283–93.

――――. "Southern Violence." *American Historical Review*, LXXIV (February, 1969), 906–925.

Hall, Grover, "We Southerners." *Scribner's Magazine*, LXXXIII (January, 1928), 82–88.

Hamill, H. M. *The Old South*. Nashville: Publishing House of the Methodist Episcopal Church South, 1913.

Hammond, John. *Leah and Rachel, or, The Two Fruitfull Sisters of Virginia and Mary-land*. London: T. Mabb, 1656.

Harper, William, and others. *The Pro-Slavery Argument*. Charleston: Walker, Richard, & Company, 1852.

Harris, Mrs. L. N. "A Southern's [sic] View of 'The Southerner.'" *Independent*, November 11, 1909, pp. 1090–91.

Hart, A. B. *The Southern South*. New York: D. Appleton, 1910.

Hartman, D. A. "The Psychological Point of View in History: Some Phases of the Slavery Struggle." *Journal of Abnormal and Social Psychology*, XVII (October-December, 1922), 261–73.

Hartz, Louis. *The Liberal Tradition in America*. New York: Harcourt, Brace, 1955.

Haygood, Atticus. *The New South*. 1880; reprint. Atlanta: Emory University, 1950.

――――. *Our Brothers in Black*. Nashville: Southern Methodist Publishing House, 1881.

Hays, Brooks. *A Southern Moderate Speaks*. Chapel Hill: University of North Carolina Press, 1959.

Helper, Hinton Rowan. *Compendium of The Impending Crisis of the South*. New York: A. B. Burdick, 1859, 1860.

――――. *The Impending Crisis of the South*. New York: A. B. Burdick, 1857.

――――. *The Land of Gold*. Baltimore: H. Taylor, 1855.

――――. *The Negroes in Negroland; The Negroes in America; and Negroes Generally*. New York: G. W. Carleton, 1868.

――――. *Nojoque: A Question for a Continent*. New York: G. W. Carleton, 1867.

――――. *Noonday Exigencies in America*. New York: Bible Brothers, 1871.

Hemphill, Paul. *The Good Old Boys*. Garden City, N.Y.: Doubleday, 1975.

Hendrick, Burton J. *The Life and Letters of Walter H. Page*. 2 vols. Garden City, N.Y.: Doubleday, Page, 1922.

――――. *The Training of an American: The Earlier Life and Letters of Walter H. Page, 1855–1913*. Boston: Houghton Mifflin, 1928.

Hesseltine, W. B. "Look Away, Dixie." *Sewanee Review*, XXXIX (January-March, 1931), 97–103.

[Heyward, DuBose]. "The New Note in Southern Literature." *Bookman*, LXI (April, 1925), 153–56.

Hibbard, Addison. "Again—A Renaissance!" *New South*, I (March, 1927), 28, 61–62.

――――. "A New Deal for Southern Literature." *Southern Magazine*, II (July, 1924), 49–53.

Highsaw, Robert, ed. *The Deep South in Transformation*. Tuscaloosa: University of Alabama Press, 1964.

Hill, Daniel H. Editorial. *The Land We Love*, VI (February, 1869), 344–52.

———. "Education." *The Land We Love*, I (May, 1866), 1–11.

Hill, Samuel S., Jr., and others. *Religion and the Solid South*. Nashville: Abingdon Press, 1972.

"The Hill Gentry." *Time*, September 28, 1942, p. 92.

Hobson, Fred. *Serpent in Eden: H. L. Mencken and the South*. Chapel Hill: University of North Carolina Press, 1974.

Holman, C. Hugh. *The Immoderate Past: The Southern Writer and History*. Athens: University of Georgia Press, 1977.

———. "Literature and Culture: The Fugitive-Agrarians." *Social Forces*, XXXVII (October, 1958), 15–19.

———. *The Roots of Southern Writing: Essays on the Literature of the American South*. Athens: University of Georgia Press, 1972.

Holmes, George Frederick. "Observation on a Passage in the Politics of Aristotle Relative to Slavery." *Southern Literary Messenger*, XVI (April, 1850), 193–205.

Hubbell, Jay B. *The South in American Literature, 1607–1900*. Durham: Duke University Press, 1954.

Hughes, Henry. *Treatise on Sociology*. 1854; reprint. New York: Negro University Press, 1965.

Hundley, Daniel R. "The Evils of Commercial Supremacy." *Hunt's Merchant's Magazine*, XXXVI (March, 1857), 316–17.

———. *Prison Echoes of the Late Rebellion*. New York: S. W. Green, printer, 1874.

———. *Social Relations in Our Southern States*. 1860; reprint. Baton Rouge: Louisiana State University Press, 1979.

———. "Traffic in Coolies." *Hunt's Merchant's Magazine*, XXXVI (May, 1857), 570–73.

———. *Work and Bread; or the Coming Winter and the Poor*. Chicago: Barnet, 1858.

Hutchens, John K. "Lillian Smith." *New York Herald Tribune Book Review*, October 30, 1949, p. 2.

I'll Take My Stand: The South and the Agrarian Tradition. By Twelve Southerners. 1930; New York: Harper Torchbooks, 1962.

Jefferson, Thomas. *Notes on the State of Virginia*. 1785; Chapel Hill: University of North Carolina Press, 1955.

Jenkins, William S. *Pro-Slavery Thought in the Old South*. Chapel Hill: University of North Carolina Press, 1935.

Johnson, Gerald W. "The Advancing South." *Virginia Quarterly Review*, II (October, 1926), 594–96.

———. "After Forty Years—Dixi." *Virginia Quarterly Review*, XLI (Spring, 1965), 192–201.

———. "Below the Potomac." *New Republic*, May 12, 1941, p. 673.

———. "The Cadets of New Market—A Reminder to Critics of the South." *Harper's*, CLX (December, 1929), 111–19.

————. "Critical Attitudes North and South." *Journal of Social Forces*, II (May, 1924), 575–79.

————. "Dixie, My Dixie." *New Republic*, September 22, 1958, p. 20.

————. "Greensboro, or What You Will." *Reviewer*, IV (April, 1924), 169–75.

————. "The Horrible South." *Virginia Quarterly Review*, XI (January, 1935), 201–217.

————. "Journalism Below the Potomac." *American Mercury*, IX (September, 1926), 77—82.

————. "The Ku Kluxer." *American Mercury*, I (February, 1924), 207–211.

————. "No More Excuses: A Southerner to Southerners." *Harper's*, CLXII (February, 1931), 331–37.

————. "Saving Souls." *American Mercury*, II (July, 1924), 364–68.

————. "Service in the Cotton Mills." *American Mercury*, V (June, 1925), 219–23.

————. "The South Faces Itself." *Virginia Quarterly Review*, VII (January, 1931), 152–57.

————. "The South Takes the Offensive." *American Mercury*, II (May, 1924), 70–78.

————. "Southern Image-Breakers." *Virginia Quarterly Review*, IV (October, 1928), 508–519.

————. "To Live and Die in Dixie." *Atlantic Monthly*, CCVI (July, 1960), 29–34.

————. *The Wasted Land*. Chapel Hill: University of North Carolina Press, 1938.

Johnson, Thomas Cary. *The Life and Letters of Robert Lewis Dabney*. Richmond: Presbyterian Committee of Publications, 1903.

Jones, Charles Colcock, Jr. *Annual Addresses to the Confederate Survivors Association*. Augusta: M. M. Hill, 1881–1892.

Jones, Howard Mumford. "The Southern Legend." *Scribner's Magazine*, LXXXV (May, 1929), 538–42.

Jones, Hugh. *The Present State of Virginia*. 1724; reprint, edited by Richard L. Morton. Chapel Hill: University of North Carolina Press, 1956.

Justus, James H. "On the Restlessness of Southerners." *Southern Review*, New Ser., XI (Winter, 1975), 65–83.

Kane, Harnett T., ed. *The Romantic South*. New York: Coward-McCann, 1961.

Karanakis, Alexander. *Tillers of a Myth: Southern Agrarians as Social and Literary Critics*. Madison: University of Wisconsin Press, 1966.

Kennedy, Stetson. *Southern Exposure*. Garden City, N.Y.: Doubleday, 1946.

Key, V. O. *Southern Politics in State and Nation*. New York: Knopf, 1949.

Killian, Lewis M. *White Southerners*. New York: Random House, 1970.

King, Edward. *The Great South*. Hartford: American Publishing Company, 1875.

King, Florence. *Southern Ladies and Gentlemen*. New York: Stein & Day, 1975.

King, Larry. *Confessions of a White Racist*. New York: Viking, 1971.

King, Richard H. *A Southern Renaissance: The Cultural Awakening of the American South, 1930–1955*. New York: Oxford University Press, 1980.

Kirby, Jack Temple. *Media-Made Dixie: The South in the American Imagination*. Baton Rouge: Louisiana State University Press, 1978.

Kirk, Russell. "Richard M. Weaver, R.I.P." *National Review*, April 23, 1963, p. 308.

Knickerbocker, William S. "Asides and Soliloquies." *Sewanee Review*, XLII (April-June, 1934), 133–34.

———. "At Break of Day." *Sewanee Review*, XLI (January-March, 1933), 122–26.

———. "Mr. Ransom and the Old South." *Sewanee Review*, XXXIX (April-June, 1931), 222–39.

———. "The Return of the Native." *Sewanee Review*, XXXVIII (December, 1930), 479–83.

Lamar, Dolly Blount. *When All Is Said and Done*. Athens: University of Georgia Press, 1952.

Leary, Lewis. *Southern Excursions: Essays on Mark Twain and Others*. Baton Rouge: Louisiana State University Press, 1971.

Lefler, Hugh T. *Hinton Rowan Helper: Advocate of a "White America."* Charlottesville: Historical Publishing Company, 1935.

Leiserson, Avery, ed. *The American South in the 1960s*. New York: Praeger, 1964.

Leland, John A. *A Voice From South Carolina*. Charleston: Walker, Evans & Cogswell, 1879.

Lerche, Charles O., Jr. *The Uncertain South: Its Changing Patterns of Politics in Foreign Policy*. Chicago: Quadrangle Books, 1964.

Lindeman, E. C. "Notes on the Changing South." *New Republic*, April 28, 1926, pp. 299–300.

Link, Arthur, and Rembert W. Patrick, eds. *Writing Southern History*. Baton Rouge: Louisiana State University Press, 1965.

Long, Margaret. "The Sense of Her Presence: A Memorial for Lillian Smith." *New South*, XXI (Fall, 1966), 71–77.

Lumpkin, Katharine DuPre. *The Making of a Southerner*. New York: Knopf, 1947.

McGill, Ralph. "A Matter of Change." *New York Times Book Review*, February 13, 1955, p. 7.

———. *The South and the Southerner*. Boston: Little, Brown, 1963.

———. "Times Unforgotten—And a Burden Passed Along." *New York Times Book Review*, August 31, 1958, p. 3.

Mack, Raymond W., ed. *The Changing South*. Chicago: Aldine, 1970.

MacKethan, Lucinda Hardwick. *The Dream of Arcady: Place and Time in Southern Literature*. Baton Rouge: Louisiana State University Press, 1980.

McKinney, John C., and Linda Brookover Bourque. "The Changing South: National Incorporation of a Region." *American Sociological Review*, XXXVI (June, 1971), 399–412.

McMillan, George. "Portrait of a Southern Liberal." *New York Review of Books*, April 18, 1974, p. 33.

McWhiney, Grady. *Southerners and Other Americans*. New York: Basic Books, 1973.

Maddex, Jack P., Jr. "Pollard's *Lost Cause Regained*: A Mask for Southern Accommodation." *Journal of Southern History*, XL (November, 1974), 595–612.

———. *The Reconstruction of Edward A. Pollard*. Chapel Hill: University of North Carolina Press, 1974.

Martin, Neal A. *The Library of James McBride Dabbs: An Inventory*. [Florence, S.C.]: Francis Marion College, 1980.

Mayo, Selz C. "Social Change, Social Movements, and the Disappearing Sectional South." *Social Forces*, XLIII (October, 1964), 1–10.

Melville, Herman. "Benito Cereno." In *Selected Tales and Poems*, edited by Richard Chase. San Francisco: Rinehart Press, 1950.

Mencken, H. L. "The Agonies of Dixie." *American Mercury*, XXVIII (February, 1933), 251–53.

———. "Beneath the Magnolias." Baltimore *Evening Sun*, October 20, 1924.

———. "Black Boy." *American Mercury*, XV (September, 1928), 126.

———. "The Calamity of Appomattox." *American Mercury*, XXI (September, 1930), 29–31.

———. "The Sahara of the Bozart." *Prejudices, Second Series*. New York: Knopf, 1920.

———. "The South Astir." *Virginia Quarterly Review*, XI (January, 1935), 47–60.

———. "The South Begins to Mutter." *Smart Set*, LXV (August, 1921), 138–44.

———. "The South Looks Ahead." *American Mercury*, VIII (August, 1926), 506–509.

———. "The South Rebels Again." Chicago *Tribune*, December 7, 1924.

Milton, George Fort. "A Southern Liberal." *Yale Review*, XXX (April, 1941), 831–33.

Mims, Edwin. *The Advancing South*. Garden City, N.Y.: Doubleday, Page, 1926.

———. "Intellectual Progress in the South." *Review of Reviews*, LXXIII (April, 1926), 367–69.

———. "The South Pleads for Just Criticism." *Independent*, November 20, 1926, pp. 589–90, 599.

———. "Why the South Is Anti-Evolution." *World's Work*, L (September, 1925), 548–52.

Mitchell, Betty L. *Edmund Ruffin: A Biography*. Bloomington: Indiana University Press, 1981.

Mitchell, Broadus. "Fleshpots in the South." *Virginia Quarterly Review*, III (April, 1927), 161–76.

———. *The Rise of Cotton Mills in the South*. Baltimore: Johns Hopkins University Press, 1921.

———. "Taking a Stand in Dixie." *Commonweal*, June 5, 1929, pp. 127–29.

Mixon, Wayne. *Southern Writers and· the New South Movement, 1865–1913*. Chapel Hill: University of North Carolina Press, 1980.

Morris, Willie. *North Toward Home*. Boston: Houghton Mifflin, 1967.

Morrison, Joseph L. "Mencken and Odum: The Dutch Uncle and the South." *Virginia Quarterly Review*, XLII (Autumn, 1966), 601–615.

———. "The Summing Up." *South Atlantic Quarterly*, LXX (Autumn, 1971), 477–86.

———. *W. J. Cash: Southern Prophet*. New York: Knopf, 1967.

Mowry, George E. *Another Look at the Twentieth-Century South*. Baton Rouge: Louisiana State University Press, 1973.

Murphy, Edgar Gardner. *The Basis of Ascendancy: A Discussion of Certain Principles of Public Policy Involved in the Development of Southern States.* New York: Longmans, Green, 1909.

――――. *Problems of the Present South: A Discussion of Certain of the Educational, Industrial, and Political Issues of the Southern States.* New York: Grosset & Dunlap, 1904.

Myers, Robert H., ed. *The Children of Pride: A True Story of Georgia and the Civil War.* New Haven: Yale University Press, 1972.

Myrdal, Gunnar. *An American Dilemma: The Negro Problem and Modern Democracy.* 1944; reprint. New York: Harper & Row, 1962.

Newman, Frances. *The Hard-Boiled Virgin.* New York: Boni & Liveright, 1926.

Nolan, Terence Hunt. "William Henry Skaggs and the Reform Challenge of 1894." *Alabama Historical Quarterly,* XXXIII (Summer, 1971), 117–34.

Norwood, Thomas Manson. *A True Vindication of the South.* Savannah: Braid & Hutton, 1917.

O'Brien, Michael. "C. Vann Woodward and the Burden of Southern Liberalism." *American Historical Review,* LXXVIII (June, 1973), 589–604.

――――. "Edwin Mims: An Aspect of the Mind of the New South Considered." *South Atlantic Quarterly,* LXXIII (Spring, 1974), 199–212; LXXIII (Summer, 1974), 324–34.

――――. "Edwin Mims and Donald Davidson: A Correspondence, 1923–1958." *Southern Review,* New Ser., X (Autumn, 1974), 904–922.

――――. *The Idea of the American South, 1920–1941.* Baltimore: Johns Hopkins University Press, 1979.

――――. "W. J. Cash, Hegel, and the South." *Journal of Southern History,* XLIV (August, 1978), 379–98.

Odum, Howard W. *An American Epoch: Southern Portraiture in the National Picture.* New York: Henry Holt, 1930.

――――. "Black Ulysses Goes to War." *American Mercury,* XVII (August, 1929), 385–400.

――――. "Black Ulysses in Camp." *American Mercury,* XVIII (September, 1929), 47–59.

――――. *Cold Blue Moon.* Indianapolis: Bobbs-Merrill, 1931.

――――. "The Duel to the Death." *Journal of Social Forces,* IV (September, 1925), 189–94.

――――. Editorial Notes. *Journal of Social Forces,* I (November, 1922), 56–61; I (January, 1923), 178–83; I (March, 1923), 315–20; I (September, 1923), 616–20; III (November, 1924), 139–46.

――――. "A More Articulate South." *Journal of Social Forces,* II (September, 1924), 730–35.

――――. "On Southern Literature and Southern Culture." In *Southern Renascence: The Literature of the Modern South,* edited by Louis D. Rubin, Jr., and Robert D. Jacobs. Baltimore: Johns Hopkins University Press, 1953.

――――. *Race and Rumors of Race.* Chapel Hill: University of North Carolina Press, 1943.

――――. *Rainbow Round My Shoulder.* Indianapolis: Bobbs-Merrill, 1928.

————. "Reading, Writing, and Leadership." *Journal of Social Forces*, I (March, 1923), 321–35.

————. "Regionalism vs. Sectionalism in the South's Place in the National Economy." *Journal of Social Forces*, XII (March, 1934), 338–54.

————. "Religious Folk-Songs of the Southern Negro." *Journal of Religious Psychology and Education*, III (July, 1909), 265–365.

————. "A Southern Promise." *Journal of Social Forces*, III (May, 1925), 739–46.

————. *Southern Regions of the United States*. Chapel Hill: University of North Carolina Press, 1936.

————. *The Way of the South: Toward the Regional Balance of America*. New York: Macmillan, 1947.

————. *Wings on My Feet*. Indianapolis: Bobbs-Merrill, 1929.

————, ed. *Southern Pioneers in Social Interpretation*. Chapel Hill: University of North Carolina Press, 1925.

Odum, Howard W., and Guy B. Johnson. *Negro Workaday Songs*. Chapel Hill: University of North Carolina Press, 1926.

Odum, Howard W., and Harry Estill Moore. *American Regionalism*. New York: Henry Holt, 1938.

Olmsted, Frederick Law. *The Cotton Kingdom: A Traveller's Observations on Cotton and Slavery in the American Slave States*. Edited, with an Introduction, by Arthur M. Schlesinger. New York: Knopf, 1953.

Osterweis, Rollin. *Romanticism and Nationalism in the Old South*. New Haven: Yale University Press, 1949.

Owsley, Frank L. "A Key to Southern Liberalism." *Southern Review*, III (Summer, 1937), 28–38.

————. "The Pillars of Agrarianism." *American Review*, IV (March, 1935), 529–47.

————. *Plain Folk of the Old South*. Baton Rouge: Louisiana State University Press, 1949.

Page, Rosewell. *Thomas Nelson Page: A Memoir of a Virginia Gentleman*. New York: Scribner's, 1923.

Page, Thomas Nelson. *Bred in the Bone*. New York: Scribner's, 1912.

————. *The Burial of the Guns*. New York: Scribner's, 1910.

————. *Gordon Keith*. New York: Scribner's, 1903.

————. *In Ole Virginia*. Rev. ed. New York: Scribner's, 1912.

————. *John Marvel, Assistant*. New York: Scribner's, 1909.

————. *Necessity for a History of the South*. [Roanoke: n.p., 1892].

————. *The Negro: The Southerner's Problem*. New York: Scribner's, 1904.

————. *The Old Dominion*. New York: Scribner's, 1908.

————. *The Old South: Essays Social and Political*. 1892; reprint. New York: Haskell House, 1968.

————. *On Newfound River*. New York: Scribner's, 1891.

————. *Pastime Stories*. New York: Harper & Brothers, 1894.

————. *The Red Riders*. New York: Scribner's, 1924.

————. *Red Rock*. New York: Scribner's, 1898.

————. *Robert E. Lee: The Southerner*. New York: Scribner's, 1908.

————. *Social Life in Old Virginia Before the War.* New York: Scribner's, 1897.

————. "A Virginia Realist." Preface to *The Old Virginia Gentleman,* by George W. Bagby. New York: Scribner's, 1910.

[Page, Walter Hines]. "The Autobiography of a Southerner Since the Civil War." *Atlantic Monthly,* XCVIII (July, August, September, October, 1906), 1–12, 157–76, 311–25, 474–88.

————. "The Forgotten Man." See *The Rebuilding of Old Commonwealths.*

————. "The Last Hold of the Southern Bully." *Forum,* XVI (November, 1893), 303–314.

————. *The Rebuilding of Old Commonwealths.* New York: Doubleday, Page, 1902.

————. "The School That Built a Town." See *The Rebuilding of Old Commonwealths.*

[————]. *The Southerner: A Novel, Being the Autobiography of Nicholas Worth.* New York: Doubleday, Page, 1909.

————. "Study of an Old Southern Borough." *Atlantic Monthly,* XLVII (May, 1881), 648–58.

Parks, Edd Winfield. *Segments of Southern Thought.* Athens: University of Georgia Press, 1938.

Paulding, J. K. "Biography." *Commonweal,* October 2, 1942, p. 369.

Percy, Walker. Introduction to *Lanterns on the Levee,* by William Alexander Percy. Baton Rouge: Louisiana State University Press, 1974.

————. *The Last Gentleman.* New York: Farrar, Straus & Giroux, 1966.

————. "Mississippi: The Fallen Paradise." *Harper's,* CCXXX (April, 1965), 166–72.

————. "Random Thoughts on Southern Literature, Southern Politics, and the American Future." *Georgia Review,* XXXII (Fall, 1978), 499–511.

————. "Stoicism in the South." *Commonweal,* July 6, 1956, pp. 342–44.

Percy, William Alexander. *Collected Poems.* New York: Knopf, 1943.

————. *Enzio's Kingdom.* New Haven: Yale University Press, 1924.

————. *In April Once and Other Poems.* New Haven: Yale University Press, 1920.

————. *Lanterns on the Levee: Recollections of a Planter's Son.* 1941; reprint. Baton Rouge: Louisiana State University Press, 1974.

————. *Sappho in Levkas and Other Poems.* New Haven: Yale University Press, 1915.

————. *Selected Poems.* New Haven: Yale University Press, 1930.

Phillips, Ulrich B. "Economic and Political Essays." In *The South in the Building of the Nation.* Vol. VII. Richmond: Southern Historical Publication Society, 1909.

————. *Life and Labor in the Old South.* Boston: Little, Brown, 1929.

————. *The Slave Economy of the Old South.* Baton Rouge: Louisiana State University Press, 1968.

Pike, James S. *The Prostrate South: South Carolina Under Negro Government.* 1874; New York: Harper Torchbooks, 1968.

Pinckney, Josephine. "Southern Writers Congress." *Saturday Review,* November 7, 1931, p. 266.

Polk, William T. "The Hated Helper." *South Atlantic Quarterly*, XXX (April, 1931), 177–89.

———. *Southern Accent: From Uncle Remus to Oak Ridge*. New York: Morrow, 1953.

Pollard, Edward A. *Life of Jefferson Davis*. Philadelphia: National Publishing Company, 1869.

———. *The Lost Cause*. New York: E. B. Treat, 1866.

———. *The Lost Cause Regained*. 1868; reprint. Freeport, N.Y.: Books for Libraries Press, 1970.

Potter, David M. "The Enigma of the South." *Yale Review*, LI (October, 1961), 142–51.

———. *The Impending Crisis, 1848–1861*. Edited and completed by Don E. Fehrenbacher. New York: Harper & Row, 1976.

———. "On Understanding the South." *Journal of Southern History*, XXX (November, 1964), 451–62.

———. *The South and the Concurrent Majority*. Baton Rouge: Louisiana State University Press, 1972.

———. *The South and the Sectional Conflict*. Baton Rouge: Louisiana State University Press, 1968.

Powledge, Fred. *Journeys Through the South*. New York: Vanguard, 1979.

The Pro-Slavery Argument. Charleston: Walker, Richards, 1852.

"Psychoanalysis of a Nation." *Time*, February, 24, 1941, p. 97.

Purdy, Rob Roy, ed. *Fugitives' Reunion*. Nashville: Vanderbilt University Press, 1959.

Quinn, Arthur Hobson. *American Fiction*. New York: D. Appleton-Century, 1936.

Ransom, John Crowe. "The Aesthetics of Regionalism." *American Review*, II (January, 1934), 290–310.

———. *God Without Thunder: An Unorthodox Defense of Orthodoxy*. London: Gerald Howe, 1931.

———. "Modern With the Southern Accent." *Virginia Quarterly Review*, XI (April, 1935), 184–98.

———. "Sociology and the Black Belt." *American Review*, IV (December, 1934), 147–54.

———. "The South Defends Its Heritage." *Harper's*, CLIX (June, 1929), 108–118.

———. "The South—Old or New?" *Sewanee Review*, XXXVI (April, 1928), 139–47.

———. "What Does the South Want?" *Virginia Quarterly Review*, XII (April, 1936), 180–94.

Raper, Arthur. *Preface to Peasantry: A Tale of Two Black Belt Counties*. Chapel Hill: University of North Carolina Press, 1936.

Reed, John Shelton. *The Enduring South: Subcultural Persistence in Mass Society*. Lexington, Mass.: Lexington Books, 1972.

Reissman, Leonard. "Social Development and the American South." *Journal of Social Issues*, XXII (January, 1966), 101–116.

Rice, Andrew. *I Came Out of the Eighteenth Century*. New York: Harper & Brothers, 1942.

Robertson, Ben. *Red Hills and Cotton: An Upcountry Memory*. New York: Knopf, 1942.

Robertson, William J. *The Changing South*. New York: Boni & Liveright, 1927.

Robinson, Jo Ann. "Lillian Smith." *Southern Exposure*, IV (Winter, 1977), 43–48.

Rocks, James C. "The Art of *Lanterns on the Levee*." *Southern Review*, New Ser., XII (Autumn, 1976), 814–23.

Roller, David C., and Robert W. Twyman, eds. *The Encyclopedia of Southern History*. Baton Rouge: Louisiana State University Press, 1979.

[Rouquette, Adrien]. *Critical Dialogue Between Aboo and Caboo on a New Book; or, a Grandissime Ascension*. [New Orleans: n.p., 1880].

Rowe, Anne E. *The Enchanted Country: Northern Writers in the South, 1865–1910*. Baton Rouge: Louisiana State University Press, 1978.

Rubin, Louis D., Jr. *The Faraway Country: Writers of the Modern South*. Seattle: University of Washington Press, 1963.

———. *George W. Cable: The Life and Times of a Southern Heretic*. New York: Pegasus, 1969.

———. "The Mind of the South." *Sewanee Review*, LXII (Autumn, 1954), 683–95.

———. "The Old Gray Mare: The Continuing Relevance of Southern Literary Issues." In *Southern Fiction Today*, edited by George Core. Athens: University of Georgia Press, 1969.

———. "The Other Side of Slavery: Thomas Nelson Page's 'No Haid Pawn.'" *Studies in the Literary Imagination*, VII (Spring, 1974), 95–99.

———. "Scarlett O'Hara and the Two Quentin Compsons." In *The South and Faulkner's Yoknapatawpha: The Actual and the Apocryphal*, edited by Evans Harrington and Ann J. Abadie. Jackson: University Press of Mississippi, 1977.

———. "Southern Writing and the Changing South." In *South: Modern Southern Literature in Its Cultural Setting*, edited by Rubin and Robert D. Jacobs. Garden City, N.Y.: Doubleday, 1961.

———. *The Wary Fugitives: Four Poets and the South*. Baton Rouge: Louisiana State University Press, 1978.

———. *William Elliott Shoots a Bear: Essays on the Southern Literary Imagination*. Baton Rouge: Louisiana State University Press, 1975.

———. *The Writer in the South: Studies in a Literary Community*. Athens: University of Georgia Press, 1972.

———, ed. *The American South: Portrait of a Culture*. Baton Rouge: Louisiana State University Press, 1980.

———, ed. *A Bibliographical Guide to the Study of Southern Literature*. Baton Rouge: Louisiana State University Press, 1969.

Rubin, Louis D., Jr., and C. Hugh Holman, eds. *Southern Literary Study: Problems and Possibilities*. Chapel Hill: University of North Carolina Press, 1975.

Rubin, Louis D., Jr., and James J. Kilpatrick, eds. *The Lasting South: Fourteen Southerners Look at Their Home*. Chicago: Regnery, 1957.

Rubin, Louis D., Jr., and Robert D. Jacobs, eds. *Southern Renascence: The Literature of the Modern South.* Baltimore: Johns Hopkins University Press, 1953.

Ruffin, Edmund. *Anticipations of the Future: To Serve as Lessons for the Present Time.* Richmond: J. W. Randolph, 1860.

———. *Consequences of Abolition Agitation.* Washington, D.C.: L. Towers, 1857.

[———]. *The Diary of Edmund Ruffin.* 2 vols. Edited by William Kauffman Scarborough. Baton Rouge: Louisiana State University Press, 1972.

———. *The Political Economy of Slavery.* [Washington, D.C.]: L. Towers, 1857.

Rutherford, Mildred Lewis. *The South in History and Literature.* Atlanta: Franklin-Turner, 1907.

———. *Truths of History.* [Athens]: n.p., 1920.

Sale, Kirkpatrick. *Power Shift: The Rise of the Southern Rim and Its Challenge to the Eastern Establishment.* New York: Random House, 1975.

Savage, Henry. *Seeds of Time: The Background of Southern Thinking.* New York: Henry Holt, 1959.

Sawyer, George S. *Southern Institutes; or, An Inquiry into the Origin and Early Prevalence of Slavery and the Slave Trade.* Philadelphia: Lippincott, 1858.

Scopes, John Thomas, and James Presley. *Center of the Storm: Memoirs of John T. Scopes.* New York: Holt, Rinehart & Winston, 1967.

Sellers, Charles Grier, Jr. "Walter Hines Page and the Spirit of the New South." *North Carolina Historical Review,* XXIX (October, 1952), 481–99.

———, ed. *The Southerner as American.* Chapel Hill: University of North Carolina Press, 1960.

Silver, James Wesley. *Mississippi: The Closed Society.* New York: Harcourt, Brace & World, 1964.

Simkins, Francis Butler. *The Everlasting South.* Baton Rouge: Louisiana State University Press, 1963.

———. "Robert Lewis Dabney, Southern Conservative." *Georgia Review,* XVIII (Winter, 1964), 393–407.

Simpson, John. "The Cult of the 'Lost Cause.'" *Tennessee Historical Quarterly,* XXXIV (Winter, 1975), 350–61.

Simpson, Lewis P. "The Antebellum South as a Symbol of Mind." *Southern Literary Journal,* XII (Spring, 1980), 125–36.

———. *The Dispossessed Garden: Pastoral and History in Southern Literature.* Athens: University of Georgia Press, 1975.

———. *The Man of Letters in New England and the South: Essays on the History of the Literary Vocation in America.* Baton Rouge: Louisiana State University Press, 1973.

———. "The South and the Poetry of Community." In *The Poetry of Community: Essays on the Southern Sensibility of History and Literature,* edited by Simpson. Atlanta: Georgia State University, 1972.

———. "The Southern Recovery of Memory and History." *Sewanee Review,* LXXXII (Winter, 1974), 1–32.

———. "The South's Reaction to Modernism: A Problem in the Study of Southern Letters." In *Southern Literary Study: Problems and Possibilities,* edited by Louis D. Rubin, Jr., and C. Hugh Holman. Chapel Hill: University of North Carolina Press, 1975.

Skaggs, William . *The Southern Oligarchy: An Appeal in Behalf of the Silent Masses of Our Country Against the Despotic Rule of the Few*. New York: Devin-Adair, 1924.

Smedes, Susan Dabney. *Memorials of a Southern Planter*. Baltimore: Cushings & Bailey, 1887.

Smith, Frank E. *Congressman from Mississippi*. New York: Pantheon, 1964.

———. *Look Away from Dixie*. Baton Rouge: Louisiana State University Press, 1965.

Smith, Lillian. *The Journey*. 1954; reprint. New York: Norton, 1965.

———. *Killers of the Dream*. 1949; revised and enlarged. Garden City, N.Y.: Anchor Books, 1963.

———. *Memory of a Large Christmas*. New York: Norton, 1962.

———. *Now Is the Time*. New York: Viking, 1955.

———. *One Hour*. New York: Harcourt, Brace, 1959.

———. *Our Faces, Our Words*. New York: Norton, 1964.

———. *Strange Fruit*. New York: Reynal & Hitchcock, 1944.

———. "A Strange Kind of Love." *Saturday Review*, October 20, 1962, pp. 18–20, 94.

———. *The Winner Names the Age*. Edited by Michelle Cliff. New York: Norton, 1978.

Snyder, Charles Lee. "How the South Came to Think and Feel as It Did." *New York Times Book Review*, February 23, 1941, p. 4.

Somers, Robert. *The Southern States Since the War*. 1871; reprint. Tuscaloosa: University of Alabama Press, 1965.

Sosna, Morton. *In Search of the Silent South: Southern Liberals and the Race Issue*. New York: Columbia University Press, 1977.

Sowder, William J. "Gerald W. Johnson, Thomas Nelson Page, and the South." *Mississippi Quarterly*, XIV (Fall, 1961), 197–203.

Spalding, Phinizy. "Mississippi and the Poet: William Alexander Percy." *Journal of Mississippi History*, XXVII (February, 1965), 63–73.

———. "A Stoic Trend in William Alexander Percy's Thought." *Georgia Review*, XII (Fall, 1958), 241–51.

Stampp, Kenneth. *The Peculiar Institution: Slavery in the Antebellum South*. New York: Knopf, 1956.

Stanley, H. M. Review of *The Southerner*, by Walter Hines Page. *Nation*, November 25, 1909, 512.

Stephens, Alexander. *A Constitutional View of the Late War Between the States*. 2 vols. Philadelphia: National Publishing Company, 1868–1870.

Stephenson, Wendell H., ed. *Southern History in the Making: Pioneer Historians of the South*. Baton Rouge: Louisiana State University Press, 1964.

Stewart, John L. *The Burden of Time: The Fugitives and the Agrarians*. Princeton: Princeton University Press, 1965.

Stowe, Harriet Beecher. *Uncle Tom's Cabin*. Boston: J. P. Jewett, 1851.

Sugg, Redding S., Jr. "Lillian Smith and the Condition of Woman." *South Atlantic Quarterly*, LXXI (Spring, 1972), 155–64.

Sullivan, Margaret. "Lillian Smith: The Public Image and the Personal Vision." *Mad River Review*, II (Summer-Fall, 1967), 3–21.

Tannenbaum, Frank. *Darker Phases of the South*. New York: G. P. Putnam's Sons, 1924.

Tate, Allen. *Essays of Four Decades*. Chicago: Swallow Press, 1968.

——. "Last Days of the Charming Lady." *Nation*, October 28, 1925, pp. 485–86.

——. "The New Provincialism." *Virginia Quarterly Review*, XXI (Spring, 1945), 262–72.

——. "The Profession of Letters in the South." *Virginia Quarterly Review*, XI (April, 1935), 161–76.

——. "Regionalism and Sectionalism." *New Republic*, December 23, 1931, pp. 158–61.

——. "A View of the Whole South." *American Review*, II (February, 1934), 411–32.

Taylor, William R. *Cavalier and Yankee: The Old South and American National Character*. New York: George Braziller, 1961.

Thomas, Emory M. *The Confederate Nation, 1861–1865*. New York: Harper & Row, 1979.

Thompson, Holland. *The New South*. New Haven: Yale University Press, 1919.

Thorpe, Earl E. *Eros and Freedom in the Old South*. Durham: printed by Seeman Printery, 1967.

——. *The Old South: A Psychohistory*. Durham: printed by Seeman Printery, 1972.

Tindall, George B. "The Benighted South: Origins of a Modern Image." *Virginia Quarterly Review*, XL (Spring, 1964), 281–94.

——. *The Emergence of the New South, 1913–1945*. Baton Rouge: Louisiana State University Press, 1967.

——. *The Ethnic Southerners*. Baton Rouge: Louisiana State University Press, 1976.

——. "Mythology: A New Frontier in Southern History." In *The Idea of the South: Pursuit of a Central Theme*, edited by Frank E. Vandiver. Chicago: University of Chicago Press, 1964.

——. "The Significance of Howard W. Odum to Southern History: A Preliminary Estimate." *Journal of Southern History*, XXIV (August, 1958), 285–307.

——, ed. *The Pursuit of Southern History: Presidential Addresses of the Southern Historical Association, 1935–1963*. Baton Rouge: Louisiana State University Press, 1964.

[Tucker, Nathaniel Beverley]. *The Partisan Leader*. 1836; reprint. New York: Knopf, 1933.

Turner, Arlin. *George W. Cable: A Biography*. 1956; reprint. Baton Rouge: Louisiana State University Press, 1966.

———, ed. *The Negro Question: A Selection of Writings on Civil Rights in the South by George W. Cable*. New York: Norton, 1958.

Twelve Southerners. See *I'll Take My Stand*.

Vance, Rupert B. "Beyond the Fleshpots: The Coming Culture Crisis in the South." *Virginia Quarterly Review*, XLI (Spring, 1965), 217–30.

Vandiver, Frank E., ed. *The Idea of the South: Pursuit of a Central Theme*. Chicago: University of Chicago Press, 1964.

Wade, John Donald. *Augustus Baldwin Longstreet*. New York: Macmillan, 1924.

———. *Selected Essays and Other Writings of John Donald Wade*. Edited by Donald Davidson. Athens: University of Georgia Press, 1966.

Warren, Robert Penn. *The Legacy of the Civil War*. New York: Random House, 1961.

———. *Segregation*. New York: Random House, 1956.

———. *Who Speaks for the Negro?* New York: Random House, 1965.

Watters, Pat. *Down to Now: Reflections on the Southern Civil Rights Movement*. New York: Pantheon, 1971.

———. *The South and the Nation*. 1969; reprint. New York: Vintage Books, 1971.

Weaver, Blanche. "D. R. Hundley: Subjective Sociologist." *Georgia Review*, X (Summer, 1956), 222–34.

Weaver, Richard M. "Agrarianism in Exile." *Sewanee Review*, LVIII (Autumn, 1950), 586–606.

———. "Aspects of the Southern Philosophy." In *Southern Renascence: The Literature of the Modern South*, edited by Louis D. Rubin, Jr., and Robert D. Jacobs. Baltimore: Johns Hopkins University Press, 1953.

———. "Contemporary Southern Literature." *Texas Quarterly*, II (Summer, 1959), 126–44.

———. *The Ethics of Rhetoric*. Chicago: Regnery, 1953.

———. *Ideas Have Consequences*. Chicago: University of Chicago Press, 1948.

———. "Lee the Philosopher." *Georgia Review*, II (Fall, 1948), 297–303.

———. *Life Without Prejudice and Other Essays*. Chicago: Regnery, 1965.

———. "The Regime of the South." *National Review*, March 14, 1959, pp. 587–89.

———. "The South and the American Union." In *The Lasting South: Fourteen Southerners Look at Their Home*, edited by Louis D. Rubin, Jr., and James J. Kilpatrick. Chicago: Regnery, 1957.

———. "The South and the Revolution of Nihilism." *South Atlantic Quarterly*, XLIII (April, 1944), 194–98.

———. "The Southern Phoenix." *Georgia Review*, XVII (Spring, 1963), 6–17.

———. *The Southern Tradition at Bay: A History of Postbellum Thought*. Edited by George Core and M. E. Bradford. New Rochelle, N.Y.: Arlington House, 1968.

———. "The Tennessee Agrarians." *Shenandoah*, III (Summer, 1952), 3–10.

———. "Two Orators." Edited by George Core and M. E. Bradford. *Modern Age*, XIV (Summer-Fall, 1970), 226–42.

Welsh, J. R. "William Alexander Percy and His Writings." *Notes on Mississippi Writers*, I (Winter, 1969), 82–99.

Weltner, Charles Longstreet. *Southerner*. Philadelphia: Lippincott, 1966.

Westbrook, John. "Twilight of Southern Regionalism." *Southwest Review*, XLII (Summer, 1957), 231–34.

Westbrook, Robert B. "C. Vann Woodward: The Southerner as Liberal Realist." *South Atlantic Quarterly*, LXXVII (Winter, 1978), 54–72.

[Whetton, Harriet Douglas]. "A Volunteer Nurse in the Civil War: The Diary of Harriet Douglas Whetton." Edited by Paul H. Hass. *Wisconsin Magazine of History*, XLVIII (Spring, 1965), 205–221.

White, Helen, and Redding S. Sugg, Jr., eds. *From the Mountain: Selections from Pseudopodia, the North Georgia Review, and South Today*. Memphis: Memphis State University Press, 1972.

Why the South Will Survive: Fifteen Southerners Look at Their Region a Half Century After I'll Take My Stand. Athens: University of Georgia Press, 1981.

Wilson, Charles Reagan. *Baptized in Blood: The Religion of the Lost Cause, 1865–1920*. Athens: University of Georgia Press, 1980.

Wilson, Clyde N., ed. *Selections from the Letters and Speeches of the Hon. James H. Hammond*. Columbia: Southern Studies Program of the University of South Carolina, 1978.

Wilson, Edmund. *Patriotic Gore: Studies in the Literature of the American Civil War*. New York: Oxford University Press, 1962.

Winston, Robert W. *It's a Far Cry*. New York: Henry Holt, 1937.

Wish, Harvey. *George Fitzhugh: Propagandist of the Old South*. Baton Rouge: Louisiana State University Press, 1943.

———, ed. *Ante-Bellum: Writings of George Fitzhugh and Hinton Rowan Helper on Slavery*. New York: G. P. Putnam's Sons, 1960.

Wiswall, J. T. "Causes of Aristocracy." *De Bow's Review*, XXVIII (May, 1860), 551–66.

Wolfe, Samuel M. *Helper's Impending Crisis Dissected*. Philadelphia: J. T. Lloyd, 1860.

Woodward, C. Vann. *American Counterpoint: Slavery and Racism in the North-South Dialogue*. Boston: Little, Brown, 1971.

———. *The Burden of Southern History*. Rev. ed. Baton Rouge: Louisiana State University Press, 1968.

———. "Double Maverick." *Nation*, November 15, 1958, p. 365.

———. "George Fitzhugh, *Sui Generis*." Introduction to *Cannibals All!*, by George Fitzhugh. Cambridge: Harvard University Press, 1960.

———. "The Irony of Southern History." In *Southern Renascence: The Literature of the Modern South*, edited by Louis D. Rubin, Jr., and Robert D. Jacobs. Baltimore: Johns Hopkins University Press, 1953.

———. "Lewis H. Blair: Prophet Without Honor." Introduction to *A Southern Prophecy: The Prosperity of the South Dependent Upon the Elevation of the Negro*, by Lewis H. Blair. Boston: Little, Brown, 1964.

———. *Origins of the New South, 1877–1913*. Baton Rouge: Louisiana State University Press, 1951.

———. Review of *Southern Legacy*, by Hodding Carter. *Journal of Southern History*, XVI (August, 1950), 381–82.

———. *The Strange Career of Jim Crow.* New York: Oxford University Press, 1957.

———. "White Man, White Mind." *New Republic,* December 9, 1967, pp. 28–30.

———, ed. *Mary Chesnut's Civil War.* New Haven: Yale University Press, 1981.

Woody, R. H. "The Second Annual Meeting of the Southern Historical Association." *Journal of Southern History,* III (February, 1937), 83–84.

Workman, William D., Jr. *The Case for the South.* New York: Devin-Adair, 1960.

Wynes, Charles E., ed. *Forgotten Voices: Dissenting Southerners in an Age of Conformity.* Baton Rouge: Louisiana State University Press, 1967.

Yoder, Edwin M., Jr. "W. J. Cash After a Quarter Century." In *The South Today: 100 Years After Appomattox,* edited by Willie Morris. New York: Harper & Row, 1965.

Young, Stark. "More Souths." *New Republic,* October 5, 1942, p. 421.

Young, Thomas Daniel, and M. Thomas Inge. *Donald Davidson.* New York: Twayne, 1971.

Zinn, Howard. *The Southern Mystique.* New York: Knopf, 1964.

General Reading in Primary Sources

JOURNALS AND MAGAZINES

American Review (New York), 1933–1937.
De Bow's Review (New Orleans), 1855–1867.
Fugitive (Nashville), 1922–1925.
Journal of Social Forces. Later, *Social Forces* (Chapel Hill), 1922–1928.
The Land We Love (Charlotte), 1866–1869.
New Eclectic (Baltimore), 1869–1870.
Richmond Eclectic (Richmond), 1866–1868.
Russell's Magazine (Charleston), 1857–1859.
Sewanee Review (Sewanee), 1929–1935.
South Atlantic Quarterly (Durham), 1929–1932.
Southern Literary Messenger (Richmond), 1850–1860.
Southern Magazine (Baltimore), 1871–1875.
Southern Review (Baltimore), 1867–1879.
Southern Review (Baton Rouge), 1935–1942.
Virginia Quarterly Review (Charlottesville), 1925–1934.

NEWSPAPERS

Cash, W. J. Book-page articles. Charlotte *News,* 1936–1940.
Davidson, Donald. "The Spyglass." Nashville *Tennessean,* 1925–1928.
———. "Critic's Almanac." Nashville *Tennessean,* 1928–1930.
Hibbard, Addison. "Literary Lantern." Greensboro *Daily News* (and other newspapers), 1923–1927.
Page, Walter Hines. Letters to the Raleigh *State Chronicle,* 1886.

Index